THE ARCHITECT'S STUDIO COMPANION

TECHNICAL GUIDELINES FOR PRELIMINARY DESIGN

THE ARCHITECT'S STUDIO COMPANION

TECHNICAL GUIDELINES FOR PRELIMINARY DESIGN

EDWARD ALLEN
JOSEPH IANO

WILEY

JOHN WILEY & SONS

NEW YORK ▪ CHICHESTER ▪ BRISBANE ▪ TORONTO ▪ SINGAPORE

Cover and text design: Karin Gerdes Kincheloe
Cover photo: Mona Zamdmer
Copyediting and production: Marcia Samuels

Library of Congress Cataloging-in-Publication Data:

Allen, Edward, 1938–
   The architect's studio companion.

   Bibliography: p.
   Includes index.
   1. Architectural design.   I. Iano, Joseph.   II. Title.
NA2750.A556 1989   721   88-28028
ISBN 0-471-63220-1
Printed in the United States of America

10 9 8 7 6 5 4 3

ACKNOWLEDGMENTS

We wish to thank the many individuals who contributed so graciously to the making of this book. Among those professionals whom we consulted during its formative stages, special mention goes to Professor Carl Bovill of the University of Tennessee, who strongly influenced the underlying philosophy of the book, and Professor Stephen Vamosi of the University of Cincinnati, who gave exceedingly generously of his technical expertise on mechanical and electrical systems. Robert Heryford, P.E., and Peter S. Watt, P.E., of R. G. Vanderweil Associates and Marvin Mass of Cosentini Associates also shared freely of their knowledge in this area. Richard J. Farley, a member of the Architecture faculty at the University of Pennsylvania, and Professor Daniel Schodek of the Graduate School of Design at Harvard University gave valuable advice on structural matters. For additional contributions of technical expertise we are indebted to Professor Harvey Bryan of Harvard University; Mark Dooling, Jerry Hicks, and Douglas Mahone, Architects, and Professor Peter Stone of Florida A. & M. University.

For a truly exceptional working relationship with the publisher, John Wiley & Sons, Inc., we thank Judith R. Joseph, the editor with whom we began the project, and Claire Thompson, who continued as editor and guided the book through its development with skill and a never-failing cheerfulness that buoyed us when we needed it most. Karin Kincheloe, a truly gifted artist, labored unstintingly on the design and production of the book. We wish to thank Marcia Samuels for an expert job of copyediting and for guiding the book through the complexities of its production with impressive skill, unending patience, and a refreshing sense of humor. Cynthia Zigmund, Erika Levy, and Barbara Tillman handled the many administrative difficulties with good cheer and solid professionalism. We also thank Paula Lininger of McFarland Graphics and Design for handling swiftly and accurately our complex needs for typesetting.

For their valuable assistance in reviewing and commenting upon preliminary drafts of the manuscript, we thank David Glasser, University of Wisconsin, Milwaukee; Roger N. Goldstein, Goody, Clancy & Associates, Inc., Boston, Massachusetts; Jack Kremers, Kent State University; Sandra Davis Lakeman, California Polytechnic University; Alan Levy, University of Pennsylvania; John Reynolds, University of Oregon; Donald Prowler, University of Pennsylvania; and Marc Schiler, Pasadena, California.

We would like, finally, to acknowledge the assistance and support of those closest to our hearts. Edward Allen wishes to thank Mary M. Allen. Joseph Iano thanks Mavra Simon Iano and Richard Peter Iano for the things that only parents can do and that they have done so well. He would especially like to thank Lesley Bain Iano for her patience, enthusiasm, and hand in marriage.

DISCLAIMER

The information in this book has been interpreted from sources that include building codes, industry standards, manufacturers' literature, engineering reference works, and personal contacts with many individuals. It is presented in good faith, but although the authors and the publisher have made every reasonable effort to make this book accurate and authoritative, they do not warrant, and assume no liability for, its accuracy or completeness or its fitness for any particular purpose. The user should note especially that this is a book of first approximations, information that is not intended to be used for final design of any building or structure. It is the responsibility of users to apply their professional knowledge in the use of information contained in this book, to consult original sources for more detailed information as needed, and to seek expert advice as needed, especially in the later stages of the process of designing a building.

CONTENTS

HOW TO USE THIS BOOK

This book is your desktop technical advisor for the earliest stages of building design. It reduces complex engineering and building code information to simple formal and spatial approximations that are readily incorporated into initial design explorations. It does not replace building codes, detailed technical handbooks, and skilled consultants; it simply helps you prepare a buildable preliminary design as a realistic basis for the more detailed design development and consultations that will follow.

After you have used this book on several projects, you will have developed a pattern for its use that suits your temperament and your own way of going about designing a building. The first time that you use it, there are two approaches you might take. One is simply to enter the book at any point that you wish, using the index tabs and following the logical paths indicated by the cross-references until your need for information is satisfied. Alternatively, you may wish to begin at the beginning, tracing the following steps as a means of finding the information you need while becoming familiar with the layout of the book:

1. Turn to the first section, Designing with Building Codes. Use the index on page 7 to determine which building code you must comply with. Then consult the Index of Use Groups for that code on pages 8–11 to find out which Use Group your building falls within. Make a note of the code and Use Group for ready reference as you progress through the other sections of the book—these pieces of information are your key to unlocking many different kinds of information.

2. Move next to the second section, Designing the Structure. Read the brief passage concerning building code requirements on page 17. Refer to the table in Appendix A that corresponds to the code and Use Group you noted earlier. List from this table the Construction Types you are permitted to use in your building.

3. Skim the explanation of Construction Types that begins on page 422 in Appendix B. Add notes to your list of permitted Construction Types to help you remember which specific structural materials and systems are associated with each Construction Type.

4. Continue the process of selecting a structural system by returning to pages 18–27, which will help you identify one or more specific structural systems that might be appropriate for the building you are designing Be sure your choices fall within one or another of the Construction Types you had previously identified as permitted under the appropriate building code.

5. Follow the page references given with each choice of structural system to learn in detail what each system looks like and what its potentials and limitations are. With the information found here, you can begin adding a structural plan and sections to the design for your building, complete with spacings and approximate sizes of all the members.

6. If you need help in laying out the overall structural system, turn to page 29 and the pages that

xi

HOW TO USE THIS BOOK

follow for general advice on configuring a structural system.

7. When you are satisfied that you have a good initial scheme for the structure of your building, move to the third section, Designing Spaces for Mechanical and Electrical Services, which begins on page 135. Decide first whether your building falls into the "large" or "small" category. Follow the references to the pages that correspond to this category, where you will find help in selecting a heating and cooling system. Follow through this section as far as you want to go, learning more about the characteristics of each system that seems appropriate and determining the sizes and configurations of the spaces it requires. Work these spaces for the mechanical and electrical systems into your developing design.

8. With the help of the fourth section, Designing for Egress, which begins on page 217, modify the circulation scheme of your building to meet code requirements for emergency egress.

9. By this time you should be finding your way through the book with ease, using the index tabs as your primary guideposts and the cross-references as clues to where to look for answers to your next questions.

As you gain experience with this book, developing your own patterns of use and adding notations wherever they are useful to you, it will become a personal handbook uniquely suited to your own way of creating buildings.

DESIGNING WITH BUILDING CODES

DESIGNING WITH BUILDING CODES

This section will help you determine which of the four model building codes applies to the project you are designing and, within that code, which Use Group your project belongs to. You will need to know these two facts to have full access to the information in this book.

BUILDING CODES AND ZONING ORDINANCES

A designer works under complex legal constraints that exert a powerful influence on the form a building may take. Local zoning ordinances control building uses, heights, areas, distances from property lines, and on-site parking capacities. Building codes enacted at the local, county, state, or provincial level regulate everything from building heights and areas to the types of interior finish materials that may be used. Further constraints are often imposed by local fire districts and by special state codes pertaining to schools, hospitals, nursing homes, and other particular uses.

While zoning laws and use-specific codes continue to be written and promulgated at the local and state levels, the building codes themselves have become increasingly standardized in North America, to the point that most codes now follow closely one or another of four "model" codes: the BOCA National Building Code, the National Building Code of Canada, the Standard Building Code, and the Uniform Building Code. This book condenses from these four model codes the provisions that have the most direct and important effects on building form: height and area limitations, beginning on page 287, and requirements for the design of egress systems, starting on page 217. Code requirements having to do with the detailed design of structural and mechanical components of buildings are reflected here indirectly through the preliminary sizing charts for structural elements (pages 45–133) and the rules of thumb for providing space for mechanical and electrical systems (pages 135–215).

In order to make use of this building code information, you should first consult the index that follows to determine which code pertains in the geographical region of your project. Then you should use the appropriate code-specific index that follows to ascertain the Use Group of the building you are designing. These two pieces of information are the keys that will unlock code-related information again and again as you refer to this book.

Many large cities and certain states and counties have written their own building codes. Some are sufficiently similar to a model code that, once you have determined the similarity, you may use the code information in this book as a reasonable approximation during the early stages of design. Others are too dissimilar to permit use of the code information given here. The picture is clouded further by the different editions of each of the model codes that are still in force in different areas, because major changes often take place between one edition of a code and the next. Before becoming too deeply immersed in a design, be sure *exactly* which code governs the site where the building will be built. If it is not one of the model codes whose provisions are condensed and simplified here, it will be necessary to work directly with the specific code from the outset.

Many buildings contain multiple uses that are classified under more than one Use Group. If you are designing such a building, consult the information on mixed-use buildings on page 12.

Multistory open spaces within a building raise fire safety problems that receive special treatment under the four model codes. These provisions are summarized in Appendix C, Mezzanines and Atriums, on pages 435–438.

WHICH BUILDING CODE TO CONSULT

Most building codes in North America are based on one of four "model" codes. To make best use of this section, you should find out from the local building department or state government which of these model codes is the basis for the code in force in the area where your building will be located. The following list indicates the model code followed most closely in each state, as interpreted from information furnished by the National Conference of States on Building Codes and Standards. (BOCA = BOCA National Building Code, NBCC = National Building Code of Canada, SBC = Standard Building Code, UBC = Uniform Building Code. Some states have state or local codes that do not follow any of the model codes.)

State	Code
Alabama	SBC
Alaska	UBC
Arizona	state code
Arkansas	SBC
California	UBC
Canada	NBCC
Colorado	UBC
Connecticut	BOCA
Delaware	county codes
District of Columbia	BOCA
Florida	local codes; mainly SBC
Georgia	SBC
Hawaii	UBC
Idaho	UBC
Illinois	local codes
Indiana	UBC
Iowa	UBC
Kansas	UBC

State	Code
Kentucky	BOCA
Louisiana	NFPA 101
Maine	BOCA
Maryland	BOCA
Massachusetts	BOCA
Michigan	BOCA
Minnesota	UBC
Mississippi	SBC
Missouri	local codes
Montana	UBC
Nebraska	BOCA
Nevada	UBC
New Hampshire	BOCA
New Jersey	BOCA
New Mexico	UBC
New York	state and local codes
North Carolina	SBC
North Dakota	UBC
Ohio	BOCA

State	Code
Oklahoma	BOCA
Oregon	UBC
Pennsylvania	BOCA
Rhode Island	BOCA
South Carolina	SBC
South Dakota	no statewide building code
Tennessee	SBC
Texas	local codes
Utah	UBC
Vermont	BOCA
Virginia	BOCA
Washington	UBC
West Virginia	BOCA
Wisconsin	state code
Wyoming	UBC
Guam	UBC
Puerto Rico	UBC
Virgin Islands	territorial code

USE GROUPS: BOCA NATIONAL BUILDING CODE

This index is compiled from those building uses that are mentioned specifically in the BOCA National Building Code.

8

*Use Group A-5 is governed under the BOCA Code by National Fire Protection Association 102, "Assembly Seating, Tents and Air Supported Structures." No information on this Use Group is furnished in the present volume.

USE GROUPS: NATIONAL BUILDING CODE OF CANADA

This index is compiled from those building uses that are mentioned specifically in the National Building Code of Canada.

Building Use	Use Group	Building Use	Use Group	Building Use	Use Group
Aircraft hangars	F-2	Factories	F-2 or F-3	Planing mills	F-2
Amusement park structures	A-4	Feed mills	F-1	Police stations with detention quarters	B-1
Apartments	C	Flour mills	F-1	Police stations without detention quarters	D
Arenas	A-3	Freight depots	F-2		
Art galleries	A-2	Garages, repair	F-2	Power plants	F-3
Auditoria	A-2	Garages, storage	F-3	Printing plants	F-2
Banks	D	Garages, storage, open air	special	Prisons	B-1
Barber shops	D			Radio stations	D
Beauty shops	D	Grain elevators	F-1	Recreational piers	A-2
Bleachers	A-4	Grandstands	A-4	Reformatories with detention quarters	B-1
Boarding houses	C	Gymnasia	A-2		
Bowling alleys	A-2	Helicopter landing areas on roofs	F-2	Restaurants	A-2
Box factories	F-2	Hospitals	B-2	Reviewing stands	A-4
Bulk plants, flammable liquids	F-1	Hospitals, psychiatric, no detention quarters	B-2	Rinks	A-3
Candy plants	F-2			Rubber processing plants	F-1
Cereal mills	F-1	Hospitals, psychiatric, with detention quarters	B-1	Salesrooms	F-2 or F-3
Chemical manufacturing plants	F-1	Hotels	C	Sample display rooms	F-3
Children's custodial homes	B-2	Houses	C	Sanitoria without detention quarters	B-2
		Infirmaries	B-2		
Churches and other places of worship	A-2	Jails	B-1	Schools, residential	C
		Laboratories	F-2 or F-3	Schools, nonresidential	A-2
Clubs, nonresidential	A-2			Service stations	F-2
Clubs, residential	C	Lacquer factories	F-1	Shops, retail	E
Cold storage plants	F-2	Laundries, self-service	D	Spray painting	F-1
Colleges, nonresidential	A-2	Laundries, other than self-service	F-2	Stadia	A-4
				Storage rooms	F-2 or F-3
Colleges, residential	C	Lecture halls	A-2		
Community halls	A-2	Libraries	A-2	Storage warehouses, hazardous substances in bulk	F-1
Convalescent homes	B-2	Licensed beverage establishments	A-2		
Convents	C				
Courtrooms	A-2	Lodging houses	C	Stores, retail	E
Creameries	F-3	Markets	E	Supermarkets	E
Dance halls	A-2	Mattress factories	F-1 or F-2	Swimming pools, indoor	A-3
Dental offices	D			Television studios with viewing audience	A-1
Department stores	E	Medical offices	D		
Distilleries	F-1	Monasteries	C	Television studios, no audience	F-2
Dormitories	C	Motels	C		
Dry cleaning plants using flammable solvents	F-1	Motion picture theaters	A-1	Theaters	A-1
		Museums	A-2	Tool and appliance rentals	D
		Nursing homes	B-2		
Dry cleaning plants, no flammable solvents	F-2	Offices	D	Undertaking premises	A-2
		Opera houses	A-1	Warehouses	F-2 or F-3
Dry cleaning, self-service, no flammable solvents	D	Orphanages	B-2		
		Paint, varnish, and pyroxylin factories	F-1	Waste paper processing	F-1
				Wholesale rooms	F-2
Electrical substations	F-2	Passenger stations and depots	A-2	Woodworking factories	F-2
Exhibition halls	A-2 or E			Workshops	F-2 or F-3
		Penitentiaries	B-1		

USE GROUPS:
STANDARD BUILDING CODE

This index is compiled from those building uses that are mentioned specifically in the Standard Building Code.

Building Use	Use Group	Building Use	Use Group	Building Use	Use Group
Academies	E	Freight depots	S	Pre-release centers	I-r*
Aircraft hangars	S	Garages	S	Processing plants	F
Amusement park buildings:		Garages, open air	special	Pyroxylin plastic manufacturing	H
1000 or more persons	A-1	Grain elevators	H	Recreation halls:	
Less than 1000 persons	A-2	Greenhouses	B	1000 or more persons	A-1
Assembly halls:		Gymnasiums:		50–999 persons	A-2
1000 or more persons	A-1	1000 or more persons	A-1	Reformatories	I-r*
50–999 persons	A-2	50–999 persons	A-2	Restaurants:	
Auditoriums:		Hospitals	I-u*	1000 or more patrons	A-1
1000 or more persons	A-1	Hotels	R	101–999 patrons	A-2
50–999 persons	A-2	Jails	I-r*	1–100 patrons	B
Banks	B	Libraries, other than in schools	B	Schools	E
Bowling alleys	B	Lodging houses	R	Service stations	B
Churches, places of worship:		Manufacturing plants	F	Shopping malls	M
1000 or more persons	A-1	Markets	M	Shops, retail	M
50–999 persons	A-2	Mental institutions	I-u*	Stadiums and grandstands:	
Colleges	E	Mills	F	1000 or more persons	A-1
Convents	R	Monasteries	R	50–999 persons	A-2
Correctional institutions	I-r*	Motels	R	Storage buildings	S
Dance halls:		Motion picture theaters:		Storage of highly combustible materials	H
1000 or more persons	A-1	1000 or more persons	A-1	Stores	M
50–999 persons	A-2	50–999 persons	A-2	Tank farms, flammable liquids or gases	H
Detention centers	I-r*	Museums:		Tents for assembly:	
Dormitories	R	1000 or more persons	A-1	1000 or more persons	A-1
Dry cleaning establishments	H	50–999 persons	A-2	50–999 persons	A-2
Dwellings, multiple	R	Nurseries, 24-hour care for persons under 6 years of age	I-u*	Theaters for stage productions:	
Dwellings, single-family	R	Nursing homes	I-u*	700 or more persons	A-1
Explosives manufacturing	H	Office buildings	B	50–699 persons	A-2
Factories	F	Paint or solvent manufacturing	H	Tire recapping	H
Film storage (combustible)	H	Parking structures, see Garages		Universities	E
		Passenger depots:		Warehouses	S
		1000 or more persons	A-1		
		Less than 1000 persons	A-2		

*I-r = Institutional, restrained
*I-u = Institutional, unrestrained

USE GROUPS: UNIFORM BUILDING CODE

This index is compiled from those building uses that are mentioned specifically in the Uniform Building Code.

Building Use	Use Group
Aircraft hangars	B-3
Aircraft repair hangars	H-5
Amusement park structures	A-4
Apartment houses	R-1
Assembly, without stage, occupant load less than 300 persons	A-3
Assembly, without stage, occupant load of 300 or more persons	A-2.1
Assembly, with stage, occupant load less than 1000 persons	A-2
Assembly, with stage, occupant load of 1000 or more persons	A-1
Bars, occupant load less than 50 persons	B-2
Bars, occupant load of 50 or more persons, see Assembly	
Box factories	H-3
Cold storage plants	B-4
Convents	R-1
Creameries	B-4
Day care facilities	E-3
Drinking and dining establishments, occupant load less than 50 persons	B-2
Drinking and dining establishments, occupant load of 50 or more persons, see Assembly	
Dry cleaning plants	H-2
Dwellings	R-3
Education, beyond 12th grade, less than 50 occupants per room	B-2
Education, through 12th grade, 50 or more persons	E-1
Education, through 12th grade, less than 50 persons	E-2
Factories, low hazard	B-2

Building Use	Use Group
Factories, noncombustible materials	B-4
Factories with loose combustible fibers or combustible dust	H-3
Fire stations	B-2
Garages, repair, no welding or hazardous liquids	B-1
Gasoline service stations	B-1
Hazardous: storage, handling, use, or sale of hazardous or highly flammable or explosive materials other than Class I, II, or III-A liquids	H-1
Hazardous: storage, handling, or sale of Class I, II, or III-A liquids	H-2
Heliports	B-3
Homes for 6 or more children 6 years of age or older	I-2
Hospitals	I-1
Hotels	R-1
Houses, 1- and 2-family	R-3
Ice plants	B-4
Jails	I-3
Lodging houses	R-3
Mental hospitals	I-3
Monasteries	R-1
Night clubs, see Assembly	
Nurseries, full-time care of at least 6 children under the age of 6	I-1
Nursing homes, ambulatory patients	I-2
Nursing homes, nonambulatory patients	I-1
Office buildings	B-2
Paint shops and spray painting rooms	H-2
Paint storage, no bulk handling	B-2
Paint stores with bulk handling	H-2

Building Use	Use Group
Parking garages, open	special
Planing mills	H-3
Police stations	B-2
Power plants	B-4
Printing plants	B-2
Prisons	I-3
Pumping plants	B-4
Reformatories	I-3
Repair garages using welding, open flame, or combustible liquids	H-4
Restaurants, occupant load less than 50 persons	B-2
Restaurants, occupant load of 50 or more persons, see Assembly	
Reviewing stands	A-4
Sales rooms, noncombustible merchandise	B-4
Sanitariums	I-1
Schools, elementary or secondary, less than 50 persons	E-2
Schools, elementary or secondary, 50 or more persons	E-1
Semiconductor research or fabrication	H-6
Stadiums	A-4
Storage, combustible materials	B-2
Storage, noncombustible materials	B-4
Storage, hazardous materials, see Hazardous	
Storage, with loose combustible fibers or dust	H-3
Stores, retail	B-2
Theaters, see Assembly	
Warehouses, see Storage	
Wholesale stores	B-2
Woodworking establishments	H-3
Workshops, low hazard	B-2

MIXED-USE BUILDINGS

A single building often incorporates more than one use—retail space on the ground floor of an office building; restaurants, bars, and meeting rooms in a hotel; parking levels beneath a commercial building. Such mixed-use buildings are treated slightly differently by different building codes. The four model building codes deal with mixed-use buildings in the following manner:

• The mixed uses generally must be separated from one another by fire walls, fire doors, and fire-resistant floor/ceiling assemblies. The exact degree of fire resistance required for each such separation must be determined by consulting the appropriate code.

• There are several situations in which a fire separation is not usually required. Assembly rooms not more than 750 sq ft (70 m^2) in area need not be separated from surrounding rooms. A kitchen does not have to be separated from the dining area it serves. Administrative offices comprising not more than a quarter of the total floor area of a building may also be built without such a separation, unless the remainder of the building falls into a hazardous Use Group.

• Each portion of a mixed-use building must conform to the normal code requirements for its Use Group.

• Under the National Building Code of Canada and the Standard Building Code, the most restrictive height and area limitations for any of the uses in a building apply to the entire building, unless the more restrictive use occupies not more than 10% of the building area, in which case the building is classified by its main use.

• Under the BOCA National Building Code and the Uniform Building Code, if the various uses are separated from one another by fire walls of specified fire-resistance ratings, each use may be considered to be in its own separate "building." BOCA allows each "building" to be built to the full height and area limitations of a separate building of that Use Group and Construction Type. The Uniform Building Code is more restrictive, specifying that the sum of the ratios of the actual constructed areas to the allowable areas for all the occupancies may not exceed one.

• If parking is provided below a building, the overall height of the building is governed by the main Use Group. Fire separations are required between the parking and the rest of the building, and structural members in the parking garage must meet the fire-resistive requirements of the building above.

DESIGNING THE STRUCTURE

SELECTING THE STRUCTURAL SYSTEM

This section will help you select a structural system for the preliminary design of a building.

15

BUILDING CODE CRITERIA FOR THE SELECTION OF STRUCTURAL SYSTEMS

When choosing a structural system for a building, you must first determine the range of structural systems that the relevant building code allows. Each of the model building codes on which most North American codes are based requires you to do this by determining first the Use Group into which a building falls, then consulting tables, formulas, and numerous detailed provisions of the code that prescribe the maximum height and floor area to which a building of a given Use Group may be built using each of a range of code-defined Construction Types. To streamline this laborious process for purposes of preliminary design, simplified tables of height and area limitations for the four model building codes are compiled on pages 287–419. You should consult the indexes on pages 7–11 first to determine which code governs in the area where your building will be built and the Use Group into which that code places your building. The Construction Type or Types into which each structural system falls are identified on pages 421–433.

DESIGN CRITERIA FOR THE SELECTION
OF STRUCTURAL SYSTEMS

If you wish to create a building with a highly irregular form:

Choose systems with simple floor and roof framing that are fabricated mostly on site, such as

  Sitecast concrete using any slab system without beams or ribs (pages 105–121)

  Light gauge steel framing (pages 86–89)

  Platform frame (pages 47–63)

  Masonry construction with either concrete slab or wood light floor framing (pages 69–83)

If you wish to leave the structure exposed while retaining a high fire-resistance rating:

Choose structural systems that are inherently resistant to fire and heat, including

  All concrete systems (although ribbed systems may require added thickness in the ribs or slab, or an applied fireproofing) (pages 105–133)

  Heavy timber frame (pages 47–67)

  Mill construction (pages 69–83)

Structural steel is extremely susceptible to loss of strength in a fire and usually must be protected with a fire-resistive finishing system.

For further information on the fire resistance of various structural systems and uses for which they are permitted, see pages 421–433.

If you wish to allow column placements that deviate from a regular grid:

Use systems that do not include beams or joists in the floor and roof structure, such as

  Sitecast concrete two-way flat plate or flat slab (pages 116–119)

  Metal space frame

If you wish to minimize floor thickness to reduce total building height or to reduce floor spandrel depth on the building facade:

The thinnest floor systems are concrete slabs without ribs, preferably prestressed, such as

  Sitecast concrete two-way flat plate or flat slab, especially when post-tensioned (pages 116–119)

  Precast prestressed hollow core or solid slab (pages 130–131)

  Posttensioned one-way solid slab (pages 112–113)

If you wish to minimize the area occupied by columns or bearing walls:

Consider long-span structural systems, such as

  Heavy wood trusses (pages 64–65)

  Glue laminated wood beams (pages 60–61)

  Glue laminated wood arches (pages 66–67)

  Conventional steel frame (pages 85–103)

  Open-web steel joists (pages 98–99)

  Single-story rigid steel frame (pages 100–101)

  Steel trusses (pages 102–103)

  Sitecast concrete waffle slab, particularly when posttensioned (pages 120–121)

  Precast concrete single or double tees (pages 132–133)

You may also wish to consider other long-span systems, such as specially fabricated steel beams, suspended systems, arches, vaults, and shells.

DESIGN CRITERIA FOR THE SELECTION OF STRUCTURAL SYSTEMS

If you wish to allow for changes to the building over time:

Consider short-span one-way systems that permit easy structural modification, such as

Light gauge or conventional steel frame (pages 85–103)

Any wood system, including those incorporating masonry construction (pages 47–77)

Sitecast concrete one-way solid slab or one-way joist construction, excluding posttensioned (pages 112–115)

Precast concrete solid or hollow core slab (pages 130–131)

If you wish to permit construction under adverse weather conditions:

Select a system that does not depend on on-site chemical processes (such as the curing of concrete or mortar) and that can be erected quickly, such as

Any steel system (pages 85–103)

Any wood system (pages 47–67)

Precast concrete systems, particularly those that minimize the use of sitecast concrete toppings and grouting (pages 123–133)

If you wish to minimize off-site fabrication time:

Consider systems in which the building is constructed on site from easily formed, relatively unprocessed materials, such as

Any sitecast concrete system (pages 105–121)

Light gauge steel framing (pages 86–89)

Platform frame (pages 47–63)

Any masonry system (pages 70–77)

If you wish to minimize on-site erection time:

Consider systems using highly preprocessed, prefabricated or modular components, such as

Single-story rigid steel frame (pages 100–101)

Conventional steel frame, particularly with hinge connections (pages 85–103)

Any precast concrete system (pages 123–133)

Heavy timber frame (pages 47–67)

If you wish to minimize construction time for a one- or two-story building:

Consider systems that are lightweight and easy to form, or prefabricated and easy to assemble, such as

Any steel system (pages 85–103)

Heavy timber frame (pages 47–67)

Platform frame (pages 47–63)

(*continued*)

SELECTING THE STRUCTURAL SYSTEM

19

DESIGN CRITERIA FOR THE SELECTION OF STRUCTURAL SYSTEMS

If you wish to minimize construction time for a 4- to 20-story building:

Choose from the following systems

    Precast concrete (pages 123–133)

    Conventional steel frame (pages 85–103)

Once the structural components for either of the above systems are prefabricated, on-site erection proceeds quickly.

    Any sitecast concrete system (pages 105–121)

The absence of lead time for the prefabrication of components in these systems allows construction of the building to begin on-site at the earliest time.

If you wish to minimize construction time for a building 30 stories or more in height:

Choose a system that is strong, lightweight, prefabricated, and easy to assemble

    Steel frame (pages 85–103)

    Systems of precast and sitecast concrete are also becoming an economical alternative to steel frame construction in some regions.

The structural design of high-rise buildings is a specialized task, and the necessary consultants should be sought out as early as possible in the design process.

20 *If you wish to minimize the need for diagonal bracing or shear walls:*

Choose a system that is capable of forming rigid joints, such as

    Any sitecast concrete system, particularly those with beams or deepened slabs around the columns (pages 105–121)

    Steel frame with welded rigid connections (pages 85–103)

    Single-story rigid steel frame (pages 100–101)

When depending on a rigid frame for lateral stiffness, the sizes of the framing members often must be increased to resist the added bending stresses produced in such systems.

If you wish to minimize the dead load on the building foundation:

Consider lightweight or short span systems, such as

    Any steel system (pages 85–103)

    Any wood system (pages 47–67)

If you wish to minimize structural distress due to unstable foundation conditions:

Frame systems without rigid joints are recommended, such as

    Steel frame, with bolted connections (pages 85–103)

    Heavy timber frame (pages 58–61)

    Precast concrete systems (pages 123–133)

    Platform framing (pages 47–63)

Welded steel frame, masonry bearing wall, and sitecast concrete frame are particularly to be avoided.

DESIGN CRITERIA FOR THE SELECTION
OF STRUCTURAL SYSTEMS

If you wish to minimize the number of separate trades and contracts required to complete the building:

Consider systems that incorporate many of the functions of a complete wall system in one operation, such as

    Masonry construction including Mill or Ordinary construction (pages 70–83)

    Precast concrete loadbearing wall panel systems (pages 126–127)

If you wish to provide concealed spaces within the structure itself for ducts, pipes, wires, and other building mechanical systems:

Consider systems that naturally provide convenient hollow spaces, such as

    Truss and open-web joist systems (pages 62–65, 98–99, 102–103)

    Light gauge steel framing (pages 86–89)

    Platform frame (pages 47–63)

Light gauge steel framing and platform frame construction are often applied as finish or infill systems in combination with other types of building structure to provide such spaces. For more information on the integration of building services and the structural system, see pages 168–183 and 196–215.

DESIGN CRITERIA: SUMMARY CHART

GIVE SPECIAL CONSIDERATION TO THE SYSTEMS INDICATED IF YOU WISH TO:	WOOD AND MASONRY				STEEL			
	Platform Frame (Pages 47–63)	Timber Frame (Pages 47–67)	Ordinary Construction (Pages 69–83)	Mill Construction (Pages 69–83)	Light Gauge Steel Framing (Pages 86–89)	Single-Story Rigid Steel Frame (Pages 100–101)	Steel Frame—Hinged Connections (Pages 85–103)	Steel Frame—Rigid Connections (Pages 85–103)
Create a highly irregular building form	●		●		●			
Expose the structure while retaining a high fire-resistance rating		●		●				
Allow column placements that deviate from a regular grid								
Minimize floor thickness								
Minimize the area occupied by columns or bearing walls						●	●	
Allow for changes in the building over time	●	●	●	●	●		●	
Permit construction under adverse weather conditions	●	●			●	●	●	
Minimize off-site fabrication time	●		●	●	●			
Minimize on-site erection time		●				●	●	
Minimize construction time for a one- or two-story building	●	●			●	●	●	
Minimize construction time for a 4- to 20-story building							●	
Minimize construction time for a building 30 stories or more in height							●	
Avoid the need for diagonal bracing or shear walls						●		
Minimize the dead load on a foundation	●	●			●	●	●	
Minimize structural distress due to unstable foundation conditions	●	●					●	
Minimize the number of separate trades needed to complete a building			●	●				
Provide concealed spaces for ducts, pipes, etc.	●		●		●			

DESIGN CRITERIA: SUMMARY CHART

	SITECAST CONCRETE										PRECAST CONCRETE			
	One-Way Solid Slab (Pages 112–113)	Posttensioned One-Way Solid Slab (Pages 112–113)	One-Way Joist (Pages 114–115)	Posttensioned One-Way Joist (Pages 114–115)	Two-Way Flat Plate (Pages 116–117)	Posttensioned Two-Way Flat Plate (Pages 116–117)	Two-Way Flat Slab (Pages 118–119)	Posttensioned Two-Way Flat Slab (Pages 118–119)	Waffle Slab (Pages 120–121)	Posttensioned Waffle Slab (Pages 120–121)	Solid Slab (Pages 130–131)	Hollow Core Slab (Pages 130–131)	Double Tee (Pages 132–133)	Single Tee (Pages 132–133)
	●	●			●	●	●	●						
	●	●	●	●	●	●	●	●	●	●	●	●	●	●
					●	●	●	●	●	●				
		●			●	●	●	●			●	●		
									●	●			●	●
	●		●								●	●		
											●	●	●	●
	●	●	●	●	●	●	●	●	●	●				
											●	●	●	●
	●	●	●	●	●	●	●	●	●	●	●	●	●	●
	●	●	●	●	●	●	●	●	●	●				
											●	●	●	●

PRACTICAL SPAN RANGES FOR STRUCTURAL SYSTEMS

This chart gives practical span ranges for various structural systems. Greater or lesser spans may be possible in some circumstances. Page references are included where a system is covered in greater detail elsewhere in this book.

STRUCTURAL SYSTEM		Pages	Span Range
			10' 3m — 20' 6m — 30' 9m — 50' 15m — 100' 30m — 200' 60m — 300' 90m — 500' 150m
WOOD	Joists	54–55	
	Decking	52–53	
	Solid Beams	58–59	
	Rafter Pairs	56–57	
	Light Floor Trusses	62–63	
	Light Roof Trusses	62–63	
	Glue Laminated Beams	60–61	
	Heavy Trusses	64–65	
	Glue Laminated Arches	66–67	
	Domes		
BRICK & CONCRETE MASONRY	Lintels	74–75 82–83	
	Arches	77	
STEEL	Corrugated Decking	94–95	
	Light Gauge Joists	88–89	
	Beams	96–97	
	Open-Web Joists	98–99	
	Single-Story Rigid Frame	100–101	
	Heavy Trusses	102–103	
	Arches and Vaults		
	Space Frame		
	Domes		
	Cable-Stayed		
	Suspension		
SITECAST CONCRETE	One-Way Slabs	112–113	
	Two-Way Slabs	116–119	
	One-Way Joists	114–115	
	Waffle Slab	120–121	
	Beams	110–111	
	Folded Plates and Shells		
	Domes		
	Arches		
PRECAST CONCRETE	Slabs	130–131	
	Beams	128–129	
	Double Tees	132–133	
	Single Tees	132–133	
PNEUMATIC	Air Inflated		
	Air Supported		

LIVE LOAD RANGES FOR BUILDING OCCUPANCIES

LIVE LOAD RANGES FOR BUILDING OCCUPANCIES

OCCUPANCY	Light Loads — 20 psf / 1.0 kPa	Medium Loads — 60 psf / 2.9 kPa	Heavy Loads — 100 psf / 4.8 kPa	Very Heavy Loads — 150 psf / 7.2 kPa	250 psf / 12.0 kPa
Assembly Areas		Fixed seats	Movable seats — Stage areas		
Building Corridors		Private	Public		
Garages		Passenger cars		Trucks and buses	
Hospitals		Private rooms	Operating rooms — Laboratories		
Hotels and Multifamily Housing	Private rooms		Public rooms		
Libraries		Reading rooms		Stacks	
Manufacturing				Light	Heavy
Office Buildings		Offices	Lobbies		
One- and Two-Family Dwellings	Attics — Bedrooms	Living spaces			
Outdoor Areas				Pedestrian	Vehicular
Roof Loads	No snow	Moderate snow	High mountains — Pedestrian		
Storage Areas				Light	Heavy
Schools		Classrooms	Assembly	Shops	
Stores			Retail	Wholesale	
Miscellaneous Public Facilities	Penal institutions — Cell blocks	Bowling alleys — Poolrooms	Gymnasiums — Dance halls — Dining rooms — Restaurants — Stadiums — Skating rinks	Armories — Drill rooms	

LIVE LOAD RANGES FOR STRUCTURAL SYSTEMS

LIVE LOAD RANGES FOR STRUCTURAL SYSTEMS

STRUCTURAL SYSTEM		Pages	Light Loads	Medium Loads	Heavy Loads	Very Heavy Loads
WOOD	Platform Frame	47–63				
	Timber Frame	47–67				
MASONRY	Ordinary Construction	69–83				
	Mill Construction	69–85				
STEEL	Light Gauge Steel Framing	86–89				
	Single-Story Rigid Steel Frame	100–101			(Roof loads only)	
	Conventional Steel Frame	85–103				
SITECAST CONCRETE	One-Way Solid Slab	112–113				
	One-Way Beam and Slab	112–113				
	One-Way Joist	114–115				
	Two-Way Flat Plate	116–117				
	Two-Way Flat Slab	118–119				
	Waffle Slab	120–121				
	Two-Way Beam and Slab	116–117				
PRECAST CONCRETE	Solid Slab	130–131				
	Hollow Core Slab	130–131				
	Double Tee	132–133				
	Single Tee	132–133				

Use the charts on these two pages to identify appropriate structural systems based on the activities planned within the building. Read the chart on the facing page first to determine the approximate live load range associated with the expected building use. Once a load range has been determined, consult the chart on this page to select systems that are recommended within that range. Roof loads are also covered to aid in the selection of roof structural systems.

If a building will have multiple uses, read from the chart for the higher load range. Or, if the different uses will be physically separate within the building, the load ranges for each use may be applied to the appropriate areas.

CONFIGURING THE STRUCTURAL SYSTEM

This section will aid you in making a preliminary layout of the structural system of a building.

29

LATERAL STABILITY AND STRUCTURAL SYSTEMS

STABILIZING ELEMENTS

All buildings must include structural elements designed specifically to resist lateral forces such as wind and earthquake. The choice and location of these elements can influence building design in important ways even at the preliminary stage. The three stabilizing mechanisms used in buildings are the shear wall, the braced frame, and the rigid frame. Any one of these can be used to stabilize a building, or they may be used in combination.

Shear Walls

Shear walls are extremely effective in resisting lateral forces. They are easily constructed from concrete, masonry, or wood, and sometimes, in tall buildings, from steel. The superior resistance of shear walls to lateral forces often makes them a good choice in situations such as across the narrow dimension of a tall, slender building, where the maximum resistance to lateral forces is required. Shear walls also are commonly integrated into the enclosure of vertical building cores or stair towers. Shear walls may or may not bear gravity loads, and for maximum performance they should have a minimum of penetrations or openings. When shear walls are incorporated into the interior of a building, their locations must be coordinated with the building plan. Shear walls at the perimeter of a building can restrict the size, number, or arrangement of openings in the building facade.

Braced Frames

Braced frames are also very effective at resisting lateral forces. They may be constructed from steel, timber, or, occasionally, from concrete. The diagonal elements that comprise this system are similar to shear walls in their impact on the plan or facade of a building. Braced frames also are often integrated into the structure of vertical cores in a building

Rigid Frames

Rigid frames depend on rigid connections between columns and beams (or slabs) to develop resistance to lateral forces. Though the least efficient of the three stabilizing mechanisms, rigid frames find use in such situations as those requiring relatively modest resistance (low, broad buildings), or in buildings where the presence of stabilizing walls or braces is undesirable. Compared to shear wall or braced frame systems, the use of rigid frames may set greater restrictions on the arrangement and sizing of the structural frame: Column spacings often must be reduced, variations or irregularities in column placements may be limited, and the depths of columns and beams may need to be increased. The rigid joints necessary in this system can easily be constructed in steel (at added cost compared to hinge connections), or in sitecast concrete, where they are formed as a normal part of the construction process. Though possible, rigid joints are difficult to construct and are rarely used in precast concrete. Rigid frames are often combined with either shear walls or braced frames for improved results over either system alone.

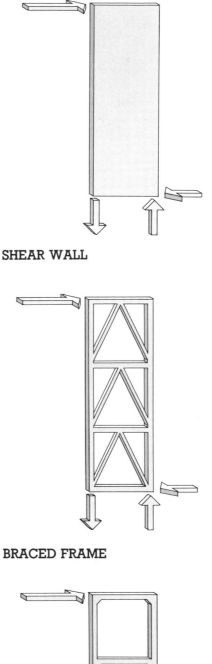

SHEAR WALL

BRACED FRAME

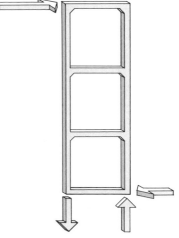

RIGID FRAME

LATERAL STABILITY AND STRUCTURAL SYSTEMS

CONFIGURING STABILIZING ELEMENTS

The proper arrangement of shear walls, diagonal braces, or rigid joints in a structure is crucial to their effectiveness in resisting lateral forces acting on the building. As illustrated in the adjacent schematic floor plans, these elements may be placed within the interior of the building or at the perimeter, and they may be combined in a variety of ways. However, they must be arranged so as to resist lateral forces acting from all directions. This is usually accomplished by aligning one set of stabilizing elements along each of the two perpendicular plan axes of a building. Stabilizing elements must also be arranged in as balanced a fashion as possible in relation to the mass of the building. Unbalanced arrangements of these elements result in the displacement of the center of resistance of the building away from its center of mass. Such a condition causes unusual building movements under lateral loads that may be difficult or impossible to control.

In general, considerations of lateral stability become increasingly important as the height of the building increases. The configuration of stabilizing elements is discussed in more detail on the following pages.

Stabilizing elements may be placed within the interior or at the perimeter of a building.

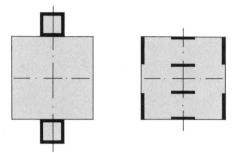

Stabilizing elements should be arranged in a balanced fashion.

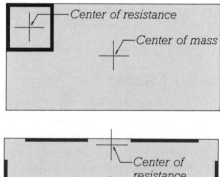

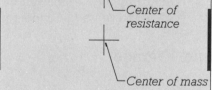

Unbalanced arrangements of stabilizing elements result in the displacement of the center of the building away from its center of mass. Such arrangements should be avoided.

LATERAL STABILITY AND STRUCTURAL SYSTEMS

This chart indicates the methods of resisting lateral forces most appropriate to each structural system. More detailed information on the individual systems can be found on the pages noted in the chart.

STRUCTURAL SYSTEM		Pages	Rigid Frame	Semi-Rigid Joints w/Supplemental Braced Frames or Shear Walls	Braced Frame	Shear Walls
WOOD	Platform Frame	47–63			● Let-in bracing	● Panel sheathing
	Timber Frame	47–67			● Timber bracing	● Diagonal or panel sheathing
MASONRY	Ordinary Construction	69–83				● Masonry walls
	Mill Construction	69–83				● Masonry walls
STEEL	Light Gauge Steel Framing	86–89			● Strap bracing	● Panel sheathing
	Single-Story Rigid Steel Frame	100–101	● Parallel to frames only		● Perpendicular to frames	
	Conventional Steel Frame	85–103	● Requires welded connections	●	●	● Sitecast concrete
SITECAST CONCRETE	One-Way Solid Slab	112–113	○ May require added structure	●		
	One-Way Beam and Slab	112–113	●	●		
	One-Way Joist	114–115	●	●		
	Two-Way Flat Plate	116–117	○ May require added structure	●		
	Two-Way Flat Slab	118–119	○ May require added structure	●		
	Waffle Slab	120–121	●	●		
	Two-Way Beam and Slab	116–117	●	●		
PRECAST CONCRETE	Solid Slab	130–131	○		○ Uncommon	●
	Hollow Core Slab	130–131	○		○ Uncommon	●
	Double Tee	132–133	○		○ Uncommon	●
	Single Tee	132–133	○		○ Uncommon	●

● Recommended
○ Possible in some circumstances

WALL AND SLAB SYSTEMS

VERTICAL LOAD RESISTING ELEMENTS

Wall and slab systems are composed of loadbearing walls spanned by horizontal slabs. The placement of walls in this system is restricted by their role as structural elements, as they must be located to support the loads from slabs and walls above. Due to the significant presence of the walls in the plan of the building, the use of a wall and slab system generally implies a close correspondence between the structural module and the planning of building functions. Furthermore, economic considerations usually dictate that the arrangement of walls be as uniform as possible, making this system particularly attractive for building types that require regular arrangements of uniformly sized spaces, such as apartments, schools, and hotels.

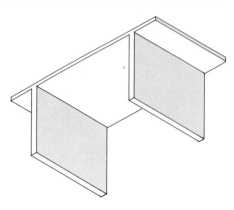

WALL AND SLAB SYSTEMS
(shown from below)

LATERAL LOAD RESISTING ELEMENTS

The regularly placed structural walls used in this system are well suited to act as shear walls for lateral stability. They may be used alone or combined with rigid frames or braced frames, for instance, where structural walls run in only one direction in a building.

    When used alone, shear walls must be arranged to resist lateral forces in all directions, such as in some variation of a complete or partial box form. Shear walls should always be placed as symmetrically as possible in the building plan, particularly in taller buildings. The sizes and spacing of openings in shear walls may need to be restricted as well.

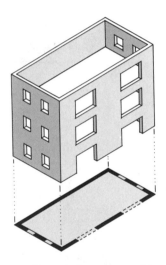

Shear walls may be arranged in a box form to resist lateral forces from all directions.

SYSTEMS WELL SUITED TO WALL AND SLAB FRAMING

Bearing walls of any type may be used to create wall and slab structural systems. See the following sections for more information:

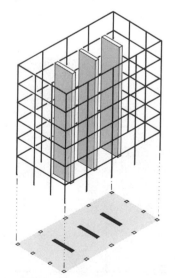

When combined with other stabilizing mechanisms, shear walls may be arranged so as to resist forces in only one direction of a building.

34

WALL AND SLAB SYSTEMS

WALL AND SLAB SYSTEM LAYOUTS

The distance between walls is equal to the span of the slab.

Walls can be any length but are required wherever slabs are supported. Where necessary, openings in walls can be made by including beams over such openings to carry loads from above. In multistory buildings the locations of bearing walls should coincide from floor to floor. However, where it is desirable to omit bearing walls from a lower floor, it may be possible to design the wall above as a deep beam supported at its ends only.

Wall and slab systems can be combined with column systems to permit greater open areas in a plan. Wherever possible, keep walls in locations that are most desirable for lateral load resistance.

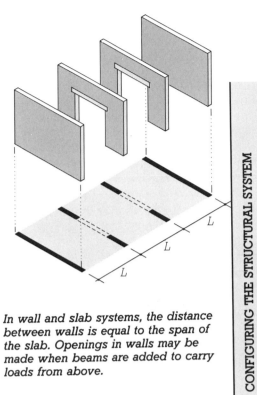

In wall and slab systems, the distance between walls is equal to the span of the slab. Openings in walls may be made when beams are added to carry loads from above.

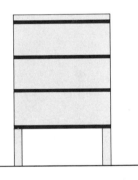

Bearing walls may act as deep beams to span across openings below, as shown in this schematic cross section.

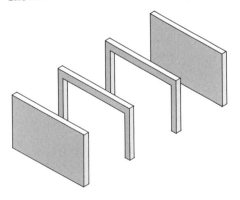

Bearing wall and column systems may be combined for more flexibility in plan layouts.

COLUMN AND BEAM SYSTEMS

VERTICAL LOAD RESISTING ELEMENTS

Column and beam systems are composed of vertical columns, horizontally spanning girders and beams, and a slab spanning between the beams. The columns in this system have less impact than loadbearing walls on the planning of spaces within a building. Where the sizes of interior spaces of a building do not correspond with a structural module or are irregular in shape or size, where maximum open space is desired, or where a high degree of flexibility in the use of space over time is desired, column and beam systems are a good choice. Compared to column and slab systems, column and beam systems are also practical over a greater range of spans and bay proportions.

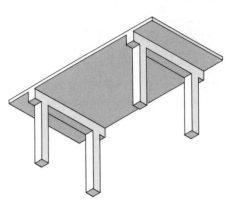

COLUMN AND BEAM SYSTEMS
(shown from below)

LATERAL LOAD RESISTING ELEMENTS

Column and beam systems of steel frame or sitecast concrete construction are well suited to rigid frame action. When used in this way, rigid joints are required at some or all column to beam connections. In sitecast concrete, rigid joints are produced as a normal feature of the system. In steel, rigid connections must be welded and may be more expensive to construct. Rigid joints are difficult to construct and are rarely used in precast concrete. Because no added braces or walls are required, rigid frame systems are often preferred for their minimal interference with the plan of a building. However, the use of rigid frames generally restricts column placements to regular, orthogonal layouts, and often requires deeper beams and more closely spaced and larger columns than would otherwise be required with either braced frame or shear walls. Rigid frames are normally not well suited for structures with unusually long spans or tall columns.

When braced frames or shear walls are used for lateral stability, columns and beams may be joined with simpler, hinged connections, such as the bolted connections normally used in steel and timber structures or the flexible welded connections used in precast concrete. The stabilizing braces or walls may be located within the interior of the building or at the perimeter, but they must be placed so as to resist lateral forces in all directions. Building cores or stair towers housing vertical circulation or other systems often can be easily designed to incorporate such elements, thus eliminating their intrusion from the remainder of the building floor plan. When located at the perimeter of the structure, these elements may influence the design of the building facade.

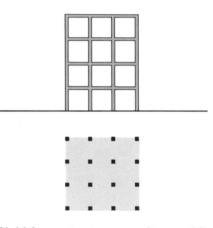

Rigid frame structures require no additional bracing or shear walls, as shown in this elevation and plan.

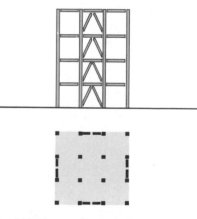

The locations of braced frames or shear walls must be considered in relation to the elevation and plan of the building.

COLUMN AND BEAM SYSTEMS

SYSTEMS WELL SUITED TO COLUMN AND BEAM FRAMING

Information on column and beam systems may be found in the following sections:

Systems	Pages
Wood Beams	58–61
Steel Beams and Girders	96–97
Sitecast Concrete Beams and Girders	110–111
Precast Concrete Beams and Girders	128–129

COLUMN AND BEAM SYSTEM LAYOUTS

Columns are located on the lines of the beams above. Although column spacings may vary within the limits of the spanning capacity of the beams, for reasons of economy, columns are typically restricted to some regular gridded arrangement.

Various combinations of beams and slabs are possible. Beams can span in one direction only, with slabs spanning perpendicular to them. With this arrangement, column spacing in one direction is equal to the span of the beams; in the other direction, it is equal to the span of the slabs.

More flexibility in the location of columns can be achieved with beams spanning in both directions. Deeper beams, termed *girders*, span the columns. The girders in turn support shallower, secondary beams, spanning perpendicular to them. Finally, the distance between the secondary beams is spanned by the slab. Column spacings with such beam and girder arrangements are limited only by the spanning capacity of the beams in either direction. The choice of the direction of the span of the girders and beams in such a structure can be influenced by a variety of factors, including the particular structural systems involved, the relative structural efficiency of either arrangement, the lateral stability requirements for the overall structure, and the integration of the floor structure with other building systems such as electrical wiring in the slab or ducts and piping running beneath the floor framing. These considerations are covered in more detail in the sections of this book covering specific structural or mechanical systems.

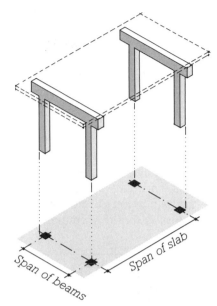

In column and beam systems, columns are located on beam lines.

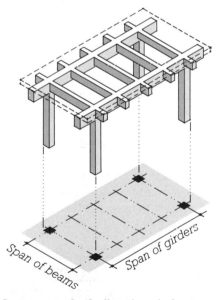

Beams span both directions in beam and girder systems.

COLUMN AND SLAB SYSTEMS

VERTICAL LOAD RESISTING ELEMENTS

Column and slab systems are composed of vertical columns directly supporting horizontally spanning slabs without the use of beams. As with column and beam systems, the reliance on columns for carrying vertical loads permits greater independence between the building plan and the structural system. The absence of beams in column and slab systems may permit even greater flexibility in column placements than with column and beam systems, because columns are not restricted to beam lines. Column and slab systems may also be attractive economically due to the simplification of construction techniques and the reduction in total floor depths that they make possible.

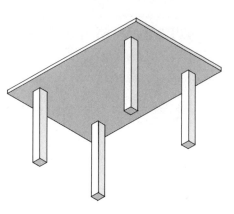

COLUMN AND SLAB SYSTEMS
(shown from below)

LATERAL LOAD RESISTING ELEMENTS

Rigid frame action is possible in column and slab systems, although its effectiveness depends on the depth of the slab, particularly in the areas close to the columns. Where large lateral forces are expected with systems with shallow slabs, a deepening of the slab or the addition of structural beams between columns may be required to achieve sufficient lateral resistance.

Shear walls or braced frames may also be used to develop lateral resistance in column and slab systems. These elements may be used either as the sole means of lateral bracing, or as enhancements to the rigid frame action of the system. They may be located within the interior of the building or at the perimeter, but they must be placed so as to resist lateral forces in all directions. The locations of interior elements must be coordinated with the building plan. Building cores housing vertical circulation or other systems can often be easily designed to incorporate such elements, thus eliminating their intrusion from the remainder of the floor plan. When located at the perimeter of the structure, shear walls or braces may influence the design of the building facade.

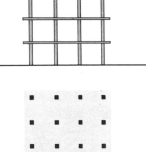

As shown in this elevation and plan, rigid frame action is possible with column and slab systems, although its effectiveness may be limited.

SYSTEMS WELL SUITED TO COLUMN AND SLAB FRAMING

Conventional structural systems that are configured as column and slab systems are metal space frame, or sitecast concrete systems, including two-way flat plate, two-way flat slab, and either one-way joist or waffle slab construction (when these two systems are used with shallow beams that do not extend below the surface of the ribs). For further information, see the following pages:

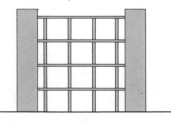

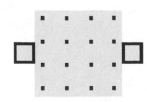

Shear walls are commonly used with column and slab systems. In this elevation and plan, the shear walls are shown incorporated into a pair of vertical cores.

COLUMN AND SLAB SYSTEMS

COLUMN AND SLAB SYSTEM LAYOUTS

Column spacing in either direction is equal to the span of the slab. For maximum economy and structural efficiency, column bays should be approximately square in proportion, and column displacements from regular lines should be minimized. However, column layouts are more flexible in column and slab systems because columns are not restricted to beam lines. Variations in column placements, changes in bay sizes, and irregular plan shapes may be more easily accommodated than in other framing systems.

STRUCTURAL LIMITATIONS OF COLUMN AND SLAB SYSTEMS

The absence of beams in sitecast concrete flat plate and flat slab construction may limit the structural performance of these systems. The relatively shallow depth of the joint between the columns and slabs can restrict their capacity to carry heavy loads on the slab and can limit their resistance to lateral forces. Though the addition of beams to these systems adds substantially to construction costs, it may be a practical alternative where longer spans are required, very heavy loads must be carried, or additional lateral resistance is needed and the use of shear walls or braced frames is undesirable. Such configurations are covered in more detail in the sections describing these structural systems.

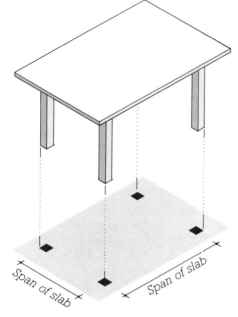

In column and slab systems, the span of the slab is equal to the column spacing in either direction.

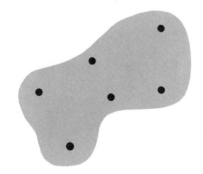

The absence of beams in column and slab systems may facilitate irregular column layouts or plan shapes.

HIGH-RISE STRUCTURAL CONFIGURATIONS

THE DESIGN OF HIGH-RISE STRUCTURES

As the proposed height of a building increases, the design of its structural system becomes increasingly specialized and complex. A variety of factors, many of them difficult to characterize at the schematic level, can have a major influence on the selection and design of a structural system. The great vertical loads on the structure, the character of wind and earthquake forces specific to the building site, the local foundation conditions, the relative costs of various construction systems within the region, unusual structural conditions within the building, and the particular expertise of the structural engineer are all important factors. For these reasons no serious attempt at the design of a high-rise structure should be made without the participation of a qualified structural engineer, even in the early phases of design. Within this context, however, the information in this section may serve to inform the architect of the basic structural systems available for tall buildings and to describe the relationship of these structural systems to the total design of the building.

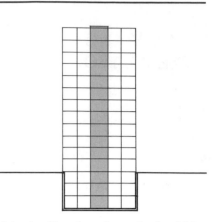

Major loadbearing elements should be continuous vertically to the foundations of the building.

VERTICAL LOAD RESISTING SYSTEMS

The vertical load resisting systems for high-rise buildings are essentially the same as those for low-rise structures discussed on the previous pages. In the tallest buildings, column and beam systems are predominant due to their efficient use of space, versatility as a structural system, and ease of construction. Because of the large gravity loads associated with tall buildings, special care should be taken that major structural elements are not interrupted vertically. Whenever possible, building cores, columns, and loadbearing walls should not shift laterally from floor to floor and should be continuous from the roof to the foundation of the building.

However, configurations may occur in which all loads do not have direct and continuous paths to the foundation. In some cases it is desirable to redistribute vertical loads in a structure outward toward the corners of the building to increase its resistance to overturning. Unique spaces in the lower portions of tall buildings, such as auditoriums, lobbies, atriums, or other public facilities, often require longer span systems that must interrupt the paths of loadbearing elements from above. And changes in the massing of a building or in programmed uses at different levels within the building may dictate changes in the arrangement or spacing of structural elements for these different areas. Where such changes in structural configuration must occur, the effects may range from the use of transfer beams or trusses designed to redistribute vertical loads horizontally to, in extreme cases, the reconsideration of the basic structural configuration or programmatic organization of the building.

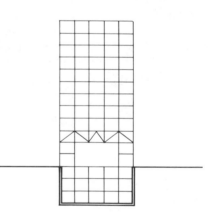

Transfer beams or trusses may be used to interrupt vertical loadbearing elements where necessary.

HIGH-RISE STRUCTURAL CONFIGURATIONS

LATERAL LOAD RESISTING SYSTEMS

Increasing the height of a building increases its sensitivity to both wind and earthquake forces. The taller the building, the more these forces will dominate the design of the entire structure, and the more attention should be given to designing for them. The following guidelines are particularly important in the design of high-rise buildings.

Tall, narrow buildings are more difficult to stabilize against lateral forces than broader buildings. In such instances more effective bracing mechanisms may be required, and bracing elements may assume more prominence in the final design of the building.

Especially in areas of high seismic activity, tall buildings that are nonsymmetrical or unbalanced in either massing or the arrangement of bracing elements can experience forces that may be difficult to control. Such conditions should be avoided whenever possible.

Parts of a building that are independent in massing can be expected to move differently under the dynamic loads associated with earthquakes. The leg of an L-shaped building, the stem of a T-shaped building, a wide base with a narrow tower, or any other forms composed of discrete masses may interact in potentially destructive ways under such conditions. All such masses should be designed as separate structures, with independent vertical and lateral load resisting systems, to minimize these effects.

Buildings of inherently unstable massing should be avoided.

Discontinuities in the stiffness of a structure at different levels may lead to excessive deflections or other unfavorable responses to lateral loads. For instance, an open space with long horizontal spans at the base of a tall building may produce excessive flexibility at that level. If such a "soft story" cannot be avoided, the addition of special bracing elements at that level may be required.

Tall buildings may interact with winds in unpredictable ways. With buildings of irregular or unusual form, or on sites where adjacent structures or other features may produce unusual air movements, specialized studies of the building's response to local wind pressures and fluctuations may be required.

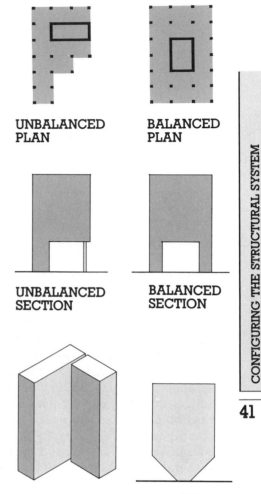

UNBALANCED PLAN   **BALANCED PLAN**

UNBALANCED SECTION   **BALANCED SECTION**

Discrete building masses should be structurally independent. Inherently unstable building masses should be avoided.

Discontinuities in the stiffness of structures at different levels should be avoided, or additional stabilizing elements may be required.

CONFIGURING THE STRUCTURAL SYSTEM

41

HIGH-RISE STRUCTURAL CONFIGURATIONS

The three mechanisms of shear wall, braced frame, and rigid frame can be configured in specialized ways for use in high-rise structures. The following systems are presented in order of increasing resistance to lateral forces. The adjacent diagrams illustrate these systems schematically in elevation above and plan below.

CONVENTIONAL CONFIGURATIONS

The conventional arrangements of stabilizing elements used in low-rise buildings may be extended for use in buildings up to 20 to 25 stories in height. The same considerations that apply to low-rise buildings apply to taller buildings as well. Stabilizing elements should be arranged so as to resist lateral forces along all major axes of the building. These elements should be arranged in a balanced manner either within the building or at the perimeter. And such elements must be integrated with the building plan or elevation.

Shear walls and braced frames are the stabilizing elements most commonly used in buildings of this height, due to their structural efficiency. They may be used either separately or in combination. The use of rigid frames as the sole means of stabilizing structures of this height is possible, although it may be less desirable because of the increased size of the beams and columns that it necessitates. For steel structures, the fabrication of welded joints required with rigid frames also becomes increasingly uneconomical as the number of these connections multiplies. Rigid frames may also be used in combination with either shear walls or braced frames to enhance the total lateral resistance of a structure.

CORE STRUCTURES

Core structures are perhaps the system that is most commonly used to stabilize all but the tallest buildings. These structures integrate the stabilizing elements of the structure into the vertical cores that house circulation and mechanical systems in tall buildings. One of the principal advantages of these structures is that with the incorporation of the resisting elements into the building core, interference with the surrounding usable space in the building is minimized. In concrete construction, core walls already intended to enclose these other building systems can easily be designed to also act as shear walls, in many cases with no increase in size. In steel construction, core structures are usually designed as braced frames.

In buildings with more than one core, the cores should be located symmetrically in the building plan so as to provide balanced resistance under lateral loads from any direction. A single core servicing an entire building should be located at the center of the building. Cores typically comprise approximately 20%–25% of the total floor area of a high-rise building. They should be formed as closed elements, approximately square or cylindrical, with openings into the core kept to a minimum.

Simple core structures can be used in buildings as high as 35 to 40 stories. Core structures can also be enhanced structurally with the addition

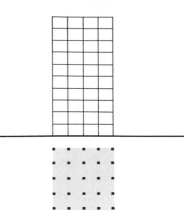

RIGID FRAME

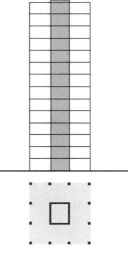

RIGID CORE

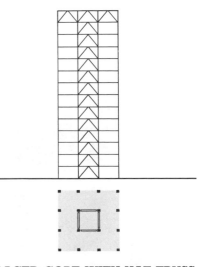

BRACED CORE WITH HAT TRUSS

of bracing in the form of "hat" trusses. Hat trusses involve the perimeter columns of the building in resisting lateral loads, thus significantly improving the overall performance of the building. Such trusses may influence the design of the building facade or the location of mechanical floors. Columns at the perimeter of the building may also increase in size with this system. These core-interactive structures are suitable for buildings up to approximately 55 stories in height.

For further information on the design of building cores to accommodate mechanical and circulation systems, see pages 168–178.

TUBE STRUCTURES

The tallest buildings currently being constructed are designed as tube structures. In this system stabilizing elements are located at the perimeter of the structure, leaving the layout of the interior of the building virtually unrestricted by considerations of lateral stability. Either braced frame or rigid frame elements, constructed from either steel or concrete, may be used. Simple tube structures and their variations are generally used for buildings approximately 50 to 55 stories or greater in height.

The use of rigid frame tubes may affect the size and spacing of framing elements at the perimeter of the building. Beams may need to be deeper and columns may need to be larger and more closely spaced than would otherwise be required. When building in steel, the welded joints required in this system may be more costly to construct, although construction systems have been developed that allow the off-site fabrication of these joints, thus minimizing this disadvantage.

Braced frame tubes are one of the most structurally efficient lateral load resisting configurations. When built in steel, these structures also rely on more easily constructed bolted connections. The diagonal braces that are an integral part of this system often have a significant impact on the appearance of the building facade.

The performance of rigid frame tube structures may be enhanced with the addition of belt trusses located at the perimeter of the structure. These trusses may be located at various levels in the structure, and as with hat trusses, they may influence the location of mechanical floors and overall facade design.

Variations on the tube structure are also possible. "Tube-in tube" structures, in which perimeter tubes interact with rigid cores, may be designed for enhanced structural performance. "Bundled tube" structures permit greater variation in the massing of a structure and can enhance the overall performance of the structure as well.

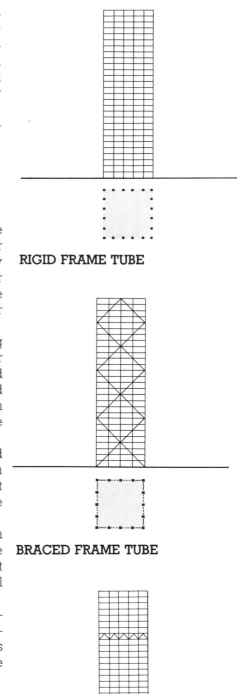

RIGID FRAME TUBE

BRACED FRAME TUBE

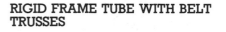

RIGID FRAME TUBE WITH BELT TRUSSES

THE DESIGN OF TALL BUILDINGS FOR MAJOR EARTHQUAKES

Particularly in areas of high seismic risk, the design of the structural system for a tall building will be strongly influenced by the behavior of the structure under the dynamic loads of an earthquake. The final selection of a structural system and material should be based on a detailed engineering analysis, as well as the preferences and experience of the structural engineer. The following guidelines may be useful for preliminary considerations.

Steel

Structural steel frames are considered particularly well suited to withstanding the extreme forces associated with major earthquakes. The light weight of steel reduces overall building mass, thereby minimizing the forces experienced by the structure under dynamic conditions. And the high ductility of steel allows the design of a structure capable of dissipating the great amounts of energy imparted to it during a major earthquake. Designing steel structures that take full advantage of these characteristics results in a building frame that is relatively flexible but highly resilient and capable of withstanding extreme forces without collapse.

Relying on structures that are flexible as a strategy for withstanding the destructive effects of earthquakes is the predominant approach used for the design of tall buildings on the North American continent. However, the large movements that can be expected in such a structure during a major earthquake present difficulties in the design of non-structural elements and their connections to the building frame. As much as possible, elements such as external cladding or interior partitions must be isolated from the structural frame so as to minimize damage to them during an earthquake and so that they do not restrict the movements of the structure itself under dynamic conditions.

Concrete

Concrete is, in contrast to steel, massive and relatively brittle. The high mass of concrete is generally disadvantageous under dynamic conditions, as greater loads will be experienced by the structure. And the brittle character of concrete lessens its capacity to absorb dynamic energy, although adequate ductility in concrete frame structures can be achieved with careful design of the steel reinforcing. These characteristics of concrete result in building frames that are relatively stiff and that depend much more on the brute strength of the frame to resist the forces of earthquakes.

The relative stiffness of concrete structures may be preferable where earthquake loads are not as severe or for buildings that are less tall. Concrete structures may also be desirable for building sites where the ground movements associated with earthquakes are such that the shorter period of vibration of a stiffer structure may be advantageous. Because building movements in concrete structures are significantly less than in steel structures, the detailing of non-structural elements and their connections to the building frame are also much simplified.

SIZING THE STRUCTURAL SYSTEM

This section will assist you in assigning approximate sizes to structural elements. Additional information on designing and building with each structural system is also provided.

45

WOOD STRUCTURAL SYSTEMS

Wood construction typically takes one of two distinct forms: Wood Light Frame construction uses relatively thin, closely spaced members to form walls, floors, and roofs in a system called Platform Frame construction. Heavy Timber construction uses larger members configured as a post and beam system. Both of these systems are fully treated in this section.

Either Wood Light Frame or Heavy Timber construction can be combined with masonry construction for increased fire resistance and load capacity. These systems are more fully described under Masonry Structural Systems, beginning on page 69.

PLATFORM FRAME CONSTRUCTION

Platform frame construction is an economical and flexible building system. It is used extensively for single-family and multifamily housing, as well as for low-rise apartment buildings and small commercial structures.

Because this system is largely fabricated on site and the individual framing members are small, it is particularly well suited for use where unusual layouts or irregular forms are desired. Where economy is a primary concern, the use of a 2- or 4-ft (0.6- or 1.2-m) modular plan dimension may be desirable. Platform frame construction easily and unobtrusively incorporates mechanical systems and other building services.

Platform framing is a wall and slab system. Lateral bracing may be supplied either by shear wall or braced frame action of the load-bearing walls.

HEAVY TIMBER CONSTRUCTION

Heavy Timber construction is characterized by high fire resistance (it has a substantially higher fire rating than unprotected steel), high load capacity, and the unique aesthetic qualities of the exposed wood frame. The framing members for Heavy Timber construction may be either solid wood or glue laminated. Heavy timber frames are used for low-rise commercial and industrial buildings and in residential construction. Because the framing members are typically prefabricated, on-site erection times can be rapid with this system. However, the larger sizes of the framing members make this system less suitable than platform framing for structures that are highly irregular in form or layout. Special provisions may also be required for the integration of mechanical and electrical systems into heavy timber framing.

As in platform framing, economy of construction may be maximized with the use of a 2- or 4-ft (0.6- or 1.2-m) design module when planning a timber frame structure.

Timber frames may be stabilized laterally by the shear resistance of the walls or panels used to enclose the frame, or with the use of diagonal bracing. The masonry bearing walls of Ordinary or Mill construction are also well suited to acting as shear walls.

SIZING THE STRUCTURAL SYSTEM

47

FIRE-RESISTANCE RATINGS FOR WOOD COLUMNS

To qualify as components of Mill construction as defined by most building codes, wood columns supporting floor loads must have a nominal size of at least 8 × 8 in. (191 × 191 mm). Columns supporting roof and ceiling loads only may be as small as 6 × 8 in. (140 × 191 mm). Columns of lesser dimension may be used in Ordinary construction and Wood Light Frame construction.

WOOD COLUMNS

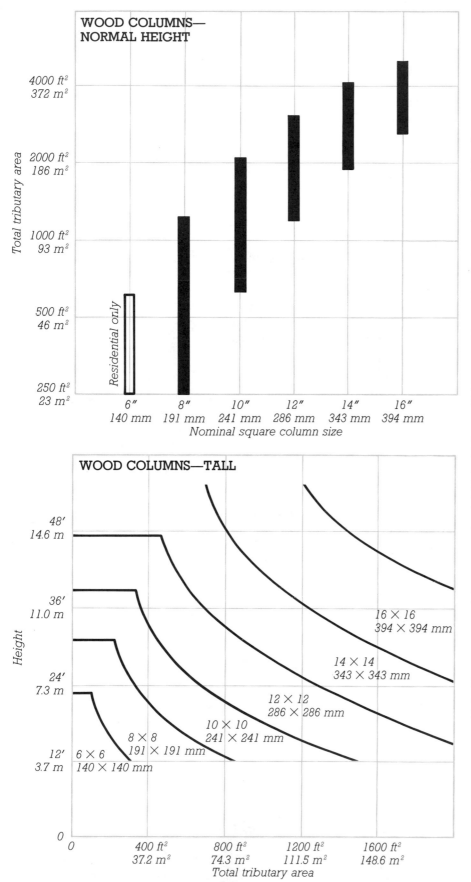

WOOD COLUMNS— NORMAL HEIGHT

Total tributary area

4000 ft² / 372 m²	
2000 ft² / 186 m²	
1000 ft² / 93 m²	
500 ft² / 46 m²	
250 ft² / 23 m²	

Residential only

6" 140 mm	8" 191 mm	10" 241 mm	12" 286 mm	14" 343 mm	16" 394 mm

Nominal square column size

WOOD COLUMNS—TALL

Height

48' / 14.6 m	
36' / 11.0 m	16 × 16 / 394 × 394 mm
24' / 7.3 m	14 × 14 / 343 × 343 mm
	12 × 12 / 286 × 286 mm
	10 × 10 / 241 × 241 mm
12' / 3.7 m	8 × 8 / 191 × 191 mm
	6 × 6 / 140 × 140 mm
0	

0	400 ft² 37.2 m²	800 ft² 74.3 m²	1200 ft² 111.5 m²	1600 ft² 148.6 m²

Total tributary area

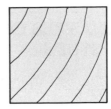

The top chart is for wood columns of up to 12 ft (3.7 m) in height between floors. For strong woods or low loads, read toward the top of the indicated areas. For heavy loads, or for columns resisting lateral or other bending forces, read toward the bottom.

☐ Strong woods include Douglas Fir, Larch, Southern Pine, and Oak.

☐ For rectangular columns, read from the square column with equivalent area.

☐ Actual column size is ½ in. (13 mm) less than nominal in each direction.

☐ *Total tributary area* is the total area of roofs and floors supported by the column.

For columns taller than 12 ft (3.7 m) between floors, read both charts on this page. Use the larger of the two sizes indicated.

☐ For light loads or strong woods, decrease column size by one size (less 2 in. or 50 mm). For heavy loads, or for columns resisting lateral or other bending forces, increase column size by one size (add 2 in. or 50 mm).

☐ For rectangular columns, read from the square column the same size as the least dimension of the rectangular column.

WOOD STUD WALLS

ACTUAL SIZES OF WALL STUDS

Nominal Size	Actual Size	
2 × 4	1½″ × 3½″	(38 × 89 mm)
2 × 6	1½″ × 5½″	(38 × 140 mm)
2 × 8	1½″ × 7¼″	(38 × 184 mm)

SPACING OF WALL STUDS

Wall studs are most commonly spaced 16 in. (406 mm) center-to-center. A 12-in. (305-mm) spacing may be used where greater strength and stiffness are required. Where the structural requirements are less, a 24-in. (610-mm) spacing may also be used so long as the applied sheathing or finishing panels are sufficiently stiff to span the greater distance between studs. In all cases studs must fall on a 4-ft (1219-mm) module in order to coordinate with the standard width of various panel products that are used as an integral part of this system.

FIRE-RESISTANCE RATINGS OF WOOD STUD WALLS

Wood stud walls are classified as Wood Light Frame construction and may qualify for a 1-hour fire rating when covered on both sides with ⅝-in. (16-mm) Type X gypsum board or its equivalent.

WOOD STUD WALLS

WOOD STUD WALLS— NORMAL HEIGHT

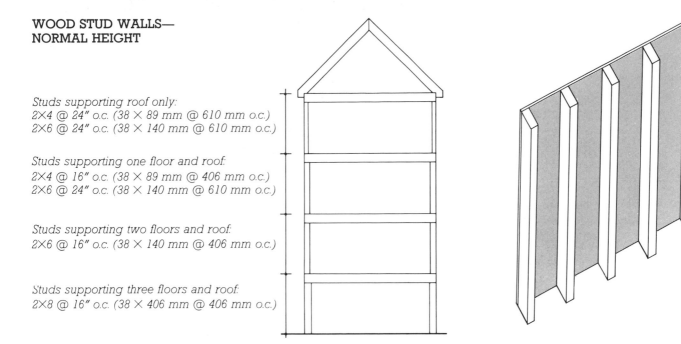

Studs supporting roof only:
2×4 @ 24″ o.c. (38 × 89 mm @ 610 mm o.c.)
2×6 @ 24″ o.c. (38 × 140 mm @ 610 mm o.c.)

Studs supporting one floor and roof:
2×4 @ 16″ o.c. (38 × 89 mm @ 406 mm o.c.)
2×6 @ 24″ o.c. (38 × 140 mm @ 610 mm o.c.)

Studs supporting two floors and roof:
2×6 @ 16″ o.c. (38 × 140 mm @ 406 mm o.c.)

Studs supporting three floors and roof:
2×8 @ 16″ o.c. (38 × 406 mm @ 406 mm o.c.)

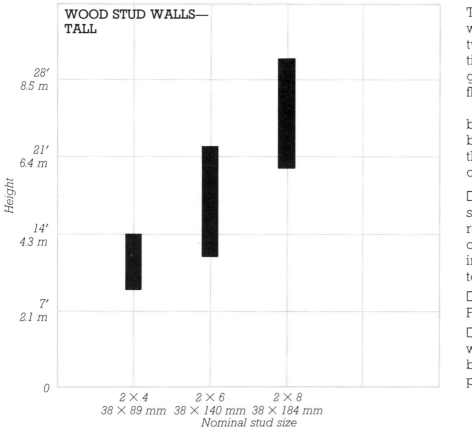

WOOD STUD WALLS— TALL

The table above is for wood stud walls up to 9 ft (2.7 m) tall between floors. Minimum combinations of stud size and spacing are given based on the total number of floors of building.

For walls taller than 9 ft (2.7 m) between floors, consult both the table above and the chart below. Use the larger of the two sizes indicated.

☐ For light loads, 12-in. (305-mm) stud spacings, or strong woods, read toward the top in the indicated areas. For heavy loads or 24-in. (610-mm) stud spacings, read toward the bottom.

☐ Strong woods include Douglas Fir, Larch, Southern Pine, and Oak.

☐ Wall heights may be increased with the addition of intermediate bracing perpendicular to the wall plane.

WOOD DECKING

FIRE-RESISTANCE RATINGS FOR WOOD DECKING

To qualify for Mill construction as defined by the building codes, wood floor decking must be at least 3 in. (64 mm) in nominal thickness, with minimum 1-in. nominal (19-mm) wood finish flooring laid over it at right angles. Roof decking for Mill construction must be at least 2 in. (38 mm) in nominal thickness. Decking of lesser thickness may be used in Ordinary construction and Wood Light Frame construction.

WOOD DECKING

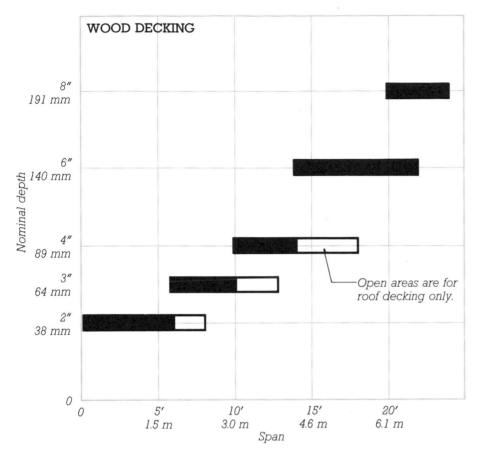

WOOD DECKING

(Vertical axis, labeled *Nominal depth*)

- 8″ / 191 mm
- 6″ / 140 mm
- 4″ / 89 mm
- 3″ / 64 mm
- 2″ / 38 mm
- 0

(Horizontal axis, labeled *Span*)

- 0
- 5′ / 1.5 m
- 10′ / 3.0 m
- 15′ / 4.6 m
- 20′ / 6.1 m

Open areas are for roof decking only.

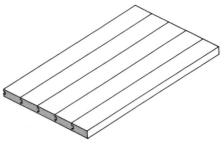

This chart is for solid or laminated wood decking. For light loads or strong woods, read toward the right in the indicated areas. For large loads or normal woods, read toward the left.

☐ Strong woods include Douglas Fir, Larch, Southern Pine, and Oak.

☐ Decking comes in various widths, 6 and 8 in. (140 and 184 mm) being the most common. Actual depth is ½ in. (13 mm) less than nominal.

☐ Allow approximately ¾ in. (19 mm) for the depth of finish flooring.

SIZING THE STRUCTURAL SYSTEM

53

WOOD FLOOR JOISTS

ACTUAL SIZES OF FLOOR JOISTS

Nominal Size	Actual Size	
2 × 6	1½" × 5½"	(38 × 140 mm)
2 × 8	1½" × 7¼"	(38 × 184 mm)
2 × 10	1½" × 9¼"	(38 × 235 mm)
2 × 12	1½" × 11¼"	(38 × 286 mm)

TOTAL FINISHED FLOOR THICKNESS

To estimate total finished floor thickness, add 2 in. (50 mm) to actual joist size for finish ceiling, subflooring, and finish flooring.

BEAMS SUPPORTING FLOOR FRAMING

Wood Beams

For sizing wood beams, see the chart on page 59. To determine clearance under a wood beam, assume the top of the beam is level with the top of the floor joists.

JOISTS WITH WOOD FLOOR BEAM

Steel Beams

Beam Size	Approximate Depth of Beam		Span of Beam	
W8	8"	(203 mm)	8'–13'	(2.4–4.0 m)
W10	10"	(254 mm)	10'–16'	(3.0–4.9 m)
W12	12"	(305 mm)	12'–18'	(3.7–5.5 m)

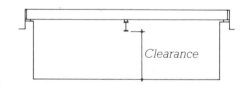

JOISTS WITH STEEL FLOOR BEAM

For lightly loaded beams, use the longer spans indicated. For heavily loaded beams, use the shorter spans.

To determine clearance under a steel beam, assume the top of the beam is level with the top of the foundation wall.

FIRE-RESISTANCE RATINGS FOR WOOD LIGHT FRAME JOISTS

Wood light frame floors with nominal 1-in. (19-mm) subflooring and finish flooring can have a 1-hour fire-resistance rating when the underside of the framing is finished with ⅝-in. (16-mm) Type X gypsum board or its equivalent.

WOOD FLOOR JOISTS

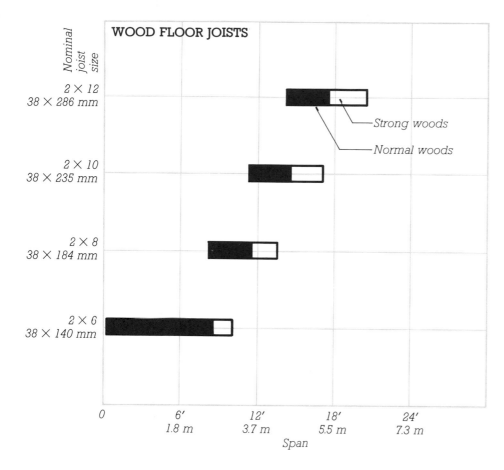

WOOD FLOOR JOISTS

Nominal joist size

2 × 12 38 × 286 mm	
2 × 10 38 × 235 mm	
2 × 8 38 × 184 mm	
2 × 6 38 × 140 mm	

Strong woods
Normal woods

0   6'
         1.8 m   12'
3.7 m   18'
5.5 m   24'
7.3 m

Span

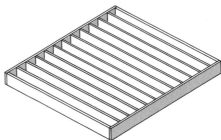

This chart is for wood floor joists with residential floor loads. For larger loads, increase the indicated joist size by one size (plus 2 in., or 50 mm). For ceiling joists supporting only residential attic loads, decrease the indicated joist size by one size (less 2 in., or 50 mm).

☐ Strong woods include Douglas Fir, Larch, Southern Pine, and Oak.

☐ For 12-in. (305-mm) joist spacings, increase allowable spans 1 to 2 ft (0.3 to 0.6 m). For 24-in. (610-mm) joist spacings, decrease allowable spans 1 to 2 ft (0.3 to 0.6 m).

☐ Most often wood floor joists are spaced 16 in. (406 mm) center-to-center. Spacings of 12 and 24 in. (305 and 610 mm) are also used. In all cases members should fall on a 4-ft. (1219-mm) module to coordinate with the standard width of various panel products that are used as an integral part of this system.

WOOD ROOF RAFTERS

ACTUAL SIZES OF ROOF RAFTERS

Nominal Size	Actual Size	
2 × 4	1½″ × 3½″	(38 × 89 mm)
2 × 6	1½″ × 5½″	(38 × 140 mm)
2 × 8	1½″ × 7¼″	(38 × 184 mm)
2 × 10	1½″ × 9¼″	(38 × 235 mm)

TIES OR BEAMS SUPPORTING ROOF RAFTERS

Rafter ties connecting rafters at their bases may be sized either as floor joists, if they are intended to support habitable space, or as ceiling joists, if they are supporting attic loads only. See the chart on the facing page.

Structural ridge beams can eliminate the need for ties at the base of the rafters. See page 95 for sizing wood beams.

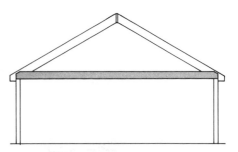

RAFTERS WITH RAFTER TIES

FIRE-RESISTANCE RATINGS FOR WOOD LIGHT FRAME RAFTERS

Wood light frame roofs can have a 1-hour fire-resistance rating when the underside of the framing is finished with ⅝-in. (16-mm) Type X gypsum board or its equivalent.

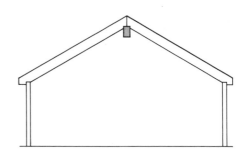

RAFTERS WITH RIDGE BEAM

WOOD ROOF RAFTERS

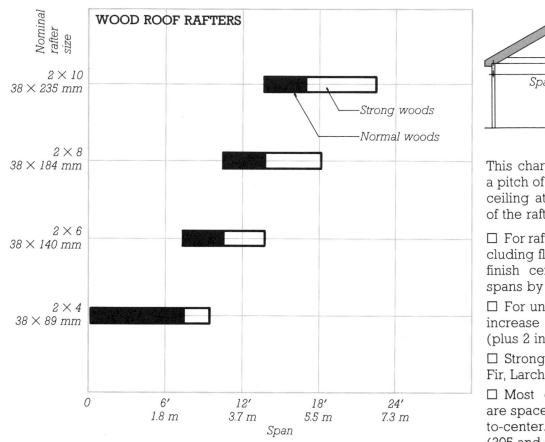

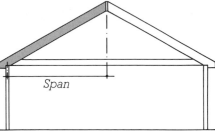

This chart is for wood rafters with a pitch of at least 3:12 and no finish ceiling attached to the underside of the rafters.

☐ For rafters with lower slopes (including flat roofs) or with attached finish ceilings, reduce allowable spans by 1 to 2 ft (0.3 to 0.6 m).

☐ For unusually heavy roof loads, increase rafter size by one size (plus 2 in., or 50 mm).

☐ Strong woods include Douglas Fir, Larch, Southern Pine, and Oak.

☐ Most often wood roof rafters are spaced 16 in. (406 mm) center-to-center. Spacings of 12 and 24 in. (305 and 610 mm) are also used. In all cases members should fall on a 4-ft. (1219-mm) module to coordinate with the standard width of various panel products that are used as an integral part of this system.

WOOD BEAMS

SIZES OF SOLID WOOD BEAMS

Nominal Depth	Actual Depth	
4″	3½″	(89 mm)
6″	5½″	(140 mm)
8″, 10″, 12″	¾″	(19 mm) less than nominal for beam widths of 2″, 3″, and 4″, and
	½″	(13 mm) less than nominal for beam widths greater than 4″
14″ or greater	½″	(13 mm) less than nominal

The actual widths of solid beams are ½ in. (13 mm) less than nominal.

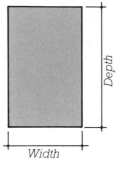

FRAMING FOR HEAVY TIMBER CONSTRUCTION

A framing system that uses both beams and joists can allow for a great range of bay sizes in heavy timber construction. With nominal 3-in. (64-mm) floor decking, joists should be spaced approximately 5 to 10 ft (1.5 to 3.0 m). For preliminary design, limit joist spans to a maximum of 20 ft (6.0 m) for solid wood joists, or 24 ft (7.3 m) for glue laminated joists.

Roof rafters spaced no greater than 4 to 8 ft (1.2 to 2.4 m) require no additional joists or purlins. Maximum practical spacing with joists or purlins is approximately 20 ft (6.0 m).

58

FIRE-RESISTANCE RATINGS FOR WOOD BEAMS

To qualify for Mill construction as defined by most building codes, wood floor beams must have a nominal size of at least 6 × 10 (140 × 241 mm). If supporting a roof and ceiling only, they may be no smaller than 4 × 6 (89 × 140 mm). Beams of lesser dimension may be used in Ordinary construction and Wood Light Frame construction.

WOOD BEAMS

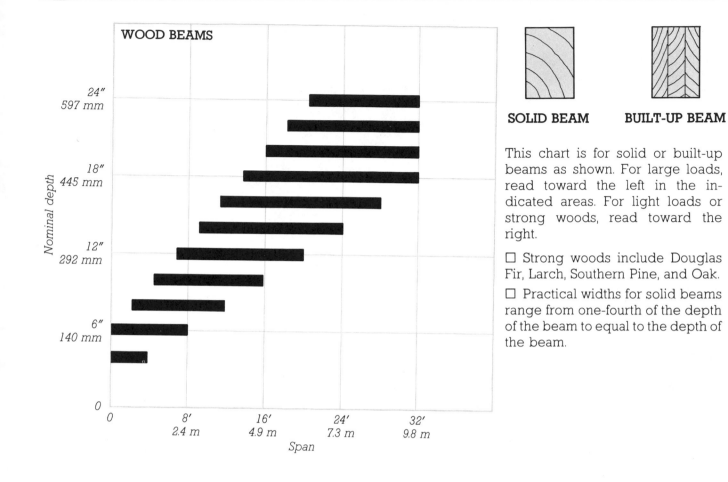

WOOD BEAMS

Nominal depth

- 24″ / 597 mm
- 18″ / 445 mm
- 12″ / 292 mm
- 6″ / 140 mm
- 0

Span

- 0
- 8′ / 2.4 m
- 16′ / 4.9 m
- 24′ / 7.3 m
- 32′ / 9.8 m

SOLID BEAM **BUILT-UP BEAM**

This chart is for solid or built-up beams as shown. For large loads, read toward the left in the indicated areas. For light loads or strong woods, read toward the right.

☐ Strong woods include Douglas Fir, Larch, Southern Pine, and Oak.

☐ Practical widths for solid beams range from one-fourth of the depth of the beam to equal to the depth of the beam.

GLUE LAMINATED WOOD BEAMS

SIZES OF GLUE LAMINATED BEAMS

Glue laminated beams are specified by their actual size. Depths must be a multiple of 1½ in. (38 mm), the depth of one lamination.

Width		Depth	
3¹/₃″	(79 mm)	3″–24″	(76–610 mm)
5¹/₈″	(130 mm)	4¹/₂″–36″	(114–914 mm)
6³/₄″	(171 mm)	6″–48″	(152–1219 mm)
8³/₄″	(222 mm)	9″–63″	(229–1600 mm)
10³/₄″	(273 mm)	10¹/₂″–75″	(267–1905 mm)

CONTINUOUS SPAN GLUE LAMINATED BEAMS

For maximum efficiency, glue laminated beams may be configured with continuous spans. For such configurations, read toward the right in the indicated area on the chart on the facing page. Practical spans for continuous span beam systems range from 25 to 65 ft (7.5 to 20.0 m).

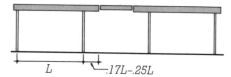

CONTINUOUS SPAN GLUE LAMINATED BEAMS

FIRE-RESISTANCE RATINGS FOR GLUE LAMINATED WOOD BEAMS

The model building codes do not distinguish between glue laminated and solid wood beams. To qualify for Mill construction as defined by most building codes, wood floor beams must have a nominal size of at least 6 × 10 (140 × 241 mm). If supporting a roof and ceiling only, they may be no smaller than 4 × 6 (89 × 140 mm). Beams of lesser dimension may be used in Ordinary construction and Wood Light Frame construction.

GLUE LAMINATED WOOD BEAMS

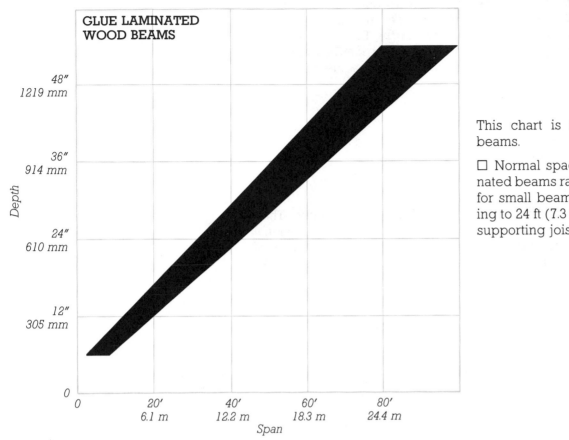

This chart is for glue laminated beams.

☐ Normal spacings for glue laminated beams range from 4 ft (1.2 m) for small beams supporting decking to 24 ft (7.3 m) for larger beams supporting joists or purlins.

WOOD FLOOR AND ROOF TRUSSES — LIGHT

Light wood floor and roof trusses are commonly used in place of conventional wood joists and rafters in platform frame construction. These prefabricated elements permit quicker erection in the field, greater clear spans, simplified framing due to the lack of interior loadbearing walls, and easier running of electrical and mechanical services due to the open spaces within the trusses.

FIRE-RESISTANCE RATINGS FOR LIGHT WOOD TRUSSES

These trusses are classified as Wood Light Frame construction. They can have a 1-hour fire-resistance rating when covered with nominal 1-in. (19-mm) subflooring and finish flooring and when the underside of the framing is finished with ⅝-in. (16-mm) Type X gypsum board or its equivalent.

WOOD FLOOR AND ROOF TRUSSES — LIGHT

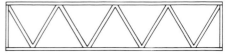

The top chart is for wood floor trusses constructed from light members (up to 6 in., or 140 mm, deep). For heavy loads, read toward the left in the indicated area. For light loads, read toward the right. For preliminary design, use depths in even 2-in. (50-mm) increments. The sizes available may vary with the manufacturer.

☐ Typical truss spacing is 16 to 48 in. (406 to 1219 mm).

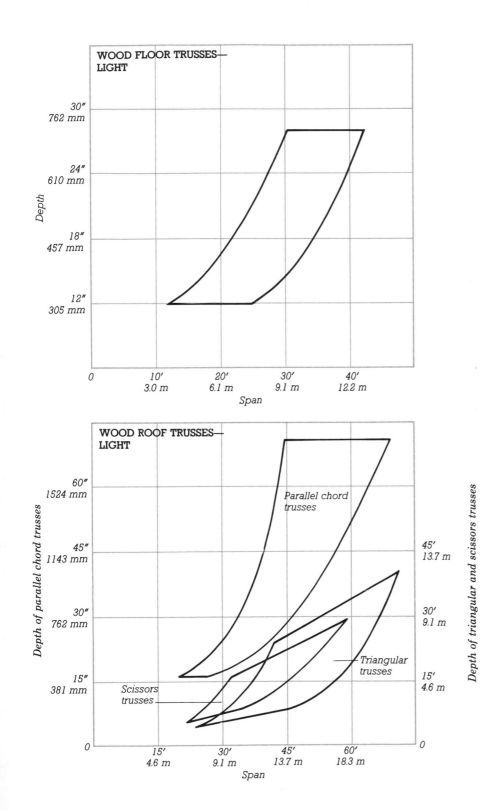

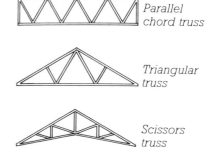

The bottom chart is for wood roof trusses constructed from light members (up to 6 in., or 140 mm, deep). For heavy loads, read toward the left in the indicated area. For light loads, read toward the right. For preliminary design, use parallel chord truss depths in even 2-in. (50-mm) increments. Triangular or scissors trusses are commonly available with top chord slopes in whole number pitches from 2:12 to 7:12. Available sizes may vary with the manufacturer.

☐ Typical truss spacing is 16 to 48 in. (406 to 1219 mm).

WOOD TRUSSES — HEAVY

SPACING OF HEAVY
WOOD ROOF TRUSSES

Roof trusses spaced no greater than 4 to 8 ft (1.2 to 2.4 m) require no additional joists or purlins. The maximum practical spacing of trusses with joists or purlins is approximately 20 ft (6.1 m).

FIRE-RESISTANCE
RATINGS FOR HEAVY
WOOD TRUSSES

To qualify for Mill construction as defined by most building codes, truss members may be no smaller in nominal dimension than 8 × 8 in. (191 × 191 mm) for floor trusses. Roof truss members may be as small in nominal dimension as 4 × 6 in. (89 × 140 mm).

WOOD TRUSSES — HEAVY

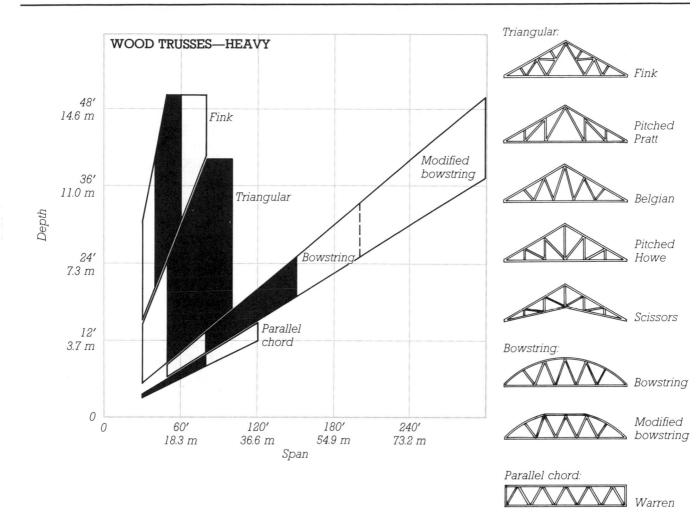

WOOD TRUSSES—HEAVY

Depth

48'
14.6 m

36'
11.0 m

24'
7.3 m

12'
3.7 m

0

Fink

Triangular

Modified bowstring

Bowstring

Parallel chord

0   60'   120'   180'   240'
     18.3 m   36.6 m   54.9 m   73.2 m

Span

Triangular:

Fink

Pitched Pratt

Belgian

Pitched Howe

Scissors

Bowstring:

Bowstring

Modified bowstring

Parallel chord:

Warren

Howe

Pratt

This chart is for wood trusses constructed from heavy members (a minimum of 4 × 6 in., or 89 × 140 mm, in nominal size).

☐ The most economical span ranges for each truss type are indicated with the solid tone.

GLUE LAMINATED WOOD ARCHES

DIMENSIONS FOR POINTED ARCHES

LOW- TO MEDIUM-PITCH ARCHES (3:12 TO 8:12)

Wall Height	Thickness of Arch	Depth of Base	Depth of Crown
10'–18' (3.0–5.5 m)	3$\frac{1}{8}$", 5$\frac{1}{8}$", 6$\frac{3}{4}$" (79, 130, 171 mm)	7$\frac{1}{2}$"–18" for short spans (191–457 mm)	7$\frac{1}{2}$"–27" (191–686 mm)
		8"–30" for medium spans (203–762 mm)	
		8$\frac{1}{2}$"–35" for long spans (216–889 mm)	

HIGH-PITCH ARCHES (10:12 TO 16:12)

Wall Height	Thickness of Arch	Depth of Base	Depth of Crown
8'–12' (2.4–3.7 m)	5$\frac{1}{8}$" (130 mm)	7$\frac{1}{2}$" for short spans (191 mm)	7$\frac{3}{4}$"–24$\frac{1}{2}$" (197–622 mm)
		7$\frac{3}{4}$" for medium spans (197 mm)	
		9$\frac{1}{2}$"–10" for long spans (241–254 mm)	

66

FIRE-RESISTANCE RATINGS FOR GLUE LAMINATED ARCHES

Glue laminated arches supporting only a roof and ceiling qualify as components of Mill construction under most building codes if they are no smaller than nominal 4 × 6 in. (89 × 140 mm) at any point.

GLUE LAMINATED WOOD ARCHES

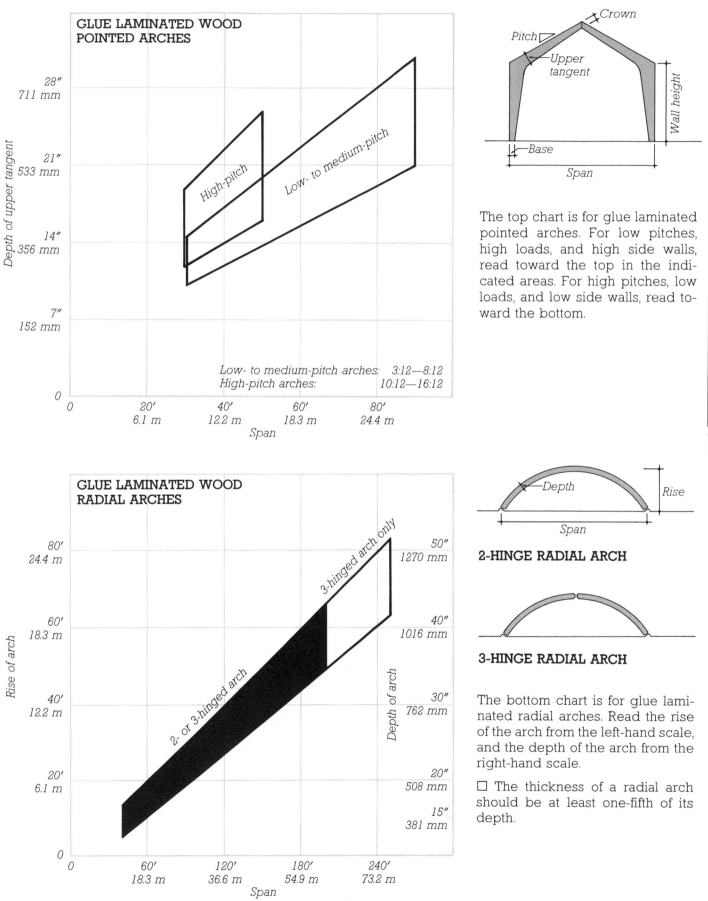

GLUE LAMINATED WOOD POINTED ARCHES

Depth of upper tangent

28″ / 711 mm
21″ / 533 mm
14″ / 356 mm
7″ / 152 mm
0

High-pitch

Low- to medium-pitch

Low- to medium-pitch arches: 3:12—8:12
High-pitch arches: 10:12—16:12

Span

0
20′ / 6.1 m
40′ / 12.2 m
60′ / 18.3 m
80′ / 24.4 m

Crown
Pitch
Upper tangent
Wall height
Base
Span

The top chart is for glue laminated pointed arches. For low pitches, high loads, and high side walls, read toward the top in the indicated areas. For high pitches, low loads, and low side walls, read toward the bottom.

GLUE LAMINATED WOOD RADIAL ARCHES

Rise of arch

80′ / 24.4 m
60′ / 18.3 m
40′ / 12.2 m
20′ / 6.1 m
0

3-hinged arch only

2- or 3-hinged arch

Depth of arch

50″ / 1270 mm
40″ / 1016 mm
30″ / 762 mm
20″ / 508 mm
15″ / 381 mm

Span

0
60′ / 18.3 m
120′ / 36.6 m
180′ / 54.9 m
240′ / 73.2 m

Depth
Rise
Span

2-HINGE RADIAL ARCH

3-HINGE RADIAL ARCH

The bottom chart is for glue laminated radial arches. Read the rise of the arch from the left-hand scale, and the depth of the arch from the right-hand scale.

☐ The thickness of a radial arch should be at least one-fifth of its depth.

MASONRY STRUCTURAL SYSTEMS

Masonry construction rarely forms a complete building system by its elf. Nonbearing masonry walls car be combined with other structural systems either in the form of infill between framing elements or as a veneer applied over wall or frame systems. Loadbearing masonry walls and columns can be combined with various spanning elements to form complete structural systems.

Masonry walls may be constructed in a great variety of ways. Use the following guidelines for preliminary design: Single-wythe walls are generally limited to nonbearing applications or as a veneer over other wall systems. Cavity wall construction is a preferred choice for exterior walls because of its high resistance to water penetration and its improved thermal performance. Concrete block construction is generally more economical than brick because of the reduced labor of laying the larger units and the lower material costs. Loadbearing masonry walls and columns must be steel reinforced in all but the smallest structures.

Since masonry construction takes place on site and utilizes elements of small size, it is well suited for use in the construction of buildings of irregular form. Modular dimensions should be used, however, to minimize the need for partial bricks in construction. Use a module of one-half the nominal length of a masonry unit in plan, and the height of one brick or block course in elevation.

MASONRY AND WOOD CONSTRUCTION

Masonry can form the exterior (and sometimes interior) loadbearing walls for either Wood Light Frame construction or Heavy Timber construction, systems named Ordinary construction and Mill construction, respectively. Both of these systems have higher fire-resistance ratings than all-wood construction and are permitted for use in larger and taller buildings. For more information on the fire resistance of these systems and the building types for which their use is permitted, see pages 430–431. For sizing the wood elements of Ordinary or Heavy Timber construction, see the appropriate pages under Wood Structural Systems beginning on page 47.

MASONRY AND STEEL CONSTRUCTION

Open-web joists are the steel spanning elements most commonly used with loadbearing masonry construction because of the relatively small concentrated loads produced where the joists bear on the walls. Where steel beams and girders bear upon masonry walls, pilasters may be required at points of support. For economy and strength, interior columns in such systems are typically structural steel rather than masonry. See pages 85–103 for information on steel construction.

MASONRY AND CONCRETE CONSTRUCTION

The sitecast and precast concrete spanning elements most commonly used with loadbearing masonry walls are shorter span slabs without ribs or beams. These systems are often highly economical due to the minimal floor depths associated with these spanning elements, the absence of any requirement for added fire-resistive finishes, and the acoustical and energy performance of these high-mass materials. See pages 105–121 for information on sitecast concrete construction and pages 123–133 for information on precast concrete construction.

RECTANGULAR COLUMNS

For the design of rectangular columns or pilasters, read from the top chart on the facing page using a square column of equivalent area. For columns or pilasters over 12 ft (3.7 m) tall, read from the second chart using the lesser dimension of a column, or the greater dimension of a pilaster.

The widths of two sides of a rectangular column should not exceed a ratio of 3:1; those of a pilaster should not exceed 4:1.

FIRE-RESISTANCE RATINGS FOR BRICK MASONRY COLUMNS

Brick columns 12 in. (305 mm) square have a fire-resistance rating of 4 hours.

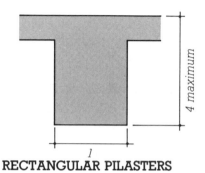

RECTANGULAR COLUMNS

RECTANGULAR PILASTERS

BRICK MASONRY COLUMNS

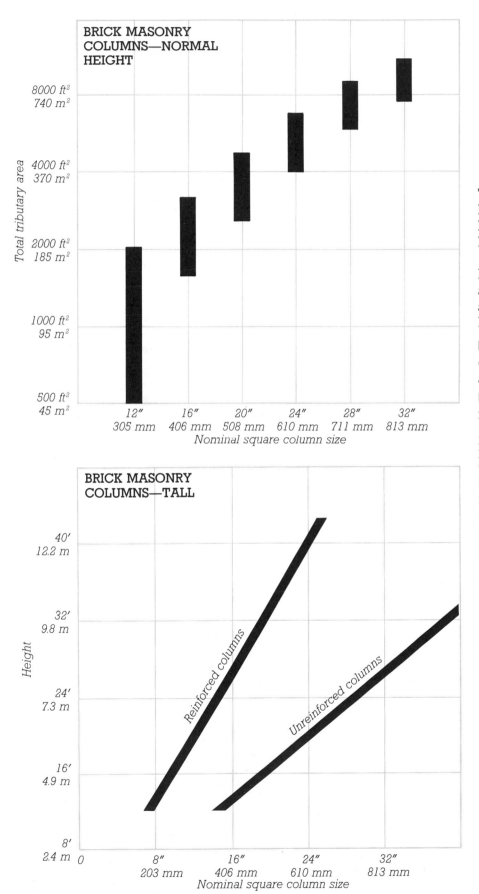

BRICK MASONRY COLUMNS—NORMAL HEIGHT

Total tributary area

- 8000 ft² / 740 m²
- 4000 ft² / 370 m²
- 2000 ft² / 185 m²
- 1000 ft² / 95 m²
- 500 ft² / 45 m²

Nominal square column size

| 12" 305 mm | 16" 406 mm | 20" 508 mm | 24" 610 mm | 28" 711 mm | 32" 813 mm |

BRICK MASONRY COLUMNS—TALL

Height

- 40' / 12.2 m
- 32' / 9.8 m
- 24' / 7.3 m
- 16' / 4.9 m
- 8' / 2.4 m

Reinforced columns

Unreinforced columns

Nominal square column size

| 0 | 8" 203 mm | 16" 406 mm | 24" 610 mm | 32" 813 mm |

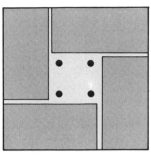

The top chart is for reinforced brick masonry columns or pilasters up to 12 ft (3.7 m) in height between floors.

For low loads or high-strength bricks, read toward the top in the solid areas. For high loads or low strength bricks, read toward the bottom.

☐ For unreinforced masonry, increase indicated column dimensions by 30%.

☐ Columns less than 12 in. (305 mm) square are restricted to supporting minor loads only. They may not be used to carry floor loads or concrete roof loads.

☐ Actual column size is equal to nominal size less ½ in. (13 mm).

☐ *Total tributary area* is the total area of roofs and floors supported by the column.

The bottom chart is for columns with unbraced heights greater than 12 ft (3.7 m). Read along the solid line for the appropriate wall type. Use the larger of the two sizes indicated by both charts on this page.

BRICK MASONRY WALLS

CAVITY WALLS

For cavity walls, use only the net width of the structural wythe when reading the charts on the facing page. For structural wythes of concrete block, see pages 80–81.

MASONRY BEARING WALLS

Brick masonry bearing walls are commonly used for a variety of low-rise structures and in high-rise structures of up to approximately 20 stories in height. The cellular nature of high-rise bearing wall configurations makes this system well suited to building types such as apartments, hotels, dormitories, hospitals, etc. In all but the smallest structures, masonry walls should be steel reinforced.

For structures of up to approximately 6 stories in height, the interior crosswalls and corridor walls typical of masonry structures are usually sufficient to provide the required lateral bracing for the structure. This permits the design of the exterior walls to remain relatively open. At greater heights, lateral stability requirements will increasingly dictate a more complete cellular configuration of walls. In this case the sizes and distribution of openings in the exterior walls may be more restricted.

Loadbearing walls should be aligned consistently from floor to floor and should be continuous from the roof to the building foundation. Where it is desirable to omit walls on a lower floor, it may be possible to design the wall above to act as a deep beam spanning between columns at each end. Such wall-beams may span 20 to 30 ft (6 to 9 m).

WALL PILASTERS

Pilasters are used both to carry concentrated vertical loads and to brace a wall against lateral forces and buckling.

When designing for vertical loads, locate the pilaster directly below the point of load application, and size the pilaster using the charts on pages 70–71.

Pilasters are used to brace walls laterally when the distance between other supports such as floor slabs or crosswalls is insufficient for this purpose. Use the bottom chart on the facing page to determine the maximum permissible spacing between such supports for any particular wall type and thickness. If the spacing is too great, the wall thickness may be increased, or pilasters may be added at the required spacing.

FIRE-RESISTANCE RATINGS FOR BRICK MASONRY WALLS

Brick masonry walls 6 in. (152 mm) thick have a fire-resistance rating of 2 hours. At a thickness of 8 in. (203 mm), a 4-hour rating is achieved.

72

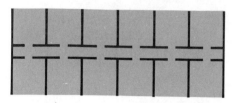

LOW-RISE BEARING WALL CONFIGURATION (*shown in plan*)

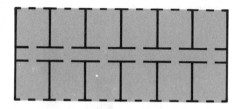

HIGH-RISE BEARING WALL CONFIGURATION (*shown in plan*)

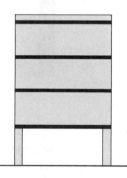

Bearing walls may act as deep beams to span across openings below, as shown in this schematic cross section.

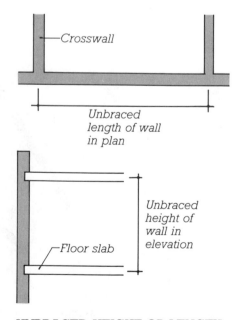

UNBRACED HEIGHT OR LENGTH OF MASONRY WALLS

BRICK MASONRY WALLS

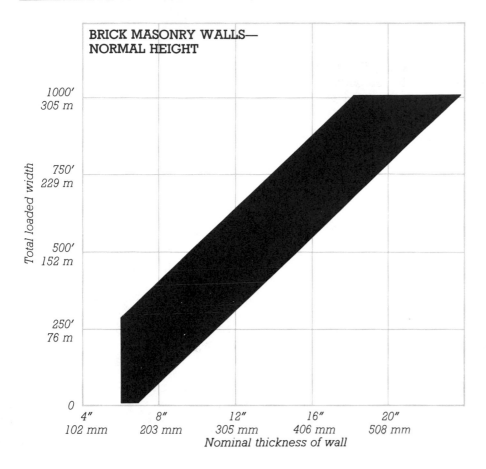

**BRICK MASONRY WALLS—
NORMAL HEIGHT**

Total loaded width

1000'
305 m

750'
229 m

500'
152 m

250'
76 m

0

4"
102 mm

8"
203 mm

12"
305 mm

16"
406 mm

20"
508 mm

Nominal thickness of wall

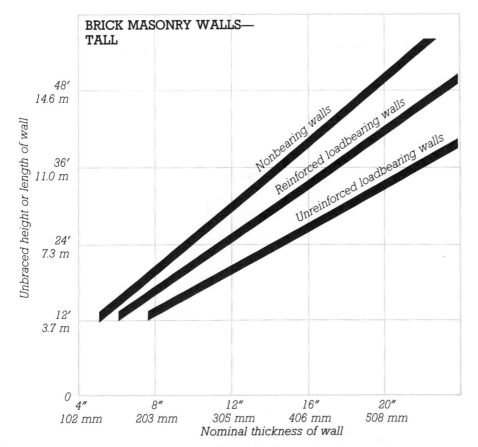

**BRICK MASONRY WALLS—
TALL**

Unbraced height or length of wall

48'
14.6 m

36'
11.0 m

24'
7.3 m

12'
3.7 m

0

Nonbearing walls

Reinforced loadbearing walls

Unreinforced loadbearing walls

4"
102 mm

8"
203 mm

12"
305 mm

16"
406 mm

20"
508 mm

Nominal thickness of wall

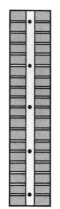

The top chart is for reinforced brick masonry loadbearing walls up to 12 ft (3.7 m) in height between floors. For light loads or high-strength bricks, read toward the top in the indicated area. For high loads or low-strength bricks, read toward the bottom.

☐ For unreinforced walls, increase the indicated wall thickness by 25%. Unreinforced bearing walls less than 12 in. (305 mm) thick are recommended for low-rise residential construction only.

☐ Nominal wall thickness may be any even number of inches. Actual wall thickness is equal to nominal thickness less ½ in. (13 mm).

☐ *Total loaded width* is one-half the span of one floor supported by the wall multiplied by the number of floors and roof above the wall.

The bottom chart is for bearing walls taller than 12 ft (3.7 m) between floors and for all nonbearing walls. Read along the solid line for the appropriate wall type. For tall bearing walls, use the larger of the sizes indicated by both charts on this page. For nonbearing walls, refer to this chart only.

☐ *Unbraced height or length of wall* is the vertical distance between floors or the horizontal distance between pilasters or crosswalls, whichever is less. (See the illustration on the facing page.)

BRICK MASONRY LINTELS

STEEL ANGLE LINTELS

The chart below is for steel angle lintels. The spans indicated are for lintels carrying wall loads only. Heavier structural shapes, such as channels or wide flange sections combined with plates, may be used where longer spans or greater load capacities are required.

Depth of Angle	Maximum Span
3" (76 mm)	5' (1.5 m)
4" (102 mm)	6' (1.8 m)
5" (127 mm)	7' (2.1 m)
6" (152 mm)	8' (2.4 m)

FIRE-RESISTANCE RATINGS FOR BRICK MASONRY LINTELS

Brick masonry lintels not less than 8 in. (203 mm) in nominal dimension may be assumed to have a fire-resistance rating of 3 hours.

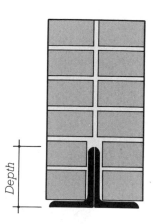

74

BRICK MASONRY LINTELS

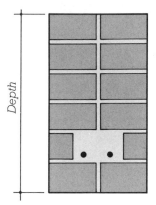

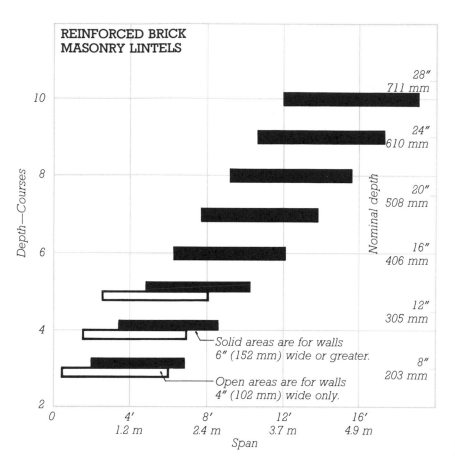

REINFORCED BRICK MASONRY LINTELS

Depth—Courses

Nominal depth

28″
711 mm

24″
610 mm

20″
508 mm

16″
406 mm

12″
305 mm

8″
203 mm

*Solid areas are for walls
6″ (152 mm) wide or greater.*

*Open areas are for walls
4″ (102 mm) wide only.*

Span

Depth

This chart is for steel reinforced brick masonry lintels. For lintels carrying only wall loads, read toward the right in the indicated areas. For additional superimposed loads, such as floor loads, read toward the left. For most applications, lintel depths of from 4 to 7 courses are sufficient.

□ Depths for this chart are based on modular brick coursing: 3 courses = 8 in. (203 mm). For other sizes, read depths in inches from the right-hand scale, and round up to a whole course height.

□ Actual depth is the thickness of one mortar joint less than the nominal depth (approximately ½ in. or 13 mm).

BRICK MASONRY ARCHES

MINOR BRICK ARCHES

The following rules apply to arches with spans of up to 6 to 8 ft (1.8 to 2.4 m): Almost any shape of arch will work at these spans, particularly when the arch is embedded in a wall. Depths of arches typically range from 4 to 16 in. (102 to 406 mm). Thicknesses of minor arches should be at least 4 to 8 in. (102 to 203 mm). Concentrated loads bearing directly on minor brick arches, especially jack arches, should be avoided. The thrusts produced by any arch must be resisted at its supports. This resistance can be provided by buttressing from an adjacent arch or an adjacent mass of masonry, or by an arch tie.

Segmental arches are most efficient when the rise of the arch is between 0.08 and 0.15 times the span of the arch.

Apply the following rules for jack arches:

Camber	Depth	Skewback
⅛″ per foot of span (1:100)	8″ (203 mm) minimum	½″ per foot of span for every 4″ of arch depth (40 mm per meter of span for every 100 mm of arch depth)

MAJOR BRICK ARCHES

Major brick arches can span to approximately 250 ft (75 m). Parabolic shapes are recommended for long span arches. The most efficient rise is approximately 0.20 to 0.25 times the span of the arch.

FIRE-RESISTANCE RATINGS FOR BRICK MASONRY ARCHES

Brick masonry arches not less than 8 in. (203 mm) in nominal dimension may be assumed to have a fire-resistance rating of 3 hours.

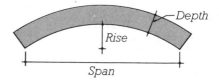

SEGMENTAL ARCH

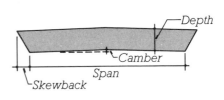

JACK ARCH

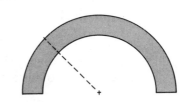

SEMICIRCULAR ARCH

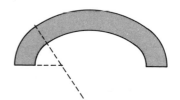

MULTI-CENTERED ARCH

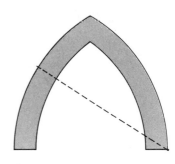

POINTED ARCH

PARABOLIC ARCH

CONCRETE BLOCK COLUMNS

RECTANGULAR COLUMNS

For the design of rectangular columns or pilasters, read from the top chart on the facing page using a square column of equivalent area. For columns or pilasters over 12 ft. (3.7 m) tall, read from the bottom chart using the lesser dimension for a column, the greater dimension for a pilaster.

The ratio of the widths of two sides of a column or pilaster should not exceed 3:1.

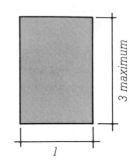

RECTANGULAR COLUMNS

FIRE-RESISTANCE RATINGS OF CONCRETE BLOCK COLUMNS

The fire resistance of concrete masonry units varies with the composition and type of unit. For preliminary design, columns at least 12 in. (305 mm) square may be assumed to have a 4-hour fire-resistance rating.

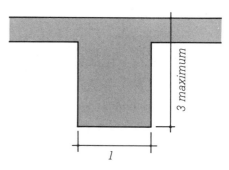

RECTANGULAR PILASTERS

CONCRETE BLOCK COLUMNS

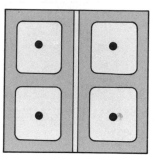

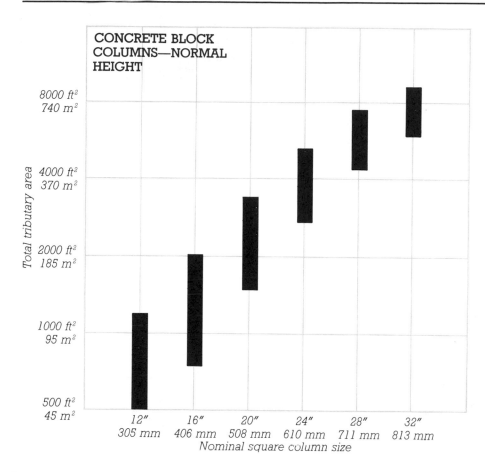

CONCRETE BLOCK COLUMNS—NORMAL HEIGHT

Total tributary area (y-axis): 500 ft² / 45 m², 1000 ft² / 95 m², 2000 ft² / 185 m², 4000 ft² / 370 m², 8000 ft² / 740 m²

Nominal square column size (x-axis): 12″ / 305 mm, 16″ / 406 mm, 20″ / 508 mm, 24″ / 610 mm, 28″ / 711 mm, 32″ / 813 mm

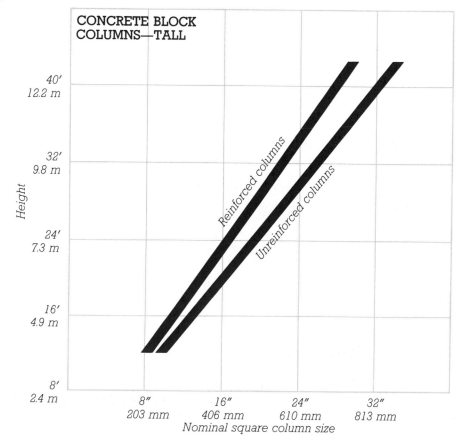

CONCRETE BLOCK COLUMNS—TALL

Height (y-axis): 8′ / 2.4 m, 16′ / 4.9 m, 24′ / 7.3 m, 32′ / 9.8 m, 40′ / 12.2 m

Reinforced columns

Unreinforced columns

Nominal square column size (x-axis): 8″ / 203 mm, 16″ / 406 mm, 24″ / 610 mm, 32″ / 813 mm

The top chart is for reinforced concrete block columns or pilasters up to 12 ft (3.7 m) in height between floors. For low loads or high-strength blocks, read toward the top in the indicated areas. For high loads or low-strength blocks, read toward the bottom.

☐ For unreinforced solid masonry, increase the indicated column size by 50%.

☐ Columns less than 12 in. (305 mm) square are not permitted, except for the support of minor loads.

☐ Actual column size is equal to nominal size less ⅜ in. (10 mm).

☐ *Total tributary area* is the total area of roofs and floors supported by the column.

The bottom chart is for columns with unbraced heights greater than 12 ft (3.7 m). Read along the solid line for the appropriate wall type. Use the larger of the two sizes indicated by both charts on this page.

CONCRETE BLOCK WALLS

CAVITY WALLS

For cavity walls, use only the net width of the structural wythe when reading the charts on the facing page.

MASONRY BEARING WALLS

Concrete masonry bearing walls are commonly used for low-rise structures and in high-rise structures of up to approximately 20 stories in height. The cellular nature of high-rise bearing wall configurations makes this system well suited to building types such as apartments, hotels, dormitories, hospitals, etc. In all but the smallest structures, masonry walls should be steel reinforced.

For structures of up to approximately 6 stories in height, the interior crosswalls and corridor walls typical of masonry structures are usually sufficient to provide the required lateral bracing for the structure. This permits the design of the exterior walls to remain relatively open. At greater heights, lateral stability requirements will increasingly dictate a more complete cellular configuration of walls, and the sizes and distribution of openings in the exterior walls may be more restricted.

Loadbearing walls should be aligned consistently from floor to floor and be continuous from the roof to the building foundation. Where it is desirable to omit walls on a lower floor, it may be possible to design the wall above to act as a deep beam spanning between columns at each end. Such wall-beams may span 20 to 30 ft (6 to 9 m).

WALL PILASTERS

Pilasters are used both to carry concentrated vertical loads and to brace a wall against lateral forces and buckling. When designing for vertical loads, locate the pilaster directly below the point of load application, and size the pilaster using the charts on pages 78–79.

Pilasters are used to brace walls laterally when the distance between other supports such as floor slabs or crosswalls is insufficient for this purpose. Use the bottom chart on the facing page to determine the maximum permissible spacing between such supports for any particular wall type and thickness. If the spacing is too great, the wall thickness may be increased, or pilasters may be added at the indicated spacing.

FIRE-RESISTANCE RATINGS FOR CONCRETE MASONRY WALLS

The fire resistance of concrete masonry walls varies with the composition and design of the masonry units themselves. For preliminary design, assume that a concrete masonry wall at least 8 in. (203 mm) thick can achieve a fire-resistance rating of 3 to 4 hours. A 2-hour rating is achieved at a thickness of 6 in. (152 mm), a 1-hour rating at 4 in. (102 mm).

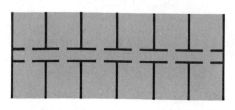

LOW-RISE BEARING WALL CONFIGURATION (*shown in plan*)

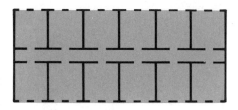

HIGH-RISE BEARING WALL CONFIGURATION (*shown in plan*)

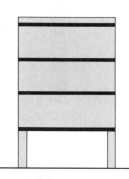

Bearing walls may act as deep beams to span across openings below, as shown in this schematic cross section.

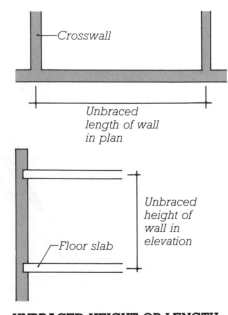

UNBRACED HEIGHT OR LENGTH OF MASONRY WALLS

CONCRETE BLOCK WALLS

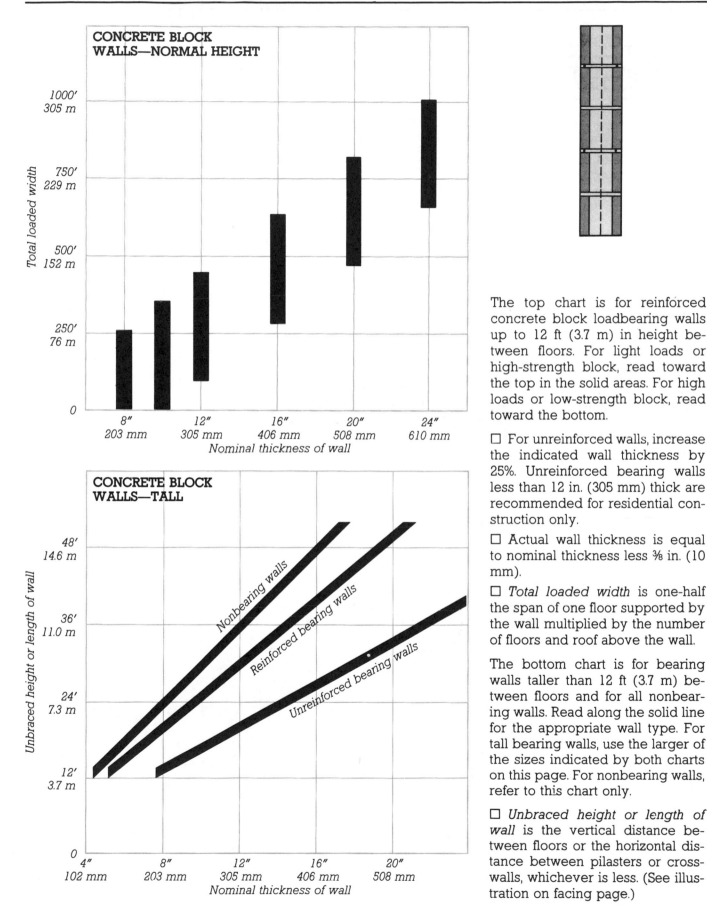

CONCRETE BLOCK WALLS—NORMAL HEIGHT

Total loaded width

1000'
305 m

750'
229 m

500'
152 m

250'
76 m

0

8"
203 mm

12"
305 mm

16"
406 mm

20"
508 mm

24"
610 mm

Nominal thickness of wall

CONCRETE BLOCK WALLS—TALL

Unbraced height or length of wall

48'
14.6 m

36'
11.0 m

24'
7.3 m

12'
3.7 m

0

Nonbearing walls

Reinforced bearing walls

Unreinforced bearing walls

4"
102 mm

8"
203 mm

12"
305 mm

16"
406 mm

20"
508 mm

Nominal thickness of wall

The top chart is for reinforced concrete block loadbearing walls up to 12 ft (3.7 m) in height between floors. For light loads or high-strength block, read toward the top in the solid areas. For high loads or low-strength block, read toward the bottom.

☐ For unreinforced walls, increase the indicated wall thickness by 25%. Unreinforced bearing walls less than 12 in. (305 mm) thick are recommended for residential construction only.

☐ Actual wall thickness is equal to nominal thickness less ⅜ in. (10 mm).

☐ *Total loaded width* is one-half the span of one floor supported by the wall multiplied by the number of floors and roof above the wall.

The bottom chart is for bearing walls taller than 12 ft (3.7 m) between floors and for all nonbearing walls. Read along the solid line for the appropriate wall type. For tall bearing walls, use the larger of the sizes indicated by both charts on this page. For nonbearing walls, refer to this chart only.

☐ *Unbraced height or length of wall* is the vertical distance between floors or the horizontal distance between pilasters or crosswalls, whichever is less. (See illustration on facing page.)

CONCRETE BLOCK LINTELS

PRECAST CONCRETE AND STRUCTURAL STEEL LINTELS

Precast concrete lintels that are 8 in. (203 mm) deep can span up to approximately 8 ft (2.4 m). Lintels 16 in. (406 mm) deep can span up to approximately 16 ft (4.9 m).

Lintels made of combinations of steel angles can span up to approximately 8 ft (2.4 m). Greater spans are possible with heavier structural steel shapes, such as channels or wide flange sections combined with plates.

FIRE-RESISTANCE RATINGS FOR CONCRETE BLOCK LINTELS

The fire resistance of concrete masonry construction varies with the composition and design of the masonry units themselves. For preliminary design, concrete masonry lintels not less than 8 in. (203 mm) in nominal dimension may be assumed to have a fire-resistance rating of 3 hours.

PRECAST CONCRETE LINTELS

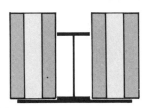

STRUCTURAL STEEL LINTELS

82

CONCRETE BLOCK LINTELS

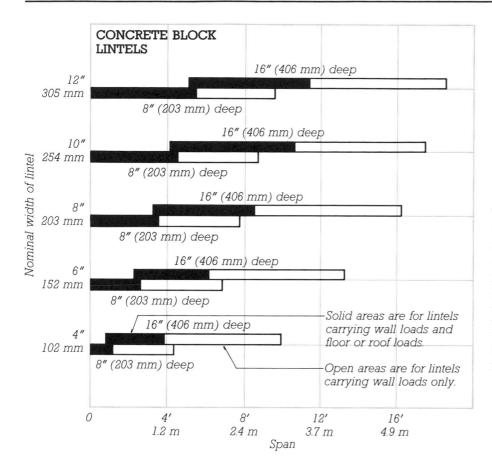

CONCRETE BLOCK LINTELS

Nominal width of lintel

12"
305 mm

16" (406 mm) deep

8" (203 mm) deep

10"
254 mm

16" (406 mm) deep

8" (203 mm) deep

8"
203 mm

16" (406 mm) deep

8" (203 mm) deep

6"
152 mm

16" (406 mm) deep

8" (203 mm) deep

4"
102 mm

16" (406 mm) deep

8" (203 mm) deep

Solid areas are for lintels carrying wall loads and floor or roof loads.

Open areas are for lintels carrying wall loads only.

| 0 | 4' 1.2 m | 8' 2.4 m | 12' 3.7 m | 16' 4.9 m |

Span

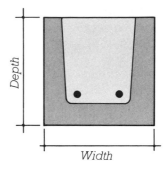

Depth

Width

This chart is for steel reinforced concrete block lintels. Open areas are for lintels carrying wall loads only. Solid areas are for lintels carrying wall loads and floor or roof loads. For light loads, read toward the right in the indicated areas. For heavy loads, read toward the left.

☐ Actual sizes are equal to nominal size less ⅜ in. (10 mm).

STEEL STRUCTURAL SYSTEMS

Steel elements are of two basic types: *Structural steel* shapes are formed into their final shapes by hot-rolling. This method produces such common elements as wide flange sections, angles, channels, bars, and plates. *Lightweight steel* members are cold-formed from thin sheets or rods. Such elements include roof and floor decking and a variety of light framing members such as channels, studs, and joists.

STRUCTURAL STEEL FRAMING

Conventional hot-rolled structural steel is a versatile, strong material that has applications ranging from single-story structures to the tallest buildings. The high level of prefabrication normally used with structural steel results in a system that is precise and fast to erect.

Structural steel elements are normally configured as a post and beam frame, with other materials or systems added to make a complete building. The slab system most commonly used with structural steel framing is a sitecast concrete slab poured over corrugated steel decking. Other sitecast or precast concrete systems are also used. Steel frames can support a great variety of cladding systems, with curtain walls of steel, aluminum, glass, masonry, and stone being the most common.

Due to the rapid loss of the strength of steel at elevated temperatures, special measures must be taken in most circumstances to protect the structural elements in a steel frame from the heat of fire. The required fire-resistive assemblies or coatings may have a significant impact on the architectural use of structural steel. See pages 422–432 for more information on the requirements for fire protection of structural steel.

LIGHTWEIGHT STEEL FRAMING

Lightweight steel framing finds applications in low-rise structures where the light weight and ease of assembly of these elements are an advantage. Many of the details of this system and the sizes of the structural elements are similar to those used in Wood Light Frame construction, a system lightweight steel framing often competes with. However, the noncombustibility of steel allows this system to be used in building types where wood construction is not permitted. (See pages 428–432 for more information on building types permitted using lightweight steel framing.) The small size of the individual structural elements and the reliance on on-site fabrication and erection also make this system a good choice where buildings of irregular or unusual form are desired.

STEEL LIGHTWEIGHT WALL STUDS

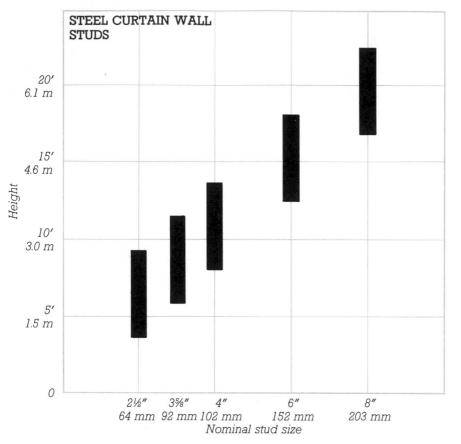

STEEL CURTAIN WALL STUDS

Height

20′ / 6.1 m

15′ / 4.6 m

10′ / 3.0 m

5′ / 1.5 m

0

2½″ / 64 mm · 3⅝″ / 92 mm · 4″ / 102 mm · 6″ / 152 mm · 8″ / 203 mm

Nominal stud size

This chart is for curtain wall studs—nonbearing studs resisting wind loads only. For light loads, close stud spacings, or heavy-gauge studs, read toward the top in the indicated areas. For heavy loads, wide stud spacings, or light-gauge studs, read toward the bottom.

☐ For brittle facings such as a masonry veneer requiring increased stiffness, read toward the bottom in the indicated areas.

☐ Typical stud spacings are 12, 16, and 24 in. (305, 406, and 610 mm).

☐ Stud widths vary from 1 to 2½ in. (25 to 64 mm) or more.

☐ Actual stud size is usually equal to nominal size. Availability of sizes varies with the manufacturer.

☐ Stud heights may be increased with the addition of intermediate bracing perpendicular to the wall plane.

FIRE-RESISTANCE RATINGS FOR LIGHTWEIGHT STEEL FRAMING

Lightweight steel construction may be used without fire protection in Unprotected Noncombustible construction, but this is seldom practical, because an interior surface material generally must be attached to the studs and joists to stabilize them against buckling.

Gypsum board or gypsum veneer plaster base, the most common interior finishes, can be applied in thicknesses sufficient to achieve a classification as 1-Hour Noncombustible construction.

STEEL LIGHTWEIGHT WALL STUDS

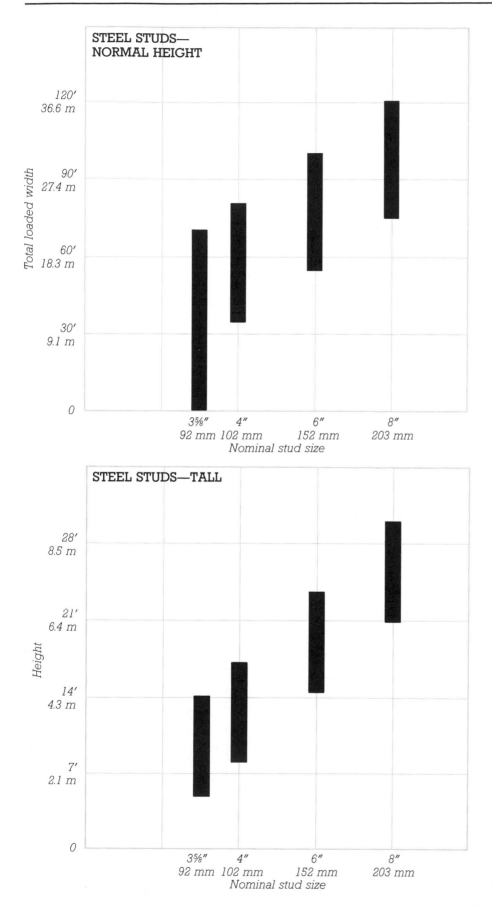

STEEL STUDS—NORMAL HEIGHT

Total loaded width

120'
36.6 m

90'
27.4 m

60'
18.3 m

30'
9.1 m

0

3⅝"
92 mm
4"
102 mm
6"
152 mm
8"
203 mm
Nominal stud size

STEEL STUDS—TALL

Height

28'
8.5 m

21'
6.4 m

14'
4.3 m

7'
2.1 m

0

3⅝"
92 mm
4"
102 mm
6"
152 mm
8"
203 mm
Nominal stud size

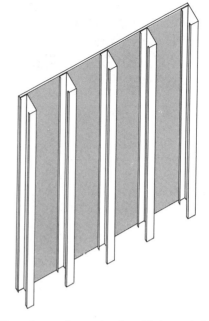

The top chart is for lightweight steel loadbearing studs up to 9 ft (2.7 m) tall between floors. For light loads, close stud spacings, or heavy-gauge studs, read toward the top in the indicated areas. For heavy loads, wide stud spacings, or light-gauge studs, read toward the bottom.

☐ Typical stud spacings are 12, 16, and 24 in. (305, 406, and 610 mm).

☐ Stud widths vary from 1 to 2½ in. (25 to 64 mm) or more.

☐ Actual stud size is usually equal to nominal size. Availability of sizes varies with the manufacturer.

☐ *Total loaded width* is the width of one floor supported by the wall multiplied by the number of floors and roof above the wall.

For stud walls taller than 9 ft (2.7 m) between floors, read both charts on this page. Use the larger of the two sizes indicated.

☐ For light loads, close stud spacings, or heavy-gauge studs, read toward the top in the indicated areas. For heavy loads, wide stud spacings, or light-gauge studs, read toward the bottom.

☐ Stud heights may be increased with the addition of intermediate bracing perpendicular to the wall plane.

STEEL LIGHTWEIGHT FLOOR JOISTS

FIRE-RESISTANCE RATINGS FOR LIGHTWEIGHT STEEL FRAMING

Lightweight steel construction may be used without fire protection in Unprotected Noncombustible construction, but this is seldom practical, because an interior surface material generally must be attached to the studs and joists to stabilize them against buckling.

Gypsum board or gypsum veneer plaster base, the most common interior finishes, can be applied in thicknesses sufficient to achieve a classification as 1-Hour Noncombustible construction.

STEEL LIGHTWEIGHT FLOOR JOISTS

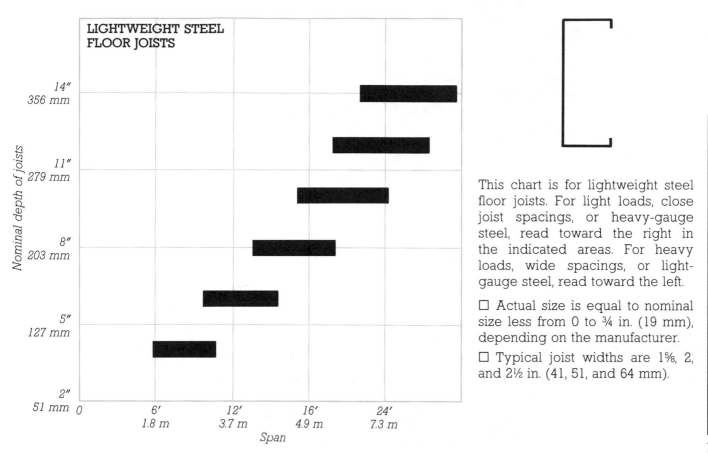

LIGHTWEIGHT STEEL
FLOOR JOISTS

Nominal depth of joists

14″ / 356 mm
11″ / 279 mm
8″ / 203 mm
5″ / 127 mm
2″ / 51 mm

Span

0   6′ / 1.8 m   12′ / 3.7 m   16′ / 4.9 m   24′ / 7.3 m

This chart is for lightweight steel floor joists. For light loads, close joist spacings, or heavy-gauge steel, read toward the right in the indicated areas. For heavy loads, wide spacings, or light-gauge steel, read toward the left.

☐ Actual size is equal to nominal size less from 0 to ¾ in. (19 mm), depending on the manufacturer.

☐ Typical joist widths are 1⅝, 2, and 2½ in. (41, 51, and 64 mm).

STEEL COLUMNS

COLUMN LAYOUT

All columns at the perimeter of a building should be oriented with their flanges facing outward to facilitate the attachment of cladding to the structural frame of the building. Elsewhere, columns should be oriented with their webs parallel to the short axis of a building whenever possible. This permits the maximum contribution from the columns to the stability of the building in the direction in which the building is most susceptible to lateral forces.

Columns above and below each other at the perimeter of a multistory building are also often aligned on their outer faces. Despite the misalignment of column centers that occurs as the column size reduces on upper floors, this arrangement is desirable for the consistent curtain-wall fastening detail that it produces.

See pages 96–97 for additional information on the sizing of column bays.

FINISH DIMENSIONS OF STEEL COLUMNS

The finish dimension of a steel column must be increased from the actual size of the section to account for applied fireproofing, protective cover or other finishes, and the added depth of connecting plates and protruding bolt heads where column sections are joined. The total finish dimension may range from 2 to 8 in. (50 to 200 mm) greater than the actual column size.

90

FIRE-RESISTANCE RATINGS FOR STEEL COLUMNS

Exposed steel columns may be used in Unprotected Noncombustible construction. Fire-resistance ratings of up to 4 hours are easily achieved with applied fireproofing.

STEEL COLUMNS

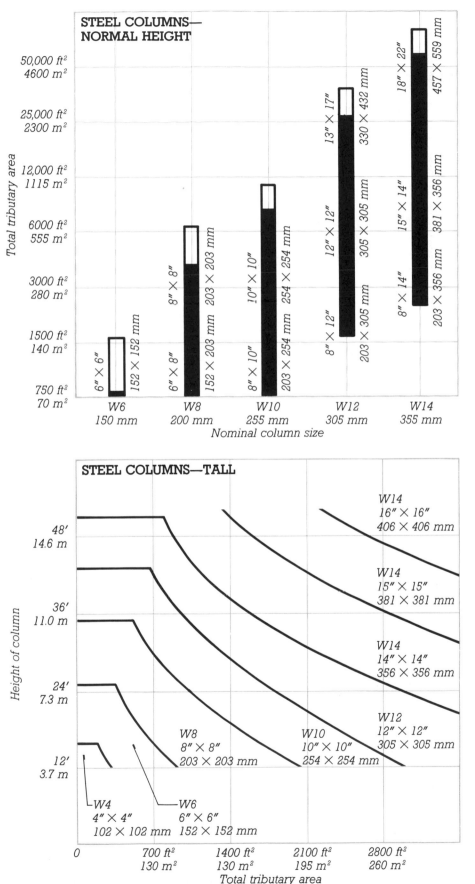

STEEL COLUMNS—NORMAL HEIGHT

Total tributary area:
- 50,000 ft² / 4600 m²
- 25,000 ft² / 2300 m²
- 12,000 ft² / 1115 m²
- 6000 ft² / 555 m²
- 3000 ft² / 280 m²
- 1500 ft² / 140 m²
- 750 ft² / 70 m²

Data bar labels:
- W6: 6″ × 6″ / 152 × 152 mm
- W8: 6″ × 8″ / 152 × 203 mm; 8″ × 8″ / 203 × 203 mm
- W10: 8″ × 10″ / 203 × 254 mm; 10″ × 10″ / 254 × 254 mm
- W12: 8″ × 12″ / 203 × 305 mm; 12″ × 12″ / 305 × 305 mm; 13″ × 17″ / 330 × 432 mm
- W14: 8″ × 14″ / 203 × 356 mm; 15″ × 14″ / 381 × 356 mm; 18″ × 22″ / 457 × 559 mm

Nominal column size:
- W6 / 150 mm
- W8 / 200 mm
- W10 / 255 mm
- W12 / 305 mm
- W14 / 355 mm

STEEL COLUMNS—TALL

Height of column:
- 48′ / 14.6 m
- 36′ / 11.0 m
- 24′ / 7.3 m
- 12′ / 3.7 m

Curve labels:
- W14 16″ × 16″ 406 × 406 mm
- W14 15″ × 15″ 381 × 381 mm
- W14 14″ × 14″ 356 × 356 mm
- W12 12″ × 12″ 305 × 305 mm
- W10 10″ × 10″ 254 × 254 mm
- W8 8″ × 8″ 203 × 203 mm
- W6 6″ × 6″ 152 × 152 mm
- W4 4″ × 4″ 102 × 102 mm

Total tributary area:
- 0
- 700 ft² / 130 m²
- 1400 ft² / 130 m²
- 2100 ft² / 195 m²
- 2800 ft² / 260 m²

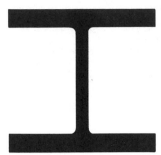

The top chart is for steel wide flange section columns up to 12 ft (3.7 m) tall between floors. The open areas indicated are for high-strength (50 ksi or 345 MPa) steel only.

☐ For light loads, read toward the top in the indicated areas. For heavy loads, read toward the bottom.

☐ Approximate actual column sizes are shown in inches and millimeters to the sides of the data bars.

☐ Columns that contribute to the lateral stability of a building may be larger in size than shown on this chart.

☐ W14 sections are the largest standard rolled sizes commonly used as columns. Larger built-up sections capable of carrying greater loads may be shop fabricated.

☐ *Total tributary area* is the total area of roofs and floors supported by the column.

For columns taller than 12 ft (3.7 m) between floors, read both charts on this page. Use the larger of the two sizes indicated. Nominal and approximate actual column sizes are shown on the chart. Column size may increase for heavy loads.

☐ Column size will increase for columns that contribute to the lateral stability of a building, particularly with taller columns.

☐ Column height may be increased with the use of intermediate bracing.

STEEL TUBE COLUMNS

STRUCTURAL STEEL TUBING

Standard shapes for structural steel tubing include square tubes, rectangular tubes, and round pipes. Compared to wide flange sections or other shapes of similar size, tubes and pipes are more resistant to buckling forces, making them good choices for columns and compressive struts in all types of steel systems. They are employed as columns in long-span steel structures for their greater efficiency, and because they are available in lighter weights than other standard shapes, they are frequently used in one- or two-story steel structures as well. Tube and pipe sections are popular choices for use in the fabrication of steel trusses and space frames, and their high torsional resistance makes them excellent choices for single post supports such as for signs or platforms.

The simple profiles and clean appearance of steel tubes and pipes also make them popular for use where the steel may remain visible in the finished structure, or for structures exposed to the weather where the absence of moisture- and dirt-trapping profiles and ease of maintenance are desirable characteristics.

SIZES FOR STEEL TUBES AND PIPES

Tubes and pipes are generally available in whole-inch (25-mm) sizes up to 6 or 8 in. (152 or 203 mm). Greater sizes are available in even-inch (51-mm) increments.

Shape	Width of Tube or Diameter of Pipe	Thickness of Wall
Square tubes	3″ × 3″–16″ × 16″ (76 × 76 mm–406 × 406 mm)	.188″–.625″ (5–16 mm)
Rectangular tubes	3″ × 2″–16″ × 12″ (76 × 51 mm–406 × 305 mm)	.188″–.625″ (5–16 mm)
Pipes	3″–12″ (76–305 mm)	.216″–.875″ (5–22 mm)

FINISH DIMENSIONS OF STEEL COLUMNS

The finish dimension of a steel column must be increased from the actual size of the section to account for applied fireproofing, protective cover or other finishes, and the added depth of connecting plates and protruding bolt heads where column sections are joined. The total finish dimension may range from 2 to 8 in. (50 to 200 mm) greater than the actual column size.

STEEL TUBE COLUMNS

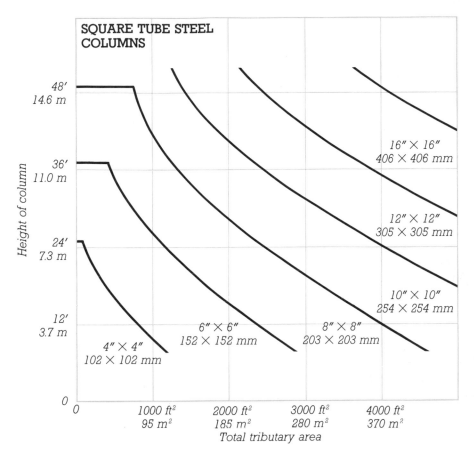

SQUARE TUBE STEEL COLUMNS

16″ × 16″
406 × 406 mm

12″ × 12″
305 × 305 mm

10″ × 10″
254 × 254 mm

8″ × 8″
203 × 203 mm

6″ × 6″
152 × 152 mm

4″ × 4″
102 × 102 mm

Height of column

48′	14.6 m
36′	11.0 m
24′	7.3 m
12′	3.7 m
0	

1000 ft²	95 m²
2000 ft²	185 m²
3000 ft²	280 m²
4000 ft²	370 m²

Total tributary area

This chart is for square tube steel columns. Column size may increase with heavy loads, or where columns contribute to the lateral stability of a building, particularly with taller columns.

☐ Actual column size is equal to nominal size.

☐ *Total tributary area* is the total area of roofs and floors supported by the column.

FIRE-RESISTANCE RATINGS FOR STEEL TUBE AND PIPE COLUMNS

Exposed steel columns or other framing elements may be used in Unprotected Noncombustible construction. Fire-resistance ratings of up to 4 hours are easily achieved with applied fireproofing. When used in roof framing systems, some building codes allow reduced fire protection of exposed steel for structures that are 15 to 25 ft (4.6 to 7.6 m) or more above the floor.

STEEL FLOOR AND ROOF DECKING

STEEL FLOOR DECKING

Corrugated steel floor decking with a sitecast concrete topping is the slab system most commonly used over structural steel framing. Typical span ranges for steel floor decking when used with structural steel framing are from 6 to 15 ft (1.8 to 4.6 m). Longer spans or shallower depths than those indicated on the chart on the facing page may be possible, although increased construction costs may result from the need for additional temporary shoring of the decking during erection.

CELLULAR FLOOR DECKING

The use of cellular decking to provide protected spaces within the floor slab for the running of electrical and communications wiring may influence the overall framing plan for the building. The layout of such a distribution system can determine the direction in which the decking cells will run in various areas of the building plan. The orientation of the beams or joists carrying the decking will be determined from this in turn, as in all cases these elements must run perpendicular to the cells in the decking. See page 181 for additional information on the planning of such systems. When reading from the chart for cellular deck on the facing page, read toward the bottom in the indicated area.

STEEL ROOF DECKING

Steel roof decking may have a sitecast concrete or gypsum topping or may be covered directly with a variety of board or roofing products. A common and economical configuration for roof decking is 1½ in. (38-mm) decking spanning up to approximately 8 ft (2.4 m). Many proprietary metal roof decking systems, with a wide variety of performance characteristics, are also available. For information on such systems, consult individual manufacturers.

FIRE-RESISTANCE RATINGS FOR STEEL DECKING

Steel roof decking without a concrete topping may be used in Unprotected Noncombustible construction.

The fire resistance of roof or floor decking with a concrete topping varies with the configuration of the decking and the thickness of the topping. Though resistance ratings of as high as 3 hours may be possible, for preliminary design, assume that decking must be protected with applied fireproofing or an appropriately fire-resistive ceiling to achieve ratings of more than 1 hour.

STEEL FLOOR AND ROOF DECKING

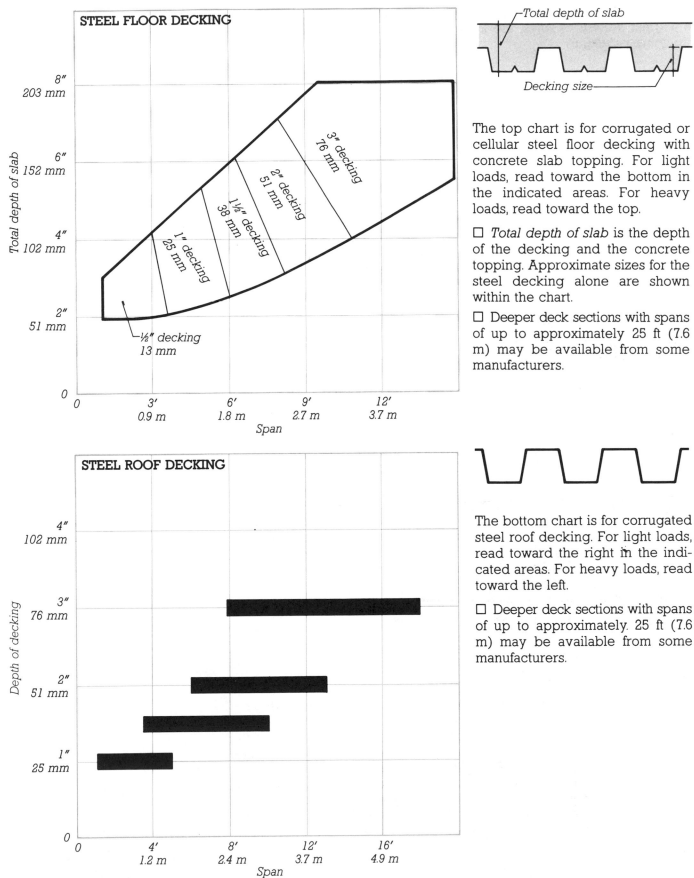

STEEL FLOOR DECKING

Total depth of slab

- 8″ / 203 mm
- 6″ / 152 mm
- 4″ / 102 mm
- 2″ / 51 mm
- 0

3″ decking 76 mm

2″ decking 51 mm

1½″ decking 38 mm

1″ decking 25 mm

½″ decking 13 mm

Span: 0 | 3′ 0.9 m | 6′ 1.8 m | 9′ 2.7 m | 12′ 3.7 m

Total depth of slab

Decking size

The top chart is for corrugated or cellular steel floor decking with concrete slab topping. For light loads, read toward the bottom in the indicated areas. For heavy loads, read toward the top.

☐ *Total depth of slab* is the depth of the decking and the concrete topping. Approximate sizes for the steel decking alone are shown within the chart.

☐ Deeper deck sections with spans of up to approximately 25 ft (7.6 m) may be available from some manufacturers.

STEEL ROOF DECKING

Depth of decking

- 4″ / 102 mm
- 3″ / 76 mm
- 2″ / 51 mm
- 1″ / 25 mm
- 0

Span: 0 | 4′ 1.2 m | 8′ 2.4 m | 12′ 3.7 m | 16′ 4.9 m

The bottom chart is for corrugated steel roof decking. For light loads, read toward the right in the indicated areas. For heavy loads, read toward the left.

☐ Deeper deck sections with spans of up to approximately. 25 ft (7.6 m) may be available from some manufacturers.

STEEL BEAMS AND GIRDERS

Structural steel is a versatile building material. Though it can be used in a great variety of ways, the following guidelines may be used for preliminary design.

FLOOR AND ROOF FRAMING

The most economical span range for conventional steel floor and roof framing is from 20 to 32 ft (6 to 10 m). Above spans of 32 to 40 ft (10 to 12 m), open-web steel joists become an increasingly economical alternative for both floor and roof framing due to their lighter weight. See pages 98–99 for the sizing and spacing of open-web steel joists.

The spacing of beams depends on the applied loads and the decking system. Spacings of from 6 to 15 ft (1.8 to 4.6 m) are common with corrugated steel floor decking. Spacings of up to approximately 8 ft (2.4 m) are typical for roof decking systems.

BEAM AND GIRDER CONFIGURATION

The orientation of beams and girders in a floor or roof framing system may depend on a variety of factors. When possible, girders should run parallel to the short axis of the building. This permits any contribution that these heavier members can make to lateral stability to be utilized in the direction along which the structure is most susceptible to lateral forces.

Beam and girder placement is also related to the arrangement of the column bays. In a rectangular bay, it is usually more economical to run the girders in the longer direction. When combined with open web steel joists, however, structural steel girders most often run along the short direction of the bay, allowing the joists to span the greater distance. Furthermore, when a floor system utilizes cellular decking as part of a communications or wiring system, the preferred direction for the cells of the decking may determine beam and girder orientations, because beams must run perpendicular to the corrugations of any steel decking.

COMPOSITE BEAMS

Composite construction, in which shear studs are used to cause the concrete deck and the steel beams to act as a unified structural element, can reduce beam depths, or increase their span and load capacity. Composite beams are almost always an economical alternative to simple beams. However, their use may be limited with electrified deck systems because of the trench headers in the slabs used with these systems. Composite beams are often spaced farther than simple beams to gain maximum advantage from the interaction of the beam and the section of concrete slab above.

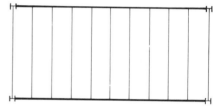

With conventional framing, it is usually more economical to run the girders in the long direction in a rectangular bay.

When used with open web steel joists, girders usually run the shorter direction in a rectangular bay.

96

STEEL BEAMS AND GIRDERS

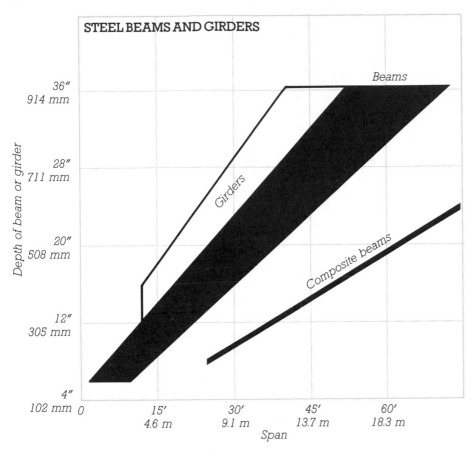

STEEL BEAMS AND GIRDERS

Depth of beam or girder

36" 914 mm
28" 711 mm
20" 508 mm
12" 305 mm
4" 102 mm

Beams
Girders
Composite beams

0   15' 4.6 m   30' 9.1 m   45' 13.7 m   60' 18.3 m

Span

This chart is for steel wide-flange sections. For heavy loads, read toward the left in the solid area. For light loads, read toward the right.

☐ For girders, read in the open area indicated. For composite beams, read along the line indicated. (For more information on girders or composite beams, see the facing page.)

☐ Beams or girders also acting to resist lateral loads may be deeper than indicated on this chart.

☐ Economical widths of beams and girders range from approximately one-third to one-half the depth of the beam. Heavy sections may be wider.

☐ Depths of up to 36 in. (914 mm) are available as standard rolled sections. Greater depth beams capable of longer spans may be shop fabricated.

FIRE-RESISTANCE RATINGS FOR STEEL BEAMS AND GIRDERS

Exposed steel beams and girders may be used in Unprotected Noncombustible construction. Fire-resistance ratings of as high as 4 hours are easily achieved with applied fireproofing or an appropriately fire resistive ceiling. Some building codes also allow reduced fire protection or exposed steel for roof structures that are 15 to 25 ft (4.6 to 7.6 m) or more above the floor.

OPEN-WEB JOIST FRAMING

The light weight of open-web steel joists makes them an economical alternative to conventional structural steel members for spans greater than 30 to 40 ft (9 to 12 m). Where significant concentrated loads exist, open-web joists may need to be supplemented with additional structural members.

Girders used with open-web joists may be joist girders (a heavier version of an open-web joist) or conventional structural steel members. For greater loads and spans, heavy steel trusses may also be used. For rectangular bays, the joists usually span the longer direction. (See pages 96–97 for structural steel beams and girders and pages 102–103 for heavy steel trusses.)

A variety of proprietary composite systems are also available. Such systems are particularly effective at overcoming the excessive flexibility sometimes encountered with long-span joist systems.

FIRE-RESISTANCE RATINGS FOR OPEN-WEB STEEL JOISTS

Exposed open-web joists and joist girders may be used in Unprotected Noncombustible construction. Fire-resistance ratings of as high as 3 hours are easily achieved with applied fireproofing or an appropriately fire-resistive ceiling. The fire-resistive ceiling is used more commonly, due to the difficulty of applying fireproofing directly to the complex surfaces of an open-web joist. Some building codes also permit reduced fire protection or exposed steel for roof structures that are 15 to 25 ft (4.6 to 7.6 m) or more above the floor.

STEEL OPEN-WEB JOISTS

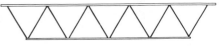

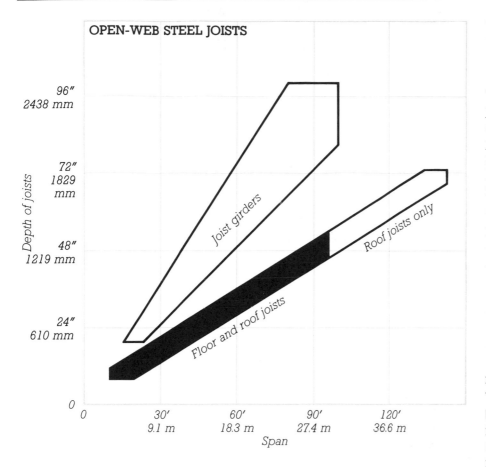

OPEN-WEB STEEL JOISTS

Depth of joists

96″
2438 mm

72″
1829 mm

48″
1219 mm

24″
610 mm

0

Joist girders

Floor and roof joists

Roof joists only

0

30′
9.1 m

60′
18.3 m

90′
27.4 m

120′
36.6 m

Span

This chart is for open-web steel joists and joist girders for floors and roofs. For light loads or close joist spacings, read toward the right in the indicated areas. For heavy loads or large joist spacings, read toward the left.

☐ Joist spacings range from 2 to 10 ft (0.6 to 3.0 m) or more, depending on the floor loads and the decking system applied over the joists.

☐ Joists generally come in depths of from 8 to 32 in. in 2-in. increments (from 203 to 813 mm in 51-mm increments) and from 32 to 72 in. in 4-in. increments (from 813 to 1829 mm in 102-mm increments). Availability of sizes varies with the manufacturer.

☐ Joist girders come in depths of from 20 to 96 in. in 4-in. increments (from 508 to 2438 mm in 102-mm increments).

SINGLE-STORY RIGID STEEL FRAMES

RELATED DIMENSIONS FOR SINGLE-STORY RIGID STEEL FRAMES

For the span ranges indicated on the chart on the facing page, the following dimensions may be used:

Wall Height	Depth at Base	Roof Pitch
8'-30' (2.4-9.1 m)	7"-21" (178-533 mm)	1:12-4:12

Typical spacing of frames is 20 or 25 ft (6.1 or 7.6 m).

For variations on the rigid frame system, or for sizes outside the range of those shown in the chart, consult with individual manufacturers.

FIRE-RESISTANCE RATINGS FOR SINGLE-STORY RIGID STEEL FRAME STRUCTURES

Exposed steel frames may be used in Unprotected Noncombustible construction. Fire-resistance ratings of as high as 4 hours are easily achieved with applied fireproofing or an appropriately fire-resistive ceiling. Some building codes also allow reduced fire protection or exposed steel for roof structures that are 15 to 25 ft (4.6 to 7.6 m) or more above the floor.

SINGLE-STORY RIGID STEEL FRAMES

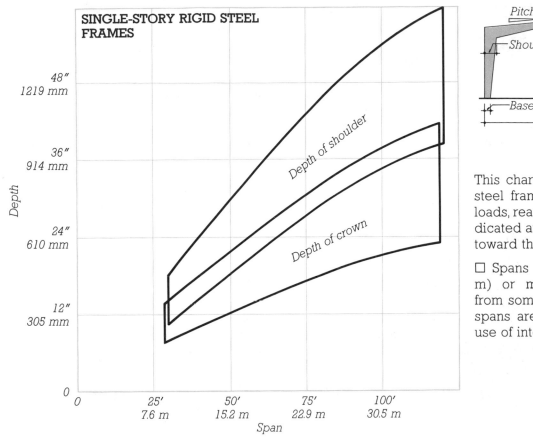

SINGLE-STORY RIGID STEEL
FRAMES

Depth

48"
1219 mm

36"
914 mm

24"
610 mm

12"
305 mm

0

Depth of shoulder

Depth of crown

0
25'
7.6 m
50'
15.2 m
75'
22.9 m
100'
30.5 m

Span

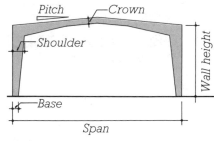

Pitch Crown
Shoulder
Base
Span
Wall height

This chart is for single-story rigid steel frame structures. For heavy loads, read toward the top in the indicated areas. For light loads, read toward the bottom.

☐ Spans as great as 200 ft (61.0 m) or more may be available from some manufacturers. Greater spans are also available with the use of intermediate columns.

STEEL TRUSSES

ECONOMICAL SPAN RANGES FOR PARALLEL CHORD TRUSSES

Parallel chord trusses are most economical for spans of up to 120 to 140 ft (35 to 45 m), due to the increased difficulty of shipping elements greater than 12 ft (3.7 m) deep. Triangular and bowstring trusses can be shipped at slightly greater depths. Trusses spanning 300 ft (90 m) or more may be fabricated on site.

FIRE-RESISTANCE RATINGS FOR STEEL TRUSSES

Exposed steel trusses may be used in Unprotected Noncombustible construction. Fire-resistance ratings of as high as 4 hours are easily achieved with applied fireproofing or an appropriately fire-resistive ceiling. Some building codes also allow reduced fire protection or exposed steel for roof structures that are 15 to 25 ft (4.6 to 7.6 m) or more above the floor.

STEEL TRUSSES

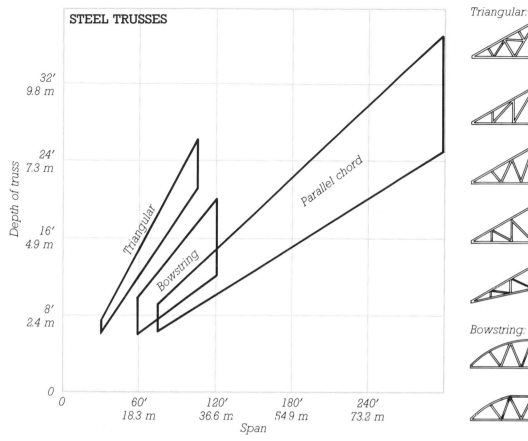

STEEL TRUSSES

Depth of truss

32'
9.8 m

24'
7.3 m

16'
4.9 m

8'
2.4 m

0

Triangular

Bowstring

Parallel chord

0

60'
18.3 m

120'
36.6 m

180'
54.9 m

240'
73.2 m

Span

Triangular:

Fink

Pitched Pratt

Belgian

Pitched Howe

Scissors

Bowstring:

Bowstring

Modified bowstring

Parallel chord:

Warren

Howe

Pratt

This chart is for steel trusses fabricated from structural steel members. Because these trusses are custom designed and fabricated, a great variety of shapes and configurations are possible.

SITECAST CONCRETE STRUCTURAL SYSTEMS

The initial choice of a sitecast concrete framing system is most often based on the desired spans or column spacings of the structure and on the expected magnitude of the in-service loads on the building. The following systems are listed in order of increasing spans, load capacity, and cost:

- One-Way Solid Slab
- Two-Way Flat Plate
- Two-Way Flat Slab
- One-Way Joist
- Waffle Slab
- One-Way Beam and Slab
- Two-Way Beam and Slab

For short-span, light-load conditions, systems from the top of this list are the most economical. For long spans and heavy loads, systems from the bottom of the list may be required.

POSTTENSIONING

The span ranges of sitecast concrete systems can be increased by the use of posttensioned reinforcing. Charts for the sizing of posttensioned systems are included in this section. Posttensioning also substantially reduces the depth of spanning members and may be desirable where total floor-to-floor heights must be kept to a minimum. The extensive use of posttensioning in a concrete structure may limit the ease with which such a structure can be modified in the future, since penetrations in slabs and beams must not interrupt the continuity of the reinforcing or surrounding concrete. This may make posttensioning an undesirable choice for buildings where significant change in program or structure must be anticipated.

ARCHITECTURAL SITECAST CONCRETE CONSTRUCTION

The inherent fire-resistive qualities of concrete construction allow concrete systems to remain wholly or partially exposed in a finished building. Furthermore, the process by which concrete is formed on site, and its monolithic and plastic qualities as a finished product give this material unique architectural potential. For these reasons, the choice of a concrete framing system may have significant architectural implications that should be considered early in the design process. Factors to consider in the architectural use of sitecast concrete include: the added cost and difficulty of achieving acceptable levels of finish quality and dimensional accuracy with exposed concrete, the ease of integrating building mechanical and electrical services into the exposed structure, and the potential aesthetic qualities of the various construction elements and systems. If an extensive use of architectural concrete is being considered for a project, the necessary consultants should be sought out at the earliest possible time, as the use of architectural concrete will have a major impact on the design and construction of the building.

SITECAST CONCRETE COLUMNS

CONCRETE STRENGTH AND COLUMN SIZE

The top chart on the facing page is based on a concrete strength of 5000 psi (35 MPa). Higher-strength concretes may be used to reduce the required column size. For other concrete strengths, multiply the indicated column size by the amount in the table to the right:

Concrete Strength		Multiply Column Size by
3000 psi	(21 MPa)	1.20
7000 psi	(48 MPa)	0.95
9000 psi	(62 MPa)	0.80
11,000 psi	(76 MPa)	0.75

COLUMN SIZE AND CONCRETE SLAB SYSTEMS

For the two-way slab systems in the table to the right, column size may be limited by the depth of the slab. For further information see the pages indicated.

Systems	Pages
Sitecast Concrete Two-Way Flat Plate	116–117
Sitecast Concrete Two-Way Flat Slab	118–119
Sitecast Concrete Waffle Slab	120–121

ECONOMICAL CONCRETE COLUMN DESIGN

Column sizes should change as little as possible throughout a building. Column strength can be varied where required by changing the strength of the concrete mix or by adjusting the amount of steel reinforcing. Where size increases cannot be avoided, increasing only one dimension of a column at a time, in even 2-in. (50-mm) increments, is usually preferred.

Column locations should be continuous to the building foundation. Where columns on floors above cannot be supported directly below, large transfer beams are required.

Column placements should be as uniform and ordered as possible. Irregular column placements prevent the use of the most economical forming methods.

Rectangular or square columns should conform to standard orthogonal alignments. Deviations from the normal complicate formwork where the column and the slab meet.

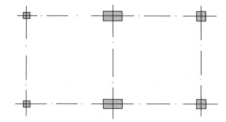

VARIATIONS IN COLUMN SIZE

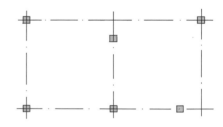

IRREGULAR COLUMN PLACEMENTS

FIRE-RESISTANCE RATINGS FOR SITECAST CONCRETE COLUMNS

Fire-resistance ratings for concrete construction vary with the type and density of concrete used. Use the following guidelines for preliminary design:

To achieve a 4-hour rating, a concrete column must be at least 14 in. (356 mm) in minimum dimension. For a 3-hour rating, the minimum dimension is 12 in. (305 mm). For 2 hours, a column must be at least 10 in. (254 mm) on a side, and for 1 hour, 8 in. (203 mm).

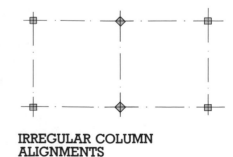

IRREGULAR COLUMN ALIGNMENTS

SITECAST CONCRETE COLUMNS

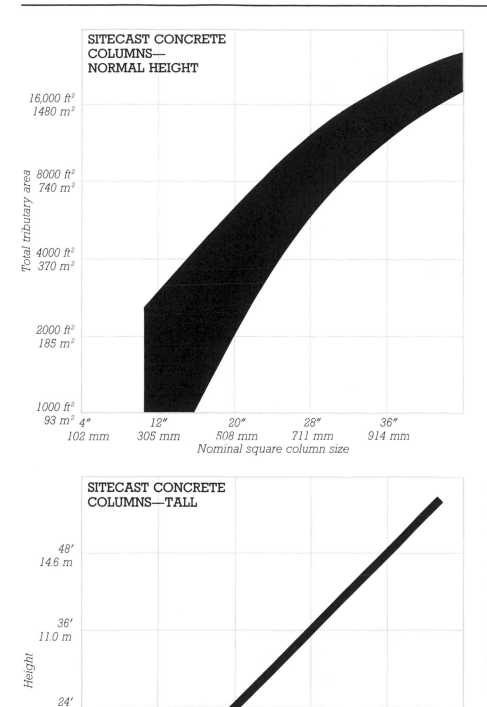

SITECAST CONCRETE COLUMNS— NORMAL HEIGHT

Total tributary area

16,000 ft²
1480 m²

8000 ft²
740 m²

4000 ft²
370 m²

2000 ft²
185 m²

1000 ft²
93 m²   4"
102 mm

12"
305 mm

20"
508 mm

28"
711 mm

36"
914 mm

Nominal square column size

SITECAST CONCRETE COLUMNS—TALL

Height

48'
14.6 m

36'
11.0 m

24'
7.3 m

12'
3.7 m

0

0   12"
305 mm

24"
610 mm

36"
914 mm

48"
1219 mm

Nominal square column size

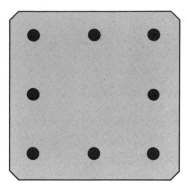

The top chart is for sitecast concrete columns up to 12 ft (3.7 m) in height between floors. For normal loads, read toward the left in the solid area. For high loads, read toward the right.

☐ For round columns, increase the indicated column diameter by 25%.

☐ For rectangular columns, select a column of equivalent area.

☐ Actual column size is equal to the nominal column size less ½ in. (13 mm).

☐ *Total tributary area* is the total area of roofs and floors supported by the column.

The bottom chart is for columns with unbraced heights greater than 12 ft (3.7 m). Use the larger of the two sizes indicated by both charts on this page.

☐ For rectangular columns, read from this chart using the least dimension of the column.

☐ For round columns, read from this chart using the diameter of the column.

SITECAST CONCRETE WALLS

Sitecast concrete bearing walls may be used as the primary loadbearing element in a structural system or may be an integrated part of many other systems. Some of the most common uses for concrete walls include construction below grade, building structural cores, and shear walls in steel or concrete frame construction.

ECONOMICAL DESIGN OF SITECAST CONCRETE WALLS

Vary wall thicknesses as little as possible. Where necessary, changes in thickness should be in 2- or 4-in. (50- or 100-mm) increments.

Loadbearing wall locations should be consistent from floor to floor and continuous to the building foundation. Where it is desirable to omit bearing walls on a lower floor, an economical alternative may be to design the wall above to act as a deep beam spanning between columns at each end. The space between the columns may then remain open. Such wall-beams may economically span up to 20 to 30 ft (6 to 9 m).

Concrete building cores should be symmetrical and rectilinear in shape and should vary as little as possible in shape or size from floor to floor. The locations and sizes of openings in core walls and the floor should also be as consistent as possible. See pages 168–178 for additional information on the design of building cores.

The use of pilasters should be avoided. Where required, they should be regularly spaced and of consistent, standard dimensions.

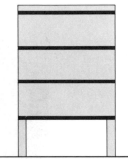

Bearing walls may act as deep beams to span across openings below.

FIRE-RESISTANCE RATINGS FOR SITECAST CONCRETE WALLS

Fire-resistance ratings for concrete construction vary with the type and density of concrete used. Use the following guidelines for preliminary design:

For a fire-resistance rating of 4 hours, sitecast concrete loadbearing walls must be at least 6.5 in. (165 mm) thick. A 3-hour rating is achieved at a thickness of 6 in. (152 mm), a 2-hour rating at 5 in. (127 mm), and a 1-hour rating at 3.5 in. (89 mm).

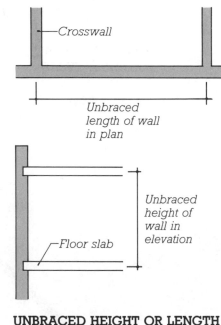

UNBRACED HEIGHT OR LENGTH OF CONCRETE WALLS

SITECAST CONCRETE WALLS

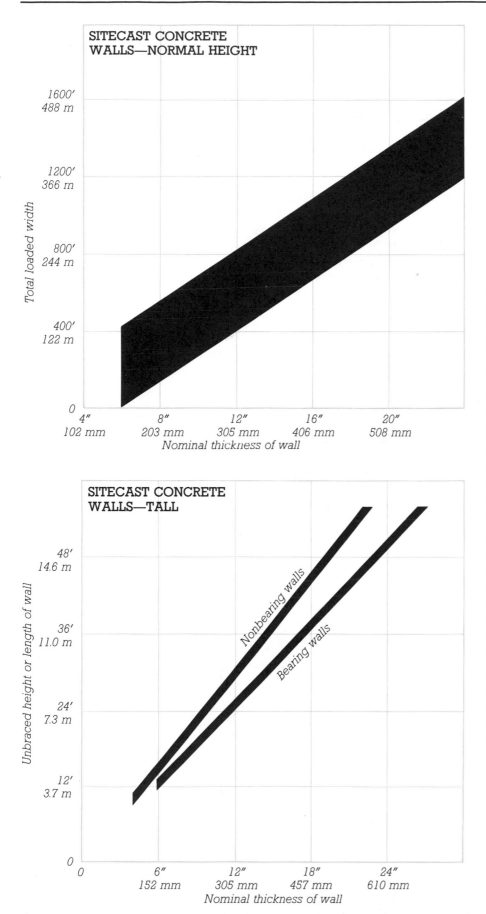

SITECAST CONCRETE WALLS—NORMAL HEIGHT

Total loaded width

1600'
488 m

1200'
366 m

800'
244 m

400'
122 m

0

4"
102 mm

8"
203 mm

12"
305 mm

16"
406 mm

20"
508 mm

Nominal thickness of wall

SITECAST CONCRETE WALLS—TALL

Unbraced height or length of wall

48'
14.6 m

36'
11.0 m

24'
7.3 m

12'
3.7 m

0

0

6"
152 mm

12"
305 mm

18"
457 mm

24"
610 mm

Nominal thickness of wall

Nonbearing walls

Bearing walls

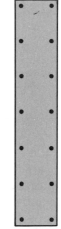

The top chart is for concrete load-bearing walls up to 12 ft (3.7 m) in height between floors. For normal loads, read toward the top in the indicated area. For high loads, read toward the bottom.

☐ Actual wall thickness is equal to the nominal thickness less ½ in. (13 mm).

☐ *Total loaded width* is one-half the span of one floor supported by the wall multiplied by the number of floors and roof above the wall.

The bottom chart is for bearing walls taller than 12 ft (3.7 m) between floors and for nonbearing walls. Read along the solid line for the appropriate wall type. For tall bearing walls, use the larger of the sizes indicated by both charts on this page. For nonbearing walls, refer to this chart only.

☐ *Unbraced height or length of wall* is the vertical distance between floors or the horizontal distance between pilasters or crosswalls, whichever is less. (See the lower diagram on the facing page.)

SITECAST CONCRETE BEAMS AND GIRDERS

ECONOMICAL BEAM DESIGN

Vary the sizes of beams throughout the building as little as possible. Size the beam with the longest span, using the chart on the facing page. Beams with shorter spans can often be the same size with reduced reinforcement.

Use beam widths equal to or greater than the widths of the columns supporting them.

In some systems an economical alternative to conventionally sized beams and girders are wide, shallow beams called either slab bands (for solid slab construction), or joist bands (for one-way joist construction). Savings in total floor-to-floor heights are possible with the reduced beam depths, and formwork costs are reduced. The depth of the slab itself may be reduced as well, since with the broader beams, the span of the slab between beams is lessened. See pages 112–113 for slab bands and pages 114–115 for joist bands.

FIRE-RESISTANCE RATINGS FOR SITECAST CONCRETE BEAMS AND GIRDERS

Fire-resistance ratings for concrete beams and girders vary with the type and density of concrete used, as well as with the proximity of the steel reinforcing to the surface of the beam. Use the following guidelines for preliminary design:

Concrete beams and girders with a minimum width of 9.5 in. (241 mm) may have a fire-resistance rating of from 1 to 4 hours.

SITECAST CONCRETE BEAMS AND GIRDERS

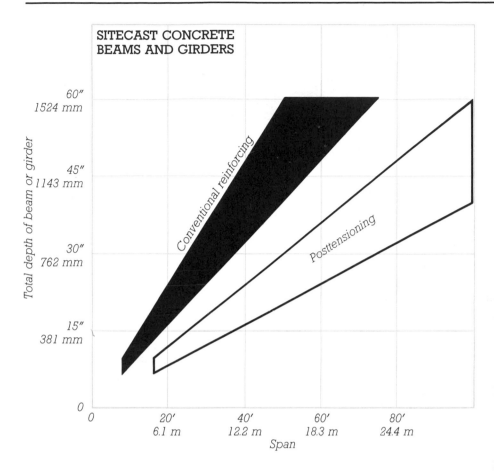

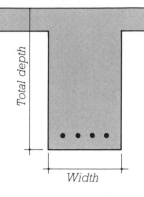

This chart is for sitecast concrete beams and girders, either conventionally reinforced or posttensioned. For light loads or continuous spans, read toward the right in the indicated areas. For heavy loads or simple spans, read toward the left.

☐ For girders, read to the extreme left in the indicated areas.

☐ Size beam depths in even 2-in. (50-mm) increments.

☐ *Total depth of beam or girder* is measured from the bottom of the beam to the top of the slab.

☐ Normal beam widths range from one-third to one-half of the beam depth. Use beam widths in multiples of 2 or 3 in. (50 or 75 mm).

SITECAST CONCRETE ONE-WAY SOLID SLAB

One-way solid slab construction supported by bearing walls is the least expensive sitecast concrete framing system for short spans and light loads. It is a popular concrete system for multiple dwelling building types such as apartments or hotels, where the regular spacing of bearing walls is easily coordinated with the layout of the small, uniformly arranged rooms typical of these buildings.

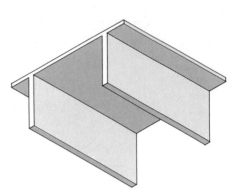

ONE-WAY SOLID SLAB WITH BEARING WALLS

ONE-WAY BEAM AND SLAB SYSTEMS

The addition of beams and girders to one-way solid slab construction can increase the load capacity and span range of the system and eliminate the need for regularly spaced walls in the building plan. The increased complexity of beam and girder systems, however, makes these one of the most expensive of all sitecast concrete systems to construct. One-way beam and slab construction is usually economical only where long spans or high loads must be accommodated, such as with industrial uses or in areas of high seismic risk.

Slab bands can be an economical alternative to conventional deeper beams when beams are used. Savings in total floor-to-floor heights are possible with the reduced beam depths, and formwork costs are reduced. The depth of the slab itself may be reduced as well, since with the broader beams, the span of the slab between the beams is lessened.

Maximum repetition of standard sizes increases the economy of slab and beam systems. Wherever possible, beam depths should be sized for the longest spans, and then the same depths should be used throughout. Beam widths and spacings, slab depths, and column sizes and spacings should also vary as little as possible within the structure.

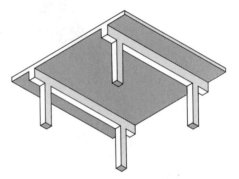

ONE-WAY SOLID SLAB WITH BEAMS

112

FIRE-RESISTANCE RATINGS FOR ONE-WAY SOLID SLAB CONSTRUCTION

Fire-resistance ratings for concrete construction vary with the type and density of concrete used. Use the following guidelines for preliminary design:

To achieve a 3-hour fire-resistance rating, a solid slab must be at least 6.5 in. (165 mm) thick. For a 2-hour rating, the minimum thickness is 5 in. (127 mm), for 1½ hours, 4.5 in. (114 mm), and for 1 hour, 3.5 in. (89 mm).

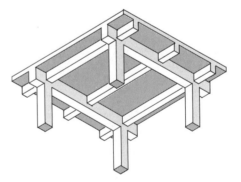

ONE-WAY SOLID SLAB WITH BEAMS AND GIRDERS

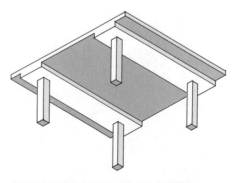

ONE-WAY SOLID SLAB WITH SLAB BANDS

SITECAST CONCRETE ONE-WAY SOLID SLAB

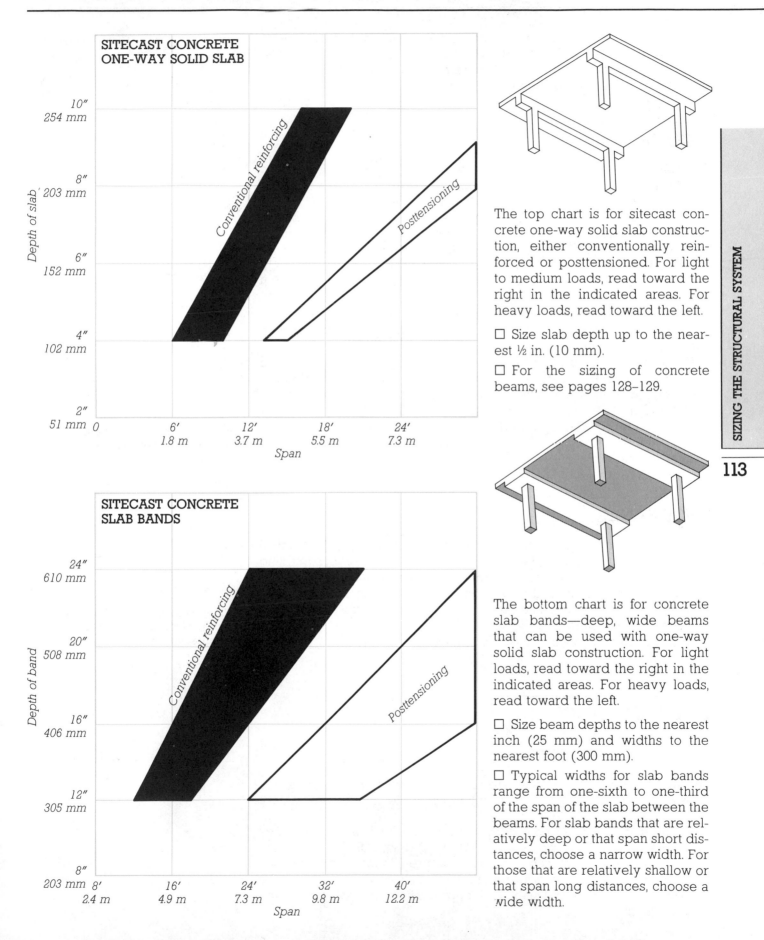

SITECAST CONCRETE ONE-WAY SOLID SLAB

Depth of slab

10″ / 254 mm
8″ / 203 mm
6″ / 152 mm
4″ / 102 mm
2″ / 51 mm

Conventional reinforcing

Posttensioning

0
6′ / 1.8 m
12′ / 3.7 m
18′ / 5.5 m
24′ / 7.3 m

Span

SITECAST CONCRETE SLAB BANDS

Depth of band

24″ / 610 mm
20″ / 508 mm
16″ / 406 mm
12″ / 305 mm
8″ / 203 mm

Conventional reinforcing

Posttensioning

8′ / 2.4 m
16′ / 4.9 m
24′ / 7.3 m
32′ / 9.8 m
40′ / 12.2 m

Span

The top chart is for sitecast concrete one-way solid slab construction, either conventionally reinforced or posttensioned. For light to medium loads, read toward the right in the indicated areas. For heavy loads, read toward the left.

☐ Size slab depth up to the nearest ½ in. (10 mm).

☐ For the sizing of concrete beams, see pages 128–129.

The bottom chart is for concrete slab bands—deep, wide beams that can be used with one-way solid slab construction. For light loads, read toward the right in the indicated areas. For heavy loads, read toward the left.

☐ Size beam depths to the nearest inch (25 mm) and widths to the nearest foot (300 mm).

☐ Typical widths for slab bands range from one-sixth to one-third of the span of the slab between the beams. For slab bands that are relatively deep or that span short distances, choose a narrow width. For those that are relatively shallow or that span long distances, choose a wide width.

SITECAST CONCRETE ONE-WAY JOISTS

One-way joist construction is an economical system for heavy loads or relatively long spans. This system is also sometimes desirable for the distinctive appearance of the underside of the slab, which may be left exposed in finished construction.

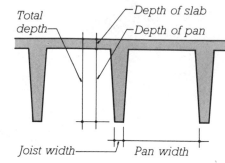

ONE-WAY JOISTS

JOIST LAYOUT

The spacing of joists depends on the widths of the pans and the joists. Standard pan widths are 20 and 30 in. (508 and 762 mm). Joists typically range in width from 5 to 9 in. (127 to 229 mm). A 6-in. (152-mm) wide joist may be assumed for preliminary purposes.

In medium- and light-load applications, alternate joists may be omitted for greater economy. This system, called wide module or skip joist construction, is economical for spans of up to approximately 40 ft (12 m). In some instances, joist spacing may be increased to as much as 9 ft (2.7 m).

In long-span or heavy-load applications, joists may be widened 2 to 2½ in. (50 to 65 mm) over the last 3 ft (1 m) toward their ends for increased capacity.

For joist spans of greater than 20 ft (6.1 m), distribution ribs running perpendicular to the joists are required. These ribs are 4 in. (102 mm) wide and the same depth as the joists. For longer spans, allow a maximum of 15 ft (4.6 m) between evenly spaced lines of ribs.

The economy of this system depends on the maximum repetition of standard forms and sizes. Depths, thicknesses, and spacings should vary as little as possible.

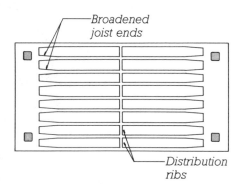

Joist bands usually run the shorter direction in rectangular bays.

JOIST BANDS

The use of joist bands the same depth as the joists is a highly economical alternative to conventional deeper beams. This system reduces building height, speeds construction, and simplifies the installation of building utilities. In some instances it may even prove economical to use a joist system deeper than otherwise necessary in order to match the required depth of the joist bands.

With rectangular column bays, joist bands should usually run in the shorter direction.

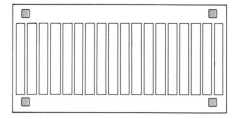

With light loads, it may be more economical to run joist bands in the long direction in a rectangular bay.

FIRE-RESISTANCE RATINGS FOR ONE-WAY JOIST CONSTRUCTION

Fire-resistance ratings for concrete construction vary with the type and density of concrete used. Use the following guidelines for preliminary design:

A slab that is 3 in. (76 mm) deep between joists has a fire-resistance rating of from 0 to 1½ hours. A 4½-in. (114-mm) deep slab provides from 1½ to 3 hours of fire protection. For higher fire-resistance ratings, the slab thickness may be increased, fireproofing materials may be applied to the underside of the joists and slab, or an appropriately fire-resistive ceiling may be used.

SITECAST CONCRETE ONE-WAY JOISTS

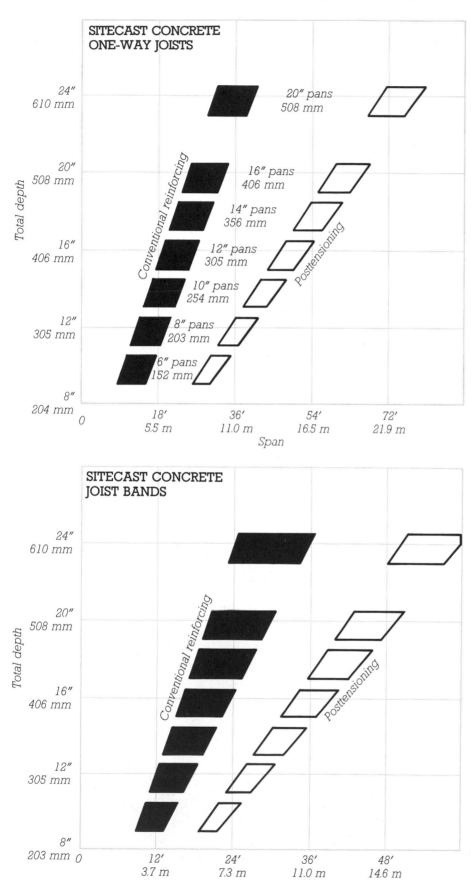

SITECAST CONCRETE ONE-WAY JOISTS

Total depth

24" 610 mm	
20" 508 mm	
16" 406 mm	
12" 305 mm	
8" 204 mm	

Conventional reinforcing

20" pans 508 mm
16" pans 406 mm
14" pans 356 mm
12" pans 305 mm
10" pans 254 mm
8" pans 203 mm
6" pans 152 mm

Posttensioning

0   18' 5.5 m   36' 11.0 m   54' 16.5 m   72' 21.9 m

Span

SITECAST CONCRETE JOIST BANDS

Total depth

24" 610 mm	
20" 508 mm	
16" 406 mm	
12" 305 mm	
8" 203 mm	

Conventional reinforcing

Posttensioning

0   12' 3.7 m   24' 7.3 m   36' 11.0 m   48' 14.6 m

Span

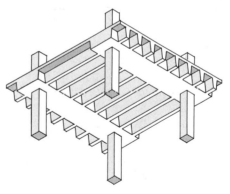

The top chart is for sitecast concrete one-way joist construction, either conventionally reinforced or posttensioned. For light loads, read toward the right in the indicated areas. For heavy loads, read toward the left.

☐ *Total depth* is measured from the bottom of the joist to the top of the slab. (See the diagram on the facing page.) Depths are indicated on the chart for slabs of from 3 to 4½ in. (76 to 114 mm) deep with standard pan sizes. The choice of the slab depth usually depends on the required fire-resistance rating for the system.

The bottom chart is for concrete joist bands—deep, wide beams used with the one-way joist system. For light loads, read toward the right in the indicated areas. For heavy loads, read toward the left.

☐ Whenever possible, use a joist band of the same depth as the joists.

☐ Typical widths for joist bands range from 1 to 6 ft (0.3 to 1.8 m).

SITECAST CONCRETE TWO-WAY FLAT PLATE

Two-way flat plate construction is one of the most economical concrete framing systems. This system can span farther than one-way slabs, and the plain form of the slab makes it simple to construct and easy to finish. This system is commonly used in apartment and hotel construction, where it is well suited to the moderate live loads, it is economical to construct, and the flexibility of its column placements permits greater ease of unit planning and layout.

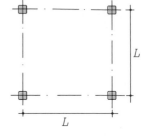

SQUARE BAYS

COLUMN LAYOUTS FOR FLAT PLATE CONSTRUCTION

For maximum economy and efficiency of the two-way structural system, the following guidelines on column placement should be followed whenever possible:

Column bays are most efficient when square or close to square. When rectangular bays are used, the sides of the bays should differ in length by a ratio of no more than 2:1.

Individual columns may be offset by as much as one-tenth of the span from regular column lines. (Columns on floors above and below an offset column must also be equally offset to maintain a vertical alignment of columns.)

Successive span lengths should not differ by more than one-third of the longer span. Slabs should also span over at least three bays in each direction.

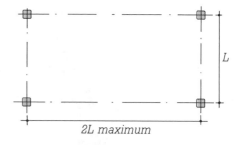

RECTANGULAR BAYS

116

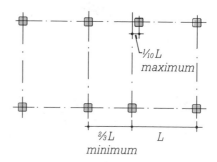

COLUMN OFFSETS AND BAY SIZE VARIATIONS

TWO-WAY SLAB AND BEAM CONSTRUCTION

Two-way slab and beam construction uses beams to support the slab between columns. The high construction costs of this system make it economical only for long spans and heavy loads, such as in heavy industrial applications, or where high resistance to lateral forces is required. For preliminary sizing of slab depths, read from the area for posttensioned construction in the chart on the facing page.

FIRE-RESISTANCE RATINGS FOR TWO-WAY FLAT PLATE CONSTRUCTION

Fire-resistance ratings for concrete construction vary with the type and density of concrete used. Use the following guidelines for preliminary design:

To achieve a 3-hour fire-resistance rating, the slab must be at least 6.5 in. (165 mm) thick. For a 2-hour rating, the minimum thickness is 5 in. (127 mm), for 1½ hours, 4.5 in. (114 mm), and for 1 hour, 3.5 in. (89 mm).

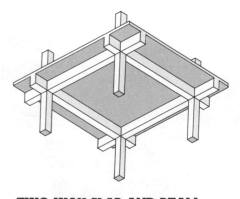

TWO-WAY SLAB AND BEAM CONSTRUCTION

SITECAST CONCRETE TWO-WAY FLAT PLATE

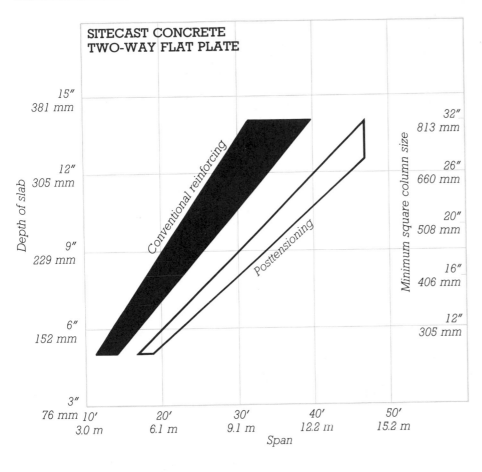

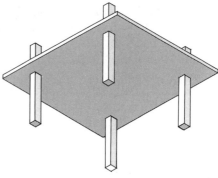

This chart is for sitecast concrete flat plate construction, either conventionally reinforced or posttensioned. For medium to light loads, read toward the right in the indicated areas. For heavy loads, read toward the left.

☐ For rectangular column bays, use the span of the longer of the two sides of the bay in reading from this chart.

☐ Size slab depth to the nearest ½ in. (10 mm).

COLUMN SIZES FOR FLAT PLATE CONSTRUCTION

The shallow depth of the junction between the slab and the column in flat plate construction restricts the minimum column size in this system. The right-hand scale on the chart above provides minimum square column sizes for various slab thicknesses. The required minimum column sizes for this system also depend on the applied loads on the structure. For light loads, reduce the indicated column size by 2 in. (50 mm). For heavy loads, increase the column size by 2 to 4 in. (50 to 100 mm).

For rectangular columns, use a column whose area is equal to that of the square column indicated. For round columns, use a column diameter one-third greater than the square column size indicated. Column sizes may also need to be increased at the edges of a slab.

For columns in multistory buildings, or for columns over 12 ft (3.7 m) tall, column size should also be checked using the charts on pages 106–107.

If smaller column sizes are desired, consider two-way flat slab construction as an alternative construction system. See pages 118–119.

SITECAST CONCRETE TWO-WAY FLAT SLAB

The two-way flat slab system is distinguished from flat plate construction by the strengthening of the column-to-slab junction, usually in the form of drop panels and/or column caps. Flat slab construction is an economical alternative to flat plate construction for heavier loads and longer spans. It also has increased resistance to lateral forces and often requires smaller columns than flat plate construction. However, the drop panels and column caps used in this system result in increased construction costs and greater overall floor depths than with flat plate construction.

DROP PANELS, COLUMN CAPS, AND SHEARHEADS

All flat slab construction requires some form of strengthening at the column-to-slab junction. Most commonly this is accomplished with the addition of drop panels, a deepening of the slab in the column region.

There are a number of alternatives to the exclusive use of drop panels in flat slab construction. Column caps, a widening of the columns toward their tops, may be used in place of drop panels where the loads on the slab are light, or in conjunction with drop panels where loads are very high. Where all such formed elements are considered undesirable, special arrangements of steel reinforcing in the slab, termed shearheads, may be an acceptable alternative to these methods.

The minimum size for drop panels is a width of one-third the span of the slab and a total depth of one and one-fourth times the depth of the slab. For heavy loads, panels may increase in width and depth.

For maximum economy, keep all drop panels the same dimensions throughout the building. The difference in depth between the slab and the drop panels should be equal to a standard lumber dimension. The edges of drop panels should be a minimum of 16 ft 6 in. (5.0 m) apart to utilize standard 16-ft (4.9-m) lumber in the formwork.

When column caps are used, their overall width should be eight to ten times the slab depth. Column caps are commonly either tapered or rectangular in profile, but should be approximately half as deep as their width at the top.

The addition of beams to flat slab construction can increase the load capacity and span range of the system, though with increased costs.

FIRE-RESISTANCE RATINGS FOR TWO-WAY FLAT SLAB CONSTRUCTION

Fire-resistance ratings for concrete construction vary with the type and density of concrete used. Use the following guidelines for preliminary design:

To achieve a 3-hour fire-resistance rating, the slab must be at least 6.5 in. (165 mm) thick. For a 2-hour rating, the minimum thickness is 5 in. (127 mm), for 1½ hours, 4.5 in. (114 mm), and for 1 hour, 3.5 in. (89 mm).

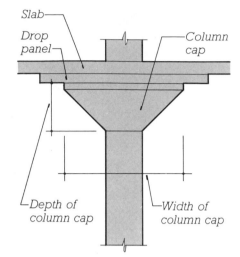

DROP PANELS AND COLUMN CAPS

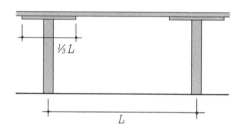

DROP PANEL WIDTH

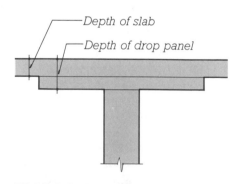

DROP PANEL DEPTH

SITECAST CONCRETE TWO-WAY FLAT SLAB

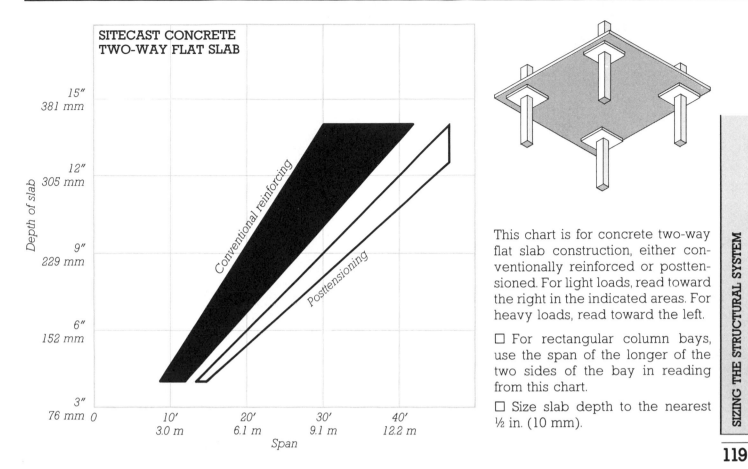

This chart is for concrete two-way flat slab construction, either conventionally reinforced or posttensioned. For light loads, read toward the right in the indicated areas. For heavy loads, read toward the left.

☐ For rectangular column bays, use the span of the longer of the two sides of the bay in reading from this chart.

☐ Size slab depth to the nearest ½ in. (10 mm).

COLUMN SIZES AND LAYOUTS FOR FLAT SLAB CONSTRUCTION

For light to moderate loads, use a minimum square column size of 12 in. (300 mm) for preliminary design. For heavier loads, larger columns or the addition of column caps may be required. Column size may be increased by 4 to 12 in. (100 to 300 mm) for extremely heavy loads.

For rectangular columns, use a column whose area is equal to that of the recommended square column size. For round columns, use a column diameter one-third greater than the recommended square column size. Column sizes may also need to be increased in multistory buildings or for columns taller than 12 ft (3.7 m). See pages 106–107 for checking column sizes for these conditions.

For maximum economy and efficiency of the two-way structural system, column layouts for flat slab construction should adhere to the same guidelines as those described for flat plate construction. Column bays should be approximately square, and column offsets from regular lines should be minimized. See page 116 for a complete discussion of these guidelines.

SITECAST CONCRETE WAFFLE SLAB

The waffle slab (or two-way joist) system is an economical system for long spans or heavy loads. This system is often desirable for the distinctive appearance of the underside of the slab, which may be left exposed in finished construction.

RIB LAYOUT FOR WAFFLE SLAB CONSTRUCTION

Standard 19-in. (483-mm) domes are used with ribs that are 5 in. (127 mm) wide to create a 24-in. (610-mm) module. Domes of 30 in. (762 mm) are used with 6-in. (152-mm) ribs to create a 36-in. (914-mm) module. Standard domes are also available for 4- and 5-ft (1.2- and 1.5-m) modules, and other square or rectangular sizes can be specially ordered.

Solid heads must be created over all columns by omitting domes in the vicinity of each column and pouring the slab flush with the bottom of the ribs. The number of domes omitted varies, increasing with longer spans and heavier loads. In some cases solid strips may extend continuously between columns in both directions.

The economy of this system depends on the maximum repetition of standard forms and sizes. Depths, thicknesses, and spacings should vary as little as possible.

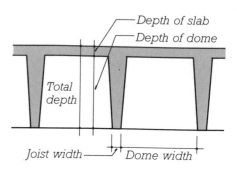

WAFFLE SLAB

EDGE CONDITIONS

When the slab ends flush with the edge columns, the area between the outermost rib and the slab edge is filled solid to create an edge beam. The slab may also cantilever beyond the columns by as much as one-third of a full span. In this case, both an edge beam and a solid strip running between the edge columns may be required.

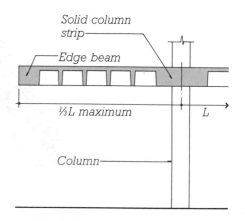

EDGE BEAMS AND CANTILEVERS

FIRE-RESISTANCE RATINGS FOR WAFFLE SLAB CONSTRUCTION

Fire-resistance ratings for concrete construction vary with the type and density of concrete used. Use the following guidelines for preliminary design:

A 3-in. (76-mm) slab thickness between ribs gives a fire-resistance rating of 0 to 1 hour. A 3½-in. (89-mm) thickness gives 1 hour, a 4½-in. (114-mm) thickness gives 1½ hours, and a 5-in. (127-mm) thickness gives 2 hours. For higher fire-resistance ratings, the slab thickness may be increased further, fireproofing materials may be applied to the underside of the ribs and slab, or an appropriately fire-resistive ceiling may be used.

SITECAST CONCRETE WAFFLE SLAB

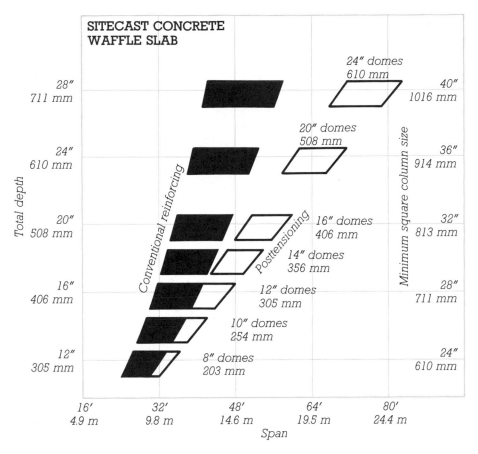

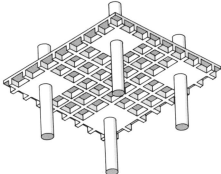

This chart is for concrete waffle slab construction, either conventionally reinforced or posttensioned. For light loads, read toward the right in the indicated areas. For heavy loads, read toward the left.

☐ For rectangular bays, use the average of the spans of the two sides of the bay when reading from this chart.

☐ *Total depth* is the sum of the depth of the ribs and the slab. (See the diagram on the facing page.) Depths are indicated on the chart for slabs from 3 to 4½ in. (76 to 114 mm) deep with standard pan sizes. The choice of the slab depth usually depends on the required fire-resistance rating for the system. See the facing page for fire-resistance information.

COLUMN SIZES AND LAYOUTS FOR WAFFLE SLAB CONSTRUCTION

In waffle slab construction, minimum column size is dependent on the overall thickness of the slab. The right-hand scale on the chart above provides minimum square column sizes for various slab thicknesses. For light loads, reduce the indicated column size by 2 to 4 in. (50 to 100 mm). For heavy loads, increase the indicated column size by 4 to 12 in. (100 to 300 mm).

For rectangular columns, use a column whose area is equal to that of the square column indicated. For round columns, use a column diameter one-third greater than the square column size indicated.

For columns in multistory buildings or for columns over 12 ft (3.7 m) tall, column size should also be checked using the charts on pages 106–107.

For maximum economy and efficiency of the two-way structural system, column layouts for waffle slab construction should adhere to the same guidelines as those described for flat plate construction. Column bays should be approximately square, and column offsets from regular lines should be minimized. See pages 116 for a complete discussion of these guidelines.

PRECAST CONCRETE STRUCTURAL SYSTEMS

Precast prestressed concrete framing systems are characterized by reduced depths and deflections for spanning members, faster construction, and increased quality and durability of the concrete itself as compared to conventional sitecast concrete. Where future changes to a structure are anticipated, precast concrete may be a preferred choice for the ease with which individual elements in the system may be removed or replaced. The difficulty of fabricating rigid joints in these systems leads to a greater reliance on shear walls or cross bracing to achieve lateral stability than in sitecast concrete structures, and makes them potentially more sensitive to vibrations produced by heavy machinery or other sources. Precast concrete spanning elements are also often used in combination with other site-fabricated vertical systems such as sitecast concrete, masonry, or steel.

SELECTING A PRECAST CONCRETE FRAMING SYSTEM

The initial choice of a framing system should be based on the desired spanning capacity or column spacings of the system and the magnitude of the expected loads on the structure. The following precast concrete systems are listed in order of increasing spans, load capacity, and cost:

- Solid Flat Slab
- Hollow Core Slab
- Double Tee
- Single Tee

For short spans and light loads, select a system from the top of the list. For longer spans and heavier loads, systems toward the bottom of the list are required.

As with sitecast concrete, the inherent fire-resistive qualities of precast concrete construction allow these systems to remain wholly or partially exposed in the finished building. For this reason, the choice of a concrete framing system often has significant architectural implications that should be considered early in the design process. Thus the designer may also wish to consider the following factors in the choice of a precast concrete system:

- The ease of integration of building services into the system.

- The possible use of the underside of the slab as a finish ceiling.

- The aesthetic qualities of the system.

LAYING OUT A PRECAST CONCRETE SYSTEM

The economy of precast concrete construction depends on the maximum repetition of standard elements and sizes. Use the following guidelines for preliminary layout of a precast concrete structure to assure maximum economy:

- In the direction of the span of the deck members, use a modular dimension of 1 ft (0.3 m). If a wall panel has been selected, use the width of the panel as the modular dimension.

- In the direction transverse to the span of the deck members, use a module of 8 ft (2.4 m). If a deck member has been selected, use the width of the member as the modular dimension.

- Floor-to-floor heights need not be designed to any particular module, though the maximum repetition of the dimension chosen is desirable. Where precast wall panels are used, floor-to-floor heights should be coordinated with the height of the wall panel.

- Restrictions due to shipping and handling of members usually limit span lengths to from 60 to 80 ft (18 to 24 m) maximum. Further transportation restrictions on depths of elements usually limit bay widths to between 24 and 40 ft (7 and 12 m) where girders are used.

In general, any design features that require unique structural elements, excessive variations in the sizes of elements, alterations in structural configuration, or deviation from the standard dimensions of the system should be avoided. Where the maximum flexibility of layout with precast concrete elements is desired, solid flat slabs or hollow core slabs may be preferred for their shorter spans and the greater ease with which they may be sawn after casting to conform to irregular conditions.

PROJECT SIZE

The economy of precast concrete construction also depends on the size of the construction project. The following figures are approximate minimum project sizes for which the production of precast concrete elements may be economical:

- 10,000 ft^2 (1000 m^2) of architectural wall panels, or,

- 15,000 ft^2 (1500 m^2) of deck or slab members, or,

- 1000 linear feet (300 m) of girders, columns, or pilings.

PRECAST CONCRETE COLUMNS

Precast concrete columns are typically combined with precast concrete beams in a post and beam configuration. Unlike in sitecast concrete systems, the fabrication of rigid joints in a precast concrete frame is difficult and rarely done. Instead, shear walls or diagonal bracing are normally incorporated into the framing system in order to stabilize the structure against lateral forces.

Precast concrete columns are usually reinforced conventionally. Pre-stressing may be used to reduce stresses on the column during transportation and handling or when significant bending or buckling stresses may be expected in service.

**PRECAST CONCRETE COLUMN
WITH TWO CORBELS**

STANDARD SIZES AND SHAPES OF PRECAST CONCRETE COLUMNS

Precast concrete columns are commonly available in square sizes from 10 to 24 in. (254 to 619 mm). Rectangular sections are also produced, although available sizes will vary with the supplier. For projects using over approximately 1000 linear feet (300 meters) of columns, a greater range of cross sections and sizes may be produced economically.

Columns in lengths of up to approximately 60 ft (18 m) can be transported easily. Columns of up to approximately 100 ft (30 m) in length can be shipped with special arrangements that may affect the overall economy of the system.

For ease of casting, columns with corbels should be restricted to corbels on two opposite sides, or at most, on three sides.

As with all precast concrete elements, precast columns should be as consistent as possible in dimensions and layout in order to achieve maximum economy.

124

CONCRETE STRENGTH AND COLUMN SIZE

The top chart on the facing page is based on a concrete strength of 5000 psi (34.5 MPa). Higher-strength concretes may be used to reduce the required column size. For higher concrete strengths, multiply the indicated column size by the amount in the table to the right:

Concrete Strength		Multiply Column Size by
7000 psi	(48 MPa)	0.95
9000 psi	(62 MPa)	0.80
11,000 psi	(76 MPa)	0.75

FIRE-RESISTANCE RATINGS FOR PRECAST CONCRETE COLUMNS

Fire-resistance ratings for concrete construction vary with the type and density of concrete used. Use the following guidelines for preliminary design:

Precast columns must be at least 14 in. (356 mm) in minimum dimension to achieve a 4-hour fire-resistance rating. For a 3-hour rating, the minimum dimension is 12 in. (305 mm). For 2 hours, a column must be at least 10 in. (254 mm) on a side.

PRECAST CONCRETE COLUMNS

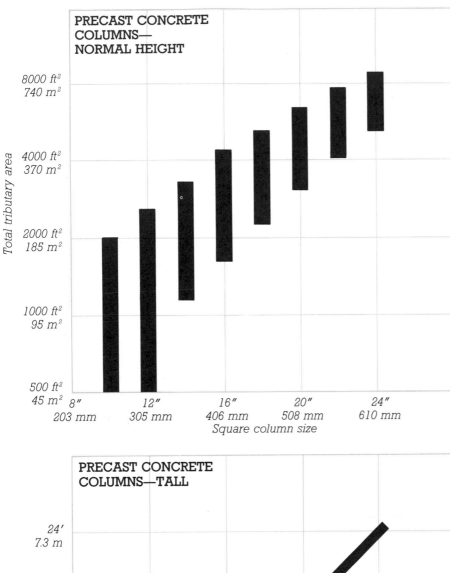

PRECAST CONCRETE COLUMNS— NORMAL HEIGHT

Total tributary area

- 8000 ft² / 740 m²
- 4000 ft² / 370 m²
- 2000 ft² / 185 m²
- 1000 ft² / 95 m²
- 500 ft² / 45 m²

Square column size:
- 8" / 203 mm
- 12" / 305 mm
- 16" / 406 mm
- 20" / 508 mm
- 24" / 610 mm

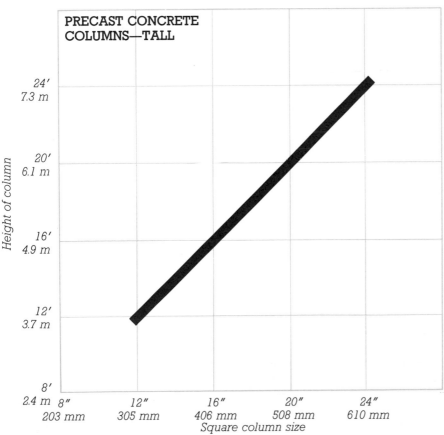

PRECAST CONCRETE COLUMNS—TALL

Height of column

- 24' / 7.3 m
- 20' / 6.1 m
- 16' / 4.9 m
- 12' / 3.7 m
- 8' / 2.4 m

Square column size:
- 8" / 203 mm
- 12" / 305 mm
- 16" / 406 mm
- 20" / 508 mm
- 24" / 610 mm

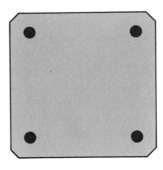

The top chart is for square precast concrete columns of up to 12 ft (3.7 m) in height between floors. For normal loads, read toward the top in the indicated areas. For high loads, read toward the bottom.

☐ For rectangular columns, select a column of equivalent area.

☐ Actual column size is equal to the nominal column size.

☐ *Total tributary area* is the total area of roofs and floors supported by the column.

The bottom chart is for columns with unbraced heights of greater than 12 ft (3.7 m). Use the larger of the two sizes indicated by both charts on this page.

☐ For rectangular columns, read from this chart using the least dimension of the column.

SIZING THE STRUCTURAL SYSTEM

125

PRECAST CONCRETE WALL PANELS

There is great variety in precast concrete wall panel types and applications. Panels may be prestressed or conventionally reinforced; they may be loadbearing or nonbearing; they may or may not contribute to the lateral stability of a building; they may be flat, ribbed, or more intricately shaped; and they may be solid, hollow, or a sandwich of concrete with an insulating core. Precast concrete wall panels may be used in conjunction with a precast concrete framing system or with other framing systems, such as steel or concrete.

PANEL TYPES

Flat panels may be one to two stories high. Ribbed panels may be one to four stories high.

Wall panels may also be formed in a great variety of original shapes. The design of such panels depends on specialized knowledge of precasting methods. When the use of such panels is planned, the necessary consultants should be sought out early in the design process. For the preliminary sizing of these panels, use the chart for ribbed panels on the facing page. Loadbearing wall panels such as these may be used in buildings of up to approximately 16 to 20 stories in height.

Panels with openings usually may not be prestressed. Panels without openings may be prestressed to reduce thickness or to limit stresses in the panels during transportation and handling.

126 SIZES OF PRECAST CONCRETE WALL PANELS

Solid panels are commonly available in thicknesses of from 3½ to 10 in. (89 to 254 mm). Sandwich or hollow core panels range in thickness from 5½ to 12 in. (140 to 305 mm). Ribbed wall panels are commonly available in thicknesses of from 12 to 24 in. (305 to 610 mm).

For preliminary design, assume an 8-ft (2.4-m) width for all panel types. With special provisions, panels in widths of up to approximately 14 ft (4.3 m) may be transported without excessive economic penalty.

FIRE-RESISTANCE RATINGS FOR PRECAST CONCRETE WALL PANELS

Fire-resistance ratings will vary with the density of concrete used in the panel, and in sandwich panels, with the type of core insulation as well. The following guidelines may be used for preliminary design:

Panels must be at least 6.5 in. (165 mm) thick to achieve a fire-resistance rating of 4 hours. A 3-hour rating is achieved at a thickness of 6 in. (152 mm), a 2-hour rating at 5 in. (127 mm), and a 1-hour rating at 3.5 in. (89 mm).

PRECAST CONCRETE WALL PANELS

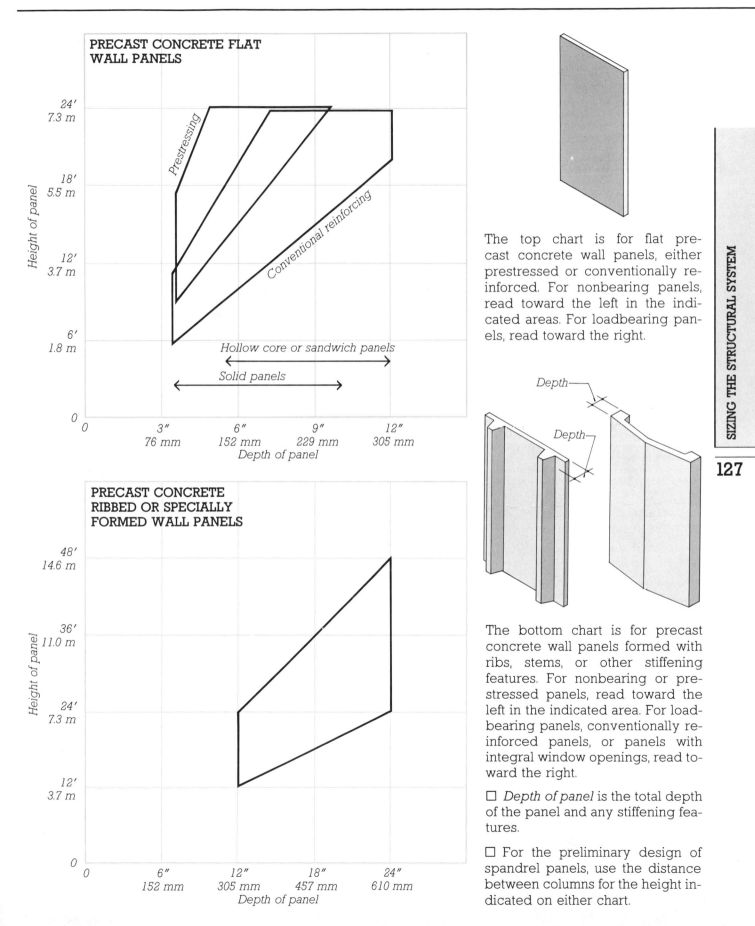

PRECAST CONCRETE FLAT WALL PANELS

Height of panel: 24' / 7.3 m, 18' / 5.5 m, 12' / 3.7 m, 6' / 1.8 m, 0

Prestressing

Conventional reinforcing

Hollow core or sandwich panels

Solid panels

Depth of panel: 0, 3" / 76 mm, 6" / 152 mm, 9" / 229 mm, 12" / 305 mm

PRECAST CONCRETE RIBBED OR SPECIALLY FORMED WALL PANELS

Height of panel: 48' / 14.6 m, 36' / 11.0 m, 24' / 7.3 m, 12' / 3.7 m, 0

Depth of panel: 0, 6" / 152 mm, 12" / 305 mm, 18" / 457 mm, 24" / 610 mm

Depth

Depth

The top chart is for flat precast concrete wall panels, either prestressed or conventionally reinforced. For nonbearing panels, read toward the left in the indicated areas. For loadbearing panels, read toward the right.

The bottom chart is for precast concrete wall panels formed with ribs, stems, or other stiffening features. For nonbearing or prestressed panels, read toward the left in the indicated area. For loadbearing panels, conventionally reinforced panels, or panels with integral window openings, read toward the right.

☐ Depth of panel is the total depth of the panel and any stiffening features.

☐ For the preliminary design of spandrel panels, use the distance between columns for the height indicated on either chart.

PRECAST CONCRETE BEAMS AND GIRDERS

Precast prestressed concrete girders are commonly used to carry all varieties of precast concrete decking elements between columns or bearing walls. They can be used in any building type where precast concrete construction is to be considered.

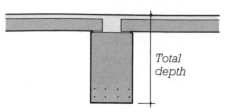

RECTANGULAR BEAM WITH SOLID OR HOLLOW CORE SLABS

TOTAL DEPTH OF FLOOR SYSTEMS

Rectangular beams are commonly used with solid or hollow core slabs resting on top of the beam. Total floor depth at the beam is the sum of the depths of the slab (and topping, if any) and the beam.

Inverted T- and L-beams are commonly used with double and single tees. When erected, the top of the tees should be level with or slightly above the top of the beam. When the tees rest directly on the beam ledge, the total floor depth at the beam is the depth of the tee (and topping, if any) plus the depth of the ledge. Deeper tees may have their ends notched or "dapped" so as to rest lower on the beam. The use of dapped tees may result in total floor depths of as little as the depth of the tee itself plus any topping.

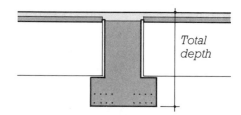

INVERTED T-BEAM WITH SINGLE OR DOUBLE TEES

FIRE-RESISTANCE RATINGS FOR PRECAST BEAMS AND GIRDERS

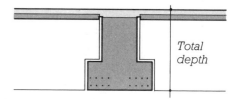

INVERTED T-BEAM WITH DAPPED TEES

Fire-resistance ratings will vary with the density of concrete used in the beams. The following guidelines may be used for preliminary design:

A prestressed concrete beam not smaller than 9.5 in. (241 mm) in width has a fire-resistance rating of 3 hours. For a 2-hour rating, the minimum width is 7 in. (178 mm), and for 1 hour, 4 in. (102 mm).

PRECAST CONCRETE BEAMS AND GIRDERS

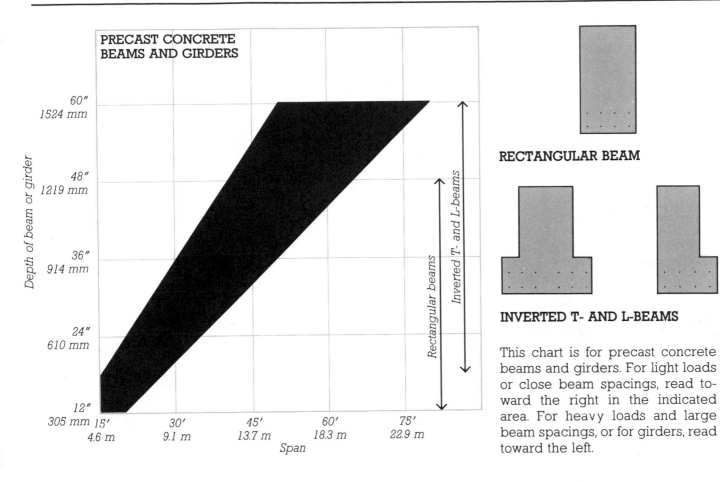

PRECAST CONCRETE
BEAMS AND GIRDERS

Depth of beam or girder

60"
1524 mm

48"
1219 mm

36"
914 mm

24"
610 mm

12"
305 mm

15'
4.6 m

30'
9.1 m

45'
13.7 m

60'
18.3 m

75'
22.9 m

Span

Rectangular beams

Inverted T- and L-beams

RECTANGULAR BEAM

INVERTED T- AND L-BEAMS

This chart is for precast concrete beams and girders. For light loads or close beam spacings, read toward the right in the indicated area. For heavy loads and large beam spacings, or for girders, read toward the left.

SIZING THE STRUCTURAL SYSTEM

129

COMMON SIZES OF PRECAST CONCRETE BEAMS AND GIRDERS

Rectangular beams commonly range in depth from 18 to 48 in. (457 to 1219 mm). Widths range from 12 to 36 in. (305 to 914 mm).

Inverted T- and L-beams commonly range in depth from 18 to 60 in. (457 to 1524 mm), although sections deeper than 48 in. (1219 mm) may be subject to shipping or handling restrictions. Widths of the beam stem (not including the ledges) range from 12 to 30 in. (305 to 762 mm).

Standard dimensions for beam ledges are 6 in. (152 mm) wide and 12 in. (305 mm) deep.

Beam sizes typically vary in increments of 2 or 4 in. (50 or 100 mm). Availability of sizes varies with suppliers.

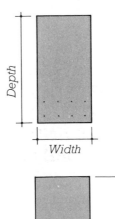

Depth

Width

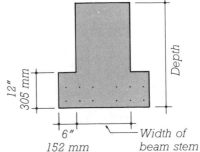

Depth

12"
305 mm

6"
152 mm

Width of beam stem

PRECAST CONCRETE SLABS

Precast prestressed concrete solid and hollow core slabs are commonly used in hotels, multifamily dwellings, commercial structures, hospitals, schools, and parking structures.

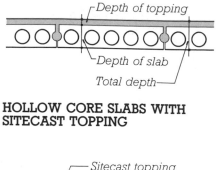

HOLLOW CORE SLABS WITH SITECAST TOPPING

CONCRETE TOPPING ON PRECAST SLABS

Sitecast concrete topping is often applied over precast concrete slabs to increase the structural performance of the slab, to increase the fire resistance of the floor system, to allow the integration of electrical and communications services into the floor, or to provide a more level and smoother floor surface in preparation for subsequent finishing. In buildings such as hotels, housing, and some parking structures, where these requirements may not exist, the use of untopped slabs may be an acceptable and economical system choice.

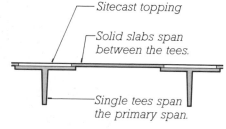

SPREAD TEE SYSTEM WITH SOLID SLABS

SPECIAL SYSTEMS

Both solid and hollow core slabs may be combined with other spanning elements to create several variations of floor systems referred to as *spread systems*. These systems can have increased economy and may allow greater flexibility in the choice of building module.

- Either slab type may be used as a secondary element spanning transversely between longer spanning single tees, double tees, or channels.

- Hollow core slabs can be spread from 2 to 3 ft (0.6 to 0.9 m), with corrugated steel decking spanning between the slabs. This system is usually topped. Where many floor penetrations are expected, this is an especially attractive system due to the ease of creating openings through the steel decking.

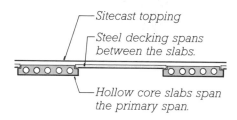

HOLLOW CORE SLAB SPREAD SYSTEM

130

FIRE-RESISTANCE RATINGS FOR SOLID FLAT SLABS AND HOLLOW CORE SLABS

Fire-resistance ratings will vary with the density of concrete used in the slabs and the topping. Use the following guidelines for preliminary design:

Solid slab floors must be at least 5.5 in. (140 mm) thick to have a fire resistance rating of 3 hours. For a 2-hour rating, the required thickness is 4.5 in. (114 mm). A 1½-hour rating requires a minimum thickness of 4 in. (102 mm), and a 1-hour rating, 3.5 in. (89 mm). These thicknesses include the depth of any topping.

Hollow core slabs at least 8 in. (203 mm) deep achieve a fire-resistance rating of 2 hours without a concrete topping. With the addition of a 2-in. (50-mm) topping, the rating rises to 3 hours.

PRECAST CONCRETE SLABS

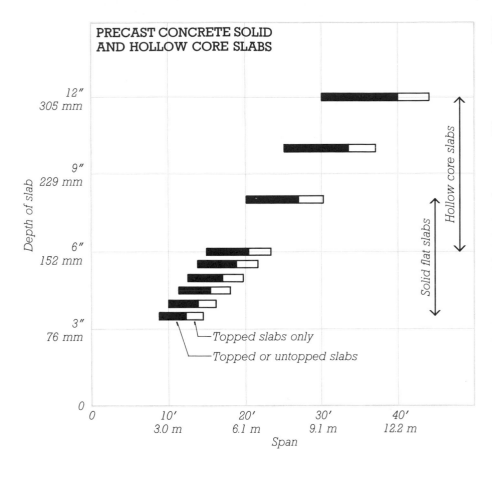

PRECAST CONCRETE SOLID AND HOLLOW CORE SLABS

Depth of slab — Span

Topped slabs only

Topped or untopped slabs

SOLID FLAT SLAB

HOLLOW CORE SLAB

This chart is for precast concrete solid flat slabs and hollow core slabs. For light loads, read toward the right in the indicated areas. For heavy loads, read toward the left.

☐ The open areas indicated on the chart are for slabs with an added sitecast concrete topping only. The solid areas are for either topped or untopped slabs. The depths indicated on the chart are for the slabs alone, without any additional topping. Where a topping is used, add 2 in. (50 mm) to the indicated depths for preliminary design. See the facing page for further information on the use of concrete toppings.

COMMON SIZES OF SOLID AND HOLLOW CORE SLABS

Solid flat slabs come in depths from 3½ to 8 in. (89 to 203 mm). For depths of 6 in. (152 mm) and above, however, hollow core slabs are usually more economical. Typical widths are 8 to 12 ft (2.4 to 3.7 m).

Hollow core slabs come in depths from 6 to 12 in. (152 to 305 mm). Typical widths are 2 ft, 3 ft 4 in., 4 ft, and 8 ft (0.6, 1.0, 1.2, and 2.4 m).

Availability of sizes varies with suppliers.

PRECAST CONCRETE SINGLE AND DOUBLE TEES

Precast prestressed single and double tees can span farther than precast slabs and are commonly used in such building types as commercial structures, schools, and parking garages.

SPREAD TEE SYSTEMS

Single and double tees may be combined with other spanning elements to create framing systems referred to as *spread systems*. In these systems, the tees are erected with spaces between. These gaps are then bridged with precast solid or hollow core slabs, or with sitecast concrete that is poured as part of the topping. These systems can increase the economy of long-span structures and may allow greater flexibility in the choice of building module.

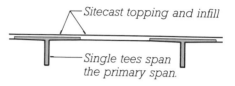

SPREAD TEE SYSTEM WITH SITECAST CONCRETE TOPPING AND INFILL

FIRE-RESISTANCE RATINGS FOR SINGLE AND DOUBLE TEES

Fire resistance will vary with the density of concrete used in the slabs and topping. Use the following guidelines for preliminary design:

For a fire-resistance rating of 3 hours, single and double tees require applied fire-protection materials or an appropriately fire-resistive ceiling. For ratings of 2 hours and less, protection may be achieved by regulating the thickness of the concrete topping: 3.5 in. (90 mm) for 2 hours, 3.0 in. (75 mm) for 1½ hours, and 2.0 in. (50 mm) for 1 hour.

132

PRECAST CONCRETE SINGLE AND DOUBLE TEES

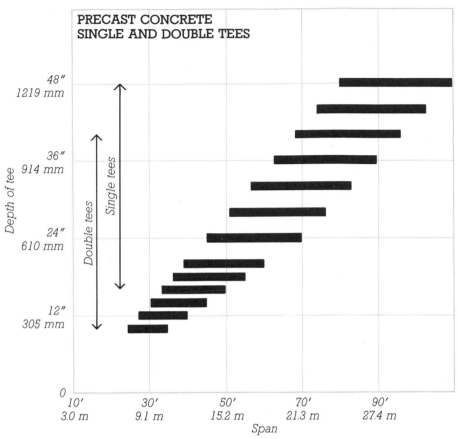

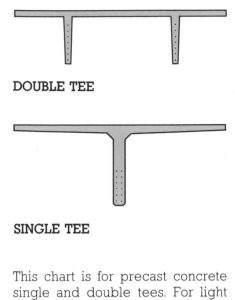

DOUBLE TEE

SINGLE TEE

This chart is for precast concrete single and double tees. For light loads, read toward the right in the indicated areas. For heavy loads, read toward the left.

☐ Because they do not require temporary support against tipping, double tees are easier and more economical to erect than single tees. Their use is preferred wherever possible.

☐ Double tees are most commonly used with a concrete topping. For preliminary purposes, add 2 in. (50 mm) to the depths indicated on the chart. Roof slabs and deep single tees may not need to be topped.

COMMON SIZES OF PRECAST SINGLE AND DOUBLE TEES

Double tees come in widths of 4, 8, 10, and 12 ft (1.2, 2.4, 3.0, and 3.7 m). Common depths are from 10 to 40 in. (254 to 1016 mm).

Single tees come in widths of 6, 8, 10, and 12 ft (1.8, 2.4, 3.0, and 3.7 m). Common depths are from 16 to 48 in. (406 to 1219 mm).

Tees longer than 60 to 80 ft (18 to 24 m) may be less economical because of increased transportation and handling costs.

Availability of sizes varies with suppliers.

DESIGNING SPACES FOR MECHANICAL AND ELECTRICAL SERVICES

SELECTING HEATING AND COOLING SYSTEMS FOR LARGE BUILDINGS

This section will help you select a heating and cooling system for the preliminary design of a large building.

DESIGN CRITERIA FOR THE SELECTION OF HEATING AND COOLING SYSTEMS FOR LARGE BUILDINGS

If you wish to minimize first cost of the heating and cooling system:

Choose the simplest possible all-air system:

    Single duct, constant air volume (pages 148–149)

or choose a system that involves no ductwork or piping:

    Through-the-wall and packaged terminal units (page 156)

If you wish to minimize operating cost:

Choose systems that convert fuel to heating and cooling energy with maximum efficiency:

    Variable air volume (pages 146–147)

    Single duct, constant air volume (pages 148–149)

    Hydronic convectors (pages 154–155)

or choose a system that uses ambient heat from the surrounding environment:

    Closed-loop heat pump system (page 153)

If you wish to maximize control of air quality and air velocity:

Choose one of the all-air heating systems:

    Variable air volume (pages 146–147)

    VAV reheat (page 147)

    VAV induction (page 147)

    Dual-duct VAV (page 147)

    Single duct, constant air volume (pages 148–149)

    Multizone (page 149)

---

138 *If you wish to maximize individual control over temperature in a number of rooms or zones:*

Choose a system that can react separately to a number of thermostats:

    Variable air volume (pages 146–147)

    VAV reheat (page 147)

    VAV induction (page 147)

    Dual-duct VAV (page 147)

    CAV reheat (page 149)

    Multizone (page 149)

    Air-water induction (pages 150–151)

    Fan-coil terminals (page 152)

    Through-the-wall and packaged terminal units (page 156)

If you wish to minimize system noise:

Choose a system that operates at low air velocities and whose moving parts are distant from the occupied spaces, such as:

    Any all-air system other than an induction system (pages 146–149)

    Hydronic convectors (pages 154–155)

DESIGN CRITERIA FOR THE SELECTION OF HEATING AND COOLING SYSTEMS FOR LARGE BUILDINGS

If you wish to minimize the visual obtrusiveness of the heating and cooling system:	Choose a system that has minimal hardware in the occupied spaces of the building, such as: Any all-air system (pages 146–149)

If you wish to minimize the floor space used for the mechanical system, or the floor-to-floor height of the building:	Choose a local system that has no ductwork or piping, such as:
	    Through-the-wall and packaged terminal units (page 156)
	or a system that minimizes the size of the ductwork, such as:
	    Induction systems (pages 147, 150–151)
	    Hydronic convectors (pages 154–155)

If you wish to minimize maintenance requirements of the heating and cooling system:	Choose systems that are very simple and have few moving parts in the occupied spaces of the building:
	    Variable air volume (pages 146–147)
	    Single duct, constant air volume (pages 148–149)
	    Hydronic convectors (pages 154–155)

If you wish to avoid having a chimney in the building:	Choose systems that are electrically powered:
	    Electric boilers (pages 146–155)
	    Through-the-wall and packaged terminal units (page 156)
	    Closed-loop heat pumps (page 153)

If you wish to maximize the speed of construction:	Choose systems that can be installed by a single trade, such as: Through-the-wall and packaged terminal units (page 156)

HEATING AND COOLING SYSTEMS FOR LARGE BUILDINGS: SUMMARY CHART

GIVE SPECIAL CONSIDERATION TO THE SYSTEMS INDICATED IF YOU WISH TO:	Variable Air Volume (VAV) (page 146)	VAV Reheat (page 147)	VAV Induction (page 147)	Dual-Duct VAV (page 147)	Single-Duct, Constant Air Volume (CAV) (page 148)
Minimize first cost					●
Minimize operating cost	●				●
Maximize control of air velocity and air quality	●	●		○	●
Maximize individual control over temperature	●	●	○	○	
Minimize system noise	●	●		○	●
Minimize visual obtrusiveness	●	●	○	○	●
Maximize flexibility of rental space	●	●	○	○	●
Minimize floor space used for the heating and cooling system			○		
Minimize floor-to-floor height			○		
Minimize system maintenance	●				●
Avoid having a chimney					
Maximize the speed of construction					

● Frequently used
○ Infrequently used
†System for heating only

140

CAV Reheat (page 149)	Multizone (page 149)	Air-Water Induction (page 150)	Fan-Coil Terminals (page 152)	Closed-Loop Heat Pumps (page 153)	Hydronic Convectors† (page 154)	Packaged Terminal Units or Through-the-Wall Units (page 156)
						●
				●	●	
○	○					
○	○	○	●	●		●
○	○				●	
○	○				●	
○	○	○	●		●	●
		○	●	●	●	●
		○	●	●	●	●
					●	
						●
						●

SOME TYPICAL CHOICES OF HEATING AND COOLING SYSTEMS FOR LARGE BUILDINGS

OCCUPANCY	Variable Air Volume (VAV) (page 146)	VAV Reheat (page 147)	VAV Induction (page 147)	Dual-Duct VAV (page 147)	Single-Duct, Constant Air Volume (CAV) (page 148)
Apartments					
Arenas, Exhibition Halls	●*				●*
Auditoriums, Theaters	●				●
Factories	●*	●			●*
Hospitals	●	●		●	
Hotels, Motels, Dormitories	●				
Laboratories	●	●		●	●
Libraries	●				
Nursing Homes	●				
Offices	●*		●		
Places of Worship	●				●
Schools	●*	●			
Shopping Centers	●*				
Stores	●*				

● Frequently used
○ Infrequently used

*Sometimes installed as packaged systems
†System for heating only

142

SOME TYPICAL CHOICES OF HEATING AND COOLING SYSTEMS FOR LARGE BUILDINGS

CAV Reheat (page 149)	Multizone (page 149)	Air-Water Induction (page 150)	Fan-Coil Terminals (page 152)	Closed-Loop Heat Pumps (page 153)	Hydronic Convectors† (page 154)	Packaged Terminal Units or Through-the-Wall Units (page 156)
			●	●	●	●
			●			
	●					
	●*	○	●		●	
●	●	○	●			
		○	●	●		●
●						
	●					
			●			●
	●*	○			●	
	●				●	
			●			
	●*					
	●*					

ZONING A BUILDING FOR HEATING AND COOLING

Before attempting to select a heating and cooling system, rough out a zoning scheme for the building. Separately controlled zones are established so that thermal comfort can be achieved throughout a building despite conditions that differ between one space and another. Sometimes a zone should be no larger than a single room (a classroom, a hotel room). Sometimes a number of spaces with similar thermal requirements can be grouped into a larger zone (a group of offices that are occupied during the day but not at night; a group of galleries in a museum). Sometimes rooms must be put on separate zones because they have differing requirements for air quality or temperature (locker rooms in a gymnasium complex, cast dressing rooms in a theater). Sometimes different zones must be established to deal effectively with different rates of internal generation of heat (a kitchen in a restaurant or dining hall, a computer room in a school, a metal casting area in an industrial building).

Buildings in which solar heat gain through windows is a major component of the cooling load need to be zoned according to the various window orientations of the rooms. In commercial buildings where each tenant will be billed separately for heating and cooling costs, each tenant space will constitute a separate zone. A large business or mercantile building might be divided into several large zones of approximately equal size to fit the capacities of the fans and ductwork or the capacities of packaged air conditioning systems. A multiuse building may incorporate parking, retail shops, lobbies, offices, and apartments, each requiring a different type of heating and cooling system.

The zoning of a building is significant in the early stages of design because it may suggest a choice of heating and cooling system: Room-by-room zoning suggests an all-water fan coil system or packaged terminal units for an apartment building, for example, meaning that the building does not have to be designed to accommodate major ductwork. Zoning may also have an impact on where the major equipment spaces are placed. It often makes sense to put major equipment on the "seam" between two zones. An example of this might be placing the major heating and cooling equipment on the second or third floor of a multiuse downtown building, above retail and lobby spaces and below multiple floors of office space.

CENTRAL SYSTEMS VERSUS LOCAL SYSTEMS

In a *central system,* heat is supplied to a building or extracted from it by large equipment situated in one or several large mechanical spaces. Air or water is heated or cooled in these spaces and distributed to the inhabited areas of the building by ductwork or piping to maintain comfortable temperatures.

In a *local system,* independent, self-contained pieces of heating and cooling equipment are situated throughout the building, one or more in each room.

Central systems are generally quieter and more energy efficient than local systems and offer better control of indoor air quality. Central equipment tends to last longer than local equipment and is more convenient to service. Local systems occupy less space in a building than central systems because they do not require central mechanical spaces, ductwork, or piping. They are often more economical to buy and install. They can be advantageous in buildings that have many small spaces requiring individual temperature control.

Pages 146–155 describe alternative choices of central heating and cooling systems for large buildings. Local systems are described on page 156.

FUELS

Heating and cooling equipment in large buildings may be powered by oil, gas, electricity, steam, or hot water. In central areas of many large cities, utility-generated pipeline steam is available. In some large complexes of buildings, such as university campuses, steam or hot water is furnished to each structure, along with chilled water for cooling, via underground pipelines from a single central boiler/chiller plant. Steam and hot water, where available, are ideal energy sources for heating and cooling, because no chimney is needed and the necessary heat exchange equipment for steam or hot water is more compact than the fuel-burning boilers that would otherwise be required. Electricity is also an ideal energy source, because it is clean, it is distributed through compact lines, and electrical equipment tends to be quieter and smaller than fuel-burning equipment. In most geographic areas, however, electricity converted directly into heat is a very costly fuel as compared to oil or gas. Gas burns cleanly and requires no on-site storage of fuel. In areas where it is more economical than gas, fuel oil is favored despite its need for on-site storage tanks.

144

MEANS OF DISTRIBUTION

The distribution of heating and cooling energy in central systems involves the circulation of air or water or both to the inhabited spaces.

• In *all-air systems,* central fans circulate conditioned air to and from the spaces through long runs of ductwork.

• In *air and water systems,* air is ducted to each space. Heated water and chilled water are also piped to each space, where they are used to modify the temperature of the circulated air at each outlet to meet local demands. Air and water systems circulate less air than all-air systems, which makes them somewhat more compact and easier to house in a building.

• In *all-water systems,* air is circulated locally rather than from a central source, so ductwork is eliminated. Only heated water and chilled water are furnished to each space. The water piping is much smaller than equivalent ductwork, making all-water systems the most compact of all.

All-air systems offer excellent control of interior air quality. The central air-handling equipment can be designed for precise control of fresh air, filtration, humidification, dehumidification, heating, and cooling. When the outdoor air is cool, an all-air system can switch to an economizer cycle, in which it cools the building by circulating a maximum amount of outdoor air. All-air systems concentrate maintenance activities in unoccupied areas of the building because there are no water pipes, condensate drains, valves, fans, or filters outside the mechanical equipment rooms.

Air-and-water and all-water systems, besides saving space, can offer better individual control of temperature in the occupied spaces than some all-air systems, but they are inherently more complicated, and much of the maintenance activity must be carried out in the occupied spaces.

SELECTING HEATING AND COOLING SYSTEMS FOR LARGE BUILDINGS

The next few pages summarize the choices of heating and cooling systems for large buildings. To determine the space required by any system, look first at the list of major components that is included with each system description. The dimensions of any components that are unique to the system are given immediately following this list. Components that are common to more than one system may be sized using the charts on pages 184–187.

CENTRAL ALL-AIR SYSTEMS: SINGLE DUCT, VARIABLE AIR VOLUME (VAV)

Description

Air is conditioned (mixed with a percentage of outdoor air, filtered, heated or cooled, and humidified or dehumidified) at a central source. Supply and return fans circulate the conditioned air through ducts to the occupied spaces of the building. At each zone, a thermostat controls room temperature by regulating the volume of air that is discharged through the diffusers in the zone.

Typical Applications

VAV is the most versatile and most widely used system for heating and cooling large buildings.

Advantages

This system offers a high degree of local temperature control at moderate cost. It is economical to operate and virtually self-balancing.

Disadvantages

VAV is limited in the range of heating or cooling demand that may be accommodated within a single system. When one area of a building needs heating while another needs cooling, a VAV system cannot serve both areas without help from a secondary system (see *Variations*, following).

Major Components

Boilers and chimney, chilled water plant, cooling tower, fan room, outdoor fresh air and exhaust louvers,

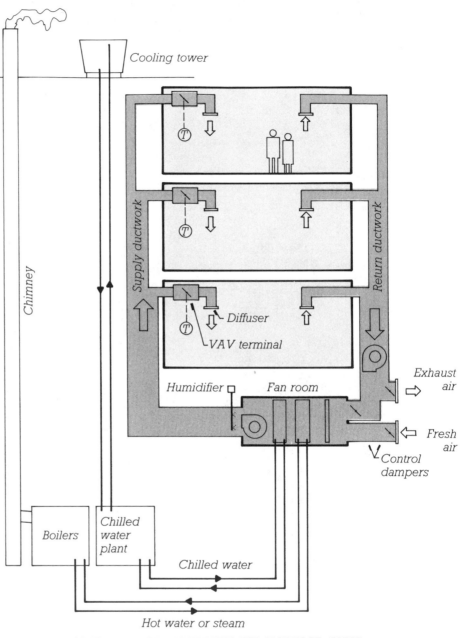

SINGLE DUCT, VARIABLE AIR VOLUME (VAV)

CENTRAL ALL-AIR SYSTEMS:
SINGLE DUCT, VARIABLE AIR VOLUME (VAV)

vertical supply and return ducts, horizontal supply and return ducts, VAV control box for each zone, supply diffusers, return grilles. (For an illustration of typical diffusers and grilles, see page 183.)

Alternately, in buildings of moderate size, a *packaged system* may be used in place of all components other than ducts, VAV control boxes, diffusers, and grilles. A *single-packaged system*, incorporating all central components in a single metal box, may be installed on the roof or outside an exterior wall, or a *split-packaged system* may be installed, with a compressor and condensing unit in an outdoor box and an air handling unit in an indoor box. Multiple packaged systems are often used to serve buildings that are large in horizontal extent. For more detailed information on packaged units, see pages 164–165.

Sizing the Components

The VAV control box is usually concealed above a suspended ceiling. It is approximately 8 to 11 in. (200 to 280 mm) high for zones up to 1500 sq ft (150 m²) in area, and up to 18 in. (460 mm) high for zones up to 7000 sq ft (700 m²). Its horizontal dimensions vary with its capacity, up to a maximum length of about 5 ft (1.5 m). To size the other components of a VAV system, use the charts on pages 184–187.

Variations

1. In buildings with large areas of windows, VAV is often combined with a second system around the perimeter of the building to deal with the large differences in heating and cooling demand between interior and perimeter rooms. The second system is most commonly either an induction system (see variation 3, following) or hydronic convectors (see pages 154–155).

2. A single duct *variable air volume reheat system* is identical to the basic VAV system, up to the point at which the air enters the local ductwork for each zone. In a reheat system, the air then passes through a reheat coil before it is distributed to the local diffusers. The reheat coil may be either an electric resistance coil or a pipe coil that carries hot water circulated from the boiler room. A local thermostat controls the flow of water or electricity through the reheat coil, allowing for close individual control of room temperature. This variation can overcome the inability of VAV systems to cope with a wide range of heating and cooling demands. VAV reheat systems are more energy-efficient than constant air volume reheat systems (page 149) because in the VAV systems the reheat coil is not activated unless the VAV system is incapable of meeting the local requirement for temperature control, and a much smaller amount of tempered air is circulated.

3. In the *variable air volume induction system*, a smaller volume of conditioned air is circulated through small high-velocity ducts from a central source. Each outlet is designed so that the air discharging from the duct continually pulls air from the room into the outlet, mixes it with air from the duct, and discharges the mixture into the room. This variation is used where limited space is available for ducts. It is also used to maintain a sufficient level of air movement in spaces that do not have a high demand for heating or cooling.

4. In a *dual-duct variable air volume system*, paired side-by-side ducts carry both heated and cooled air to each zone in the building. At each zone, the two airstreams are proportioned and mixed under thermostatic control to achieve the desired room temperature. This variation gives excellent local temperature control, but it requires an expensive and space-consuming dual system of ductwork, and it is not energy-efficient.

CENTRAL ALL-AIR SYSTEMS: SINGLE DUCT, CONSTANT AIR VOLUME (CAV)

Description
Air is conditioned (mixed with a percentage of outdoor air, filtered, heated or cooled, and humidified or dehumidified) at a central source. Supply and return fans circulate the air through ducts to the occupied spaces of the building. A master thermostat controls the central heating and cooling coils to regulate the temperature of the building.

Typical Applications
Spaces that have large open areas, few windows, and uniform loads, such as lobbies, department stores, theaters, auditoriums, and exhibition halls.

Advantages
This system offers a high degree of control of air quality. It is comparatively simple and easy to maintain.

Disadvantages
The entire area served by the system is a single zone, with no possibility for individual temperature control.

148

Major Components
Boilers and chimney, chilled water plant, cooling tower, fan room, outdoor fresh air and exhaust louvers, vertical supply and return ducts, horizontal supply and return ducts, supply diffusers, and return grilles. (For an illustration of typical diffusers and grilles, see page 183.)

Alternately, in buildings of moderate size, a *packaged system* may be used in place of all components other than ducts, diffusers, and grilles. A *single-packaged system*, incorporating all central components in a single metal box, may be installed on the roof or outside an exterior wall, or a *split-packaged system* may be installed, with a compressor and a condensing unit

in an outdoor box and an air handling unit in an indoor box. Multiple packaged systems are often used to serve buildings that are large in horizontal extent. For more detailed information on packaged units, see pages 164–165.

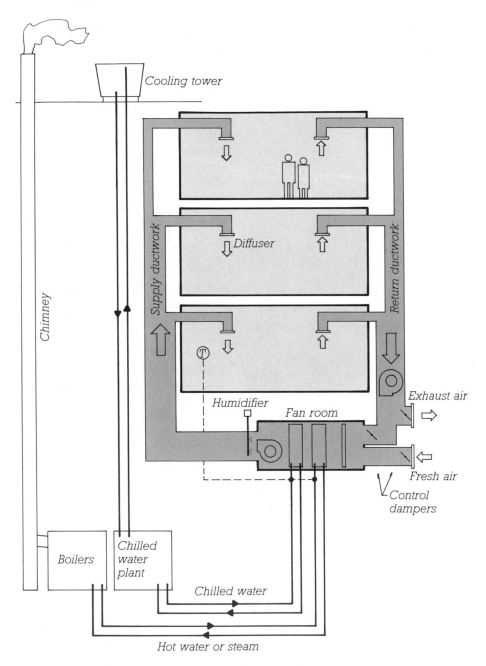

SINGLE DUCT, CONSTANT AIR VOLUME (CAV)

Sizing the Components
For the dimensions of these components, see the charts on pages 184–187.

CENTRAL ALL-AIR SYSTEMS: SINGLE DUCT, CONSTANT AIR VOLUME (CAV)

Variations

1. A *furnace* is an indoor unit that incorporates a source of heat and an air circulating fan into a single metal box. The source of heat may be a gas burner, an oil burner, an electric resistance coil, or a heat pump coil. Cooling coils may also be incorporated if desired. The capacity of furnaces is limited to such an extent that they are used mostly in single-family houses and other very small buildings; multiple furnaces are sometimes used to heat and cool somewhat larger buildings. For a more extended discussion of furnaces, see pages 197–199.

2. A single duct, *constant air volume reheat system* is identical to the CAV system first described, up to the point at which the air enters the local ductwork for each zone. In reheat systems, the air then passes through a reheat coil. The reheat coil may carry hot water or steam piped from the boiler room, or it may be an electric resistance coil. A local thermostat controls the temperature of the reheat coil, allowing for close individual control of room temperature. Reheat systems are typically used in situations requiring precise temperature control and constant airflow, such as laboratories, hospital operating rooms, or specialized industrial processes. Because constant air volume reheat systems are inherently wasteful of energy, first cooling air and then heating it, they are not often specified for new buildings.

3. In the *multizone system*, several ducts from a central fan serve each of several zones. In one type of multizone system, dampers blend hot and cold air at the fan to send air into each duct at the temperature requested by the thermostat in that zone. In another type (the one illustrated here), reheat coils in the fan room regulate the temperature of the air supplied to each zone. Multizone systems require a large amount of space for ductwork in the vicinity of the fan, so they are generally restricted to a small number of zones with short runs of ductwork. Packaged multizone units are available.

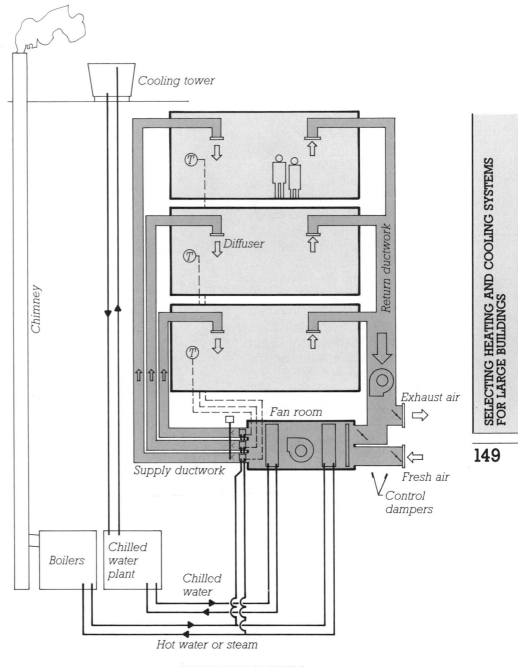

MULTIZONE SYSTEM

CENTRAL AIR AND WATER SYSTEMS: AIR-WATER INDUCTION SYSTEM

Description

Fresh air is heated or cooled, filtered, and humidified or dehumidified at a central source and circulated in small high-velocity ducts to the occupied spaces of the building. Each outlet is designed so that the air discharging from the duct (called *primary air*) draws a much larger volume of room air through a filter. The mixture of primary air and room air passes over a coil that is either heated or cooled by *secondary water* piped from the boiler room and chilled water plant. The primary air (about 15% to 25% of the total airflow through the outlet) and the heated or cooled room air that has been induced into the outlet (75% to 85% of the total airflow) are mixed and discharged into the room. A local thermostat controls water flow through the coil to regulate the temperature of the air. Condensate that drips from the chilled water coil is caught in a pan and removed through a system of drainage piping (not shown in the accompanying diagram).

Typical Applications

Exterior spaces of buildings with a wide range of heating and cooling loads where close control of humidity is not required, especially office buildings.

Advantages

This system offers good local temperature control. Space require-

150

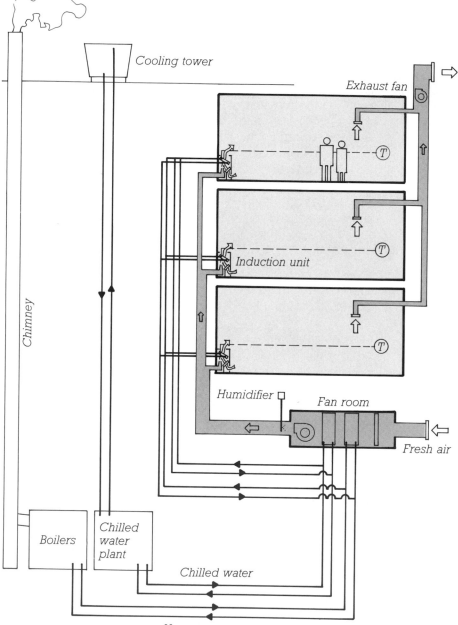

AIR-WATER INDUCTION SYSTEM

CENTRAL AIR AND WATER SYSTEMS: AIR-WATER INDUCTION SYSTEM

ments for ductwork and fans are less than for all-air systems. There are no fans in the occupied spaces.

Disadvantages

This is a relatively complicated system to design, install, maintain, and manage. It tends to be noisy, and it is very inefficient in its use of energy. Humidity cannot be closely controlled. It is rarely designed or specified today.

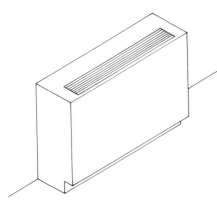

AIR-WATER INDUCTION UNIT

Major Components

Boilers and chimney, chilled water plant, cooling tower, fan room, outdoor fresh air and exhaust louvers, vertical supply and return ducts, horizontal supply and return ducts, vertical supply and return piping, horizontal supply and return piping, condensate drainage piping, air-water induction units. The water piping to each unit may consist of two, three, or four pipes, depending on whether a single coil is used for both heating and cooling or separate coils are provided for each. An additional pipe is required for condensate drainage.

Sizing the Components

Induction units are usually sized to fit beneath a window. Heights range from 25 to 28 in. (635 to 710 mm), depths from 9 to 12 in. (230 to 305 mm), and lengths from 30 to 84 in. (760 to 2130 mm). For the dimensions of the other components of the system, see the charts on pages 184–187.

Variations

Fan-coil units with primary air supply are similar to induction units, but use a fan to blow air through the coils instead of relying on the induction action of the primary airstream to circulate air from the room. The advantage of the fan-coil unit is that it can continue to circulate air even when the primary air is turned off. The primary air can be supplied through either the fan-coil unit or a separate diffuser.

CENTRAL ALL-WATER SYSTEMS: FAN-COIL TERMINALS

Description

Hot and/or chilled water are piped to fan-coil terminals. At each terminal, a fan draws a mixture of room air and outdoor air through a filter and blows it across a coil of heated or chilled water and then back into the room. A thermostat controls the flow of hot and chilled water to the coils to control the room temperature. Condensate that drips from the chilled water coil is caught in a pan and removed through a system of drainage piping (not shown in this diagram). In most installations the additional volume of air brought from the outdoors is used to pressurize the building to prevent infiltration or is exhausted through toilet exhaust vents.

Typical Applications

Buildings with many zones, all located on exterior walls, such as schools, hotels, motels, apartments, and office buildings.

Advantages

No fan rooms or ductwork spaces are required in the building. The temperature of each space is individually controlled.

Disadvantages

Humidity cannot be closely controlled. This system requires considerable maintenance, most of which must take place in the occupied space of the building.

Major Components

Boilers and chimney, chilled water plant, cooling tower, vertical supply and return piping, horizontal supply and return piping, condensate drainage piping, fan-coil terminals, outside air grilles.

Sizing the Components

Fan-coil terminals are usually sized to fit beneath a window. Heights range from 25 to 28 in. (635 to 710 mm), depths from 9 to 12 in. (230 to 305 mm), and lengths from 30 to 84 in. (760 to 2130 mm). For the dimensions of the other components of the system, see the chart on pages 184–185.

Variations

Fan-coil terminals are also manufactured in a horizontal ceiling-hung configuration and in a tall, slender configuration for mounting in vertical chases.

152

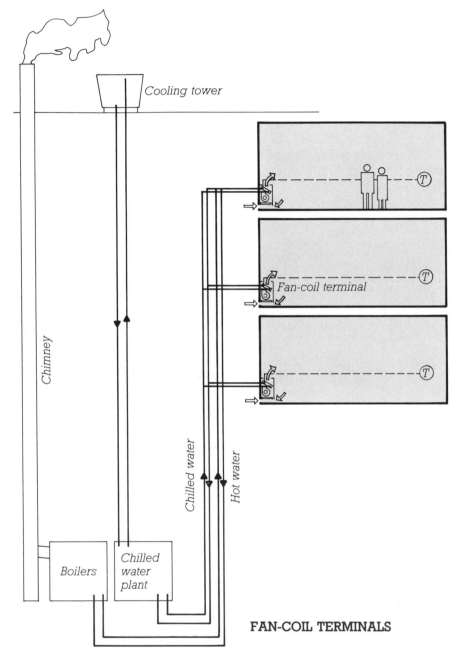

FAN-COIL TERMINALS

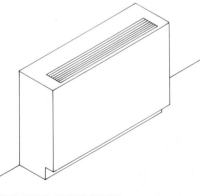

FAN-COIL TERMINAL

CENTRAL ALL-WATER SYSTEMS: CLOSED-LOOP HEAT PUMPS

Description
A water-to-air heat pump unit in each space provides heating, cooling, and fresh air. The water source for all the heat pumps in the building circulates in a closed loop of piping. Control valves allow the water source to circulate through a cooling tower in the summer and a boiler in the winter and to bypass both the boiler and the cooling tower in spring and fall and at any other time when the heating and cooling needs of the various rooms in the building balance one another.

Typical Applications
Hotels containing chronically overheated areas (kitchens, laundry, assembly rooms, restaurants).

Advantages
This is an efficient system in which heat extracted from chronically overheated areas can be used to heat underheated areas (guest rooms).

Disadvantages
This is an expensive system to install, and careful economic analysis is needed to determine if the high installation costs can be balanced by energy savings. The heat pumps require that much of the routine maintenance take place in the occupied spaces.

Major Components
Heat pump units, boiler room, cooling tower

Sizing the Components
The heat pumps may be located above a dropped ceiling over the bathroom and dressing areas in hotel rooms, or below windows. A typical under-window heat pump unit is approximately 30 in. (760 mm) high, 12 in. (305 mm) deep, and 60 in. (1525 mm) long. An above-ceiling unit has approximately the same dimensions, with the 12-in. (305-mm) dimension vertical. For the dimensions of the other components of the system, see the chart on pages 184–185.

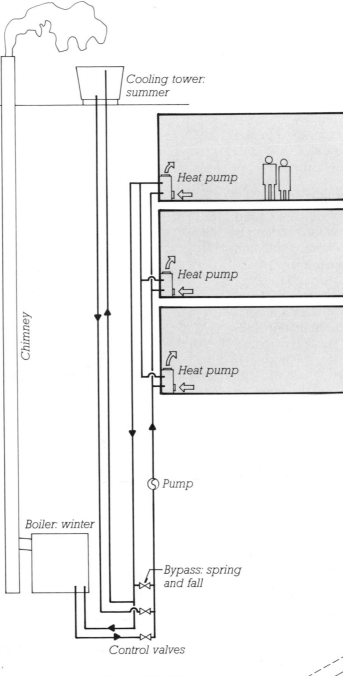

CLOSED-LOOP HEAT PUMPS

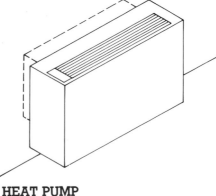

HEAT PUMP

CENTRAL ALL-WATER SYSTEMS: HYDRONIC CONVECTORS

Description

Hot water from the boiler room is circulated through fin-tube convectors, which are horizontal pipes with closely spaced vertical fins, usually mounted in a simple metal enclosure with inlet louvers below and outlet louvers above. The heated fins, working by convection, draw cool room air into the enclosure from below, heat it, and discharge it out the top.

Typical Applications

Hydronic convectors are used alone in buildings where cooling is not required and where ventilation may be accomplished by opening windows or through a supplemental ventilation system. They are also used as a supplemental source of heat in combination with other heating and cooling systems.

Advantages

This is an economical system to install and operate. It provides excellent comfort during the heating season. Convectors are available in configurations ranging from continuous horizontal strips to cabinet units, either recessed or surface-mounted. Local control of temperature is possible through thermostatically controlled zone pumps or zone valves, through self-contained, thermostatically controlled valves at each convector or, in some types of convectors, through manually controlled dampers.

154

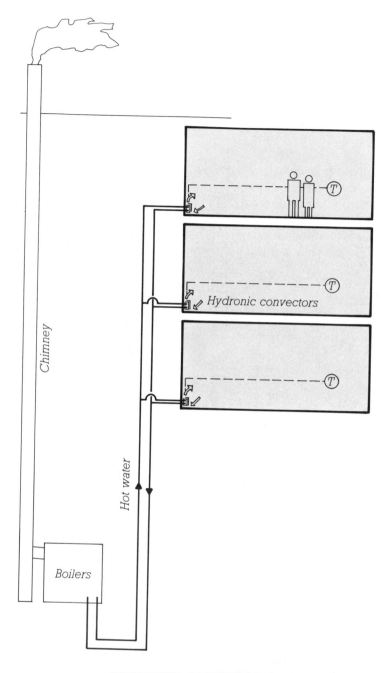

HYDRONIC CONVECTORS

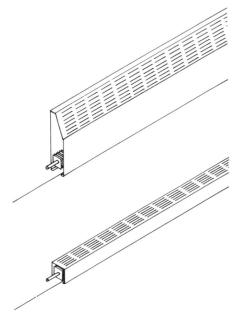

HYDRONIC CONVECTORS

Disadvantages

This is a system for heating only. Cooling, humidity control, and ventilation must be provided by separate means.

Major Components

Boilers and chimney, vertical supply and return piping, horizontal supply and return piping, convectors.

Sizing the Components

Hydronic convectors usually run continuously around the perimeter of a building. Each contains one or sometimes two continuous fin-tubes. The sheet metal enclosures for the fin-tubes are available in a variety of configurations: The smallest is about 5 in. (127 mm) square in cross section and should be mounted at least 4 in. (100 mm) above the floor. Enclosures up to 28 in. (710 mm) high and 6 in. (152 mm) deep are often used for improved thermal performance. The top of the enclosure contains small louvers and may be sloping or flat. For the dimensions of the other components of a hydronic heating system, see the chart on pages 184–185.

Variations

1. Hydronic heating is useful in buildings down to the scale of single-family residences. See pages 200–201.

2. In spaces where insufficient perimeter is available for convectors, or where the presence of convectors is undesirable, *fan-forced unit heaters* may be used. These are housed in metal cabinets that may be recessed in a wall, mounted on the surface of a wall, or suspended from the ceiling structure. Each heater contains a hot-water coil fed from the boiler room and an electric fan to circulate air across the coil. Unit heaters are very compact in relation to their heating capacity as compared to convectors.

SELECTING HEATING AND COOLING SYSTEMS FOR LARGE BUILDINGS

LOCAL SYSTEMS: PACKAGED TERMINAL UNITS AND THROUGH-THE-WALL UNITS

Description

One or several through-the-wall units or packaged terminal units are mounted on the exterior wall of each room. Within each unit, an electric-powered compressor and evaporator coil provide cooling capability. Heating is supplied either by electric resistance coils or by utilizing the compressor in a reversible cycle as a heat pump. A fan draws indoor air through a filter, adds a portion of outdoor air, passes the air across the cooling and heating coils, and blows it back into the room. Another fan circulates outdoor air independently through the unit to cool the condensing coils (and, in a heat pump cycle, to furnish heat to the evaporator coils). A control thermostat is built into each unit.

There are several alternative types of equipment that fit into this category. *Packaged terminal units* are contained primarily in an indoor metal cabinet that fits beneath a window; they are connected to outdoor air with a wall box and an outdoor grille. *Through-the-wall units* are contained in a rectangular metal box that is mounted directly in an opening in the exterior wall of the building. A variation of the through-the-wall unit is the familiar *window-mounted unit*, used only for low-cost retrofitting of existing buildings. The only service distribution to any of these types of units is an electric cable or conduit.

Typical Applications

Apartments, dormitories, motels, hotels, office buildings, schools, nursing homes.

TYPICAL DIMENSIONS OF PACKAGED TERMINAL UNITS AND THROUGH-THE-WALL UNITS

	Width	Depth	Height
Packaged Terminal Units	43" (1100 mm)	14"–20" (360–510 mm)	16" (410 mm)
Through-the-Wall Units	24"–26" (610–660 mm)	17"–30" (430–760 mm)	16"–18" (410–460 mm)

Advantages

Units are readily available and easily installed. Initial costs are often lower than for central systems. Each room has individual control of temperature. No building space is utilized for central equipment, ductwork, or piping. Operating costs may be lower than for central systems in buildings in which not all spaces need to be heated or cooled all the time, such as motels.

Disadvantages

Maintenance costs are high and equipment life is relatively short. Maintenance must be carried out in the occupied spaces. The equipment is often noisy and inefficient. Air distribution can be uneven. Wintertime humidification is not possible. Operating costs are high in areas with very cold winters and costly electricity. Through-the-wall and window-mounted units can be unsightly.

Major Components

Packaged terminal units or through-the-wall units. Typical dimensions of these units are given in the table above.

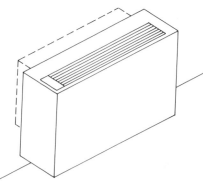

PACKAGED TERMINAL UNIT

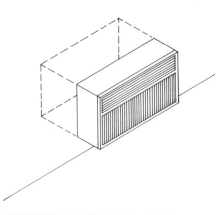

THROUGH-THE-WALL UNIT

CONFIGURING AND SIZING MECHANICAL AND ELECTRICAL SERVICES FOR LARGE BUILDINGS

This section will help you lay out the necessary spaces for mechanical and electrical equipment in a preliminary design for a large building.

157

The major equipment spaces for a large building are discussed in alphabetical order on the pages that follow.

BOILER ROOM AND CHIMNEY

The boiler room produces hot water or, less commonly, steam, to heat the building and to heat domestic water. Sometimes steam is also used to power absorption chilling equipment. A boiler room for a large building normally contains at least two boilers so that one may be in service even if the other is being cleaned or repaired. All boilers are connected to a single chimney. The boiler room may be placed anywhere in a building; common locations are a basement, a mechanical room on grade, a mechanical floor, or the roof. It should be on an outside wall because it needs an intake grille for combustion air and a door or removable panel to allow for removal and replacement of boilers. Because of the noise and heat it gives off, a boiler room should be placed below or adjacent to areas such as loading docks and lobbies that will not be adversely affected. It is helpful to locate the boiler room next to the chilled water plant; the two facilities are often combined in a single room. Hot water supply and return pipes run from the boilers through vertical shafts to reach the other floors of the building.

Boilers and their associated equipment create very heavy floor loadings that need to be taken into account when designing the supporting structure.

Boilers may be fueled by gas, electricity, or oil. Electric boilers, which generally are economical only in areas where electricity costs are very low, eliminate the need for combustion air inlets and a chimney. Generally, a two-week supply of fuel for an oil-fired boiler is stored in tanks in or near the building. The filler pipes must be accessible to oil delivery vehicles. These tanks are usually buried next to the building if space permits. If the tanks are inside the building, they must be installed in a naturally ventilated room that is designed so that it can contain the full contents of a tank and keep the contents from escaping into the building if the tank should spring a leak. A basement location on an outside wall is preferred. Oil for a boiler on an upper floor of a building is pumped up a shaft from the tanks below.

An approximate floor area for a boiler room may be determined using the chart on pages 184–185. In larger buildings, a long, narrow room is usually preferable to a square one. The ceiling height of a boiler room varies from a minimum of 12 ft (3.66 m) for a building of moderate size to a maximum of 16 ft (4.88 m) for a large building.

The size of the chimney that is associated with fuel-burning boilers varies with the type of fuel, the height of the chimney, the type of draft (natural, forced, or induced) that is employed, and other factors. For preliminary design purposes, allow a floor area of 2 ft × 2 ft (610 mm square) for a chimney in a very small building, and 6 ft × 6 ft (1.83 m square) in a very large building, interpolating between these extremes for buildings of other sizes. Keep in mind that the chimney runs through every floor of the building above the boiler room.

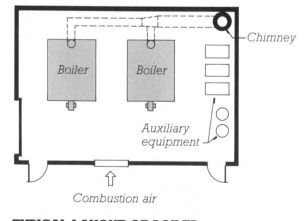

TYPICAL LAYOUT OF BOILER ROOM

MAJOR EQUIPMENT SPACES FOR LARGE BUILDINGS

CHILLED WATER PLANT

The chilled water plant produces cold water (usually 42° to 45°F, or 5° to 6°C) that is used for cooling the building. The chillers are fueled by electricity, gas, or steam. The chillers give off heat, noise, and vibration, and should not be located near spaces they will adversely affect. They may be placed anywhere in the building from basement to roof, but they are heavy and require deeper-than-normal structural members for support. An outside wall location is desirable to allow for the necessary ventilation and maintenance access. Ideally the chilled water plant should be adjacent to the boiler room; the two are often housed in the same room in a building of moderate size. Chilled water supply and return pipes run from the chilled water pumps to the fan rooms or terminals that they serve. Condenser water supply and return pipes run between the chillers and the cooling towers.

An approximate floor area for a chilled water plant may be determined using the chart on pages 184–185. In larger buildings a long, narrow room is usually preferable to a square one. The ceiling height of a chilled water plant varies from a minimum of 12 ft (3.66 m) for a building of moderate size to a maximum of 16 ft (4.88 m) for a very large building.

COOLING TOWERS

Cooling towers extract heat from the water that is used to cool the condenser coils of the chilled water plant. In effect, the cooling towers are the mechanism by which the heat removed from a building by the air conditioning system is dissipated into the atmosphere. Most cooling towers are "wet," meaning that the hot water from the condensers splashes down through the tower, giving off heat by evaporation and convection to a stream of air that is forced through the tower by fans. The cooled water is collected in a pan at the bottom of the tower and circulated back to the chillers.

The size and number of cooling towers are related to the cooling requirements of the building. Cooling towers may be located on the ground if they are at least 100 ft (30 m) from any building or parking lot, to avoid property damage and unhealthful conditions from the splash, fog, and microorganisms given off by the towers. An alternate location is the roof of the building, but because of the noise and vibration they generate, the towers should be isolated acoustically from the frame of the building, and noise-sensitive areas such as auditoriums and meeting rooms should not be located directly below them. Rooftop cooling towers must be located well away from windows and fresh air louvers.

A preliminary estimate of the roof or ground area occupied by cooling towers may be obtained from the chart on pages 184–185. Cooling towers range between 13 and 40 ft (4 and 12 m) in height; the height for a given building can be estimated by interpolating between these two extremes. The towers usually have a 4-ft (1.2-m) crawlspace beneath. For free airflow, they should be located one full width apart and at least 10 to 15 ft (3 to 5 m) from any screen wall or parapet wall unless the wall has very large louvers at the base to allow for intake air.

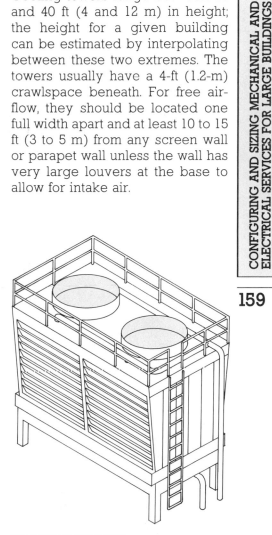

COOLING TOWER

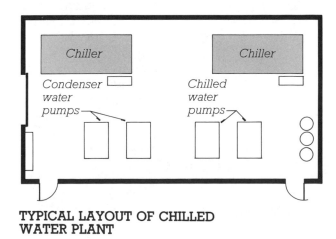

TYPICAL LAYOUT OF CHILLED WATER PLANT

ELECTRICAL SERVICE ENTRANCE, TRANSFORMERS, SWITCHGEAR, AND EMERGENCY POWER SUPPLY

Every building has an electrical transformer or transformers, a meter or meters, and a panel or switchgear that distributes the power to the interior wiring that services the building. The locations and sizes of these elements vary considerably, depending on the size and purpose of the building, the type of electric service provided by the local utility, the standards and practices of the utility company, the preferences of the building owner, the judgement of the electrical engineer, and local electrical codes.

For reasons of efficiency, electric utilities transmit electricity at high voltages. Transformers reduce this to lower voltages that can be utilized directly in the building—typically 120/208 volts or 115/230 volts in wall and floor receptacles, and up to 480/277 volts in some types of machinery and lighting fixtures. A commercial building of up to 25,000 sq ft (2500 m²) or a residential building up to twice this size will most often buy its electricity at these lower voltages. For buildings in this size range, the transformer is provided by the utility company and is mounted either overhead on a transmission pole, on the ground (especially where transmission lines are underground), or, in some dense urban situations, in a nearby building or underground vault. A meter or meters belonging to the utility company are installed on or in the building where the service wires enter, and distribution within is usually by means of panels of circuit breakers that are lo-

cated in an adjacent utility space or a small electrical closet.

Owners of larger buildings will sometimes prefer to buy electricity at these lower voltages, but they can obtain energy more economically by providing their own transformers and purchasing electricity at the higher transmission voltage. One typical pattern is to bring electricity to the building at 13,800 volts and then to step down to 480/277 volts with a large primary transformer or transformers at the service entrance. The 277-volt electricity is used directly in many types of commercial and industrial lighting, and at 480 volts, electricity can be distributed efficiently to electrical closets in various parts of the building. Each electrical closet houses one or more small secondary transformers to step down from 480 volts to the lower voltages needed for convenience receptacles and machinery.

Primary transformers may be located either outside or inside the building. Where space is available, an outdoor transformer mounted on a ground-level concrete pad is preferred to an indoor transformer, because it is less expensive, cools better, is easier to service, transmits less noise to the building, and is safer against fire. Some common

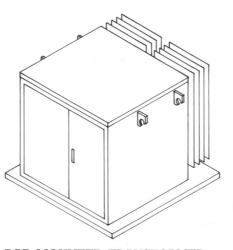

PAD-MOUNTED TRANSFORMER

dimensions of pad-mounted transformers are shown in the upper table on the facing page. A transformer of this type does not need to be fenced unless for visual concealment, in which case there must be a clear space of 4 ft (1.2 m) all around the pad for ventilation and servicing. The pad should be within 30 ft (9 m) of a service road and requires a clear service lane 6 ft (1.83 m) wide between the transformer and the road. Multiple outdoor transformers are often used to serve larger buildings and are usually placed at intervals around the perimeter of the building to supply electricity as close as possible to its point of final use.

In a dense urban situation, or where the building owner finds outdoor placement objectionable, the primary transformer or transformers must be located within the building. Oil-filled transformers of the type the utility company provides for large buildings must be placed in a transformer vault, which is a fire-rated enclosure with two exits. In a few large cities, it is customary to place the transformer vault under the sidewalk, covered with metal gratings for ventilation. Dry-type transformers of the kind usually bought by owners of small- and medium-sized buildings do not need a vault; they may be placed in the main electric room. The transformer vault or main electric room is often placed in the basement or on the ground floor, but may be located on higher floors. Primary transformers are very heavy and require a heavier, deeper supporting structure than the rest of the building.

In buildings with dry-type transformers, the switchgear, consisting of disconnect switches, secondary switches, fuses, and circuit breakers, may be housed in the same enclosure with the transformers in a configuration known as a unit substation. In large build-

MAJOR EQUIPMENT SPACES FOR LARGE BUILDINGS

ings with oil-filled transformers, the switchgear is located in a room adjacent to the transformer vault.

Transformers and switchgear must be ventilated because they give off large quantities of heat. It is best to locate them against an outside wall so that high and low convective ventilation openings can be provided. If this is not possible, ventilation can be accomplished by ductwork and fans connected to outdoor air louvers. Access panels or doors must be provided for servicing and replacing switchgear and transformers. Some examples of sizes of transformer vaults and switchgear rooms are given in the lower table on this page.

In many buildings an emergency generator is required to furnish electricity during power outages. The emergency generator is driven by an engine fueled with propane gas or diesel oil. This engine needs large quantities of air

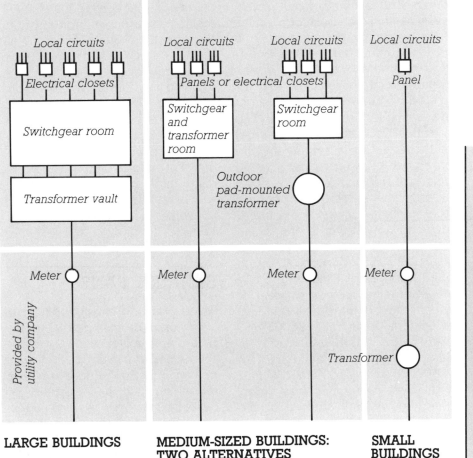

LARGE BUILDINGS

MEDIUM-SIZED BUILDINGS: TWO ALTERNATIVES

SMALL BUILDINGS

TYPICAL DIMENSIONS OF PAD-MOUNTED TRANSFORMERS

Floor Area of Commercial Building in Ft² (m²)	Number of Residential Units	Pad Size in Inches (m)
180,000 (17,000)	—	96 × 96 (2.4 × 2.4)
60,000 (5,700)	160	52 × 50 (1.3 × 1.3)
18,000 (1,700)	50	52 × 44 (1.3 × 1.2)

TYPICAL SIZES OF TRANSFORMER VAULTS AND SWITCHGEAR ROOMS

Floor Area of Commercial Building in Ft² (m²)	Floor Area of Residential Building in Ft²(m²)	Size of Combined Room for Transformers and Switchgear in Ft (m)	Size of Transformer Vault in Ft (m)	Size of Switchgear Room in Ft (m)
150,000 (15,000)	300,000 (30,000)	30 × 30 × 11 (9.14 × 9.14 × 2.44)		
100,000 (10,000)	200,000 (20,000)		20 × 20 × 11 (6.0 × 6.0 × 3.35)	30 × 20 × 11 (9.0 × 6.0 × 3.35)
300,000 (30,000)	600,000 (60,000)		20 × 40 × 11 (6.0 × 12.0 × 3.35)	30 × 40 × 11 (9.0 × 12.0 × 3.35)
1,000,000 (100,000)	2,000,000 (200,000)		20 × 80 × 11 (6.0 × 24.0 × 3.35)	30 × 80 × 11 (9.0 × 24.0 × 3.35)

for combustion and cooling, and it gives off exhaust gases, noise, and vibration. The best location for the emergency power supply is on the ground outside the building, near the switchgear room. Engine-generator sets in prefabricated weather-resistant housings are available for this purpose. The next-best location is on the roof of the building; alternatively, the emergency power supply may be placed inside the building on an exterior wall, as remote as possible from occupied areas of the building. The housing or room for an emergency power supply is usually 12 ft (3.66 m) wide. A length of 18 ft (5.5 m) will accommodate an emergency power supply for an average commercial building of up to 150,000 sq ft (14,000 m²); 22-ft (6.7-m) length will accommodate the supply for a building of up to 400,000 sq ft (37,000 m²). Where a building owner requires emergency power for other than life safety loads, these space requirements can grow very rapidly.

There is a loss of power for a period of up to 10 seconds between the time a power interruption occurs and the time the emergency generator takes over. This is usually acceptable, but in some buildings with specialized medical equipment, computers, communications equipment, certain types of lighting, or an extraordinary need for security, an uninterruptible power supply (UPS) is needed to keep electricity flowing during the brief transition from utility electricity to that generated on-site. Where a UPS is needed, it requires, in addition to the emergency power supply, a room for batteries and an adjacent room for specialized circuit breakers and electronic controls. These should be located close to the area that utilizes the UPS power. A typical computer room of 10,000 sq ft (1,000 m²) requires two rooms to house UPS equipment, an outside-

ventilated battery room of 500 sq ft (47 m²), and a room of 200 sq ft (19 m²) for electronic equipment. Both these rooms require air conditioning.

Several large conductors run from the transformers to the switchgear and from the switchgear to the vertical and horizontal distribution components that feed electrical closets throughout the building. For information on vertical distribution and electrical closets, see page 171. For information on horizontal distribution, see pages 179–183.

EXHAUST FANS

Exhaust fans draw air constantly from toilet rooms, locker rooms, bathrooms, janitor closets, storage rooms, corridors, and kitchens and deliver it to the outdoors to keep the air fresh in these spaces. Exhaust fans are also used to evacuate air from laboratory fume hoods and many industrial processes. The fans are usually housed in small mushroom ventilators on the

roof and are connected to the spaces they serve by ducts that run through the vertical shafts in the cores of the building. It is extremely difficult to generalize about the sizes of exhaust ducts and fans; they tend not to be extremely large, so it is usually sufficient to allow a small amount of shaft space and roof space that can later be adjusted in consultation with the mechanical engineer.

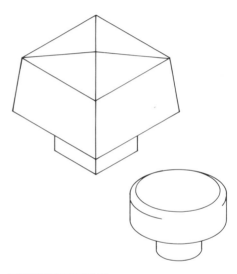

EXHAUST FANS

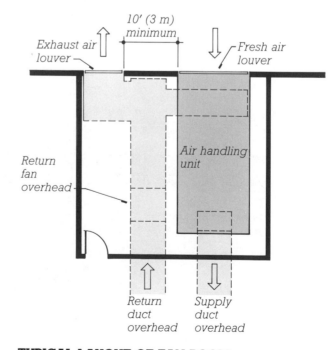

TYPICAL LAYOUT OF FAN ROOM

MAJOR EQUIPMENT SPACES FOR LARGE BUILDINGS

FAN ROOMS AND OUTDOOR AIR LOUVERS

In an all-air system, an air handling unit in a fan room circulates air through a filter and thermostatically controlled hot water and chilled water coils to condition it. The conditioned air is ducted to the occupied spaces of the building. A return fan draws air from the occupied spaces into return grilles and back to the fan room through return ducts. Just before it passes through the heating and cooling coils again, a portion of the air is diverted by a damper and exhausted through a louver to the outdoors. An equal portion of fresh air is drawn in through another outdoor louver and added to the stream of return air.

Fan rooms may be located anywhere in the building; they are supplied with hot and chilled water through insulated pipes from the boiler room and chilled water plant. A floor plan of a typical fan room is shown on the facing page. If only a single fan room is used, it may be placed in the basement, on the ground floor, on the roof, or on any intermediate floor, as close to the vertical distribution shafts as possible. It is convenient to locate this room near an outside wall, but if an outside wall location is not possible, ducts to the outdoors are used to convey fresh air and exhaust air to and from the fan. These ducts may run horizontally, above a ceiling, or vertically, in a shaft.

The maximum vertical "reach" of a fan room is approximately 25 stories up and/or down; more typically, fan rooms are located so none needs to circulate air more than 11 to 13 stories in each direction.

Multiple fans distributed throughout the building are often desirable because they allow the building to be zoned for better local control and they reduce the total volume of ductwork in the building. It can be advantageous to have a separate fan room for each floor of a building, because this saves floor space by eliminating most or all of the vertical runs of ductwork. Separate fan rooms are used in buildings that bill tenants individually for heating and cooling costs. Again, it is preferable to locate each fan room at the perimeter of the building.

Fan room equipment is often heavy enough to require stronger structural support than the surrounding areas of the building. Noise-sensitive areas such as meeting rooms and auditoriums should not be located adjacent to fan rooms, which produce vibration and air noise.

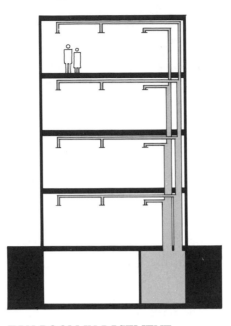

FAN ROOM IN BASEMENT

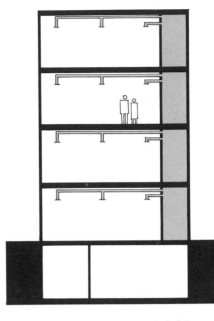

FAN ROOM ON EACH FLOOR

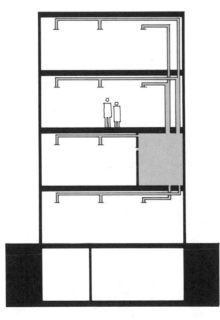

FAN ROOM ON INTERMEDIATE FLOOR

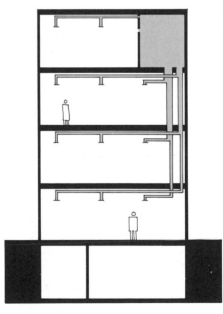

FAN ROOM AT TOP OF BUILDING

The fresh air and exhaust air louvers associated with a fan room are noisy and create local winds. They need to be located a short distance apart, usually at least 10 ft (3 m), on the exterior wall, so that the outgoing and incoming air will not mix. Louvers for small pieces of equipment such as fan-coil units are very small. With careful design work, they can be integrated unobtrusively into the fabric of the wall. Louvers for larger pieces of equipment grow progressively larger with the floor area each serves. They are large and conspicuous for central fans serving a number of floors and require special attention on the part of the architect.

Use the graph on pages 186–187 as a means of determining the approximate sizes of outdoor louvers for preliminary design purposes. The same graph gives information on sizing fan rooms as a function of floor area served. Using this graph, one may quickly evaluate a number of schemes for air distribution, using one fan room or many, to determine the effect of each scheme on the space planning and exterior appearance of the building.

LOADING DOCK AND ASSOCIATED SPACES

Every large building needs at least a single loading dock and freight room for receiving and sending mail and major shipments, moving tenant furniture in and out, removing rubbish, and facilitating the servicing of mechanical and electrical equipment. The dock needs to be situated so that trucks may back up to it easily without obstructing traffic on the street. The freight room inside the dock area should open directly to the rubbish compactor and the freight ele-

vators and should be connected to the major mechanical equipment spaces and the mail room. It is often appropriate to locate the oil filler pipes next to the truck ramp that leads to the loading dock. If possible, the access doors to the major equipment spaces should also open to the dock or ramp area. For dimensional information on truck ramps and loading docks, consult *Architectural Graphic Standards*.

PACKAGED CENTRAL HEATING AND COOLING EQUIPMENT

Packaged central heating and cooling equipment comes in two different configurations:

☐ *Single-packaged* heating and cooling equipment combines the functions of a boiler room and chimney, a chilled water plant, and a fan room into a compact, rectangular, weatherproof unit that is specified, purchased, and installed as a single piece of equipment. The supply and return ducts from the building are connected through the roof or the wall of the building to the fan inside the packaged unit.

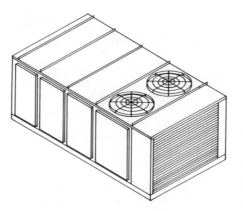

SPLIT-PACKAGED SYSTEMS

☐ *Split-packaged* units are furnished in two parts, an outdoor package that incorporates the compressor and condensing coils, and an indoor package that contains the cooling and heating coils and the circulating fan. The two packages are connected by insulated refrigerant tubing and control wiring. Split-packaged units cost slightly more than single-packaged units, but they are slightly more energy efficient because none of their ductwork is located outside the insulated shell of the building.

Packaged units, whether single or split, are fueled entirely by electricity or by a combination of electricity and gas. Packaged equipment is simple for the designer to select and specify and is easy to purchase and install because it is supplied as off-the-shelf units that need only external connections to fuel, electricity, control wiring, and air ducts.

Packaged units are available in single-zone and multizone configurations in a variety of sizes to serve a wide range of demands for cooling and heating. They can be purchased as variable air volume or constant air volume (VAV or CAV) systems (see pages 146–149).

Single-packaged units are generally located either on the roof or on a concrete pad alongside the building. If alongside, the supply and return ducts are connected to the end of the unit and pass through the side wall of the building before branching out to the spaces inside. In a rooftop installation, the ducts pass through the bottom of the unit and into the building. The ducts from single-packaged units can serve low multistory buildings through vertical shafts that connect to above-ceiling branch ducts on each floor. Rooftop units may be placed at

MAJOR EQUIPMENT SPACES FOR LARGE BUILDINGS

intervals to serve a building of any horizontal extent. The same is true of units located alongside the building, although the depth of the building is somewhat restricted by the maximum practical reach of the ducts. Using the chart on pages 186–187, you may select a combination of unit size and numbers of units to serve any desired size and shape of building. For buildings taller than four or five stories, or large buildings where only one central plant may be installed, conventional central equipment assembled from components must be used because of the relatively limited capacity range of packaged units.

The table below will help to determine preliminary sizes for split-packaged equipment. The inside package may be obtained as a horizontal unit that hangs from the roof structure, or as a vertical unit that stands on the floor. The outside package may be located on the roof or on a concrete pad next to the building.

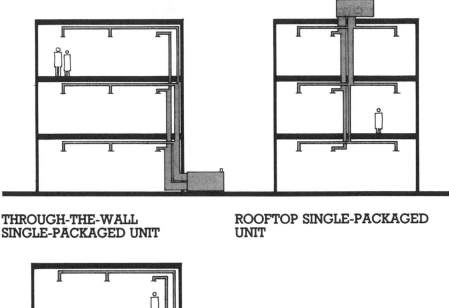

**THROUGH-THE-WALL
SINGLE-PACKAGED UNIT**

**ROOFTOP SINGLE-PACKAGED
UNIT**

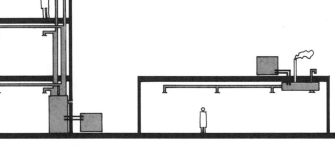

SPLIT-PACKAGED UNIT

TYPICAL DIMENSIONS OF SPLIT-PACKAGED COMPONENTS

Cooling Capacity in Tons (Mcal/sec)		10 (35)	20 (70)	30 (106)	40 (141)	50 (176)
Outdoor Unit	Length	6'-4" (1.93 m)	12'-11" (3.94 m)	12'-11" (3.94 m)	12'-11" (3.94 m)	12'-11" (3.94 m)
	Width	3'-8" (1.12 m)	4'-0" (1.22 m)	4'-10" (1.47 m)	7'-1" (2.16 m)	7'-1" (2.16 m)
	Height	3'-4" (1.02 m)	2'-4" (0.71 m)	3'-2" (0.71 m)	4'-9" (1.45 m)	5'-8" (1.73 m)
Indoor Ceiling-Suspended Unit	Length	8'-3" (2.51 m)	7'-10" (2.39 m)	9'-0" (2.74 m)	9'-8" (2.95 m)	9'-8" (2.95 m)
	Width	5'-3" (1.60 m)	6'-8" (2.03 m)	7'-10" (2.39 m)	10'-7" (3.23 m)	10'-7" (3.23 m)
	Height	2'-2" (0.66 m)	2'-6" (0.76 m)	3'-0" (0.91 m)	3'-10" (1.17 m)	3'-10" (1.17 m)
Indoor Floor-Mounted Unit	Length	5'-3" (1.60 m)	6'-8" (2.03 m)	7'-10" (2.39 m)	10'-7" (3.23 m)	10'-7" (3.23 m)
	Width	2'-2" (0.66 m)	2'-6" (0.76 m)	3'-0" (0.91 m)	3'-10" (1.17 m)	3'-10" (1.17 m)
	Height	8'-3" (2.51 m)	7'-10" (2.39 m)	9'-0" (2.74 m)	9'-8" (2.95 m)	9'-8" (2.95 m)

Use the chart on pages 184–185 to estimate the required cooling capacity.

SEWAGE EJECTOR PIT

If the lowest level of a building lies below the level of the sewer or septic tank, sewage is collected in an underfloor pit and pumped up to the sewer. The pumps do not necessarily occupy floor space, because they are usually contained within the pit, but the pit must lie beneath unobstructed floor space so it can be inspected and serviced through a removable cover.

TELEPHONE SWITCHGEAR

Telephone wiring, with its low voltage, is small in diameter and poses no safety problems. Central switching rooms for large buildings should be located in the basement or on the ground floor as close to the telephone service entrance as possible. Space requirements for telephone switching are modest compared to those for electric power: A 6 × 10 ft (1.83 × 3.0 m) room is sufficient for a building with several hundred telephones. A 14 × 14 ft (4.3 m square) room will serve 1000 telephones, and a room 20 ft (6 m) square is the maximum usually required in any building. An 8-ft (2.44-m) ceiling height is sufficient. Local closets for telephone wiring are generally fed from the main telephone switching room (see page 171).

WASTE COMPACTOR

A waste compactor is necessary in most large buildings. It may be coupled with a container system to facilitate the trucking of the compacted rubbish.

The compactor is often served by a vertical refuse chute from the upper floors of the building. The chute must be placed in a fire-rated enclosure and must be provided with an automatic sprinkler head above the top opening. Some codes also require the provision of a 2-hour enclosed chute room outside the chute opening at each floor. Inside diameters of chutes range from 15 to 30 in. (380 to 760 mm), with 24 in. (610 mm) being a typical dimension.

The waste compactor should be located directly beneath the refuse chute and adjacent to the loading dock. The size and shape of the compactor itself varies widely with the manufacturer and the capacity of the unit. A compactor room of 60 sq ft (5.6 m²) is sufficient for a small apartment building. A larger building will require 150 to 200 sq ft (14.0 to 18.6 m²), and industrial waste compacting facilities can be much larger.

WATER PUMPS

Where the water service enters the building, a room is required to house the water meter and the sprinkler and standpipe valves. In a building taller than three or four stories, a suction tank and a pair of water pumps are needed to boost the water pressure in the domestic water system. A similar pair of pumps are required for a sprinkler system. A chiller for drinking water and a heat exchanger to heat domestic hot water are often located in the same area. The table below will assist in determining the necessary floor areas for water pumps.

In a few large cities, local codes require the provision of a large gravity tank on the roof of the building to furnish a reserve of water in case of fire. In most areas, however, the pumps alone are sufficient.

WORKROOMS, CONTROL ROOMS, AND OFFICES

Operating and maintenance personnel in large buildings need space in which to work. Offices should be provided for operating engineers and maintenance supervisors. A room is required to house the control console for a large-building heating and cooling system. Lockers and workrooms are needed for mechanics, plumbers, electricians, and custodial workers. Storage facilities should be provided near the loading dock and service elevator for tools, spare parts, and custodial equipment and supplies.

SPACE REQUIREMENTS FOR WATER PUMPS

Domestic Water Pumps	
Area Served	*Room Dimensions*
Up to 200,000 ft² (Up to 18,600 m²)	8′ × 12′ (2.44 × 3.66 m)
200,000 to 1,000,000 ft² (18,600 to 93,000 m²)	16′ × 12′ (4.88 × 3.66 m)

Fire Pumps (assuming sprinklers)	
Area Served	*Room Dimensions*
Up to 100,000 ft² (Up to 9,300 m²)	8′ × 12′ (2.44 × 3.66 m)
100,000 to 200,000 ft² (9,300 to 18,600 m²)	20′ × 12′ (6.1 × 3.66 m)
1,000,000 ft² (93,000 m²)	30′ × 24′ (9.15 × 7.32 m)

VERTICAL DISTRIBUTION OF SERVICES FOR LARGE BUILDINGS

PLANNING SERVICE CORES

Spaces for the vertical distribution of mechanical and electrical services in a large building need to be planned simultaneously with other building elements that are vertically continuous or that tend to occur in stacks—principally the structural columns, bearing walls, shear walls, and wind bracing; exit stairways; elevators and elevator lobbies; and rooms with plumbing: toilet rooms, bathrooms, kitchens, and janitor closets. These elements tend to coalesce into one or more core areas where the vertically continuous elements are concentrated into efficient, neatly packaged blocks of floor space, leaving most of each floor open for maximum flexibility of layout.

Different types of buildings call for different sorts of core arrangements. In high-rise office buildings, where a maximum amount of unobstructed, rentable area is the major criterion for floor layout, a single central core is almost universal. In low-rise commercial and institutional buildings, horizontal distances are often great enough that a single core would be inefficient, and vertical elements are divided into several cores of varied internal composition. These are likely to be located asymmetrically in response to particular requirements relating to the servicing and circulation patterns of the building. In a dormitory, apartment building, or hotel, a common pattern of vertical services features slender shafts sandwiched between the units. Shafts next to the interior corridor carry the plumbing for the bathrooms and kitchens that back up to them. If the heating and cooling equipment for the units is located over the bathrooms and kitchens, the hot and chilled water piping and ductwork may share these same

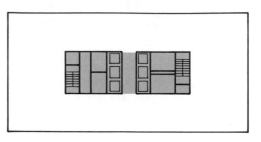

HIGH-RISE OFFICE BUILDING: VERTICAL SERVICES IN A CONCENTRATED CORE

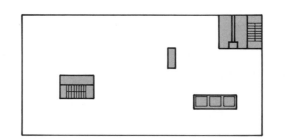

LOW-RISE BUILDING: VERTICAL SERVICES IN SCATTERED LOCATIONS

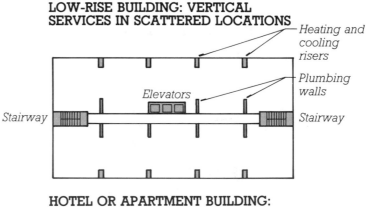

HOTEL OR APARTMENT BUILDING: VERTICAL SERVICES BETWEEN UNITS

shafts. If the heating and cooling are done along the outside walls, another set of shafts may be created between units around the perimeter of the building to serve this equipment.

Vertical distribution shafts need to connect directly with the major equipment spaces that feed them and the horizontal distribution lines they serve. The boiler room, chilled water plant, central fan room, exhaust fans, water pumps, sewage ejector, waste compactor, and cooling towers need to cluster closely around the vertical distribution shafts. The electric and telephone switchgear should not be far away. The electrical and telephone closets must stack up along the wiring shafts at each floor. The toilet rooms, bathrooms, kitchens, and janitor closets must back up to plumbing walls. Horizontal supply and return ducts need to join easily with the vertical ducts in the shafts, and horizontal piping for hot and chilled water distribution must branch off conveniently from the riser pipes.

VERTICAL DISTRIBUTION OF SERVICES FOR LARGE BUILDINGS

LOCATING THE CORES IN THE BUILDING

A centrally located core leaves the daylit perimeter area of the building open for use. It also works efficiently with a scheme that distributes services horizontally from one set of shafts, because it minimizes duct and pipe sizes. The central location can be undesirable, however, because it interrupts the open space of the floor. A core at one edge of the building does not have this problem, but it may not be able to incorporate exit stairways that are separated widely enough (see page 222), and it obstructs a portion of the daylit perimeter. Either of these core locations connects well to major equipment at the ground, the roof, and any intermediate mechanical floors.

A core located in a corner, on the other hand, is undesirable because horizontal distribution lines from the core are long, exit stairways are too close together, and connections to major equipment are congested. Two or more corner cores used in combination can overcome some of these problems.

Multiple cores often work well, particularly in broad, low-rise buildings. Exit stairways can be widely separated and connected to a simple, clear system of corridors and elevators. Vertical risers for mechanical services can be located where they work best, minimizing the congestion of ducts and pipes at points of connection to horizontal networks.

Core locations may also be dictated in part by the structural scheme that provides lateral stability to the building. A large, centrally located core or two symmetrically placed cores can furnish ideal locations for wind bracing. A core at the edge of the building or a detached core cannot house all the wind bracing for the building because it is located asymmetrically with respect to one of the principal axes of the building (see pages 31–33). Scattered cores and corner cores may not be large enough to develop the required depth of wind trusses.

The chart below summarizes some of the advantages and disadvantages of different options for core placement.

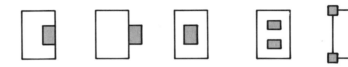

CHARACTERISTICS OF CORE PLACEMENTS

1 = Best
5 = Worst

	Edge	Detached	Central	Two	Corners	Scattered
Flexibility of typical rental areas	2	1	3	4	2	5
Perimeter for rental areas	4	3	1	1	5	2
Ground floor high-rent area	3	1	3	4	2	5
Typical distance of travel from core	4	5	2	1	3	3
Clarity of circulation	3	4	2	1	3	5
Daylight and view for core spaces	2	1	5	5	1	4
Service connections at roof	3	5	1	2	4	3
Service connections at ground	3	4	2	1	5	3
Suitability for lateral bracing	4	5	1	1	2	3

This table is adapted by permission of John Wiley & Sons, Inc., from Benjamin Stein, John S. Reynolds, and William J. McGuinness, *Mechanical and Electrical Equipment for Buildings,* 7th ed., copyright © 1986, by John Wiley & Sons, Inc.

PLANNING THE INTERNAL ARRANGEMENT OF THE CORES

The ratio of the total floor area of the core or cores of a building to the floor area served varies widely from one building to the next. The average total area of the cores in 40- to 70-story New York City office buildings, including the stairways, toilets, elevators, and elevator lobbies, is approximately 27% of the open area of each floor served by the core. This ratio runs as high as 38% in some older buildings, but ranges around 20% to 24% in office towers of recent design. At the other extreme, the total core area of a three-story suburban office building is likely to be in the range of 7% of the floor area served, because there are few elevators, much less lobby space for elevators, and much smaller shafts for mechanical and electrical services.

These percentages also vary with the relative requirements for mechanical and electrical services; they can be higher in a hospital or laboratory and are much lower in a hotel or apartment building. Core area is directly related to the type of heating and cooling system used: The percentages quoted in the preceding paragraph apply to buildings with all-air systems. Buildings with air-and-water and all-water systems require somewhat less shaft space.

A building with a fan room on each floor will need very little core area for ductwork, but the fan room is likely to occupy at least as much floor space as the vertical ductwork it eliminates.

The structural scheme of a building can also have a direct effect on core area. Of the total core area of a tall office building, about 12% is usually occupied by columns, bracing, walls, and partitions. This percentage is lower for lower buildings and can be very low in buildings whose core areas contain no columns or lateral bracing.

The most critical elements of the core, those that should be located first in at least a tentative way, are the columns and bracing, the exit stairways, and the elevators and elevator lobbies. Next should come the plumbing walls and the shafts for ductwork. For help in laying out the structural elements, see pages 31–44. Details of the location and configuration of exit stairways are given on pages 226–231. Pages 175 and 176 give advice on the number, size, and layout of elevator shafts and lobbies. Plumbing walls are illustrated on page 173, and ductwork shafts can be sized using the chart on pages 186–187.

The chimney is another element for which there may be little flexibility of location. Usually the chimney exits from a corner of the boiler room. It may be sloped at an angle not less than 60° to the horizontal to bring it to a more convenient position in the core. For sizing information on chimneys, refer to page 158.

TOTAL SHAFT AREA

The total open area of all the mechanical and electrical shafts in a tall office building is normally equal to about 4% of the area served on each floor, and can be estimated at about half this amount for a low-rise building. This should be divided into at least two separate shafts to relieve the congestion that would otherwise occur where the vertical and horizontal distribution networks connect. It is especially effective to provide separate shafts for supply and return ducts because it is often possible to use a separate return shaft as a plenum, a shaft that is itself the duct. Separate supply and return shafts also minimize conflict in the bulky ductwork connections and crossovers. For maximum utility, the horizontal proportions of each shaft should lie in the range of 1:2 to 1:4. To allow sufficient space for connections to horizontal distribution networks at each floor, no shaft should adjoin stair towers or elevator shafts on more than one long side and one short side. All shafts must be enclosed with 2-hour noncombustible walls, except in buildings of Wood Light Frame construction, where shaft enclosures do not need to be fire rated.

VERTICAL DISTRIBUTION OF SERVICES FOR LARGE BUILDINGS

ELECTRICAL CLOSETS AND TELEPHONE CLOSETS

The electrical and telephone closets must be stacked above one another and must include wiring shafts. Typical sizes and configurations for electrical closets are illustrated in the accompanying diagrams. In an office building, major electrical closets should be located in such a way that no point on a floor lies more than 125 ft (40 m) away. If this is difficult to arrange, satellite closets served by cables from the major closets may be used to feed electricity to the more distant areas. In smaller buildings or buildings other than offices, satellite-size closets may serve in place of major closets.

Telephone closets do not require as much space as electrical closets. The table below gives some typical sizes.

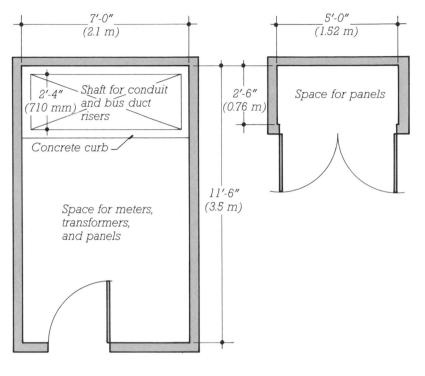

MAJOR ELECTRICAL CLOSET

SMALL OR SATELLITE ELECTRICAL CLOSET

SOME TYPICAL SIZES OF TELEPHONE CLOSETS

Area Served: Office Building	Closet Dimension
5,000 ft² (465 m²)	1'-6" × 11'-0" (460 × 3350 mm)
10,000 ft² (930 m²)	4'-0" × 7'-0" (1220 × 2135 mm)
20,000 ft² (1860 m²)	8'-0" × 8'-0" (2440 × 2440 mm)

Telephone closet requirements are considerably less in types of buildings other than offices.

FAN ROOMS

Local fan rooms, if their fresh air and exhaust air connections are provided by means of duct risers, should be placed against shafts. If local fan rooms need only hot and chilled water from central equipment, it is better to put them against outside walls, so that they may exchange air directly with the outdoors, and to serve them with water via horizontal piping from the core. (Alternatively, centrally-located local fan rooms can be connected to fresh air and exhaust louvers by horizontal ducts.) If fan rooms on an outside wall are stacked above one another, of course, it is usually possible to provide an immediately adjacent shaft, separate from the main core, for the water riser piping. See pages 162–164 and 186–187 for information on planning fan rooms.

MAIL FACILITIES

Vertical gravity chutes for mail deposit are often provided in multistory buildings. The chute occupies an area of about 5 × 15 in. (125 × 375 mm) in plan and terminates in a receiving box in the base of the building.

Vertical mail conveyors are sometimes provided for delivery of mail in a large multistory office building. The mailroom at the base of the conveyor should be adjacent to the loading dock and can be sized at about $\frac{2}{10}$ of 1% of the area it serves. The walls around the conveyor shaft itself will vary in plan from 4 ft × 4 ft 6 in. (1220 × 1370 mm) to 7 ft 3 in. × 8 ft 6 in. (2210 × 2590 mm) inside dimensions, depending on the system's capacity and manufacturer. The conveyor should discharge into a service mailroom of at least 6 × 7 ft (1830 × 2135 mm) on each floor. A 2-hour fire enclosure is required around the conveyor shaft.

PIPE RISERS FOR HEATING AND COOLING

The insulated pipes that conduct heated and chilled water to and from the spaces in a building require considerable space. In a tall apartment building or hotel, a clear shaft of 12 × 48 in. (300 × 1200 mm) is generally sufficient to serve two stacks of units. This may be sandwiched between units at the perimeter of the building or located adjacent to the central corridor, depending on where the heating and cooling equipment is located in the units.

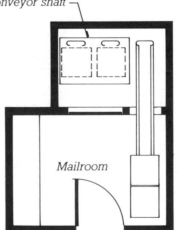

Mail conveyor shaft

Mailroom

VERTICAL DISTRIBUTION OF SERVICES FOR LARGE BUILDINGS

PLUMBING WALLS, JANITOR CLOSETS, AND TOILET ROOMS

Fixtures in bathrooms, toilet rooms, shower rooms, kitchens, laundries, and other areas with plumbing should back up to plumbing walls. A plumbing wall has an internal cavity large enough to house the supply, waste, and vent piping necessary to serve the fixtures. Plumbing walls should be stacked vertically from the bottom of the building to the top. It is possible to offset plumbing walls a few feet from one floor to the next, but the horizontal offsets are expensive and cause maintenance headaches. A typical plumbing wall arrangement, complete with janitor closet, is illustrated and dimensioned on the diagram to the right.

Fixture requirements for toilet rooms are established by plumbing codes and vary widely from one code to the next. The fixture requirements for the model plumbing codes in North America are reproduced in Appendix D, beginning on page 439. The designer must also keep in mind the general requirement that toilet rooms be usable by handicapped persons. For detailed layout dimensions of toilet rooms and accessible facilities, consult *Architectural Graphic Standards*.

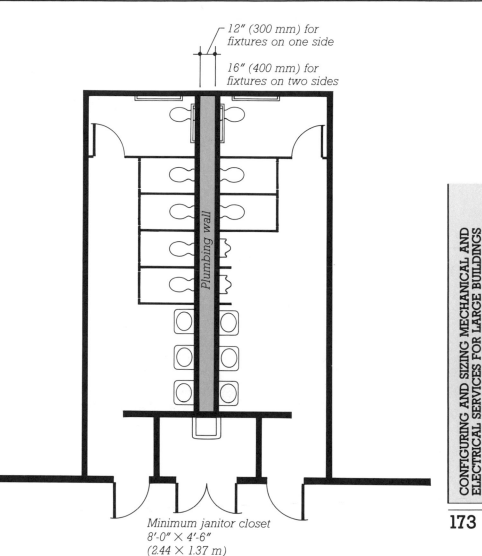

12" (300 mm) for fixtures on one side

16" (400 mm) for fixtures on two sides

Plumbing wall

Minimum janitor closet
8'-0" × 4'-6"
(2.44 × 1.37 m)

173

STANDPIPES

A standpipe is a large-diameter steel water pipe extending vertically through a building, with fire hose connections at every floor. There are two types of standpipes: A *wet standpipe* is continually filled with water and is fitted with hoses for emergency use by building occupants. A *dry standpipe* contains no water and is reserved for use by firefighters. In case of fire, the firefighters supply water to the dry standpipe by connecting pumper trucks to a Y-shaped Siamese connection on the front of the building at street level, and they carry their own hoses into the building to connect to the standpipe.

Standpipe requirements in the building codes are fairly complex. A safe initial assumption is that there is a dry standpipe in a corner of every exit stairway enclosure or in the vestibule of a smokeproof stair enclosure. Some fire departments prefer that the dry standpipes be located on the landings between floors, where each hose connection can serve two floors. It should also be assumed that wet standpipes and fire hose cabinets will be located in such a way that every point on a floor lies within

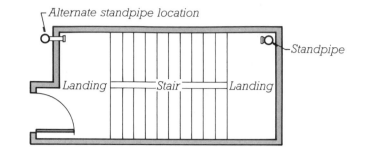

reach of a 30-ft (9-m) stream from the end of a 100-ft (30-m) hose. A typical recessed wall cabinet for a wet standpipe hose and a fire extinguisher is 2 ft 9 in. (840 mm) wide, 9 in. (230 mm) deep, and 2 ft 9 in. (840 mm) high.

Under some codes, a wet standpipe may also serve as the riser to supply water to an automatic sprinkler system, but usually a separate sprinkler riser is required. The horizontal piping for the sprinkler system branches from the standpipe at each floor and, if it is concealed, runs just above the ceiling. An assembly of valves and alarm fittings must be furnished at the point where the sprinkler system joins the domestic water system, usually in the same room with the domestic water pumps. Two Siamese fittings are required in readily accessible locations on the outside of the building to allow the fire department to attach hoses from pumper trucks to the dry standpipe and to the sprinkler riser.

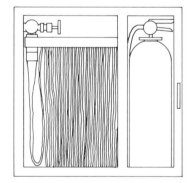

HOSE CABINET

SIAMESE FITTING

174

VERTICAL DISTRIBUTION OF SERVICES FOR LARGE BUILDINGS

DESIGNING ELEVATORS AND ELEVATOR LOBBIES

Because of its many complexities, an elevator system is usually designed by an elevator consultant or the engineering department of an elevator manufacturer. The discussion that follows will help you in making a preliminary allocation of spaces for vertical transportation and in communicating with the final designer of the system.

Number and Size of Elevators

The tables to the right can be used to arrive at an approximate number of elevators and appropriate sizes for the cars. In very tall buildings, the number of shafts can be reduced somewhat with schemes of express and local elevators. Local elevators in high and low zones of the building can even run in the same shaft to save floor space. In very tall buildings, two-story elevators served by two-story lobbies can reduce the number of shafts by as much as one-third.

Laying Out Banks of Elevators

Elevators serving the same zone of the building should be arranged in a single bank so that waiting persons can keep all the doors in sight at one time. A bank of three in a row is the largest that is desirable; four in a row is acceptable. Banks of elevators serving different zones of the building may open on opposite walls of the same elevator lobby or onto separate lobbies. The minimum width of an elevator lobby serving a single bank of elevators is 8 ft (2.45 m); and for a lobby with banks of elevators on both sides, the minimum width is 10 ft (3 m).

APPROXIMATE NUMBERS OF ELEVATOR SHAFTS

Use	Number of Shafts	Capacity of Elevator (lb)
Apartment Buildings	1 per 75 units, plus 1 service elevator for 300 units or more in a high-rise building	2000 or 2500
Hotels	1 per 90 to 100 rooms, plus 1 service elevator for up to 100 rooms and 1 service elevator for each additional 200 rooms	2000 or 2500
Office Buildings	1 per 35,000 sq ft (3250 m²) of area served, plus 1 service elevator for 265,000 sq ft (24,600 m²) of area served	2500 to 3500

ELEVATOR DIMENSIONS

Use	Capacity (lb)	Inside Car Dimensions	Inside Shaft Dimensions
Apartments, Hotels	2000	6'-0" × 3'-6" (1828 × 1067 mm)	7'-8" × 6'-1" (2337 × 1855 mm)
Apartments, Hotels, Office Buildings, Stores	2500	6'-8" × 4'-3" (2032 × 1295 mm)	8'-4" × 6'-8" (2540 × 2032 mm)
Office Buildings, Stores	3000	6'-8" × 4'-9" (2032 × 1448 mm)	8'-4" × 7'-5" (2540 × 2261 mm)
Office Buildings, Stores	3500	6'-8" × 5'-5" (2032 × 1651 mm)	8-'4" × 8'-1" (2540 × 2464 mm)
Hospitals, Nursing Homes	4500	5'-4" × 8'-5" (1626 × 2565 mm)	7'-9" × 10'-2" (2362 × 3100 mm)
Freight, Service	4000–6000	8'-4" × 10'-0" (2540 × 3050 mm)	10'-10" × 10'-8" (3300 × 3250 mm)

Elevator shafts are noisy and should not be located next to occupied space, especially in hotels and residential buildings.

Elevator cars ordinarily have doors on one side only. Cars with doors on opposing sides are available; this necessitates a shaft that is slightly wider than normal, to allow the counterweights to be placed next to the side of the car.

Freight and service elevators should open to separate service rooms or workrooms. Mailrooms, receiving rooms, and maintenance and housekeeping facilities should relate closely to service elevators.

See the following page for information on elevator types, penthouses, pits, and machine rooms.

ELEVATOR TYPES, PENTHOUSES, PITS, AND MACHINE ROOMS

The most widely useful elevator type for most buildings, including very tall ones, is an electric traction elevator with its machine room in a penthouse at the top of the shaft. A penthouse machine room is approximately 9 ft (2.7 m) high, as wide as the shaft itself, and 16 to 18 ft (5 to 5.5 m) long, inside dimensions. It exactly covers the top of the shaft and extends beyond the shaft on the side above the elevator doors.

In buildings of modest height, the penthouse may be reduced in height and restricted in area to the area of the shaft itself by using an underslung traction elevator, which has its machine room at the bottom.

The penthouse may be minimized or eliminated entirely in buildings of up to six floors in height by using a hydraulic elevator. The ceiling of the shaft may be as little as 12 ft (3.7 m) above the surface of the top floor. The hydraulic piston that lifts the car is placed in a drilled well at the bottom of the shaft; the depth of the well must be equal to the rise of the elevator. A machine room of approximately 40 sq ft (3.7 m²) is required; it may be located anywhere in the building, although a location near the shaft on the lowest floor is preferred.

Every type of elevator shaft must terminate in a pit at the bottom. For electric traction elevators, the inside depth of the pit below the lowest floor varies from 5 ft to 11 ft 6 in. (1.52 to 3.51 m), depending on the speed and capacity of the elevator; the bigger and

176

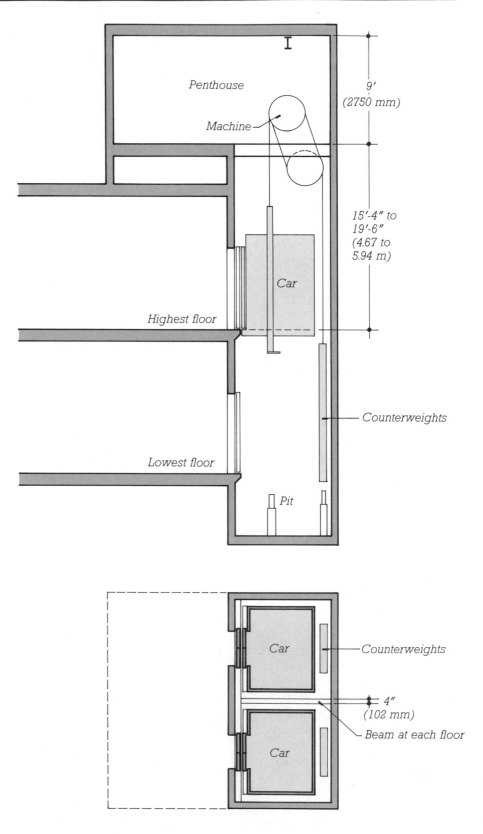

VERTICAL DISTRIBUTION OF SERVICES FOR LARGE BUILDINGS

faster the elevator, the deeper the pit. Hydraulic elevator pits are 4 ft (1.22 m) deep.

ESCALATORS

Escalators are useful in situations where large numbers of people wish to circulate among a small number of floors on a more or less continual basis. The structural and mechanical necessities of an escalator are contained in the integral box that lies beneath the moving stairway. Structural support is required only at the two ends of the unit. Some basic dimensional information on escalators is tabulated to the right.

	32" Escalator	48" Escalator
A	3'-9" (1145 mm)	5'-1" (1550 mm)
B	3'-7" (1090 mm)	4'-11" (1500 mm)

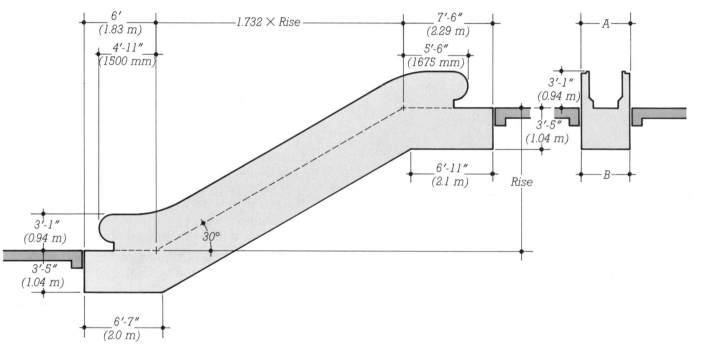

VERTICAL DISTRIBUTION OF SERVICES FOR LARGE BUILDINGS

A CHECKLIST OF CORE COMPONENTS

The following is an alphabetical listing of components that are often incorporated into the cores of a building. For more information on any component, follow the accompanying page reference.

Chimneys (page 158)

Drinking fountains and water coolers

Electrical closets (page 171)

Elevators (page 175)

    Dumbwaiters and vertical conveyors

    Elevator lobbies

    Freight elevators and freight rooms

    Passenger elevators

    Service elevators and service lobbies

Escalators (page 178)

Fan rooms (page 163)

Fire hose and fire extinguisher cabinets (page 174)

Janitor closets (page 173)

Kitchens

Mail facilities (page 172)

    Mail chutes

    Mail conveyors

    Mailrooms

Plumbing walls (including waste and vent pipes) (page 173)

Refuse facilities (page 166)

    Refuse chute

    Refuse room

Shafts (pages 168–173)

    Domestic water piping:

        Chilled drinking water supply and return piping

        Domestic cold water supply and return piping

        Domestic hot water supply and return piping

        Liquid soap supply piping to toilet rooms

        Supply riser to rooftop gravity tank

    Electrical and communications shafts:

        Electrical wires or bus bars

        First communications wiring: Alarms, smoke and heat detectors, firefighter communications

        Telephone, telex, local area networks, cable television, community antenna, etc.

    Heating and cooling shafts:

        Control wiring

        Ducts (page 186)

            Exhaust ducts from toilets, baths, janitor closets, shower rooms, locker rooms, storage rooms, kitchens, corridors, fume hoods, laboratory areas, workshop areas, industrial processes (page 162)

            Fire exhaust and pressurization ducts

            Outdoor air and exhaust air ducts to local fan rooms

            Supply ducts (page 186)

            Return ducts (page 186)

        Piping

            Air piping for controls

            Chilled water supply and return

            Condenser water supply and return between chilled water plant and cooling towers

            Fuel oil piping

            Gas piping

            Hot water and/or steam supply and return

    Piping, miscellaneous: Compressed air, vacuum, deionized water, distilled water, fuel gas, medical gases, scientific gases, industrial gases

    Piping, plumbing waste and vent (page 173)

    Piping, storm drainage risers from roofs and balconies

Sprinkler riser (page 174)

Stairways (pages 267–283)

Standpipes, fire (page 174)

Structure (pages 13–133)

    Beams and girders, including special support around shafts and under heavy equipment

    Bracing

    Columns

    Shear walls

Telephone and communications closets (page 171)

Toilet rooms (pages 173, 439–457)

HORIZONTAL DISTRIBUTION OF SERVICES FOR LARGE BUILDINGS

The horizontal distribution system for mechanical and electrical services in a large building should be planned simultaneously with the structural frame and the interior finish systems, because the three are strongly interrelated. The floor-to-floor height of a building is determined in part by the vertical dimension needed at each story for horizontal runs of ductwork and piping. The selection of finish ceiling, partition, and floor systems is often based in part on their ability to contain the necessary electrical and mechanical services and to adjust to future changes in these services. All these strategies involve close cooperation among the architect and the structural and mechanical engineers.

CONNECTING HORIZONTAL AND VERTICAL DISTRIBUTION LINES

Horizontal mechanical and electrical lines must be fed by vertical lines through smooth, functional connections. Plumbing waste lines, which must be sloped to drain by gravity, have top priority in the planning of horizontal service lines; if they are confined to vertical plumbing walls, they will not interfere with other services. Sprinkler heads, which have next-highest priority in the layout of horizontal services, are served from the fire standpipe by horizontal piping that seldom exceeds 4 in. (100 mm) in outside diameter. The spacing of the heads is coordinated with the placement of walls and partitions; the maximum coverage per head is about 200 sq ft (18.6 m²) in light-hazard buildings such as churches, schools, hospitals, offices, museums, apartments, hotels, theaters, and auditoriums. Coverage in industrial and storage buildings ranges from 130 to 90 sq ft (12.1 to 8.4 m²) per head, depending on the substances handled in the building.

Air conditioning ducts, the next priority, branch out from a local fan room or from vertical ducts in supply and return shafts. Return ducts are often very short and confined to the interior areas of the building. Supply ducts extend from the main ducts through VAV or mixing boxes, then through low-velocity secondary ducts to air diffusers throughout the occupied area of the floor, with special emphasis on the perimeter, which may be on an independent, separately zoned set of ducts. Diffusers are generally required at the rate of 4 to 7 diffusers per 1000 sq ft (100 m²). For some typical diffuser designs, see the illustration on page 183.

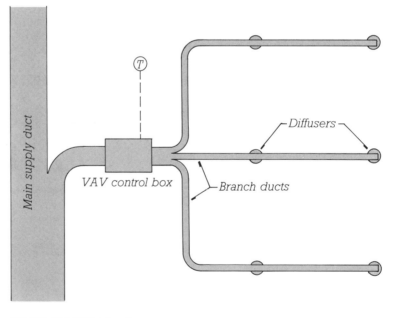

Main supply duct

VAV control box

Diffusers

Branch ducts

PLAN OF VAV DUCTING

GROUPED HORIZONTAL DISTRIBUTION

Sometimes the major runs of ductwork, piping, and wiring can be grouped in the ceiling area above the central corridor of each floor of a building, leaving the ceilings of the surrounding rooms essentially "clean." This works especially well in hotels, dormitories, and apartment buildings that rely on above-ceiling all-water or electric equipment in the area adjacent to the corridor for heating, cooling, and ventilating. A low corridor ceiling is readily accepted in exchange for high, unobstructed space in the occupied rooms, where the structure may be left exposed as the finish ceiling, saving cost and floor-to-floor height. If the building has a two-way flat plate or hollow-core precast slab floor structure, the overall thickness of the ceiling–floor structure can be reduced to as little as 8 in. (200 mm). Conduits containing wiring for the lighting fixtures may be cast into the floor slabs or exposed on the surface of the ceilings. Wiring to wall outlets is easily accommodated in permanently located partitions.

180

FLOORWIDE HORIZONTAL DISTRIBUTION

In broad expanses of floor space, particularly where all electrical and communications services must be available at any point in the area, an entire horizontal layer of space is reserved on each story for mechanical and electrical equipment. This layer may be beneath a raised access floor just above the structural floor. It may also lie within the structural floor, or just

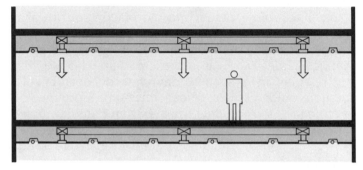

GROUPED HORIZONTAL DISTRIBUTION OVER A CENTRAL CORRIDOR

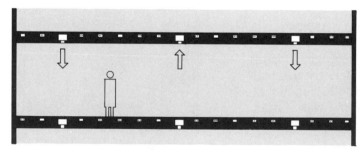

FLOORWIDE ABOVE-CEILING HORIZONTAL DISTRIBUTION

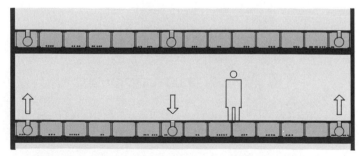

FLOORWIDE IN-FLOOR HORIZONTAL DISTRIBUTION

FLOORWIDE RAISED ACCESS FLOOR HORIZONTAL DISTRIBUTION

HORIZONTAL DISTRIBUTION OF SERVICES FOR LARGE BUILDINGS

beneath the floor, above a suspended ceiling. Sometimes combinations of these locations are used.

Distribution above a Suspended Ceiling

Above a ceiling, wiring is run in conduits or cable trays attached to the structure above. Lighting fixtures are served directly from this horizontal wiring. Outlets on the floor below may be served by electrified partitions or power poles. Outlets on the floor above may be fed via poke-through fixtures that are cut through the structural floor. Poke-through fixtures can be added or removed at any time during the life of the building; their major disadvantage is that electrical work being done for the convenience of a tenant on one floor is done at the inconvenience of the tenant on the floor below.

Distribution within the Structural Floor

Electrical and communications wiring may be embedded in the floor slab in conventional conduits. For greater flexibility in buildings where patterns of use are likely to change over time, systems of cellular steel decking over steel framing, or cellular raceways cast into a topping over concrete slabs, may be selected. These provide a tree-like structure: The trunk is a wiring trench that runs from the electrical closet to the outside wall of the building, and the branches are the hollow cells that run in the perpendicular direction. Electrical and communications wires and outlets can be added, removed, or changed at any time during the life of the building. Cellular steel decking can affect the layout of the beams and girders in a steel-

framed building: For optimum distribution of wiring, the cells in the decking generally run parallel to the wall of the core, and for structural reasons the cells must run perpendicular to the beams. This requires close coordination among the architect and the electrical and structural engineers.

Distribution above the Structural Floor

A raised access floor system allows maximum flexibility in running services because it can accommodate piping, ductwork, and wiring with equal ease. It is especially useful in industrial or office areas where large numbers of computers or computer terminals are used and where frequent wiring changes are likely. It is also valuable in retrofitting old buildings for modern services. The floor may be raised to any desired height above the structural floor; 12 in. (300 mm) is typical.

Undercarpet flat wiring may be used instead of a raised access floor in buildings with moderate needs for future wiring changes. Flat wiring does not increase the overall height of the building as raised access floors usually do, but it does not offer the unlimited capacity and complete freedom of wire location of the raised floors. Flat wiring is used in both new buildings and retrofit work.

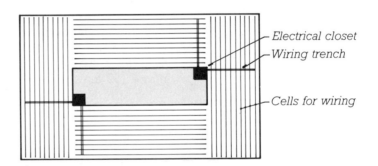

PLAN OF CELLULAR STEEL DECKING

- Electrical closet
- Wiring trench
- Cells for wiring

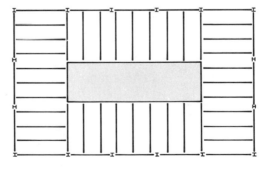

STEEL FRAMING PLAN FOR CELLULAR STEEL DECKING

HORIZONTAL DISTRIBUTION OF SERVICES FOR LARGE BUILDINGS

DESIGNING THE CEILING/FLOOR SPACE

An above-ceiling location is ordinarily best for ductwork, which is often too large and bulky to fit above or within the structural floor. The wiring and ductwork must share the above-ceiling space with lighting fixtures and sprinkler piping. This requires careful planning. Generally the lowest stratum, about 8 in. (200 mm) thick, is reserved for the sprinkler piping and lighting fixtures. Lighting fixture selection plays an important role in determining the thickness of this stratum, because some types of lighting fixtures require more space than others. The ducts, which are usually 8 to 10 in. (200 to 250 mm) deep, run between this layer and the beams and girders. Adding about 2 in. (50 mm) for the thickness of a suspended ceiling, we see that a minimum height of about 18 in. (460 mm), and preferably 20 in. (500 mm), must be added to the thickness of the floor structure and fireproofing in a typical building to allow for mechanical and electrical services. A larger dimension is often called for, depending on the requirements of the combination of systems that is chosen.

As an example, let us assume that a steel-framed building has a maximum girder depth of 27 in. (690 mm) and a 4-in. (100-mm) floor slab, for a total floor structure height of 31 in. (790 mm). Adding 20 in. (510 mm) for ceiling and services, we arrive at an overall ceiling-to-floor height of

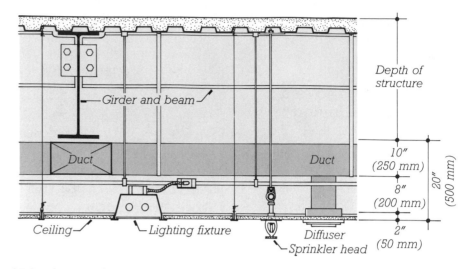

SECTION THROUGH CEILING/FLOOR ASSEMBLY

51 in. (1300 mm) that must be added to the desired room height to give the floor-to-floor height of the building. If fireproofing must be added to the girders, this dimension will increase by a couple of inches (50 mm or so).

There is tremendous economic pressure to reduce this height to a practical minimum in a tall building. A few inches per floor adds up to an enormous saving in the cost of structure, core components, and cladding. Sometimes it is possible to arrange the framing so that ductwork never passes beneath a girder. If the ductwork must cross the girders, the designers should explore such options as shallower ducts, running the ducts through holes cut in the webs of the girders, or reducing the depth of the girders by using a heavier steel shape. In the average tall office building,

the height of the ceiling-floor assembly is about 46 in. (1170 mm).

In some medical, research, and industrial buildings, the underfloor services are unusually complex, bulky, and subject to change. In these cases the layer above the ceiling and below the floor structure is expanded to a height that allows workers to walk freely in it, and the ceiling is strengthened into a structure that can support their weight. This arrangement, called an *interstitial ceiling,* allows workers to maintain and change the services without disrupting the occupied spaces above or below.

With all its service penetrations —lighting fixtures, air diffusers and grilles, sprinkler heads, smoke detectors, intercom speakers—a ceiling can take on a visually chaotic appearance. It is advisable to compose the relationships of these penetrations carefully on a reflected ceiling plan.

182

HORIZONTAL DISTRIBUTION OF SERVICES FOR LARGE BUILDINGS

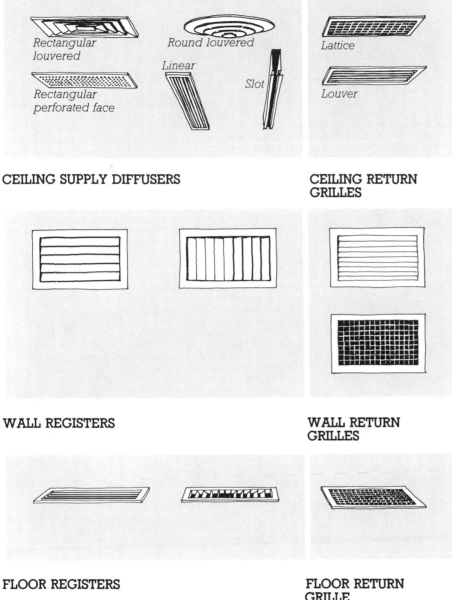

CEILING SUPPLY DIFFUSERS

Rectangular louvered

Round louvered

Linear

Slot

Rectangular perforated face

Lattice

Louver

CEILING RETURN GRILLES

WALL REGISTERS

WALL RETURN GRILLES

FLOOR REGISTERS

FLOOR RETURN GRILLE

TYPICAL GRILLE AND DIFFUSER DESIGNS

EXPOSED VERSUS CONCEALED SERVICES

In many buildings, the designer has a choice between exposing the mechanical and electrical services and concealing them above a suspended ceiling. Exposed services are the rule in warehouses and industrial buildings. In other types of buildings, exposed pipes and ducts can have an attractive, sculptural complexity. They are easy to reach for maintenance and revision. They make sense in many large, open buildings (athletic arenas, exhibition halls), as well as in certain other kinds of buildings in which partitions are not often changed and a frank, functional appearance is appropriate (schools, art galleries, pubs and restaurants, avant-garde stores). There are some disadvantages: Exposed services that must look good are more expensive to design and install, and usually the cost of painting them must be added to the bill. They also need to be cleaned from time to time. Although exposed services are readily accessible for changes, any changes must be made with care, and a painter has to follow after the mechanics who do the work. For these reasons, it is usually cheaper to install a suspended ceiling than to omit one.

SIZING SPACES FOR MAJOR HEATING AND COOLING EQUIPMENT

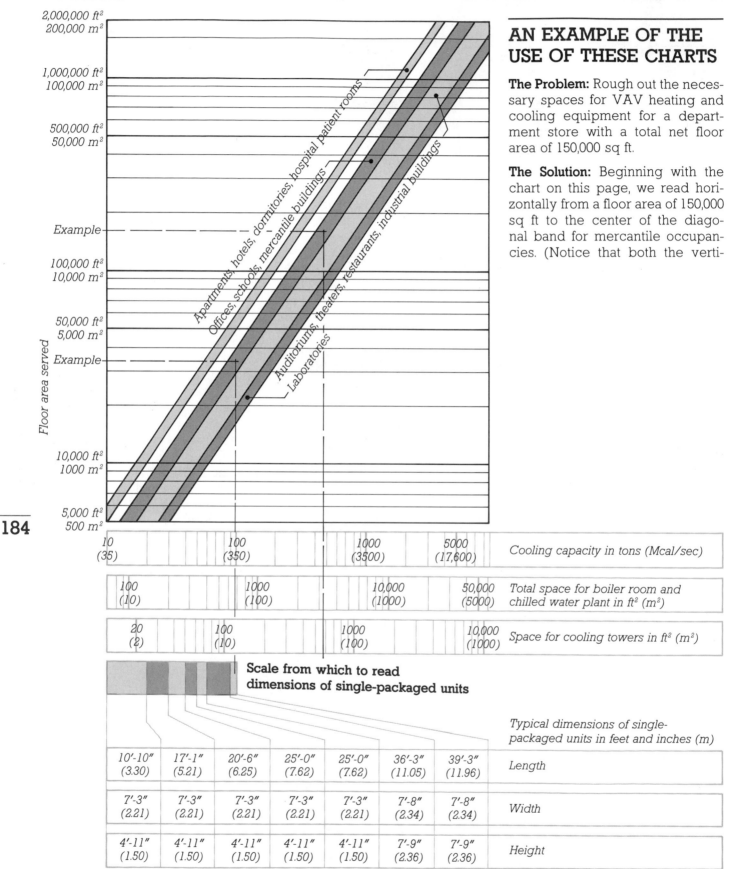

AN EXAMPLE OF THE USE OF THESE CHARTS

The Problem: Rough out the necessary spaces for VAV heating and cooling equipment for a department store with a total net floor area of 150,000 sq ft.

The Solution: Beginning with the chart on this page, we read horizontally from a floor area of 150,000 sq ft to the center of the diagonal band for mercantile occupancies. (Notice that both the verti-

Cooling capacity in tons (Mcal/sec)
10 (35)   100 (350)   1000 (3500)   5000 (17,600)

Total space for boiler room and chilled water plant in ft² (m²)
100 (10)   1000 (100)   10,000 (1000)   50,000 (5000)

Space for cooling towers in ft² (m²)
20 (2)   100 (10)   1000 (100)   10,000 (1000)

Scale from which to read dimensions of single-packaged units

Typical dimensions of single-packaged units in feet and inches (m)

10'-10" (3.30)	17'-1" (5.21)	20'-6" (6.25)	25'-0" (7.62)	25'-0" (7.62)	36'-3" (11.05)	39'-3" (11.96)	Length
7'-3" (2.21)	7'-3" (2.21)	7'-3" (2.21)	7'-3" (2.21)	7'-3" (2.21)	7'-8" (2.34)	7'-8" (2.34)	Width
4'-11" (1.50)	4'-11" (1.50)	4'-11" (1.50)	4'-11" (1.50)	4'-11" (1.50)	7'-9" (2.36)	7'-9" (2.36)	Height

SIZING SPACES FOR MAJOR HEATING AND COOLING EQUIPMENT

cal and horizontal scales for this chart are logarithmic; 150,000 lies much closer to 200,000 than to 100,000.) Reading downward, we find that the required cooling capacity for this building is approximately 450 tons, requiring a chilled water plant and boiler room that together will occupy an area of approximately 3200 sq ft. Cooling towers will occupy about 560 sq ft on the roof or alongside the building. The width of the diagonal band from which we have read gives us a range of 400 to 520 tons for the cooling requirement, so we know that these space re-quirements may grow somewhat smaller or larger as the system is designed in detail.

These values assume a central plant for heating and cooling. Could rooftop single-packaged units be used instead? We see at the bottom of the chart that no single-packaged unit is large enough to handle the entire load. Starting from the largest available packaged unit and reading upward, we intersect the diagonal band and read to the left to find that the unit could serve about 33,000 sq ft of this building. Five such units could be distributed about the roof to furnish heating and air conditioning for the entire building, each serving about 30,000 sq ft. Each would need a capacity of about 90 tons and would measure 39 ft 3 in. long, 7 ft 8 in. wide, and 7 ft 9 in. high. A larger number of smaller units could also be used.

For more detailed information on boiler rooms, see page 158. Chilled water plants and cooling towers are explained on page 159 and single packaged units on page 164.

Move to the following page to continue this example.

SIZING SPACES FOR AIR HANDLING

Using the chart on this page, we can determine the approximate sizes of the air handling components of the two choices developed on the preceding pages. The central system would move an air volume of about 200,000 cu ft per minute. This would call for a total cross-sectional area of main supply ducts equal to about 120 sq ft and branch supply ducts of about 200 sq ft total. If the branch supply ducts were 2 ft deep, for example, their aggregate width

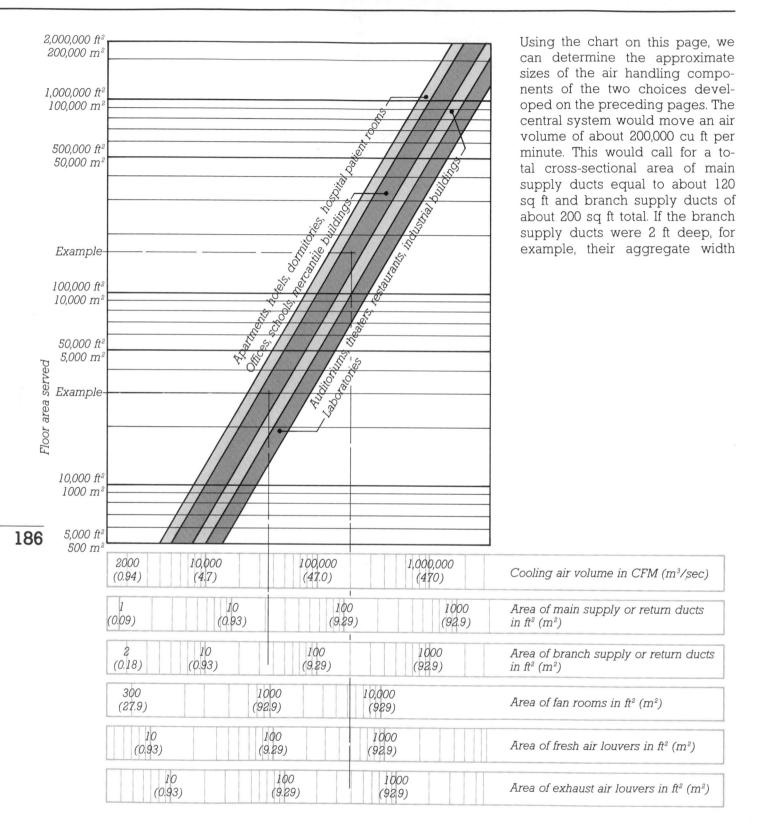

2000 (0.94)	10,000 (4.7)	100,000 (47.0)	1,000,000 (470)	Cooling air volume in CFM (m³/sec)

| 1 (0.09) | 10 (0.93) | 100 (9.29) | 1000 (92.9) | Area of main supply or return ducts in ft² (m²) |

| 2 (0.18) | 10 (0.93) | 100 (9.29) | 1000 (92.9) | Area of branch supply or return ducts in ft² (m²) |

| 300 (27.9) | 1000 (92.9) | 10,000 (929) | | Area of fan rooms in ft² (m²) |

| 10 (0.93) | 100 (9.29) | 1000 (92.9) | | Area of fresh air louvers in ft² (m²) |

| 10 (0.93) | 100 (9.29) | 1000 (92.9) | | Area of exhaust air louvers in ft² (m²) |

would be about 100 ft. Similar areas of return ducting would also be needed. Reading from the last three scales, we further determine that fan rooms totaling about 5200 sq ft are needed, served by fresh air louvers adding up to about 500 sq ft in area and exhaust air louvers totaling nearly 400 sq ft. The location and distribution of this louver area on the outside surfaces of the building are of obvious architectural importance.

Each of the rooftop single-packaged units would need about 21 sq ft of main duct for supply air and the same for return, with a total area of 35 sq ft for branch ducts. Fans and louvers are incorporated into the units and do not need to be provided separately.

For further information on fan rooms and louvers, see page 163.

MECHANICAL AND ELECTRICAL SYSTEMS FOR SMALL BUILDINGS

This section will help you select a heating and cooling system for the preliminary design of a small building. It also summarizes typical plumbing and electrical systems for small buildings.

DESIGNING SPACES FOR MECHANICAL AND ELECTRICAL SERVICES FOR SMALL BUILDINGS

Small buildings are defined for purposes of this section as those that use residential-scale mechanical and electrical systems. This category includes small educational, commercial, retail, industrial, and institutional buildings as well as houses, rowhouses, and small apartment buildings.

Heating and cooling loads in small buildings are usually dominated by heat gains and losses through the skin of the building. In many small buildings, mechanical fresh air ventilation is not an issue because of the low density of occupancy and the ability of operable windows and normal air leakage through the skin of the building to provide adequate ventilation. Most of the distribution lines for the mechanical and electrical systems in small buildings can be concealed within the hollow cavities that are a normal part of the floor, wall, and ceiling structures. A basement, crawlspace, or attic is often available as a location for the major mechanical equipment and larger horizontal distribution lines. There is an enormous variety of heating and cooling systems from which the designer may choose. This section summarizes the choices of heating and cooling systems and the typical plumbing and electrical systems. Approximate dimensions of the components of the various systems are also given.

Decide first if the building needs a heating system only, or both heating and cooling:

Some systems are capable of heating only, such as:

    Hydronic heating (pages 200–201)

    Solar heating (pages 202, 210–211)

    Electric convectors and heaters (pages 205–206)

    Radiant panel heating (page 207)

    Wall furnace (page 208)

    Heating stoves (page 209)

Some systems are capable of both heating and cooling the building, such as:

    Forced air (pages 197–199)

    Heat pump (pages 156, 198–199)

    Packaged terminal units or through-the-wall units (page 204)

    Single-packaged and split-packaged systems (pages 164–165)

If you wish to minimize the first cost of the system:

Choose systems that do not require the installation of extensive piping or ductwork, such as:

    Evaporative cooler (page 203)

    Packaged terminal units or through-the-wall units (page 204)

    Electric convectors or fan-forced heaters (pages 205–206)

    Wall furnace (page 208)

    Heating stoves (page 209)

If you wish to minimize operating costs in cold climates:

Choose systems that burn fossil fuels efficiently, systems that utilize solar heat, or systems that burn locally available, low-cost fuels, such as:

    Forced air (pages 197–199)

    Hydronic heating (pages 200–201)

    Active and passive solar (pages 202, 210–211)

    Heating stoves (page 209)

192

If you wish to minimize operating costs in moderate climates:

Choose systems that utilize ambient energy sources, such as:

    Heat pump systems (pages 156, 198–199)

    Solar heating systems (pages 202, 210–211)

    Heating stoves (page 209)

    Evaporative cooler (page 203)

If you wish to maximize control of air quality and air velocity for maximum comfort:

Choose a system that filters and moves the air mechanically, namely:

    Forced air (pages 197–199)

If you wish to maximize individual control over temperature:

Choose systems that offer separate thermostats in a number of rooms or zones, such as:

    Hydronic heating (pages 200–201)

    Packaged terminal units or through-the-wall units (page 204)

    Electric convectors or fan-forced heaters (pages 205–206)

DESIGN CRITERIA FOR THE SELECTION OF HEATING AND COOLING SYSTEMS FOR SMALL BUILDINGS

If you wish to minimize the noise created by the heating and cooling system:

Choose systems in which motors, pumps, and fans are distant from the occupied space, such as:

    Forced air (pages 197–199)

    Hydronic heating (pages 200–201)

    Electric convectors and radiant heating (pages 205–207)

    Passive solar heating (pages 210–211)

If you wish to minimize the visual obtrusiveness of the heating and cooling system:

Choose systems that place as little hardware as possible in the occupied spaces, such as:

    Forced air (pages 197–199)

    Electric radiant heating (page 207)

If you wish to maximize the inhabitants' enjoyment of the changing weather and seasons:

Choose systems that change prominently with the seasons, such as:

    Passive solar heating (pages 210–211)

    Heating stoves (page 209)

If you wish to minimize the amount of floorspace occupied by heating and cooling equipment:

Choose systems that do not occupy floorspace, such as:

    Evaporative cooler (page 203)

    Packaged terminal units or through-the-wall units (page 204)

    Electric fan-forced heaters (page 206)

    Electric radiant heating (page 207)

    Wall furnace (page 208)

    Passive solar heating (pages 210–211)

If you wish to minimize system maintenance:

Choose systems with few or no moving parts, such as:

    Forced air (pages 197–199)

    Hydronic heating (pages 200–201)

    Electric convectors (page 205)

    Electric radiant heating (page 207)

    Wall furnace (page 208)

    Passive solar heating (pages 210–211)

If you wish to avoid having a chimney in the building:

Choose systems that do not burn fuel in the building, such as:

    Heat pump furnace (pages 198–199)

    Single-packaged and split-packaged systems (pages 164–165)

    Packaged terminal units or through-the-wall units (page 204)

    All types of electric heat (pages 197–198, 205–207)

If you wish to maximize the speed of construction:

Choose systems that involve as few components and as few trades as possible, such as:

    Packaged terminal and through-the-wall units (page 204)

    All types of electric heat (pages 205–207)

HEATING AND COOLING SYSTEMS FOR SMALL BUILDINGS: SUMMARY CHART

GIVE SPECIAL CONSIDERATION TO THE SYSTEMS INDICATED IF YOU WISH TO:	Forced Air (page 197)	Heat Pump Furnace (page 198)	Hydronic Heating† (page 200)	Active Solar Heating† (page 202)	Evaporative Cooler‡ (page 203)
Combine heating and cooling in one system	●	●			
Minimize first cost					●
Minimize operating cost in very cold climates	●		●	●	
Minimize operating costs in moderate climates		●		●	●
Maximize control of air velocity and air quality	●	●			
Maximize individual control over temperature			●		
Minimize system noise	●	●	●	●	
Minimize visual obtrusiveness	●	●			
Maximize enjoyment of the seasons					
Minimize floor space used for the mechanical system					●
Minimize system maintenance	●		●		
Avoid having a chimney		●			
Maximize the speed of construction					

†System for heating only
‡System for cooling only

194

HEATING AND COOLING SYSTEMS FOR SMALL BUILDINGS: SUMMARY CHART

Packaged Terminal Units or Through-the-Wall Units (page 204)	Electric Baseboard Convectors† (page 205)	Electric Fan-Forced Unit Heaters† (page 206)	Electric Radiant Heating† (page 207)	Wall Furnace† (page 208)	Heating Stoves† (page 209)	Passive Solar Heating† (page 210)
●						
●	●	●		●	●	
					●	●
				●	●	●
●	●	●				
	●		●			●
			●			
					●	●
●	●	●	●	●		●
	●	●	●	●		●
●	●	●	●			
●	●	●		●		

CENTRAL SYSTEMS VERSUS LOCAL SYSTEMS

In a *central system,* heat is supplied to a building or extracted from it by equipment situated in a mechanical space—a furnace or a boiler in a basement, for example. Air or water is heated or cooled in this space and distributed to the inhabited areas of the building by ductwork or piping to maintain comfortable temperatures. In a *local system,* independent, self-contained pieces of heating and cooling equipment are situated throughout the building, one or more in each room. Central systems are generally quieter and more energy efficient than local systems and offer better control of indoor air quality. Central equipment tends to last longer than local equipment and is easier to service. Local systems occupy less space in a building than central systems because they do not require a central mechanical space, ductwork, or piping. They are often more economical to buy and install. They can be advantageous in buildings that have many small spaces requiring individual temperature control.

Pages 197–202 describe central heating and cooling systems for small buildings, and pages 203–211 describe local systems.

FUELS

Heating equipment in small buildings may be fueled by oil, pipeline gas, liquid propane gas, electricity, sunlight, or solid fuels—coal or wood. Cooling equipment is almost always powered by electricity. In functional respects electricity is the ideal fuel: It is clean, it is distributed through small wires, no chimney is needed, and electrical heating and cooling equipment is compact and often lower in first cost than equivalent fossil-fuel-burning equipment. In most geographic areas, however, electricity is a very costly fuel as compared to oil or gas. Gas and oil are usually the fuels of choice for small buildings. Sunlight, wood, and coal are generally less convenient energy sources than electricity, gas, and oil. They are appropriate in particular buildings where owner preferences and building occupancy patterns permit or encourage their use.

On-site storage requirements for the various fuels are summarized in the table below.

TYPICAL DIMENSIONS OF FUEL STORAGE COMPONENTS

Component	Width	Depth	Height
Coal storage, minimum, 1 ton (1 tonne)	4'-0" (1.2 m)	4'-0" (1.2 m)	4'-0" (1.2 m)
Firewood storage, minimum, 1/2 cord	4'-0" (1.2 m)	4'-0" (1.2 m)	4'-0" (1.2 m)
Liquid propane tanks, upright cylinders	16" (410 mm) diameter		60" (1525 mm)
Liquid propane tank, horizontal	41" (1040 mm) diameter		16'-3" (5.0 m)

There are many sizes of propane tanks, of which these are two of the most common. Upright cylinders are located outdoors, usually against the wall of the building, often in pairs. They may not be closer than 36" (915 mm) to a door or a basement window. The horizontal tank must be at least 25' (7.6 m) from the building or a property line and may be buried if desired.

Component	Width	Depth	Height
Oil storage tank, 275 gal (1000 l)	27" (685 mm)	60" (1525 mm)	54" (1375 mm)

For greater capacity, multiple tanks may be installed inside the building, or a larger tank may be buried just outside the foundation.

FORCED AIR HEATING AND COOLING

Description

A furnace heats air with a gas flame, an oil flame, or electric resistance coils. The heated air is circulated through the inhabited space by a fan and a system of ductwork. With an upflow furnace, the horizontal ducts are located above the furnace at the ceiling of the floor on which the furnace is located. With a downflow furnace, the ducts are located beneath the furnace in the crawlspace or floor slab. A third type, the horizontal furnace, is designed to fit in a low attic or underfloor crawlspace.

Cooling capability may be added to the furnace by installing evaporator coils in the main supply ductwork adjacent to the furnace. An outdoor compressor and condensing unit supplies cold refrigerant to the evaporator coils through small-diameter insulated tubing.

Typical Applications

Forced air heating and air conditioning is the most versatile and most widely used system for heating and cooling small buildings. Multiple furnaces may be installed to establish multiple zones of control and to heat and cool buildings of up to 10,000 sq ft (100 m²) and more.

Advantages

A forced air system can incorporate every type of humidification, dehumidification, air filtration, and

(continued)

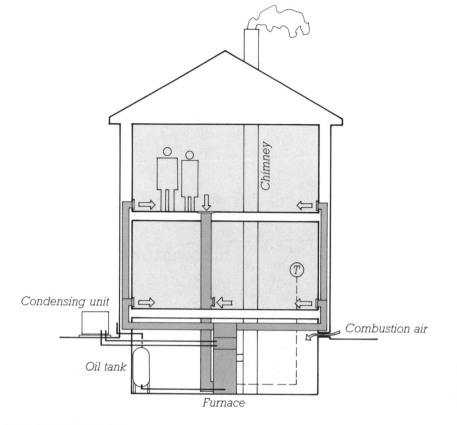

UPFLOW FURNACE

cooling equipment. If properly designed, installed, and maintained, it is quiet and fuel efficient and distributes heat evenly.

Disadvantages

Multiple zones of control are possible only by using multiple furnaces.

Major Components

Furnace, fuel storage, chimney, ductwork, and, if cooling capability is included, an outdoor condensing unit. Some high-efficiency furnaces may be vented through the wall and do not require a chimney. Typical dimensions for these components are summarized in the table on the facing page. For dimensions of fuel storage components, see page 196.

Variations

1. A *heat pump furnace* uses a reversible refrigeration cycle to create and circulate either heated or cooled air as required. An outdoor heat pump unit either extracts heat from the outdoor air and releases it through coils in the furnace, or extracts heat from the coils in the furnace and releases it to the outdoor air, depending on whether heating or cooling is required. A heat pump furnace is generally economical to operate in moderate climates, but when outdoor temperatures fall well below freezing, the heat pump cycle be-

198

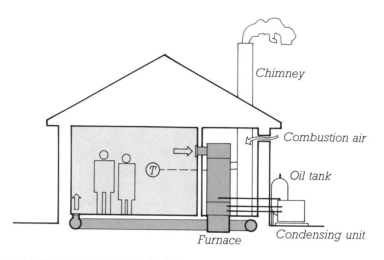

DOWNFLOW FURNACE ON SLAB

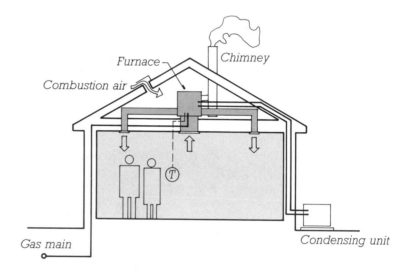

HORIZONTAL FURNACE IN ATTIC

FORCED AIR HEATING AND COOLING

comes inefficient and is turned off automatically. Electric resistance coils are then activated to generate heat, which raises operating costs dramatically. For this reason, heat pumps are not usually used in severe climates unless they use water or earth as a heat source rather than air. Heat pump furnaces are available in vertical upflow, vertical downflow, and horizontal configurations, and are similar in dimension to other furnaces.

2. A *multifuel furnace* is designed to burn solid fuel (wood or coal) as well as a backup fuel (gas or oil). It is larger and more expensive than a single-fuel furnace.

3. A *packaged system,* either a single-packaged or a split-packaged system, is often used to heat and cool small commercial, industrial, and institutional buildings. For information on packaged systems, see pages 164–165.

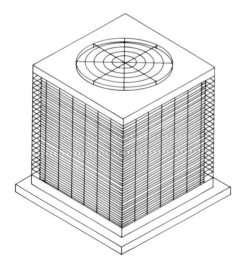

CONDENSING UNIT

TYPICAL DIMENSIONS OF COMPONENTS OF FORCED AIR HEATING SYSTEMS

Component	Width	Depth	Height
Chimney, masonry	20" (510 mm)	20" (510 mm)	*
Chimney, metal	10" (255 mm) diameter		*
Condensing unit, outdoor			
Small	24" (610 mm)	24" (610 mm)	24" (610 mm)
Large	40" (1015 mm)	50" (1270 mm)	33" (840 mm)
Ducts, sheet metal			
Main horizontal supply and return ducts, each	24" (610 mm)		12" (305 mm)
Supply risers, typical (notice that these are made to fit between wall studs)	10" (255 mm)	3.25" (83 mm)	
	12" (305 mm)	3.25" (83 mm)	
	7" oval (175 mm oval)		
Return risers (these are usually fewer in number than the supply risers and require special wall framing provisions)	8" (200 mm)	14" (360 mm)	

For duct insulation, add 1" (25 mm) all around. Insulation is recommended on heating duct and is mandatory on cooling ducts that run through non-air-conditioned space.

Fuel storage—see page 196

Furnaces, including adjacent primary ductwork			
Horizontal furnace	24" (610 mm)	84" (1170 mm)	28" (710 mm)
Upright furnace, upflow or downflow	24" (610 mm)	30" (760 mm)	84" (1170 mm)
Multifuel furnace, upright, upflow	48" (1220 mm)	60" (1525 mm)	84" (1170 mm)

A working space 3' (900 mm) square is required on the side of the furnace adjacent to the burner. Furnaces have varying requirements for installation clearances to combustible materials; some need only an inch or two.

*Under most codes a chimney must extend at least 3' (900 mm) above the highest point where it passes through the roof and at least 2' (600 mm) above any roof surface within a horizontal distance of 10' (3 m).

HYDRONIC (FORCED HOT WATER) HEATING

Description

A flame or electric resistance coil heats water in a boiler. Small pumps circulate the hot water through fin-tube convectors, which are horizontal pipes with closely-spaced vertical fins, mounted in a simple metal enclosure with inlet louvers below and outlet louvers above. The heated fins, working by convection, draw cool room air into the enclosure from below, heat it, and discharge it out the top. Instead of fin-tube convectors, especially where space is tight, fan-coil units, either surface-mounted or wall-recessed, may be used. The fan in a fan-coil unit blows room air past a hot water coil to heat it.

Typical Applications

Hydronic heating is a premium-quality heating system for any type of building.

Advantages

Hydronic heating is quiet if properly installed and maintained. It gives excellent heat distribution and is easily zoned for room-by-room control by adding thermostatically controlled zone valves or zone pumps at the boiler. The boilers for small-building systems are very compact—some gas or electric boilers are so small they can be mounted on a wall.

Disadvantages

Cooling, air filtration, and humidification, if desired, must be accomplished with independent systems, which raises the overall system cost.

Major Components

Boiler, chimney, fuel storage, expansion tank, circulator pumps, zone valves, convector or fan-coil units. Some high-efficiency boilers may be vented through a wall and do not require a chimney. Typical dimensions for these components are summarized in the table to the

200

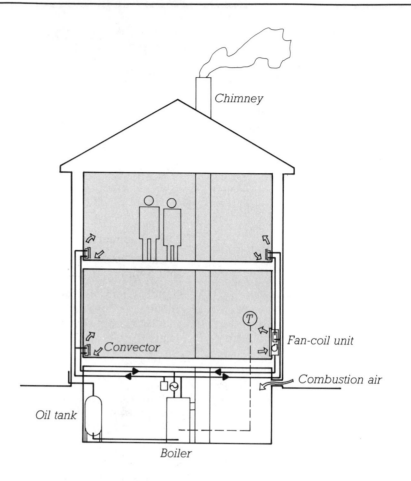

Chimney

Convector

Fan-coil unit

Combustion air

Oil tank

Boiler

HYDRONIC (FORCED HOT WATER) HEATING

right. For dimensions of fuel storage components, see page 196.

Variations

1. A *multifuel boiler* is designed to burn both solid fuel (coal or wood) and a backup fuel (gas or oil). It is larger and more expensive than a single-fuel boiler.

2. Radiant heating panels in ceilings or floors may be warmed with hot water from a hydronic boiler (see pages 200–201).

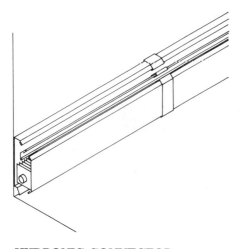

HYDRONIC CONVECTOR

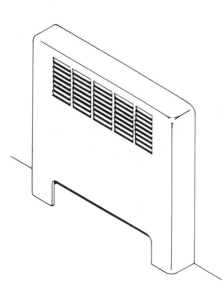

FAN-COIL UNIT

TYPICAL DIMENSIONS OF COMPONENTS OF A HYDRONIC HEATING SYSTEM

Component	Width	Depth	Height
Chimney, masonry	16" (400 mm)	16" (400 mm)	*
Chimney, metal	8" (200 mm) diameter		*
Boiler, hydronic, with expansion tank, valves, and pumps (add 10" or 250 mm on two adjacent sides for piping)			
Upright	25" (635 mm)	25" (635 mm)	84" (2135 mm)
Wall-mounted, gas or electric	30" (760 mm)	24" (610 mm)	84" (2135 mm)
Solid fuel or combination fuel	36" (900 mm)	60" (1530 mm)	84" (2135 mm)

A boiler requires a working space 3' (910 mm) square on the side adjacent to the burner. Required clearances to combustible surfaces vary depending on the design of the boiler; for some boilers they may be as little as an inch or two.

Component	Width	Depth	Height
Convector, baseboard		3" (75 mm)	7.5" (190 mm)
Fan-coil units			
Recessed or surface-mounted	24" (610 mm)	4" (100 mm)	30" (760 mm)
Toespace heater	21" (535 mm)	18" (460 mm)	4" (100 mm)

*Under most codes a chimney must extend at least 3' (900 mm) above the highest point where it passes through the roof and at least 2' (600 mm) above any roof surface within a horizontal distance of 10' (3 m).

MECHANICAL AND ELECTRICAL SYSTEMS FOR SMALL BUILDINGS

ACTIVE SOLAR SPACE HEATING

Description
Outdoor south-facing collector panels, usually mounted on the roof of the building, are heated by sunlight. A pump or fan circulates liquid or air to withdraw the heat from the panels and store it in a tank of liquid or a bin of rocks or phase-change salts. This storage is usually located in the basement or a mechanical equipment room. A fan circulates indoor air through a heat exchanger coil filled with the warm storage liquid, or through the rock bin, and distributes the heated air to the inhabited space of the building through a system of ductwork.

Typical Applications
Active solar heating is feasible in buildings that are exposed to sunlight throughout the day in climates with a high percentage of sunny weather during the winter.

Advantages
Solar heating has zero fuel cost and does not pollute the air.

Disadvantages
The initial cost of active solar heating systems tends to be so high that they are uneconomical at present fuel prices. The collector surfaces become a very prominent and often dominating part of the architecture of the building. A full backup heating system (such as forced air or hydronic heating) is required to heat the building during extended sunless periods. Cooling must be done by a separate system.

Major Components
Solar collector panels, heat storage tank or bin, ductwork for air collectors or piping for water collectors, heat exchanger, and building heating ductwork. Typical dimensions for these components are summarized in the table to the right. For dimensions of fuel storage components, see page 196.

202

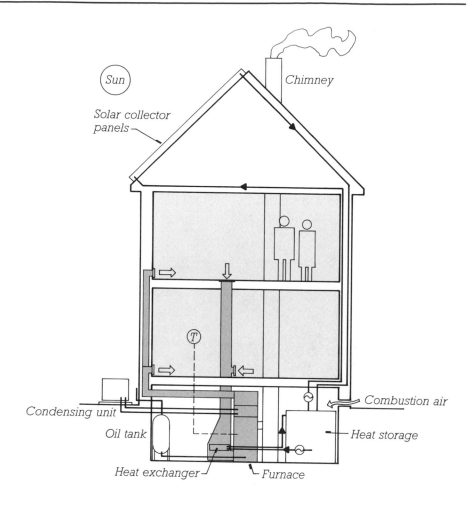

Variations
A heat pump may be added to the system to draw heat from the storage medium at relatively low temperatures and distribute it to the occupied spaces at higher temperatures. This provides a higher degree of comfort and increases the efficiency of the solar collectors.

TYPICAL DIMENSIONS OF ACTIVE SOLAR HEATING COMPONENTS

Component	Width	Depth	Height
For dimensions of the backup furnace, chimney, fuel storage, and ductwork, see pages 196 and 199.			
Collector panels, average residence	24' (7.3 m)	6" (150 mm)	20' (6 m)
Collector panels should face within 20° of true south and should be sloped at an angle to the ground equal to or up to 15° more than the latitude of the site.			
Heat exchanger with ductwork	30" (760 mm)	30" (760 mm)	30" (760 mm)
Heat storage			
Rock bed	minimum of 600 ft³ (17 m³)		
Water storage tank	8' (2.4 m) diameter		7' (2.1 m)

EVAPORATIVE COOLER

Description

A fan blows air through a wetted pad. Water evaporates from the pad into the air, cooling the air by extracting from it the latent heat of vaporization. The fan circulates the cooled air through the building. The metal cabinet in which the pad and fan are located is usually located on the roof or adjacent to the building.

Typical Applications

The cooling of buildings in which humidity control is not critical in hot, dry climates.

Advantages

Cooling costs are low.

Disadvantages

The humidity inside the building is difficult to control and may become excessive. The system is inefficient in humid climates. A separate system is required for heating the building.

Major Components

Evaporative cooling unit, ductwork. Typical dimensions for these components are summarized in the accompanying table.

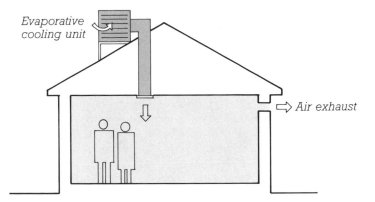

TYPICAL DIMENSIONS OF EVAPORATIVE COOLING SYSTEM COMPONENTS

Component	Width	Depth	Height
Evaporative cooler, average	36" (915 mm)	36" (915 mm)	36" (915 mm)
Duct	18" (460 mm)	18" (460 mm)	

PACKAGED TERMINAL UNITS AND THROUGH-THE-WALL UNITS

Packaged terminal units and through-the-wall units are used extensively in small buildings as well as large. See page 156 for more detailed information on these systems.

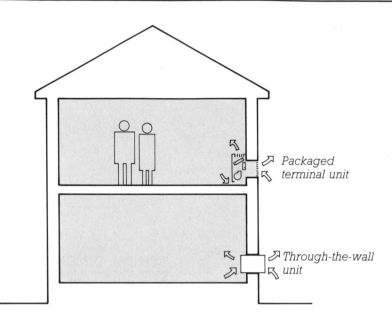

Packaged terminal unit

Through-the-wall unit

ELECTRIC BASEBOARD CONVECTORS

Description
Electric resistance wires in sheet metal enclosures are installed around the perimeter of the room at the junction of the floor and the wall. Room air circulates through slots in the enclosures by means of convection and is heated by the resistance wires.

Typical Applications
Heating systems in buildings of any type, especially where electric rates are low.

Advantages
Electric baseboard convectors are quiet and distribute heat evenly. Each room has individual temperature control. Installation costs are low. No chimney is required.

Disadvantages
The baseboard convectors occupy considerable wall space and can interfere with furniture placement. There is no means of controlling humidity or air quality. Electricity is an expensive fuel in most areas. A separate system is required for cooling.

Major Components
Electric baseboard convector units. A typical convector is 3 in. (75 mm) deep and 7.5 in. (190 mm) high and extends for some feet along a wall.

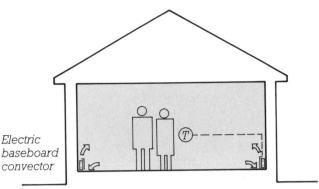

Electric baseboard convector

ELECTRIC FAN-FORCED UNIT HEATERS

Description
Fan-forced electric unit heaters are compact units inside which a fan draws in room air and heats it by passing it over electric resistance wires before blowing it back into the room.

Typical Applications
Any room or building that requires electric heating from small sources.

Advantages
They are economical to buy and install, and they do not interfere with furniture placement as much as baseboard convectors. Each room has individual temperature control. No chimney is required.

Disadvantages
Heat distribution in the room can be uneven, and the fans become noisy unless they are maintained regularly. There is no means of controlling humidity or air quality. Electricity is an expensive fuel in most areas. Separate systems are required for humidification and cooling.

Major Components
Electric fan-forced unit heaters. Typical dimensions for these components are summarized in the table to the right.

Variations
Fan-forced unit heaters are available for wall mounting in recessed or surface-mounted configurations. Toespace heaters are designed for use in the low, restricted space under kitchen cabinets or shelves. Recessed floor units lie beneath a simple floor register. Industrial unit heaters are mounted in rectangular metal cabinets that are designed to be suspended from the roof or ceiling structure.

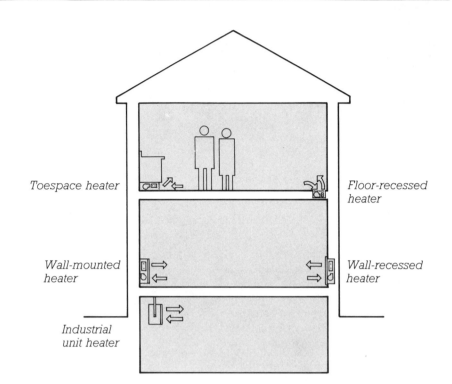

Toespace heater

Floor-recessed heater

Wall-mounted heater

Wall-recessed heater

Industrial unit heater

TYPICAL DIMENSIONS OF ELECTRIC FAN-FORCED UNIT HEATERS

Component	Width	Depth	Height
Floor-recessed heater	16" (400 mm)	8" (200 mm)	8" (200 mm)
Industrial unit heater	16" (400 mm)	12" (300 mm)	16" (400 mm)
Toespace heater	24" (610 mm)	12" (300 mm)	4" (100 mm)
Wall-recessed or wall surface-mounted heater	16" (400 mm)	4" (100 mm)	20" (510 mm)

ELECTRIC RADIANT HEATING

Description
Electric resistance heating wires are embedded in the ceiling or floor. The warm surface radiates heat directly to the body and also warms the air in the room.

Typical Applications
Residences, nursing homes.

Advantages
Heating is even and comfortable. No heating equipment is visible in the room.

Disadvantages
The system is slow to react to changing needs for heat. Tables and desktops beneath a radiant ceiling cast cold "shadows" on the legs and feet. Carpeting and furniture reduce the effectiveness of radiant floor panels. Cooling and humidity control must be provided by a separate system. Electricity is an expensive fuel in most areas.

Major Components
Resistance wires, resistance mats, or prefabricated, electrified ceiling panels.

Variations
Ceiling or floor radiant panels may be heated by hot water coils fed from a hydronic boiler.

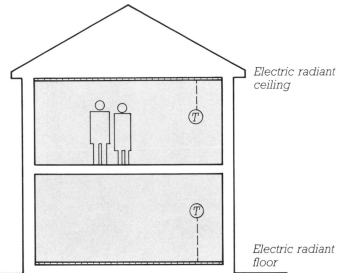

Electric radiant ceiling

Electric radiant floor

WALL FURNACE

Description
A wall furnace is a tall, wall-recessed or surface-mounted heating unit in which air flows from the room and circulates by convection past metal heat exchange surfaces warmed by a gas flame. Most wall furnaces can heat the spaces on both sides of the wall. Sometimes a short run of ductwork can be added to circulate heat to a third room.

Typical Applications
Low-cost dwellings, offices, and motels in mild climates.

Advantages
Wall furnaces are inexpensive to buy and install.

Disadvantages
They require insulated vent pipes to the outdoors, they distribute heat unevenly, and they are unattractive visually. Cooling and humidity control must be provided by separate systems.

Major Components
Gas meter and service entrance or propane tank and regulator, gas piping, wall furnace, vent pipes through the wall or to the roof. A typical wall furnace is 14 in. wide, 12 in. deep, and 84 in. high (360 × 305 × 2135 mm). The vent pipe to the roof is typically a 4-in. (100-mm) oval that may be concealed between the studs in a wall.

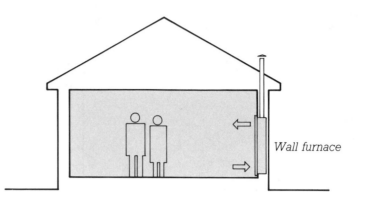

Wall furnace

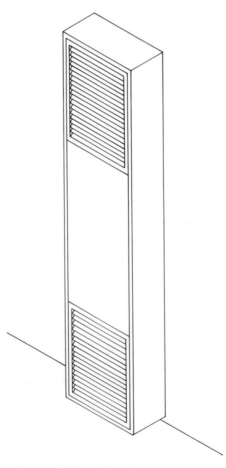

WALL FURNACE

HEATING STOVES

Description

Heating stoves are small appliances that sit conspicuously within each room they heat. They burn wood, coal, gas, oil, or kerosene, and transmit heat to the room and its occupants by a combination of convection and radiation.

Typical Applications

Residential, industrial, and commercial buildings, especially in areas where firewood or coal is inexpensive and readily available. Wood- and coal-burning stoves are frequently used as supplementary sources of heat in centrally-heated houses.

Advantages

Wood and coal are cheap fuels in many areas, and the experience of tending a stove and basking in its warmth can be aesthetically satisfying. Some stoves are visually attractive.

Disadvantages

Heating stoves use a surprisingly large amount of floor space and require chimneys. Most stoves are hot enough to burn the skin. They do not distribute heat evenly. Solid fuel stoves require constant tending and are difficult to control precisely. Solid fuel and ashes generate considerable dirt within the building. A stove becomes a fire hazard unless it and its chimney are conscientiously maintained and operated. Most solid-fuel stoves pollute the air through incomplete combustion.

Major Components

Chimney, stove and stovepipe, floor protection, wall protection, fuel storage, ash storage for solid-fuel stoves. Typical dimensions for these components are summarized in the table to the right. For dimensions of fuel storage components, see page 196.

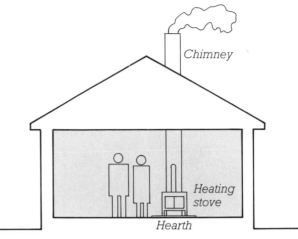

TYPICAL DIMENSIONS OF HEATING STOVES

Component	Width	Depth	Height
Ash storage	Covered metal bucket 14″ (360 mm) in diameter		
Chimney, masonry			
One stove	20″ (510 mm)	20″ (510 mm)	*
Two stoves	20″ (510 mm)	28″ (710 mm)	*
Chimney, metal	10″ (254 mm) diameter		
Fuel storage: see page 196			
Stove			
Gas-fired	38″ (965 mm)	13″ (330 mm)	40″ (1015 mm)
Oil-fired	32″ (815 mm)	30″ (760 mm)	40″ (1015 mm)
Wood-fired	Varies widely, up to the dimensions shown for gas-fired and oil-fired stoves		
Stovepipe, uninsulated, typical	7″ (180 mm) diameter		
Stovepipe, insulated, typical	9″ (230 mm) diameter		

Heating stoves typically require a clearance of 36″ (914 mm) to combustible or plaster surfaces. They also require a noncombustible hearth that extends 12″ (305 mm) to each side and to the back of the stove and 18″ (460 mm) to the front. Some stoves are shielded to allow them to be as close as 12″ to combustible surfaces to the back and sides. An uninsulated metal stovepipe may not come closer than 18″ (460 mm) to the ceiling. Insulated pipes are usually designed for a 2″ (51 mm) clearance to combustible materials.

*Under most codes a chimney must extend at least 3′ (900 mm) above the highest point where it passes through the roof and at least 2′ (600 mm) above any roof surface within a horizontal distance of 10′ (3 m).

PASSIVE SOLAR HEATING

Description
The interior space of the building acts as a solar collector, receiving sunlight directly through large south-facing windows and storing excess heat in concrete, masonry, or containers of water or phase-change salts. During sunless periods, as the room temperature drops below the temperature of the heat storage materials, the stored heat is released into the interior air.

Typical Applications
Dwellings, schools, offices, industrial buildings.

Advantages
Passive solar heating has zero fuel cost, does not pollute the air, requires little or no maintenance, and can be aesthetically satisfying.

Disadvantages
Construction cost is high for passive solar heating schemes, and a full backup heating system must be provided to heat the building during long sunless periods. Relatively large swings in interior temperature must be expected. Most passive solar systems require the occupants of the building to perform daily control duties such as opening and closing insulating shutters or curtains. The architecture of solar heated buildings is strongly influenced by the need to orient and configure the building for optimum solar collection. Cooling and humidity control must be accomplished with separate systems.

Variations
1. In *direct gain* passive solar heating, sunlight enters south-facing windows and warms the interior directly. Roof overhangs or louvers are configured to block out high summer sun. Internal mass (masonry, concrete, large containers of water, or small containers of phase-change salts) must be pro-

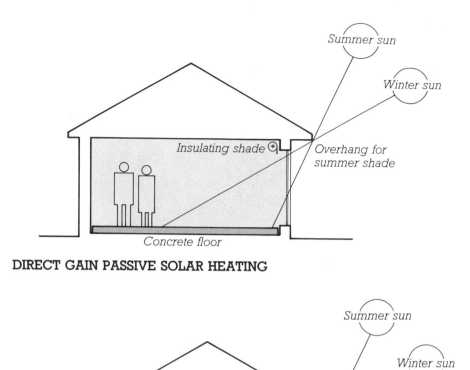

DIRECT GAIN PASSIVE SOLAR HEATING

ATTACHED SUNSPACE PASSIVE SOLAR HEATING

vided, preferably in direct sunlight, to absorb excess heat. Insulating closures are needed to cover the glass during sunless periods. This is a simple, enjoyable way of bringing heat into a building, one that puts the occupants into a very intimate relationship with the seasons and the weather. However, the direct sunlight causes visual glare, and it fades and deteriorates interior materials. Heat loss through the large glass areas during nights and cloudy days is considerable. Temperature control is often unsatisfactory.

2. In *attached sunspace passive solar heating*, an intermittently occupied greenhouse or glassy

atrium attached to the building collects solar heat by direct gain. Heated air is "borrowed" by the adjacent, fully inhabited spaces of the building by means of convection or small circulating fans. Undesirable glare and fading are largely or wholly confined to the sunspace. The sunspace can be closed off during sunless periods and allowed to grow cold. The extreme range of temperatures that occurs in the sunspace allows it to be inhabited only during limited periods and prevents plant growth unless additional temperature control mechanisms are provided.

3. *Fan-forced rock bed solar heating* is a hybrid of passive and active systems. Sunlight is received

PASSIVE SOLAR HEATING

directly into the inhabited space of the building. When the interior air becomes heated above the comfort level, a thermostat actuates a fan that draws the overheated air through a large container of stones, where the excess heat is absorbed. During sunless periods, the fan is actuated again to warm the room air by passing it through the heated stones. Compared to direct gain solar heating, a fan-forced rock bed system gives better control of temperature and does not require the presence of massive materials within the inhabited spaces. The rock bed is large and expensive to construct. Glare and fading are a problem unless the system is coupled with an attached sunspace.

4. *Trombe wall passive solar heating* features a massive wall made of masonry, concrete, or containers of water. This wall is located immediately inside the windows that receive sunlight. The interior of the building is warmed by the heat that is conducted through the Trombe wall, by allowing room air to convect between the wall and the glass, or both. As compared to direct gain solar heating, a Trombe wall system blocks most or all direct sunlight from the inhabited space, preventing glare and fading. The wall occupies considerable space, however, and obstructs desirable visual contact between the inhabitants and the sun. The room temperature is difficult to control. An insulating closure is needed to reduce heat losses through the glass during sunless periods.

Typical dimensions of passive solar components are summarized in the table to the right. A backup heating system must also be provided; the backup system may be selected from the other heating systems described in this section.

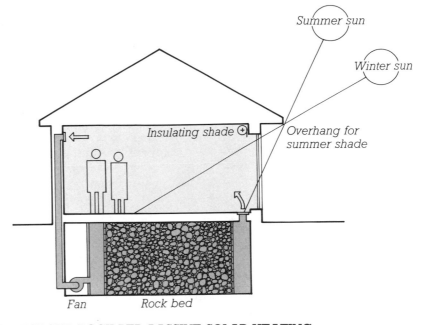

FAN-FORCED ROCK BED PASSIVE SOLAR HEATING

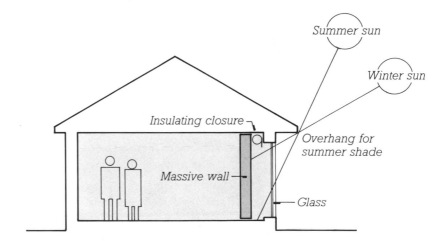

TROMBE WALL PASSIVE SOLAR HEATING

TYPICAL DIMENSIONS OF PASSIVE SOLAR HEATING COMPONENTS

Component

South-facing windows for passive solar heating for an average house should total at least 150 sq ft (14 m²) in area.

If the floor is used for thermal storage, it should be made of masonry or concrete at least 4″ (100 mm) thick.

An attached sunspace should have a minimum floor area of 10′ × 12′ (3 × 3.7 m).

A rock bed should have a minimum volume of 600 ft³ (17 m³).

A Trombe wall is typically 12″ (300 mm) thick and as tall as the adjacent windows. There is usually a space of a foot or two between the glass and the wall.

WATER SUPPLY

Water from a municipal main reaches the building via an underground service pipe and a water meter. In warm climates, the meter may be outside the building, but in cold climates, it must be installed in a heated space, usually the basement or the mechanical equipment room. In many areas a tiny electronic readout, connected by wires to the inside water meter, is mounted on the outside of the building so that the meter reader does not need to enter the building.

From the water meter, domestic cold water flows directly to the fixtures by means of small diameter copper or plastic pipes. If the water is "hard" (contains a heavy concentration of calcium ions), a water softener may be installed to remove these ions from the water that goes to the domestic water heater. The water heater uses a gas flame, an oil flame, solar-heated liquid, or electric resistance heating to warm the water to a preset temperature at which it is held in an insulated tank for subsequent use. A tree of hot water piping parallels the cold water piping as it branches to the various fixtures in the building. Supply piping should be kept out of exterior walls of buildings in cold climates to prevent wintertime freeze-ups.

If water is obtained from a private well, it is lifted from the well and pressurized by a pump. If the well is deep, the pump is usually placed at the bottom of the well. If the well is shallow (less than 20 to 25 ft, or 6 to 8 meters), the pump may be located inside the building. In either case, the pump pushes the water into a pressure tank, from which it flows on demand into the hot and cold water piping. The pressure tank may be located inside the well, or in the basement or mechanical equipment room of the building.

WASTE PIPING AND SEWAGE DISPOSAL

Sewage flows from each fixture through a trap into waste pipes that drain by gravity. To assure that the traps do not siphon dry and to maintain constant atmospheric pressure in the waste piping, a vent pipe is attached to the waste system near each trap. The vent pipes rise upward through the building until they penetrate the roof, where they are left open to the air. The vent pipes may be gathered together into a single pipe in the attic of the building to minimize the number of roof penetrations. A horizontal run of vent be used to move a plumbing vent to a less prominent rooftop location.

The waste piping descends through the building, gathering waste from all the fixtures, until it reaches the ground, the crawlspace, or the basement. If it lies above the sewer or the private disposal system at this point, it turns to an almost horizontal orientation, sloping toward its outlet (the sewer main or the septic tank) at a pitch of at least 1 in 100. If it lies below the elevation of its outlet at this point, an automatically oper-

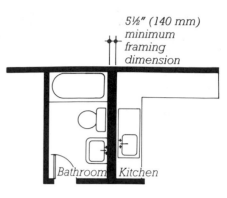

5½" (140 mm) minimum framing dimension

Bathroom   Kitchen

TYPICAL DIMENSIONS OF PLUMBING COMPONENTS

Component	Width	Depth	Height
Gas meter and piping	18" (460 mm)	12" (305 mm)	24" (610 mm)

Sewage disposal, private

The size and configuration of private sewage disposal systems vary widely depending on soil conditions, topography, local laws, and the required capacity of the system. As a starting point, allow an area of level or nearly level ground 40' × 80' (12 × 25 m), with its short side against the building. No part of this area may be closer than 100' (30 m) to a well, pond, lake, stream, or river.

Water heater			
Gas-fired	20" (510 mm) diameter		60" (1525 mm)
Electric	24" (610 mm) diameter		53" (1350 mm)
Water meter and piping	20" (510 mm)	12" (305 mm)	10" (255 mm)
Water pressure tank for a pump that is located in a well	20" (510 mm) diameter		64" (1625 mm)
Water pump and pressure tank for a shallow well	36" (915 mm)	20" (510 mm)	64" (1625 mm)
Water softener	18" (460 mm) diameter		42" (1070 mm)

212

PLUMBING SYSTEMS FOR SMALL BUILDINGS

ated underground ejector pump must be installed to lift the sewage and empty it into the outlet.

Waste and vent piping is larger in diameter than supply piping and requires careful planning to fit gracefully and efficiently into a building. Bathrooms and toilet rooms should be stacked to avoid horizontal displacements of the waste and vent stacks. For maximum economy, fixtures should be aligned along thickened plumbing walls, and rooms containing fixtures should be clustered back-to-back around the plumbing walls. The major horizontal runs of waste piping should be located in a crawlspace, beneath a slab, or just inside the perimeter of a basement. Some typical wood framing details for plumbing walls are shown in the diagram to the right.

Private sewage disposal systems vary considerably in configuration and size, depending chiefly on soil conditions and local health regulations. The most common type includes a septic tank, usually 1000 to 1500 gal (4000 to 6000 l) in capacity, in which the sewage is digested by anaerobic action. Effluent from the septic tank flows by gravity to a disposal field of open-jointed pipe laid below ground in a bed of crushed stone. In nearly all areas of North America, private sewage disposal systems may be designed only by a registered sanitary engineer. The engineer's design is based on soil tests that may be performed only during those limited periods of the year when the soil is saturated, and a building permit will not be issued until a permit has been granted for the construction of the disposal system. This often delays the start of a construction project for many months.

Typical dimensions of plumbing components are summarized in the table on the facing page.

(continued)

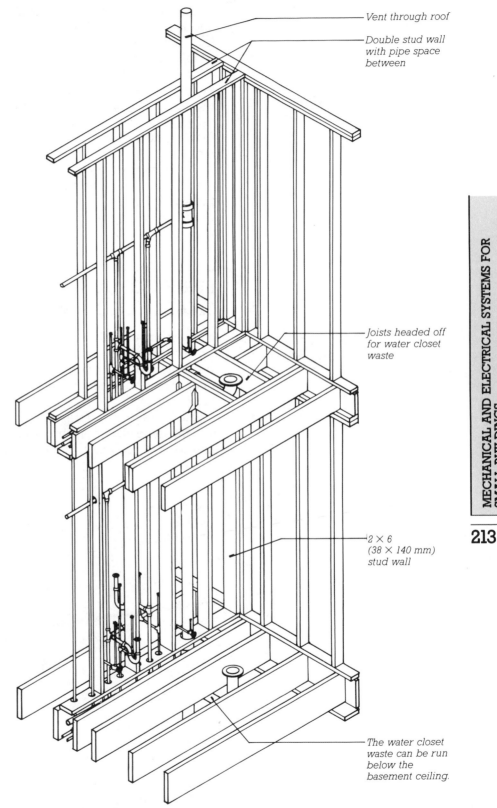

Vent through roof

Double stud wall with pipe space between

Joists headed off for water closet waste

2 × 6 (38 × 140 mm) stud wall

The water closet waste can be run below the basement ceiling.

FRAMING DETAILS FOR PLUMBING WALLS

GAS SERVICE

Natural gas is distributed to buildings through mains located beneath the street. Each building is served by an underground pipe that surfaces at a gas meter and pressure regulator next to or just inside the building. From this service entrance, the gas is piped through the building to the various appliances—furnaces, boilers, water heaters, clothes dryers, fireplaces, barbecues, kitchen ranges, and industrial equipment.

Where there are no gas mains, liquid propane gas can be delivered by tanker truck to pressurized tanks outside the building. The gas flows from the tanks through a pressure regulator and evaporator into the building's gas piping system.

Gas piping is small in diameter and is made up of threaded black iron pipe and fittings. It does not usually require special consideration in the design of the building, but space does need to be provided, usually at the basement ceiling or in the crawlspace or slab, for long horizontal runs of gas piping.

For dimensions of gas meters in a small building, see the table on page 212. For dimensions of liquid propane storage tanks, see the table on page 196.

SPRINKLER SYSTEMS IN SMALL BUILDINGS

In most small buildings, sprinkler protection, when it is required, can be provided at a maximum rate of one sprinkler head per 144 sq ft (13.4 m^2) of floor area. The average coverage per sprinkler head will be somewhat less than this because of the problems of fitting sprinkler layouts to rooms of varying sizes and shapes. The horizontal piping to the sprinklers is small in diameter and must run below the roof insulation in cold climates, either above a suspended ceiling or just on top of the ceiling material and between the joists. Vertical risers must be installed on the warm side of the wall insulation or in interior partitions. A small assembly of valves and alarm fittings must be furnished at the point where the sprinkler system joins the domestic water system, and a Siamese fitting is required for many installations. If the available water supply is inadequate to feed the sprinkler system, a backup water supply has to be furnished in the form of a gravity tank, an air-pressurized tank, or a reservoir and pump, any of which is custom designed for the given situation.

ELECTRICAL AND COMMUNICATIONS WIRING FOR SMALL BUILDINGS

Electrical, telephone, and cable television services reach the building via either overhead or underground wires, depending on the practices of the local utilities. Overhead wires at the street may be converted to an underground service to the building by running the service wires down the face of the pole to the required depth and then laterally to the building.

An electric meter is mounted at eye level in an accessible location on the outside surface of the building. Wires from an overhead service arrive at the building high above the meter and descend to it in a large cable or a metal conduit mounted on the exterior wall surface. Wires from an underground service are brought up to the meter in a conduit. A cable or conduit from the meter enters the building at the basement or main floor level and connects to the main electric panel, which should be as close to the meter as possible.

From the main panel, wiring fans out to branch panels and individual circuits. Exposed wiring or wiring in masonry or concrete must be placed in metal or plastic conduits. In frame buildings, most wiring is done with flexible plastic-sheathed cable that is routed through the cavities of the frame. In a very small building, all the branch circuits connect directly to the main panel. In a larger building, especially one with multiple tenant spaces, most circuits connect to branch panels scattered at convenient points around the building. The branch panels, in turn, are connected by cables or conduits to the main panel.

Panel locations need to be worked out fairly early in the building design process. In small framed buildings, the designer seldom needs to be concerned about providing space for the wires and cables, unless the construction system features exposed framing members and decking. In this case, conduit routes for the wiring must be carefully planned to avoid visual chaos.

Wires for telephone service, cable television, burglar alarms, smoke alarms, intercoms, local area networks, antennas, and so on, are very small in diameter and generally have no effect on the overall planning of a building in the early stages of design. Small wall-mounted panels may be required for some of these systems in a small building; these are usually located in the basement or the mechanical equipment room.

Typical dimensions of components of electrical systems in small buildings are summarized in the table below.

TYPICAL DIMENSIONS OF COMPONENTS OF ELECTRICAL SYSTEMS

Component	Width	Depth	Height
Electric meter	12" (305 mm)	9" (230 mm)	15" (380 mm)
Main panel	14" (360 mm)	4" (100 mm)	27" (685 mm)
Branch panel	14" (360 mm)	4" (100 mm)	20" (685 mm)

DESIGNING
FOR
EGRESS

CONFIGURING THE EGRESS SYSTEM

This section will assist you in laying out doors, corridors, stairways, and exit discharges for a preliminary building design in accordance with the egress requirements of the model building codes.

COMPONENTS OF AN EGRESS SYSTEM

The function of a building egress system is to conduct the occupants of the building to a safe place in case of a fire or other emergency. In most instances that safe place is a public way or other large open space at ground level. For the occupants of the upper floors of a tall building, or for people who are incapacitated or physically restrained, the safe place may be a fire-protected area of refuge within the building itself.

Although the four model building codes differ in their approaches to sizing the components of an egress system, their requirements for the configuration of egress systems are similar and are summarized together in this section.

A building egress system has three components:

1. *The exit access* conducts occupants to an exit. The most common type of exit access is an exit access corridor, but it may also be an aisle, a path across a room, or a short stair or ramp.

2. *The exit* is an enclosed, protected way of travel leading from the exit access to the exit discharge. From a ground floor room or exit access corridor, it may be simply a door opening to the outdoors, or an enclosed, protected exit passageway leading to such a door. From a room or an exit access corridor on a story above or below grade, it is usually an enclosed exit stairway, or sometimes an enclosed exit ramp.

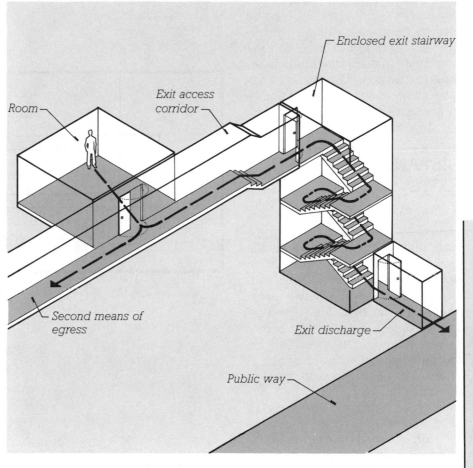

3. *The exit discharge* is a means of moving from an exit to a public way. It may be as simple as a door opening from an enclosed exit stairway to the street, but it can also be a protected exit corridor to an exterior door, or a path across a ground floor vestibule or lobby.

These three components of an egress system are discussed in greater detail on the pages that follow. Also included are simplified standards for the preliminary design of these components, condensed from the four model building codes used in North America.

The standards summarized here apply to new buildings. For existing buildings, certain of the standards are more permissive; consult the appropriate building code for details.

THE EXIT ACCESS

Most buildings require at least two separate exits. These must be as remote from each other as possible and arranged to minimize the possibility that a single fire or other emergency condition could simultaneously render both exits unsafe or inaccessible.

DISTANCE BETWEEN EXITS

The minimum distance between exits is one-half the diagonal measurement of the building or the space served by the exits. On an open floor, this is measured as a straight-line distance between exits. Where the exits are joined by an exit access corridor that is protected from fire as specified by the building code, this distance is measured along the path through the corridor.

With only minor exceptions, an exit access path may not pass through kitchens, restrooms, storerooms, workrooms, bedrooms, hazardous areas, or rooms subject to being locked.

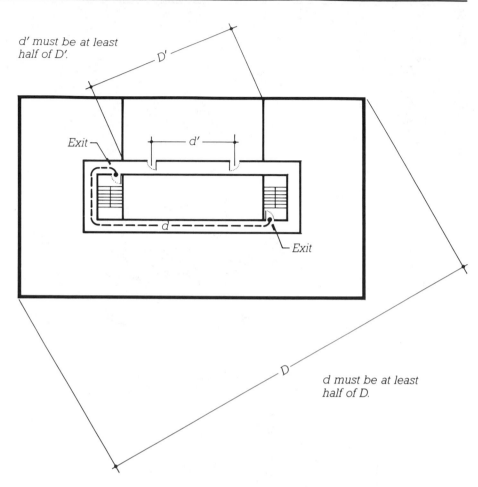

d′ must be at least half of D′.

Exit

d′

d

— Exit

D′

D

d must be at least half of D.

THE EXIT ACCESS

EXTERIOR CORRIDORS

Exit access corridors may be open balconies on the exterior of a building, but in snowy climates such corridors must be protected by roofs.

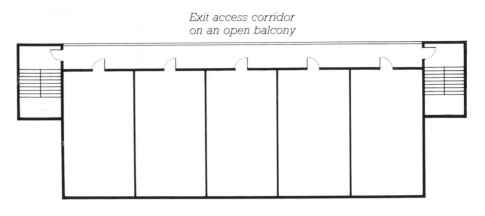

Exit access corridor on an open balcony

DEAD-END CORRIDORS

Dead-end pockets in exit access corridors are undesirable, but they are tolerated for most building occupancies within the length restrictions listed for each model code on pages 237–265.

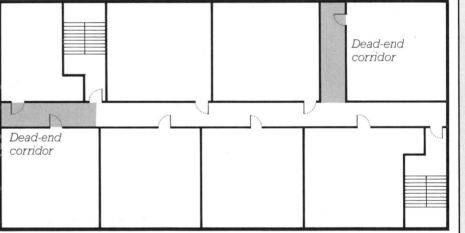

Dead-end corridor

Dead-end corridor

THE EXIT ACCESS

MAXIMUM TRAVEL DISTANCE

Maximum travel distance to the nearest exit is specified by code and Use Group on pages 240, 248, 254, and 262. Travel distance is always measured along the actual path an occupant must take to reach an exit. It is sometimes specified from the door of a room to the door of the nearest exit, and sometimes from the most remote point on a floor to the nearest exit—be sure which of these distances is being specified in the code table you consult.

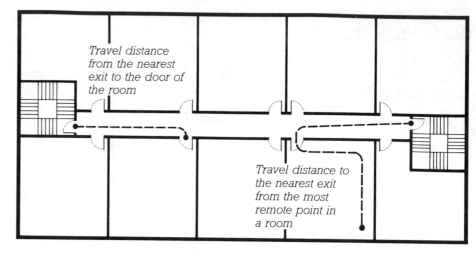

Travel distance from the nearest exit to the door of the room

Travel distance to the nearest exit from the most remote point in a room

224

THE EXIT ACCESS

DOORS

Doors should always swing in the direction of egress travel. Doors are permitted to swing contrary to travel, however, in single-family dwellings and in rooms with fewer than 50 occupants (or 60 occupants under the National Building Code of Canada).

Ideally, doors should be arranged so that their swing does not obstruct the required width of an aisle, corridor, stair landing, or stair. Building codes typically permit some obstruction, however: Up to one-half of the required width can be obstructed during the swing of the door, and when the door is fully open, it may project as much as 3½ in. (89 mm) into the required width of a stair or stair landing and as much as 7 in. (178 mm) into the required width of an aisle or corridor.

Even when locked, doors along an exit path must be easily openable in the direction of egress travel.

Exit access corridors must be enclosed in fire-resistant walls and accessed via fire-resistant doors. One-hour walls with 20-minute doors are required except in some very small buildings and in certain

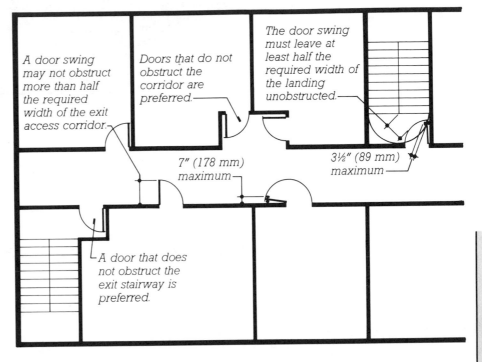

A door swing may not obstruct more than half the required width of the exit access corridor.

Doors that do not obstruct the corridor are preferred.

The door swing must leave at least half the required width of the landing unobstructed.

7" (178 mm) maximum

3½" (89 mm) maximum

A door that does not obstruct the exit stairway is preferred.

buildings with automatic sprinkler systems.

The widths of exit access doors, aisles, and corridors must be determined according to the building occupancy and the number of occupants they must serve. The tables on pages 233–265 give the quantities needed to make these determinations.

The model building codes also contain detailed provisions relating to illumination and emergency illumination of exit access facilities, marking of exit paths, combustibility of finish materials in exit access corridors, alarm systems, door hardware, and other safety concerns. Consult the appropriate building code for details.

DIRECT EXIT

The simplest exit is a door opening directly from an interior room to a public way, as it might from an exhibition hall, theater, or classroom.

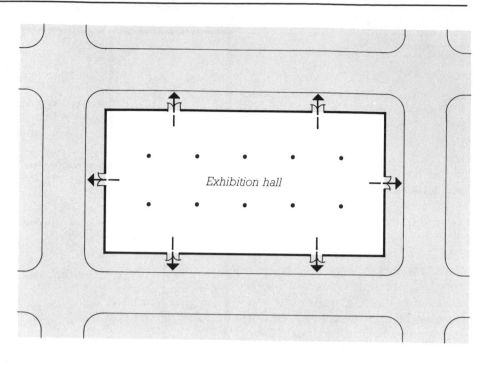

EXIT STAIRWAYS

The most common type of exit is an enclosed stairway. The enclosure must be of 2-hour construction with 1½-hour self-closing doors that swing in the direction of egress travel. (In other words, doors must swing into the stairway enclosure except at the level of exit discharge, where they must swing out.)

Stairway and landing widths are determined in accordance with the occupant load they serve. Dimensions and typical designs for stairways and stair enclosures are detailed on pages 267–283.

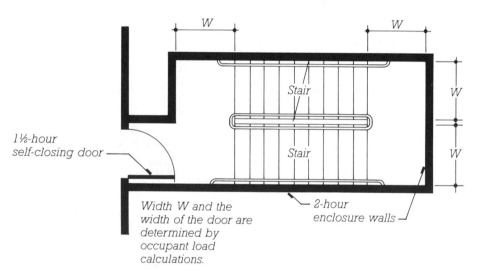

1½-hour self-closing door

Width W and the width of the door are determined by occupant load calculations.

2-hour enclosure walls

THE EXIT

SMOKEPROOF ENCLOSURES

In tall buildings it is often required that one or more of the exit stairways be placed in a smokeproof enclosure. A smokeproof enclosure is designed to limit the penetration of smoke and heat from a fire into an exit stairway to such an extent that the stairway is likely to remain usable thoughout the course of a fire in the building.

There are two ways to make a smokeproof enclosure, as illustrated to the right: natural ventilation and mechanical ventilation. (In fully sprinklered buildings, a smokeproof enclosure may also be created by means of mechanical pressurization without the need for the vestibule that is shown in the bottom drawing on this page.) A mechanical ventilating system must be backed up with a standby power supply so that it will continue operating if the main source of power is interrupted during a fire. A stairway in a smokeproof enclosure must discharge directly into a public way, an outdoor space having direct access to a public way, or an enclosed exit passageway with no other openings—it may not discharge through a vestibule or lobby at the exit discharge level. Code requirements for smokeproof enclosures are summarized on page 227.

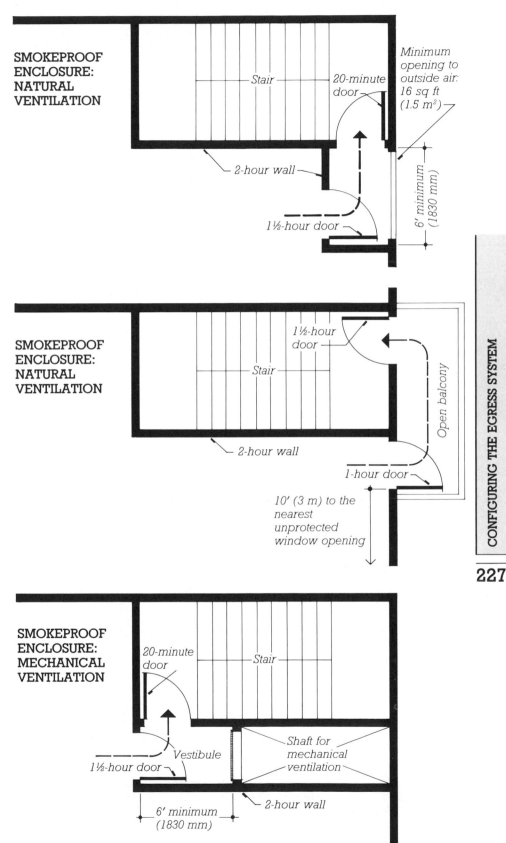

SMOKEPROOF ENCLOSURE: NATURAL VENTILATION

Stair — 20-minute door

Minimum opening to outside air: 16 sq ft (1.5 m²)

2-hour wall

1½-hour door

6' minimum (1830 mm)

SMOKEPROOF ENCLOSURE: NATURAL VENTILATION

1½-hour door

Stair

Open balcony

2-hour wall

1-hour door

10' (3 m) to the nearest unprotected window opening

SMOKEPROOF ENCLOSURE: MECHANICAL VENTILATION

20-minute door

Stair

Vestibule

1½-hour door

Shaft for mechanical ventilation

2-hour wall

6' minimum (1830 mm)

THE EXIT

OUTSIDE STAIRWAYS AND FIRE ESCAPES

Outside stairways may be used as exits. An outside stairway must be constructed with solid treads (as distinct from the open metal gratings used for treads of outside fire escapes). It must be built to the same fire-resistive requirements as an interior stair, including separation from the interior of the building by walls and openings with fire-resistance ratings as specified for interior stairs. If an outside stair is more than three stories high, it must be provided with a wall, screen, or grill at least 4 ft (1220 mm) high along its outside edge to avoid any handicap to persons with fear of high places.

A traditional metal fire escape is not permitted as an exit except as a second exit on existing buildings where it is impractical to construct a stair to current standards. Escape slides, rope ladders, escalators, and elevators cannot be counted as required exits. Fixed ladders are permitted as required exits only in certain situations in mechanical rooms and industrial occupancies where a very limited number of able-bodied workers are served by the ladder, and then the ladder may serve only as a second means of egress from the space.

THE EXIT

HORIZONTAL EXITS

A horizontal exit is a way of passage through a fire-resistant wall to an area of refuge on the same level in the same building or in an adjacent building. A horizontal exit may be designed to function for travel in one direction only, as in the case of a building that has one exit stairway and a horizontal exit to an adjoining building that has two or more exit stairways. In this case the corridors and lobbies of the adjoining building serve as the area of refuge. A horizontal exit may also be designed to function for travel in both directions, as shown on the drawing to the right. Here the corridor on the left side of the building serves as an area of refuge for the occupants of the right side of the building, and vice-versa.

The fire-resistant wall must be of 2-hour construction with no penetrations for ductwork. Wall penetrations for pipes or conduits must be tightly sealed. The exit doors must be rated at 1½ hours, must fit tightly, and must be self-closing.

The doors must swing in the direction of exit. If the area on each side of the wall serves reciprocally as an area of refuge for the area on the other side, the doors must be furnished in oppositely-swinging pairs so that at least one door will swing in the direction of exit travel for a person approaching from either side. In sizing the doors for oc-

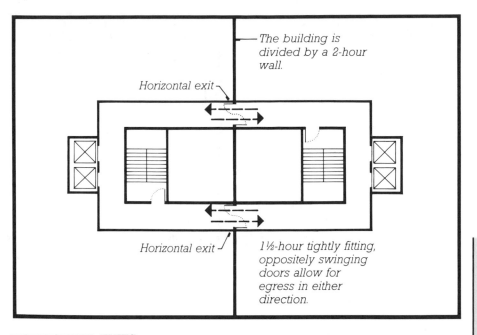

The building is divided by a 2-hour wall.

Horizontal exit

Horizontal exit

1½-hour tightly fitting, oppositely swinging doors allow for egress in either direction.

HORIZONTAL EXITS

cupant load, only doors swinging in the direction of egress may be counted.

Horizontal exits are advantageous in tall buildings, because they allow a person to escape the danger of a fire much more quickly than a stairway to the ground. They are also useful in hospitals, because they allow patients to be moved to safety while still in their beds. Horizontal exits may provide up to half of the required exit capacity of a story of a building except in health care and correctional occupancies, where they

may constitute a larger proportion of the exit capacity (up to two-thirds for health care, and 100% for correctional occupancies).

The area of refuge on either side of a horizontal exit must be large enough to accommodate the occupants from both sides of the exit. This capacity is calculated at the rate of 3 sq ft (0.28 m²) per person except in health care buildings, where the required areas are 30 sq ft (2.79 m²) for bedridden patients and 6 sq ft (0.56 m²) for those in wheelchairs. The area on each side of a horizontal exit must also be provided with at least one exit stair and one elevator.

THE EXIT

EXIT PASSAGEWAYS

An exit passageway is a horizontal means of exit travel that is protected from fire in the same manner as an enclosed interior exit stair (2-hour walls, 1½-hour self-closing doors). An exit passageway has several uses: It may be used to preserve the continuity of enclosure for an exit stair whose location shifts laterally as it descends through the building. It may be used to eliminate excessive travel distance to an exit. And it may be used as part of an exit discharge, to connect an enclosed stair to an exterior door.

The widths of passages, doors, landings, and stairs used as exits must be determined in accordance with values given by the various codes, as shown on pages 242–245, 250–251, 256–259, and 264–265. For detailed design requirements concerning illumination, emergency illumination, marking, finish materials, and hardware of exits, consult the appropriate building code.

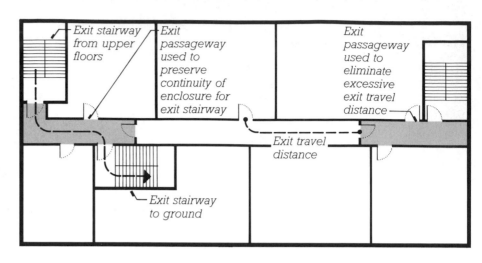

THE EXIT DISCHARGE

The exit discharge at its simplest is a door opening from an exit stair, a corridor, or the interior space of a building, directly onto a public way or an outdoor space leading to a public way. (An exit may not discharge into a courtyard from which there is no access to a public way.)

Where an exit stair is not located at the outside wall of a building, an exit passageway may lead from the base of the stair to the discharge door. This passageway may not have any openings other than required exit doorways.

A required exit may also discharge through an enclosed *foyer*, whose maximum dimensions are shown to the right. The foyer must have self-closing doors and may serve only as a means of egress. It must be separated from the other spaces of the building by at least the equivalent of wired glass in steel frames (a ¾-hour partition).

For most Use Groups, up to half the required exits from a building may discharge through a lobby area where the way to the exterior of the building is readily visible and identifiable from the point of discharge of the exit, if the entire story at the lobby level is sprinklered and the floor of the lobby level is of 2-hour construction.

Revolving doors may constitute up to half the required exit capacity of a building, providing they are constructed so as to allow free passage in a panic situation by collapsing into a book-fold position under pressure. No revolving door may be credited for an exit capacity of more than 50 persons.

For further details of exit discharge illumination, emergency illumination, marking, finish materials, and hardware, consult the appropriate building code.

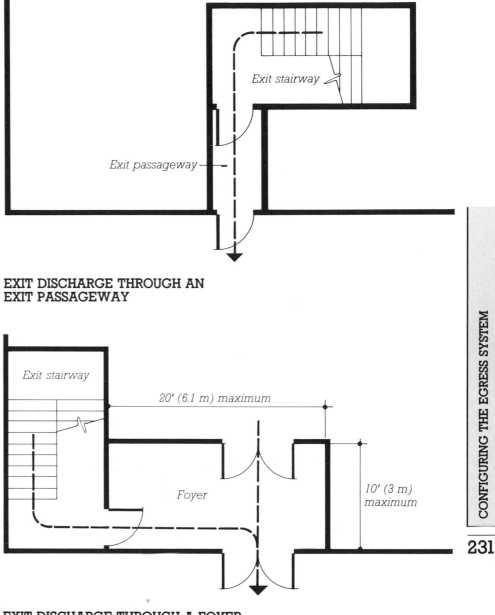

EXIT DISCHARGE THROUGH AN EXIT PASSAGEWAY

Exit stairway

20' (6.1 m) maximum

Foyer

10' (3 m) maximum

EXIT DISCHARGE THROUGH A FOYER

EGRESS FROM AUDITORIUMS, CONCERT HALLS, AND THEATERS

Assembly rooms, with their intense concentration of occupants, require a special set of egress provisions. Two types of seating arrangements are recognized by all the model building codes: conventional seating and continental seating. In conventional seating, the row length is severely limited and a network of broad aisles is laid out to conduct the audience to a relatively small number of exits. In continental seating, very long rows are permitted. In exchange for the longer row lengths, the rows must be spaced farther apart, and a larger number of exit doorways is required.

Building code egress requirements for auditoriums, concert halls, and theaters are summarized on the three following pages.

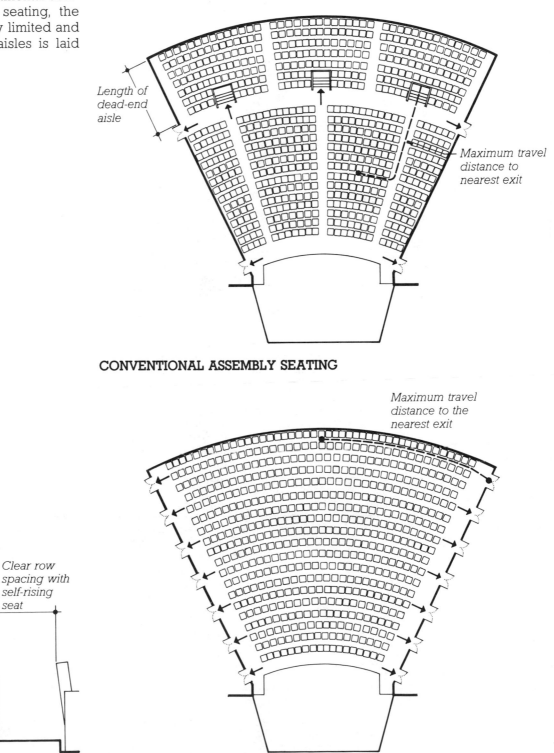

Length of dead-end aisle

Maximum travel distance to nearest exit

CONVENTIONAL ASSEMBLY SEATING

Maximum travel distance to the nearest exit

Back-to-back row spacing

Clear row spacing

Clear row spacing with self-rising seat

CONTINENTAL ASSEMBLY SEATING

EGRESS REQUIREMENTS FOR CONVENTIONAL ASSEMBLY SEATING

	Seating		Aisles			
	Maximum Row Length	Minimum Row Spacing	Minimum Aisle Width	Longest Dead-End Aisle	Cross-Aisle Width	Maximum Slope of Aisle
BOCA NATIONAL BUILDING CODE	Not more than 6 seats between any seat and the nearest aisle	12″ clear	0.2″ per person, 42″ minimum for seating on both sides; 23″ minimum for seating on one side; 36″ minimum for other aisles. See also the stair width requirements five columns to the right in this table.	20′	0.2″ per person, 36″ minimum	1:8
NATIONAL BUILDING CODE OF CANADA	Not more than 7 seats between any seat and the nearest aisle	400 mm clear	1100 mm minimum for seating on both sides, 900 mm minimum for seating on one side, 750 mm minimum for an aisle serving 60 persons or fewer, all measured at the point farthest from the exit, increasing 25 mm for each meter of length toward the exit.*	6 m	Width shall be equal to width of widest aisle served, plus 50% of remaining aisles it serves.	1:8
STANDARD BUILDING CODE	Not more than 6 seats between any seat and the nearest aisle	12″ clear, 30″ back to back	42″ minimum for seating on both sides, 36″ minimum for seating on one side, 30″ minimum for an aisle serving 60 seats or less, all measured at the point farthest from the exit, increasing 1.5″ for each 5′ of length.*	20′	4′ minimum, leading directly to an exit	1:8
UNIFORM BUILDING CODE	Not more than 6 seats between any seat and the nearest aisle	12″ clear	42″ minimum for seating on both sides, 36″ minimum for seating on one side, all measured at the point farthest from the exit, increasing 1.5″ for each 5′ of length.*	20′	Width shall be equal to width of widest aisle served, plus 50% of remaining aisles it serves.	1:8

*An aisle with egress at both ends should be of constant width.

234

EGRESS REQUIREMENTS FOR CONVENTIONAL ASSEMBLY SEATING

Stairs		Exits		
			Maximum Travel to Exit	
Stairs in Aisles	Stair Width	Main Exit Requirement	Sprinklered	Unsprinklered
Treads 11″ minimum depth, risers 8″ maximum height and 4″ minimum. Nonuniformities in tread and riser dimensions may not exceed ³/₁₆″ between adjacent steps.	0.3″ of width per person for risers 7″ or less; 0.005″ additional width for each 0.1″ of additional riser height up to a maximum of 8″. 48″ minimum width for seating on two sides; 36″ minimum for seating on one side.	A main entrance must be provided with egress capacity for half the total occupant load, and each level shall have other exits with capacity for two-thirds of the occupant load for that level.	250′	200′
Riser height 110 mm minimum, 200 mm maximum, with 6 mm maximum variation between adjacent risers allowed if the tread depth is at least 430 mm. Tread width 230 mm minimum.	See page 249.	none	45 m	45 m
See page 268.	See page 255.	A Group A—Large Assembly building must have a main entrance foyer.	200′	150′
Single riser is prohibited; see page 268.	See page 263.	A Group A-1 occupancy must have a main exit of sufficient width to accommodate 50% of the total occupant load, plus cross aisles leading to side aisles of sufficient width on each side to accommodate one-third of the total occupant load.	200′	150′

EGRESS REQUIREMENTS FOR CONTINENTAL ASSEMBLY SEATING

REQUIREMENTS FOR CONTINENTAL ASSEMBLY SEATING

	Maximum Row Length	Minimum Row Spacing	Minimum Width of Side Aisle	Side Door Requirements
BOCA National Building Code	100 seats	For a row with egress at both ends, the clear row spacing must be at least 12″ plus 0.3″ for every seat above 14. For a row with egress at one end only, the clear row spacing must be at least 12″ plus 0.6″ for every seat above 7, up to a maximum of 22″, and no seat may have a path length greater than 30′ to a point where there is a choice of two paths of travel to two exits.	0.2″ per person, 36″ minimum	0.2″ of door width per person in an unsprinklered building, or 0.15″ per person in a sprinklered building
National Building Code of Canada	100 seats	400 mm clear	1100 mm	Exit doorways must be provided at each end of each row at a rate no greater than 3 rows per doorway.
Standard Building Code	No limit	18″ clear for 18 seats or fewer, 20″ clear for 19 to 35 seats, 21″ clear for 36 to 45 seats, 22″ clear for 46 to 59 seats, and 24″ clear for 60 seats or more	44″	Exit door pairs of 66″ minimum width must be provided at each end of each row at a rate no greater than 5 rows per doorway.
Uniform Building Code	No limit	18″ clear for 18 seats or fewer, 20″ clear for 19 to 35 seats, 21″ clear for 36 to 45 seats, 22″ clear for 46 to 59 seats, and 24″ clear for 60 seats or more	44″	Exit door pairs of 66″ minimum width must be provided at each end of each row at a rate no greater than 5 rows per doorway.

Requirements for aisle slope, aisle stairs, and exit travel are the same as for conventional assembly seating—see pages 234–235.

DIMENSIONS OF WHEELCHAIR PLACES

A wheelchair place must be at least 33 in. (840 mm) wide. Its depth depends on how it is entered: If it is entered from the front or rear, it must be at least 48 in. (1220 mm) deep. For side entry, a depth of 60 in. (1525 mm) is required. Wheelchair places should be dispersed throughout the seating area, preferably in pairs.

REQUIREMENTS FOR WHEELCHAIR PLACES IN ASSEMBLY BUILDINGS

	Total Seating Capacity	Wheelchair Places Required
BOCA National Building Code		2 minimum
National Building Code of Canada	200 or fewer	2
	201–300	3
	301–400	4
	401–600	5
	601–800	6
	801–1000	7
	1000 or more	8, plus 1 per additional 1000, up to 20 maximum
Standard Building Code	500 or fewer	2
	501–750	3
	751–1000	5
	1000 or more	5, plus 1 per additional 500
Uniform Building Code		no requirements

SIZING THE EGRESS SYSTEM

This section presents simplified data for use in sizing egress components under each of the model building codes.

237

BOCA NATIONAL BUILDING CODE

MISCELLANEOUS EGRESS REQUIREMENTS

Egress Width Calculations

Stair widths and exit discharge widths are based on the occupant load of the largest single floor. Occupant loads do not accumulate from one floor to the next, except at the floor of exit discharge if people are exiting from both upper floors and basement floors and converging at the exit discharge.

Minimum Number of Exits

Occupant Load	Minimum Number of Exits
500 persons or fewer	2
501 to 1000 persons	3
More than 1000 persons	4

Buildings Requiring Only One Exit

1. Apartment buildings not more than 2 stories tall and having not more than 4 dwelling units per floor, with a maximum exit access travel of 50 ft, and a minimum fire-resistance rating of 1 hour for exit enclosure and exit doors.

2. Business and low-hazard storage buildings not more than 2 stories tall and having not more than 3500 sq ft per floor, with a maximum exit access travel of 75 ft and a minimum fire-resistance rating of 1 hour for exit enclosure and exit doors.

Window Egress

Each sleeping room below the fourth story must have at least one exterior door or operable window with a sill height of not more than 44 in., a net clear opening of at least 5.7 sq ft, a minimum clear opening height of 24 in., and a minimum clear opening width of 20 in.

Smokeproof Enclosures

At least one of the required exits must be a smokeproof enclosure in buildings having floors located more than 75 ft above the lowest level of fire department vehicle access, unless the building is fully sprinklered, or a hospital, or of Use Group B, R-1, or R-2 with horizontal exits and areas of refuge as explained on page 229.

Accessibility for Handicapped People

All buildings are required to be accessible to the handicapped except Use Groups H, S, and R-3, and buildings of Use Group I-1 with 20 occupants or fewer. Barrier-free units must be provided in hotels, motels, dormitories, and multifamily dwellings at a rate of one unit for the first 21 to 99 units per building and, in buildings of 100 units or more, at a rate of one unit per 100 units or fraction thereof. No access is required to balconies and mezzanines of Use Groups A and E if identical seating and services are available elsewhere in the assembly room. Buildings without elevators that are accessible to the handicapped at grade level and have all facilities normally sought and used by the public at grade level need not be accessible at other floors. Buildings of Use Group B without elevators, with handicapped access at grade floors, and with other floors of 1000 sq ft or less need not be accessible at other floors.

USE GROUP (see index on page 8 for specific uses)	Maximum Travel Distance from Most Remote Point to Nearest Exit Enclosure		Largest Room That May Have Only One Door
	Sprinklered	Unsprinklered	
A-1: ASSEMBLY, THEATERS	250'	200'	50 persons occupancy, or 75' of travel distance in the room
A-2: ASSEMBLY, NIGHT CLUBS AND SIMILAR USES	250'	200'	same as above
A-3: ASSEMBLY	250'	200'	same as above
A-4: ASSEMBLY, CHURCHES	250'	200'	same as above
A-5: ASSEMBLY, OUTDOOR	400'	400'	same as above
B: BUSINESS	250'	200'	same as above
E: EDUCATIONAL	250'	200'	same as above
F-1: FACTORY AND INDUSTRIAL	250'	200'	same as above
F-2: FACTORY AND INDUSTRIAL, LOW HAZARD	400'	400'	same as above
H: HIGH HAZARD	75'	not permitted	same as above
I-1: INSTITUTIONAL, RESIDENTIAL CARE	250'	200'	same as above
I-2: INSTITUTIONAL, INCAPACITATED	200'	150'	1000 square feet
I-3: INSTITUTIONAL, RESTRAINED	200'	150'	50 persons occupancy, or 75' of travel distance in the room
M: MERCANTILE	250'	200'	same as above
M: MERCANTILE, ENCLOSED SHOPPING MALLS	200' in the mall space itself	not permitted	same as above
R-1: RESIDENTIAL, HOTELS	250'	200'	same as above
R-2: RESIDENTIAL, MULTIFAMILY	250'	200'	same as above
R-3: RESIDENTIAL, ONE- AND TWO-FAMILY	250'	200'	same as above
S-1: STORAGE, MODERATE	250'	200'	same as above
S-2: STORAGE, LOW	400'	300'	same as above
OPEN PARKING GARAGES	250'	200'	not applicable

240

GENERAL GUIDELINES FOR EGRESS DESIGN

Maximum Length of Dead-End Corridor	Minimum Clear Corridor Width	Minimum Clear Door Width	Minimum Stair Width	Additional Requirements
20'	44" for occupancy of more than 50 persons, and 36" for occupancy of 50 or fewer	32"	44" for occupancy of more than 50 persons, and 36" for occupancy of 50 or fewer	See detailed requirements for row spacings, aisles, and exits on pages 234–236.
20'	same as above	32"	same as above	
20'	same as above	32"	same as above	
20'	same as above	32"	same as above	
20'	same as above	32"	same as above	
20'	same as above	32"	same as above	
20'	same, except 72" for more than 100 occupants	32"	same as above	
20'	44" for occupancy of more than 50 persons, and 36" for occupancy of 50 or fewer	32"	same as above	In a sprinklered 1-story building with automatic heat and smoke vents, the maximum travel distance is 400'.
20'	same as above	32"	same as above	
20'	same as above	32"	same as above	
20'	96" where beds must be moved	44" where beds must be moved	same as above	Window egress is required for each room in an unsprinklered building—see page 239.
20'	96" where beds must be moved	same as above	same as above	Each floor must be divided by at least one smokeproof wall with horizontal exits.
20'	44" for occupancy of more than 50 persons, and 36" for occupancy of 50 or fewer	28"	same as above	
20'	same as above	32"	same as above	
Twice the width of the mall space itself for the mall, 20' for corridors	20' for the mall space, 66" for corridors	32"	same as above	
20'	44" for occupancy of more than 50 persons, and 36" for occupancy of 50 or fewer	32"	same as above	Window egress is required for each room in an unsprinklered building—see page 239.
20'	same as above	32"	same as above	same as above
20'	same as above	28"	same as above	same as above
20'	same as above	32"	same as above	In an unsprinklered 1-story building with automatic heat and smoke vents, the maximum travel distance is 400'.
20'	same as above	32"	same as above	
20'	same as above	32"	same as above	Exit stairways may be open.

EGRESS WIDTHS: BOCA NATIONAL BUILDING CODE

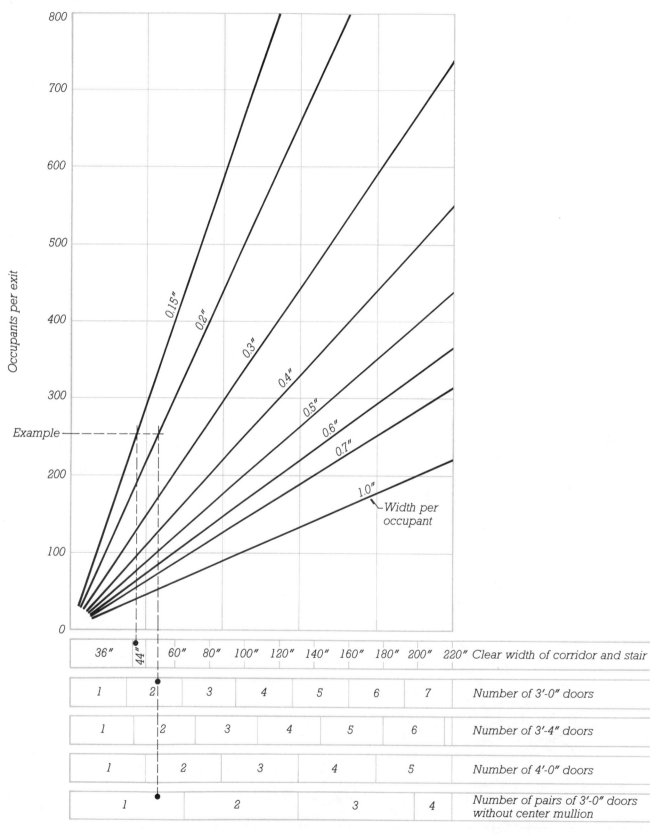

242

DETERMINING WIDTHS OF EGRESS COMPONENTS

AN EXAMPLE OF THE USE OF THIS CHART

The Problem: Design an exit for a department store basement, sprinklered, dimensions 105 × 292.55 ft.

The Solution: From the index on page 8, we find that a department store belongs to Use Group M, Mercantile. Multiplying the two dimensions of the building, we arrive at a gross floor area of 30,720 sq ft. From the table on pages 244–245, we see that for purposes of designing the exits we must allocate 30 sq ft per occupant, to arrive at an occupant load of 1024 for this floor. Assume that our design provides four exits, which is also the minimum required by the table on page 239. Dividing 1024 occupants by 4 exits gives an occupant load per exit of 256.

From the same table (pages 244–245), we find that for Use Group M, we must provide 0.15 in. of width per occupant in corridors and doorways and 0.2 in. per occupant in stairways. Moving to the chart on the facing page, we read horizontally from 256 occupants to the 0.15-in. line and then downward to find that a width of 38 in. is required for the corridor. We must round this up to the 44-in. minimum width indicated on page 241. Extending this line farther downward, we select either two 3-ft doors, a single 4-ft door, or a pair of 3-ft doors without center mullion.

Reading horizontally from 256 occupants to the 0.2-in. line, then downward, we arrive at a required stair width of 52 in. (For stair design charts, see pages 273–283.)

SIZING THE EGRESS SYSTEM

USE GROUP (see index on page 8 for specific uses)	Occupant Load: Square Feet per Occupant
A-1: ASSEMBLY, THEATERS	Actual number of fixed seats
A-2: ASSEMBLY, NIGHT CLUBS, AND SIMILAR USES	15 net
A-3: ASSEMBLY	7 net for lecture halls, 15 net for exhibition halls
A-4: ASSEMBLY, CHURCHES	18″ of pew space per occupant
A-5: ASSEMBLY, OUTDOOR	18″ of bleacher space per occupant
B: BUSINESS	100 gross
E: EDUCATIONAL	20 net for classrooms, 50 net for workshops
F-1: FACTORY AND INDUSTRIAL	100 gross
F-2: FACTORY AND INDUSTRIAL, LOW HAZARD	100 gross
H: HIGH HAZARD	100 gross
I-1: INSTITUTIONAL, RESIDENTIAL CARE	Sleeping areas 120 gross, treatment areas 240 gross
I-2: INSTITUTIONAL, INCAPACITATED	same
I-3: INSTITUTIONAL, RESTRAINED	same
M: MERCANTILE	Basement and ground floors 30 gross, other floors 60 gross. Storage, stock, and shipping areas 300 gross.
M: MERCANTILE, ENCLOSED SHOPPING MALLS	In buildings up to 150,000 sq ft: 30 gross; 150,000–300,000 sq ft: 40 gross; over 300,000 sq ft: 50 gross.
R-1: RESIDENTIAL, HOTELS	200 gross
R-2: RESIDENTIAL, MULTIFAMILY	same
R-3: RESIDENTIAL, ONE- AND TWO-FAMILY	same
S-1: STORAGE, MODERATE	300 gross
S-2: STORAGE, LOW	300 gross
OPEN PARKING GARAGES	200 gross

QUANTITIES FOR DETERMINING WIDTHS OF EGRESS COMPONENTS

Width per Occupant			
For Doors, Corridors, and Ramps		For Stairs	
Sprinklered	Unsprinklered	Sprinklered	Unsprinklered
0.15″	0.2″	0.2″	0.3″
0.15″	0.2″	0.2″	0.3″
0.15″	0.2″	0.2″	0.3″
0.15″	0.2″	0.2″	0.3″
0.15″	0.2″	0.2″	0.3″
0.15″	0.2″	0.2″	0.3″
0.15″	0.2″	0.2″	0.3″
0.15″	0.2″	0.2″	0.3″
0.15″	0.2″	0.2″	0.3″ .
0.2″	not permitted	0.3″	not permitted
0.2″	0.2″	0.2″	0.4″
0.5″	0.7″	0.6″	1.0″
0.2″	0.2″	0.3″	0.3″
0.15″	0.2″	0.2″	0.3″
0.15″	not permitted	0.2″	not permitted
0.15″	0.2″	0.2″	0.3″
0.15″	0.2″	0.2″	0.3″
0.15″	0.2″	0.2″	0.3″
0.15″	0.2″	0.2″	0.3″
0.15″	0.2″	0.2″	0.3″
0.15″	0.2″	0.2″	0.3″

MISCELLANEOUS EGRESS REQUIREMENTS

Egress Width Calculations

Stair widths and exit discharge widths are based on the occupant load of the largest single floor. Occupant loads do not accumulate from one floor to the next, except at the floor of exit discharge if people are exiting from both upper floors and basement floors and converging at the exit discharge.

Egress capacities are calculated in terms of units and half units of egress width. This is done by dividing the width of the exit by 550 mm to obtain the number of units. If the remainder is 300 mm or more, it is counted as an additional half unit.

Buildings Requiring Only One Exit

A building may have only one exit if it is not more than 2 stories in height, does not serve an occupancy load of more than 60 persons, and does not exceed the maximum floor areas and travel distances in the following table:

Firefighter Access

On unsprinklered floors from grade to 25 m above grade, firefighter access must be provided by at least one unobstructed window or access panel, minimum dimensions 1100 mm high by 550 mm wide with a sill height not greater than 900 mm, for each 15 m of wall required to face a street.

At least one elevator with a platform area of at least 2.2 m² must be provided for use by firefighters in a high building. This elevator must be protected by a ¾-hour vestibule or a 1-hour corridor enclosure at each floor and connected to a secure source of electricity.

Smoke Control in High Buildings

The National Building Code of Canada contains complex provisions relating to smoke control in high buildings. Some of these provisions relate to the use of horizontal exits and areas of refuge, the provision of balconies in residential buildings, and the area of treads and landings in exit stairways, and they may therefore have an impact on the preliminary planning of a building. Consult section 3.2.6.2 of the National Building Code of Canada for details.

Accessibility for Handicapped People

All buildings are required to be accessible to the handicapped except single-family dwellings, Use Group F-1, and buildings not intended to be occupied daily full time, such as telephone exchanges, substations, and pump houses. Every accessible floor of a building must be provided with barrier-free washrooms. Parking facilities must be accessible to the handicapped. Where barrier-free access is provided to any story above the first story of an unsprinklered building, a smoke- and fire-protected elevator must be provided, and the floor must be divided with a smokeproof wall and horizontal exits into at least two zones. Additionally, any residences on the upper floors must be furnished with balconies, and the building must have an exterior exit at ground level or with a ramp to ground level. Consult 3.3.1.5.(1) of the National Building Code of Canada for further details.

Use Groups A and E:	Maximum floor area of 150 m² and maximum travel distance of 15 m.
Use Group B:	Maximum floor area of 75 m² and maximum travel distance of 10 m.
Use Group C:	Maximum floor area of 100 m² and maximum travel distance of 15 m.
Use Group D:	Maximum floor area of 200 m² and maximum travel distance of 25 m.
Use Group F-2:	Maximum floor area of 150 m² and maximum travel distance of 10 m.
Use Group F-3:	Maximum floor area of 200 m² and maximum travel distance of 15 m.

NATIONAL BUILDING CODE OF CANADA

USE GROUP (see index on page 9 for specific uses)	Maximum Travel Distance from Most Remote Point to Nearest Exit Enclosure*		Largest Room That May Have Only One Door: Maximum Occupancy of 60 Persons, or:
	Sprinklered	Unsprinklered	
A-1: ASSEMBLY BUILDINGS	45 m	30 m	150 m² maximum area, or 15 m maximum travel distance within the room
A-2: ASSEMBLY BUILDINGS	45 m	30 m	same as above
A-3: ASSEMBLY, ARENA TYPE	45 m	30 m	same as above
A-4: ASSEMBLY, OPEN AIR	45 m	30 m	same as above
B-1: INSTITUTIONAL, DETENTION	45 m	30 m	75 m² maximum area, or 10 m maximum travel distance within the room
B-2: INSTITUTIONAL, RESTRAINED	45 m	30 m	75 m² or 10 m maximum travel distance within the room for sleeping rooms, 150 m² or 15 m for other rooms
C: RESIDENTIAL	45 m	30 m	100 m² maximum area, or 15 m maximum travel distance within the room
D: BUSINESS AND PERSONAL SERVICES	45 m	40 m	200 m² maximum area, or 25 m maximum travel distance within the room
E: MERCANTILE BUILDINGS	45 m	30 m	150 m² maximum area, or 15 m maximum travel distance within the room
F-1: INDUSTRIAL, HIGH HAZARD	25 m	25 m	not permitted
F-2: INDUSTRIAL, MEDIUM HAZARD	45 m	30 m	150 m² maximum area, or 10 m maximum travel distance within the room
F-3: INDUSTRIAL, LOW HAZARD	45 m	30 m	200 m² maximum area, or 15 m maximum travel distance within the room
OPEN AIR GARAGES	45 m	30 m	not applicable

*If a room is enclosed with at least a ¾-hour fire separation, travel distance may be measured from the door of the room.

GENERAL GUIDELINES FOR EGRESS DESIGN

Maximum Length of Dead-End Corridor	Minimum Clear Corridor Width	Minimum Clear Door Width	Minimum Stair Width	Additional Requirements
Permitted only if the areas served have a second means of egress	1100 mm	790 mm	1100 mm for a stair serving more than 3 stories, or 900 mm for a stair serving 3 stories or less	See detailed requirements for row spacings, aisles, and exits on pages 234–236.
same as above	1100 mm	790 mm	same as above	See detailed requirements for row spacings, aisles, and exits on pages 234–236.
same as above	1100 mm	790 mm	same as above	
same as above	1100 mm	790 mm	same as above	An occupant load of 1001 to 4000 persons requires at least 3 exits, and an occupant load of more than 4000 persons requires at least 4 exits.
not permitted	1100 mm	790 mm	same as above	
not permitted	same, except 2400 mm for patients in bed	1050 mm for patients in bed, 790 mm otherwise	same, except 1650 mm for patients in bed	
6 m	1100 mm	790 mm	1100 mm for a stair serving more than 3 stories, or 900 mm for a stair serving 3 stories or less	
9 m	1100 mm	790 mm	same as above	
Permitted only if the areas served have a second means of egress	1100 mm	790 mm	same as above	
same as above	1100 mm	790 mm	same as above	
same as above	1100 mm	790 mm	same as above	
same as above	1100 mm	790 mm	same as above	
9 m	1100 mm	790 mm	same as above	

QUANTITIES FOR DETERMINING WIDTHS OF EGRESS COMPONENTS

USE GROUP (see index on page 9 for specific uses)	Occupant Load: Square Meters per Occupant	Occupants per 550-mm Unit of Width	
		For Doors, Corridors, and Passageways	For Stairs and Ramps
A-1: ASSEMBLY BUILDINGS	Actual number of fixed seats	90	60
A-2: ASSEMBLY BUILDINGS	0.75	90	60
A-3: ASSEMBLY, ARENA TYPE	0.60	90	60
A-4: ASSEMBLY, OPEN AIR	0.40 standing, or 0.60 seated	300	225
B-1: INSTITUTIONAL, DETENTION	11.6	30	30
B-2: INSTITUTIONAL, RESTRAINED	10.0	30	30
C: RESIDENTIAL	4.6	30	30
D: BUSINESS AND PERSONAL SERVICES	9.3 for offices, 4.6 for personal services	90	60
E: MERCANTILE BUILDINGS	3.7 for basements and stories entered from grade, 5.6 for other stories	90	60
F-1: INDUSTRIAL, HIGH HAZARD	4.6 for manufacturing and process rooms, 28.0 for storage rooms	90	60
F-2: INDUSTRIAL, MEDIUM HAZARD	same	90	60
F-3: INDUSTRIAL, LOW HAZARD	same	90	60
OPEN AIR GARAGES	46.0	90	60

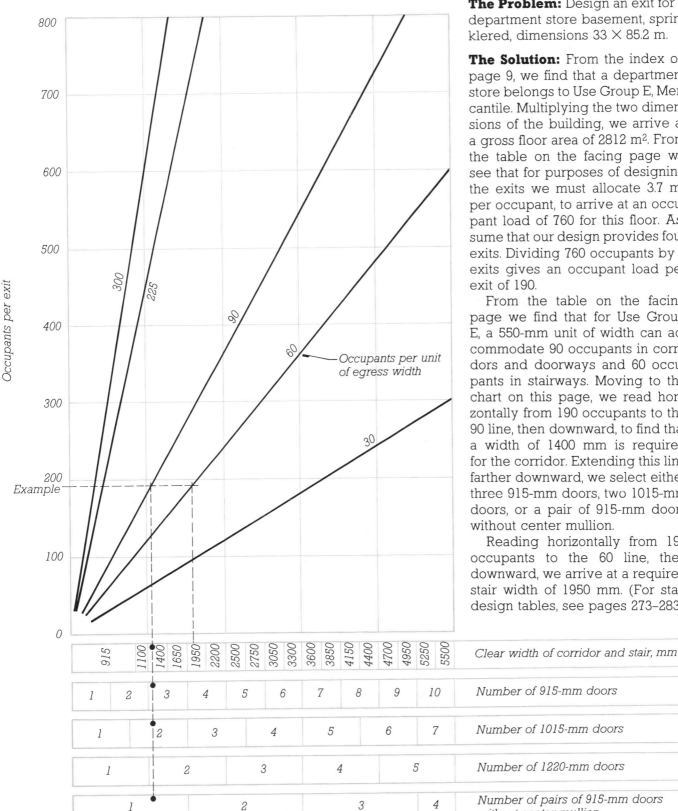

AN EXAMPLE OF THE USE OF THIS CHART

The Problem: Design an exit for a department store basement, sprinklered, dimensions 33 × 85.2 m.

The Solution: From the index on page 9, we find that a department store belongs to Use Group E, Mercantile. Multiplying the two dimensions of the building, we arrive at a gross floor area of 2812 m². From the table on the facing page we see that for purposes of designing the exits we must allocate 3.7 m² per occupant, to arrive at an occupant load of 760 for this floor. Assume that our design provides four exits. Dividing 760 occupants by 4 exits gives an occupant load per exit of 190.

From the table on the facing page we find that for Use Group E, a 550-mm unit of width can accommodate 90 occupants in corridors and doorways and 60 occupants in stairways. Moving to the chart on this page, we read horizontally from 190 occupants to the 90 line, then downward, to find that a width of 1400 mm is required for the corridor. Extending this line farther downward, we select either three 915-mm doors, two 1015-mm doors, or a pair of 915-mm doors without center mullion.

Reading horizontally from 190 occupants to the 60 line, then downward, we arrive at a required stair width of 1950 mm. (For stair design tables, see pages 273–283.)

SIZING THE EGRESS SYSTEM

251

MISCELLANEOUS EGRESS REQUIREMENTS

Egress Width Calculations

Stair widths and exit discharge widths are based on the occupant load of the largest single floor. Occupant loads do not accumulate from one floor to the next, except at the floor of exit discharge if people are exiting from both upper floors and basement floors and converging at the exit discharge.

Egress capacities are calculated in terms of units and half units of egress width. This is done by dividing the width of the exit by 22 in. to obtain the number of units. If the remainder is 12 in. or more, it is counted as an additional half unit.

Minimum Number of Exits

Occupant Load per Story	Minimum Number of Exits
500 persons or fewer	2
501 to 1000 persons	3
More than 1000 persons	4

Buildings Requiring Only One Exit

1. Use Group B buildings not more than 2 stories tall with not more than 3500 sq ft per floor and an occupancy of the upper floor by not more than 40 persons, with a maximum exit travel distance of 75 ft.

2. Single-story Use Group M buildings having a maximum of 2250 sq ft on the street floor, with a maximum exit travel distance of 50 ft.

3. Apartment buildings not more than 2 stories tall with not more than 3500 sq ft or 4 dwelling units per floor, with a maximum exit access travel of 30 ft from the door of a unit.

4. Single-story Use Group S buildings with not more than 2500 sq ft of floor area and a maximum exit travel distance of 50 ft.

Window Egress

Each sleeping room on the first and second stories of multiple dwellings and each sleeping room in a single-family dwelling must have at least one exterior door or operable window with a sill height of not more than 44 in., a net clear opening of at least 4 sq ft, a minimum clear opening height of 22 in., and a minimum clear opening width of 20 in. The glass area must be at least 5 sq ft on the ground story and 5.7 sq ft on the second story.

Smokeproof Enclosures

At least one of the required exits must be a smokeproof enclosure in buildings having floors located more than 75 ft above the lowest level of fire department vehicle access, except for Use Group B and R buildings larger than 15,000 sq ft per floor with horizontal exits and areas of refuge as explained on page 229.

Exterior Stairways

Except in Use Group I buildings, exterior stairways are limited to 6 stories or 75 ft of height.

Tall Buildings

In Use Group B and R buildings with inhabited floors more than 75 ft above the lowest level of fire department vehicle access, all elevators on all floors must open to elevator lobbies that are separated from the rest of the building by 1-hour walls and 20-minute doors. Openings to these lobbies are limited to elevator doors and doors required for egress. All rooms must have access to at least one required exit that can be reached without traveling through these lobbies. These requirements do not apply to elevators that open to an atrium, an exterior corridor, or a space on the main entrance level of the building.

Accessibility for Handicapped People

All buildings are required to be accessible to the handicapped except single-family and two-family dwellings, other residential buildings to be offered for sale, workplaces where the work cannot reasonably be performed by handicapped people, buildings without elevators where all public facilities are on an accessible ground floor, Use Group B buildings having not more than 5000 sq ft per floor that are accessible at grade level and have no elevator, and Use Group F buildings with not more than 5000 sq ft of office space. Barrier-free units must be provided in hotels, motels, dormitories, and multifamily dwellings at a rate of one unit for the first 11 to 19 units, and 5% of all units in buildings of 20 units or more, with fractions of half or more rounded up to the next whole unit. Barrier-free washrooms and drinking fountains are required. See article M-3 of the Standard Building Code for provisions relating to handicapped parking.

SIZING THE EGRESS SYSTEM

253

USE GROUP (see index on page 10 for specific uses)	Maximum Travel Distance from Most Remote Point to Nearest Exit Enclosure*		Largest Room That May Have Only One Door
	Sprinklered	Unsprinklered	
A: ASSEMBLY	200'	150'	50 persons occupancy, or 50' of travel distance in the room
B: BUSINESS	200'	150'	same as above
E: EDUCATIONAL	200'	150'	same as above
F: FACTORY-INDUSTRIAL	200'	150'	same as above
H: HAZARDOUS	75'	not permitted	same as above
I: INSTITUTIONAL, RESTRAINED	200' from any point to an exit, 100' from any point to a room door, 150' from room door to an exit, except in sleeping rooms	150' from any point to an exit, 50' from any point to a room door, 100' from room door to an exit	same as above
I: INSTITUTIONAL, UNRESTRAINED	150'	100'	same as above
M: MERCANTILE	200'	100'	same as above
M: SHOPPING MALLS	200'	not permitted	same as above
R: RESIDENTIAL	200'	150'	same as above
S: STORAGE	200'	150'	same as above
OPEN PARKING GARAGES	200'	150'	not applicable

*When egress travel within a room does not exceed 50', travel distance is measured from the door of the room.

GENERAL GUIDELINES FOR EGRESS DESIGN

Maximum Length of Dead-End Corridor	Minimum Clear Corridor Width	Minimum Clear Door Width	Minimum Stair Width	Additional Requirements
20′	44″	32″	44″ for occupancy of 50 persons or more, and 36″ for occupancy of fewer than 50 persons	See detailed requirements for row spacings, aisles, and exits on pages 234–236.
20′	44″	32″	same as above	
20′	72″ for occupancy load of 100 persons or more, 44″ otherwise	32″	same as above	
20′	44″	32″	same as above	
20′	44″	32″	same as above	
20′	44″	44″ for movement of beds, 32″ otherwise	44″	See Section 409 of the Standard Building Code for detailed requirements for Institutional Use Groups.
20′	44″	same as above	44″	See Section 409 of the Standard Building Code for detailed requirements for Institutional Use Groups.
20′	44″	32″	44″	
20′	66″	32″	66″	See Section 507 of the Standard Building Code for detailed requirements for shopping malls.
20′	36″ in one- and two-family dwellings, 44″ otherwise	32″	44″ for occupancy of 50 persons or more, and 36″ for occupancy of fewer than 50 persons	Window egress is required from sleeping rooms—see page 253.
20′	44″	32″	same as above	
20′	44″	32″	same as above	Exit stairways may be enclosed in ¼″ wired glass in steel frames.

EGRESS WIDTHS: STANDARD BUILDING CODE

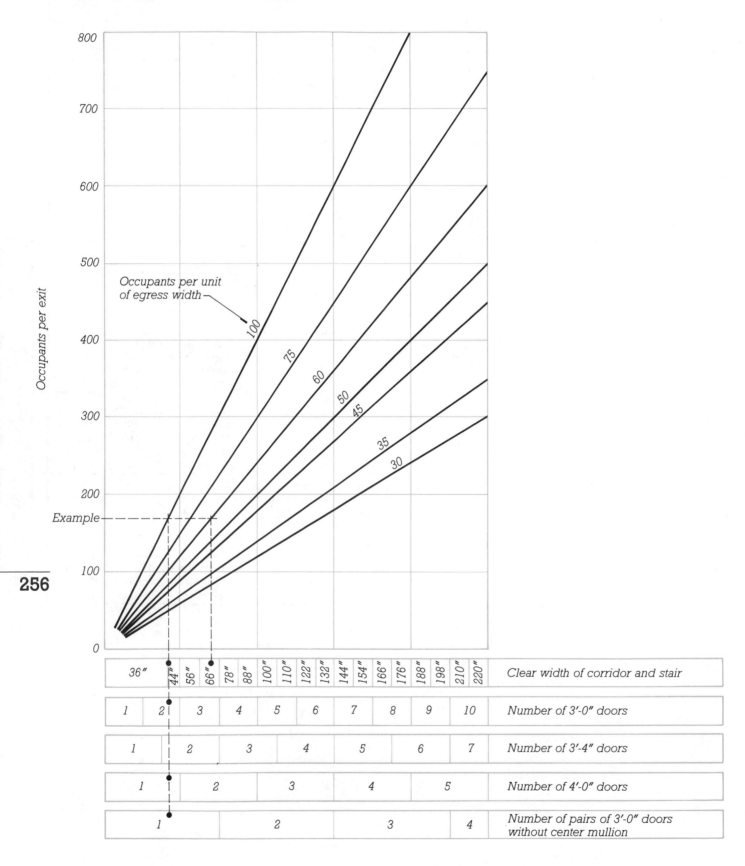

DETERMINING WIDTHS OF EGRESS COMPONENTS

AN EXAMPLE OF THE USE OF THIS CHART

The Problem: Design an exit for a department store basement, sprinklered, dimensions 103 × 203.9 ft.

The Solution: From the index on page 10, we find that a department store belongs to Use Group M, Mercantile. Multiplying the two dimensions of the building, we arrive at a gross floor area of 21,000 sq ft. From the table on pages 258–259 we see that for purposes of designing the exits we must allocate 30 sq ft per occupant, to arrive at an occupant load of 700 for this floor. Assume that our preliminary design provides four exits, one more than required by the table on page 253. Dividing 700 occupants by 4 exits gives an occupant load per exit of 175.

From the table on pages 258–259, we find that for Use Group M, a 44-in. unit of width can accommodate 100 occupants in corridors and doorways and 60 occupants in stairways. Moving to the chart on the facing page, we read horizontally from 175 occupants to the 100 line, then downward to find that a width of 44 in. is required for the corridor. Extending this line farther downward, we select either two 3-ft doors, a single 4-ft door, or a pair of 3-ft doors without center mullion.

Reading horizontally from 175 occupants to the 60 line, then downward, we arrive at a required stair width of 66 in. (For stair design tables, see pages 273–283.)

USE GROUP (see index on page 10 for specific uses)	Occupant Load: Square Feet per Occupant
A: ASSEMBLY	Actual number of fixed seats, or 7 sq ft for seated audience, 3 sq ft for standing audience, 15 sq ft for conference rooms, exhibits, gymnasiums, lounges
B: BUSINESS	100 sq ft gross, or 15 sq ft gross in small restaurants
E: EDUCATIONAL	20 sq ft net in classrooms, 50 sq ft net in shops
F: FACTORY-INDUSTRIAL	100 sq ft gross
H: HAZARDOUS	100 sq ft gross
I: INSTITUTIONAL, RESTRAINED	120 sq ft gross for sleeping rooms, 240 sq ft gross for in-patient treatment, 100 sq ft gross for outpatient treatment
I: INSTITUTIONAL, UNRESTRAINED	same
M: MERCANTILE	30 sq ft gross for basement and grade levels, 60 sq ft gross for other levels, 100 sq ft gross for storage and shipping
M: SHOPPING MALLS	30 sq ft gross for less than 150,000 sq ft, 40 sq ft gross for 150,001 to 350,000 sq ft, 50 sq ft gross over 350,000 sq ft
R: RESIDENTIAL	200 sq ft gross
S: STORAGE	300 sq ft gross
OPEN PARKING GARAGES	200 sq ft gross

QUANTITIES FOR DETERMINING WIDTHS OF EGRESS COMPONENTS

Occupants per 22-in. Unit of Width	
For Doors, Corridors, and Passageways	For Stairs and Ramps
100	75
100	60
100	75
100	60
50	30
100	60
45	35
100	60
100	60
100	75
100	60
100	60

MISCELLANEOUS EGRESS REQUIREMENTS

Egress Width Calculations

Stair widths and exit discharge widths are based on the occupant load of the largest single floor. Occupant loads do not accumulate from one floor to the next, except at the floor of exit discharge if people are exiting from both upper floors and basement floors and converging at the exit discharge. See UBC Section 3303,(b) for the method of calculation in situations where one floor exits through another floor.

Minimum Number of Exits

Occupant Load	Minimum Number of Exits
500 persons or fewer	2
501 to 1000 persons	3
More than 1000 persons	4

Buildings Requiring Only One Exit

1. The second story within an individual dwelling unit.

2. A second story with two or more dwelling units and a total occupant load of 10 or fewer.

3. Other buildings with low occupant loads, as provided in Table 33-A of the Uniform Building Code.

Window Egress

Each sleeping room in a Use Group R occupancy below the fourth story must have at least one exterior door or operable window with a sill height of not more than 44 in., a net clear opening of at least 5.7 sq ft, a minimum clear opening height of 24 in., and a minimum clear opening width of 20 in.

Smokeproof Enclosures

All the required exits must be smokeproof enclosures in buildings having floors located more than 75 ft above the lowest level of fire department vehicle access, unless the building is fully sprinklered, with horizontal exits and areas of refuge as explained on page 229, or unless the building is an open parking garage.

Accessibility for Handicapped People

All buildings are required to be accessible to the handicapped except single-family dwellings, commercial kitchens, mechanical equipment rooms, storage and stock rooms, and warehouses. Barrier-free units must be provided in hotels, motels, dormitories, and multi-family dwellings at the rate of one unit for the first 21 to 99 units per building and, in buildings of 100 units or more, at the rate of one unit per 100 units or fraction thereof.

The reference tables appearing on pages 261–265 are for preliminary design purposes only. They represent the authors' interpretation of certain major provisions of The Uniform Building Code, 1985 Edition. No official interpretation has been sought from or granted by the International Conference of Building Officials. For design development work and final preparation of building plans, you must consult the Uniform Building Code, 1985 Edition, copyright © by International Conference of Building Officials, 5360 South Workman Mill Road, Whittier, CA 90601.

SIZING THE EGRESS SYSTEM

UNIFORM BUILDING CODE

USE GROUP (see index on page 11 for specific uses)	Maximum Travel Distance from Most Remote Point to Nearest Exit Enclosure*		Largest Room That May Have Only One Door†
	Sprinklered	Unsprinklered	
A-1: ASSEMBLY BUILDING WITH STAGE AND WITH OCCUPANT LOAD OF 1000 OR MORE	200′	150′	49 occupants
A-2, A-2.1, A-3, A-4: ASSEMBLY	200′	150′	same as above
B-1: SERVICE STATIONS AND GARAGES	200′	150′	same as above
B-2: OFFICES	200′	150′	29 occupants
B-2: DRINKING AND DINING ESTABLISHMENTS	200′	150′	49 occupants
B-2: STORES	200′	150′	10 occupants in basement, 49 occupants on ground floor, 9 occupants on upper floors
B-2: SHOPPING MALLS	200′	not permitted	49 occupants or 75′ of exit travel
B-2: WORKSHOPS AND FACTORIES	200′	150′	49 occupants
B-2: CLASSROOMS	200′	150′	49 occupants
B-3: AIRCRAFT HANGARS, NO REPAIRS	200′	150′	9 occupants
B-4: INDUSTRIAL, LOW HAZARD	200′	150′	29 occupants
E: EDUCATIONAL	225′	150′	49 occupants
H-1 and H-2: HAZARDOUS	75′	75′	29 occupants or 200 square feet
H-3, H-4, H-5: HAZARDOUS	200′	150′	same as above
H-6: HAZARDOUS	100′	not permitted	same as above
I-1, I-2, I-3: INSTITUTIONAL	200′	150′	5 occupants
R-1: HOTELS, APARTMENT HOUSES, CONVENTS, MONASTERIES	200′	150′	9 occupants
R-3: DWELLINGS AND LODGING HOUSES	200′	150′	9 occupants
OPEN PARKING GARAGES	200′	150′	29 occupants

*The maximum travel distance may be increased by 100 feet when the last 150 feet of travel is in a 1-hour corridor with 20-minute doors.

262

GENERAL GUIDELINES FOR EGRESS DESIGN

Maximum Length of Dead-End Corridor	Minimum Clear Corridor Width	Minimum Clear Door Width	Minimum Stair Width	Additional Requirements
20'	44"	32"	44" for occupancy of more than 50 persons, and 36" for occupancy of 50 or fewer persons	See detailed requirements for row spacings, aisles, and exits on pages 234–236.
20'	44"	32"	same as above	See detailed requirements for row spacings, aisles, and exits on pages 234–236.
20'	44"	32"	same as above	
20'	44"	32"	same as above	
20'	44"	32"	same as above	
20'	44"	32"	same as above	
20'	44"	32"	same as above	See Appendix, Chapter 17, of the Uniform Building Code for detailed requirements.
20'	44"	32"	same as above	
20'	44"	32"	same as above	
20'	44"	32"	same as above	
20'	44"	32"	same as above	
20'	72" for Group E-1, 44" otherwise	32"	same, except 60" minimum for occupant load of 100 or more	See Section 3319 of the Uniform Building Code for further details.
20'	44"	32"	44" for occupancy of more than 50 persons, and 36" for occupancy of 50 or fewer	
20'	44"	32"	same as above	
20'	44"	32"	same as above	
20'	same, except 96" for an area housing nonambulatory patients	44" for moving patients in beds, 32" otherwise	same as above	
20'	36" within dwellings, 44" elsewhere	32"	same as above	Window egress is required from sleeping rooms—see page 261.
20'	36"	32"	same as above	Window egress is required from sleeping rooms—see page 261.
20'	44"	32"	same as above	

†A second story of a building must have at least two exits when the occupant load is 10 or more persons.

QUANTITIES FOR DETERMINING WIDTHS OF EGRESS COMPONENTS

USE GROUP (see index on page 11 for specific uses)	Occupant Load: Square Feet per Occupant	Exit Width in Feet
A-1: ASSEMBLY BUILDING WITH STAGE AND WITH OCCUPANT LOAD OF 1000 OR MORE	7	Occupant load divided by 50
A-2, A-2.1, A-3, A-4: ASSEMBLY	7 for concentrated seating, 15 for other uses	same as above
B-1: SERVICE STATIONS AND GARAGES	100	same as above
B-2: OFFICES	100	same as above
B-2: DRINKING AND DINING ESTABLISHMENTS	15	same as above
B-2: STORES	20 in basement, 30 on ground floor, 50 on upper floors, 300 in storerooms and stockrooms	same as above
B-2: SHOPPING MALLS	30 for up to 150,000 sq ft of gross leasable area, 40 for 150,001 to 350,000 sq ft, 50 for more than 350,000 sq ft	same, with 66" minimum width
B-2: WORKSHOPS AND FACTORIES	200	Occupant load divided by 50
B-2: CLASSROOMS	20	same as above
B-3: AIRCRAFT HANGARS, NO REPAIRS	500	same as above
B-4: INDUSTRIAL, LOW HAZARD	200	same as above
E: EDUCATIONAL	20 for classrooms, 50 for shops	same as above
H-1 and H-2: HAZARDOUS	200 for manufacturing, 300 for storage	same as above
H-3, H-4, H-5: HAZARDOUS	same as above	same as above
H-6: HAZARDOUS	same as above	same as above
I-1, I-2, I-3: INSTITUTIONAL	80	same as above
R-1: HOTELS, APARTMENT HOUSES, CONVENTS, MONASTERIES	200	same as above
R-3: DWELLINGS AND LODGING HOUSES	300	same as above
OPEN PARKING GARAGES	200	same as above

AN EXAMPLE OF THE USE OF THIS CHART

The Problem: Design an exit for a department store basement, sprinklered, dimensions 100 × 208 ft.

The Solution: From the index on page 11, we find that a department store belongs to Use Group B-2, Stores. Multiplying the two dimensions of the building, we arrive at a gross floor area of 20,800 sq ft. From the table on the facing page we see that for purposes of designing the exits we must allocate 20 sq ft per occupant, to arrive at an occupant load of 1040 for this floor. Assume that our design provides four exits, which is the minimum permitted for this building according to the table on page 261. Dividing 1040 occupants by 4 exits gives an occupant load per exit of 260.

Moving to the chart on this page, we read horizontally from 260 occupants to the diagonal line, then downward, to find that a width of 65 in. is required for the corridor and stairway. Extending this line farther downward, we select three 3-ft doors, two 3-ft, 4-in. doors, or a pair of 3-ft doors without center mullion. (For stair design tables, see pages 273–283.)

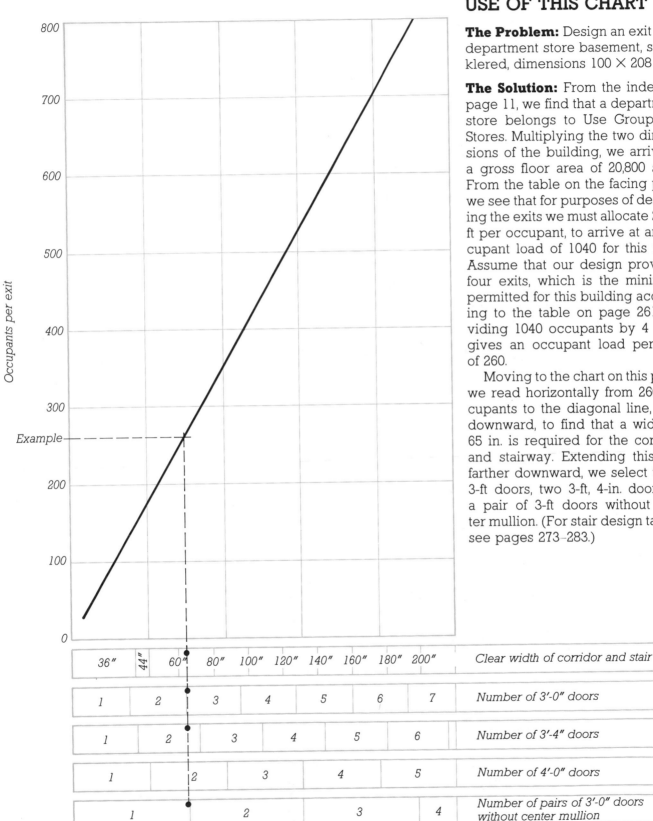

	Clear width of corridor and stair
36″ 44″ 60″ 80″ 100″ 120″ 140″ 160″ 180″ 200″	

							Number of 3′-0″ doors
1	2	3	4	5	6	7	

						Number of 3′-4″ doors
1	2	3	4	5	6	

					Number of 4′-0″ doors
1	2	3	4	5	

				Number of pairs of 3′-0″ doors without center mullion
1	2	3	4	

SIZING THE EGRESS SYSTEM

265

STAIRWAY AND RAMP DESIGN

This section will help you design stairways and ramps in accordance with the model building codes.

STAIRWAY PROPORTIONS

| | Buildings Other Than Single-Family Residential | | | | | Single-Family Residential | |
	Maximum Riser Height (R)	Minimum Tread Depth (T)	Proportioning Formula	Maximum Rise between Landings	Minimum Number of Risers per Flight	Maximum Riser Height	Minimum Tread Depth
BOCA National Building Code	7"	11"	none	12'	no requirement	8.25"	9"
National Building Code of Canada	200 mm	230 mm	none	3.7 m	3	200 mm	230 mm
Standard Building Code	7.75"	9"	2R+T=24 to 25	12'	3 in Group A occupancies	7.75"	9"
Uniform Building Code	7"	11"	none	12'	2 in aisles of assembly occupanices	8"	9"

Stairway widths may be determined rapidly by using the tables and graphs on pages 239–265.

RAMP PROPORTIONS

	Maximum Ramp Slope for Required Exits	Landing Requirements
BOCA National Building Code	1:8 (Requirements for handicapped ramps are more complex; 1:12 is a good rule of thumb.)	Landings are required at points of turning, ramp entrances, ramp exits, and doors opening onto ramps. The maximum rise between landings is 12' for slopes steeper than 1:10 and 30" for handicapped ramps. The minimum length of a landing is 60".
National Building Code of Canada	1:10 for Use Groups A, B, and C; 1:6 for Use Groups E and F; 1:8 for interior ramps other than required exit ramps; 1:10 for outdoor ramps.	Landings are required at side entrances to ramps. The width of the landing must not be less than the width of the entrance opening plus 300 mm on each side of the opening.
Standard Building Code	1:8 (1:12 for handicapped ramps.)	Ramps steeper than 1:15 must have landings top and bottom and an intermediate landing for every 5' of rise. The top and intermediate landings must be at least 5' long and the bottom landing at least 6' long.
Uniform Building Code	1:12 (1:8 for ramps other than required exit ramps.)	Ramps steeper than 1:15 must have landings top and bottom and an intermediate landing for every 5' of rise. The top and intermediate landings must be at least 5' long and the bottom landing at least 6' long.

CURVED AND SPIRAL STAIRS

	May a curved stair serve as a required exit?	Dimensional Restrictions
BOCA National Building Code	Yes.	Risers may not exceed 7″ in height, and treads may not be less than 11″ deep. The smaller radius of the stair may not be less than twice the width of the stair.
National Building Code of Canada	No, unless the stair conforms fully to the dimensional requirements for exit stairs.	If the stair is not a required exit, risers may not exceed 200 mm in height, treads may not be less than 150 mm in depth, and the tread depth must average at least 200 mm.
Standard Building Code	Yes.	The tread depth may not be less than 10″ at any point. The smaller radius of the stair may not be less than twice the width of the stair.
Uniform Building Code	Yes.	The tread depth may not be less than 10″ at any point. The smaller radius of the stair may not be less than twice the width of the stair.

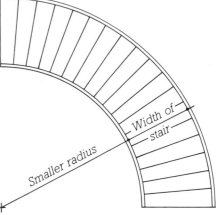

CURVED STAIR

	May a spiral stair serve as a required exit?	Dimensional Restrictions
BOCA National Building Code	A spiral stair may serve as a required exit only within a dwelling unit, for 1- and 2-family dwellings, and for mezzanines not larger than 250 sq ft with not more than 5 occupants.	The tread may not measure less than 7.5″ at a distance of 12″ from the narrow end of the tread. The riser height may not exceed 9.5″. The clear width of the stair must be at least 27″.
National Building Code of Canada	No.	The tread may not measure less than 150 mm in depth at any point, and the tread depth must average at least 200 mm. The riser height may not exceed 200 mm.
Standard Building Code	A spiral stair may serve as a required exit only within a dwelling unit, for 1- and 2-family dwellings, and for mezzanines not larger than 250 sq ft with not more than 5 occupants.	The tread may not measure less than 7.5″ at a distance of 12″ from the narrow end of the tread. The riser height may not exceed 9.5″. The clear width of the stair must be at least 27″.
Uniform Building Code	A spiral stair may serve as a required exit for an area not larger than 400 sq ft within a single dwelling unit.	The tread may not measure less than 7.5″ at a distance of 12″ from the narrow end of the tread. The riser height may not exceed 9.5″. The clear width of the stair must be at least 26″.

SPIRAL STAIR

WINDING STAIRS

	May winders be used in a required exit stairway?	Dimensional Restrictions
BOCA National Building Code	Winders may be used in a required exit stairway only within a dwelling unit and for 1- and 2-family dwellings.	The tread may not measure less than 9″ at a distance of 12″ from the narrow end. The narrow end of the tread may not be less than 6″ in depth.
National Building Code of Canada	No.	Winders may be used within dwelling units only. Treads may converge to a point. The angle of each tread may not be less than 30°, and the maximum total angle of winders per floor may not exceed 90°.
Standard Building Code	Winders may be used in a required exit stairway only within a dwelling unit and for 1- and 2-family dwellings.	The tread may not measure less than 9″ at a distance of 12″ from the narrow end. The narrow end of the tread may not be less than 6″ in depth.
Uniform Building Code	Winders may be used in a required exit stairway only within a dwelling unit.	The tread may not measure less than 9″ at a distance of 12″ from the narrow end. The narrow end of the tread may not be less than 6″ in depth.

Winders

WINDERS

EXIT STAIRWAY DESIGN TABLES

The tables that follow allow you to make a very rapid preliminary design for an exit stairway. After selecting the desired stairway configuration, consult an accompanying table to find the required interior dimensions and the tread and riser proportions of a stairway that corresponds to the stair width and floor-to-floor height for which you are designing.

The tread and riser proportions on which the English-unit tables are based conform to the requirements of the BOCA National Building Code and the Uniform Building Code. If you are working under the Standard Building Code, a somewhat steeper stairway, and therefore a somewhat smaller stairway enclosure, is possible. The metric stairway tables for the National Building Code of Canada take partial advantage of the more permissive tread and riser restrictions of that code, but do not represent the steepest stairs that are legally possible.

The "Overall Inside Length of Stair Enclosure" figures represent an absolute minimum configuration. The handrail extension requirements of the Uniform Building Code and the National Building Code of Canada will usually dictate either that the door be recessed into an alcove that falls outside this length or that the length of the stair enclosure be increased, in order to satisfy the limitations on obstruction of the width of the landing by the open door. The minimum overall inside width for a stair enclosure is twice the required width of the stair itself, but construction of the stair may be facilitated by increasing this dimension by several inches. Under all four model building codes, the handrails may be included within the required width of the stair for purposes of computing its occupant capacity.

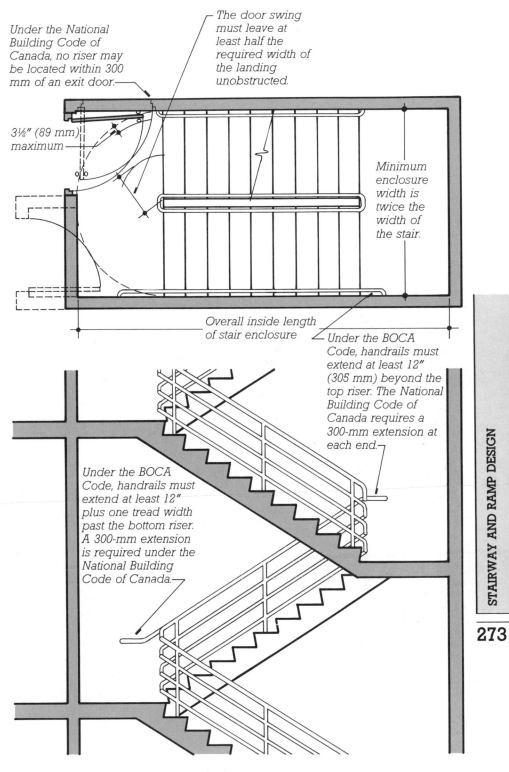

Under the National Building Code of Canada, no riser may be located within 300 mm of an exit door.

3½" (89 mm) maximum

The door swing must leave at least half the required width of the landing unobstructed.

Minimum enclosure width is twice the width of the stair.

Overall inside length of stair enclosure

Under the BOCA Code, handrails must extend at least 12" (305 mm) beyond the top riser. The National Building Code of Canada requires a 300-mm extension at each end.

Under the BOCA Code, handrails must extend at least 12" plus one tread width past the bottom riser. A 300-mm extension is required under the National Building Code of Canada.

ONE-FLIGHT STAIR

ONE-FLIGHT STAIR: ENGLISH UNITS

Floor-to-Floor Height (ft-in.)	Number of Risers	Riser Height (in.)	Tread Depth (in.)	Overall Inside Length of Stair Enclosure (ft-in.)				
				36" Width	44" Width	56" Width	66" Width	88" Width
1-8	3	6.67	11	7-10	9-2	11-2	12-10	16-6
2-0	4	6.00	11	8-9	10-1	12-1	13-9	17-5
2-4	4	7.00	11	8-9	10-1	12-1	13-9	17-5
2-8	5	6.40	11	9-8	11-0	13-0	14-8	18-4
3-0	6	6.00	11	10-7	11-11	13-11	15-7	19-3
3-4	6	6.67	11	10-7	11-11	13-11	15-7	19-3
3-8	7	6.29	11	11-6	12-10	14-10	16-6	20-2
4-0	7	6.86	11	11-6	12-10	14-10	16-6	20-2
4-4	8	6.50	11	12-5	13-9	15-9	17-5	21-1
4-8	8	7.00	11	12-5	13-9	15-9	17-5	21-1
5-0	9	6.67	11	13-4	14-8	16-8	18-4	22-0
5-4	10	6.40	11	14-3	15-7	17-7	19-3	22-11
5-8	10	6.80	11	14-3	15-7	17-7	19-3	22-11
6-0	11	6.55	11	15-2	16-6	18-6	20-2	23-10
6-4	11	6.91	11	15-2	16-6	18-6	20-2	23-10
6-8	12	6.67	11	16-1	17-5	19-5	21-1	24-9
7-0	12	7.00	11	16-1	17-5	19-5	21-1	24-9
7-4	13	6.77	11	17-0	18-4	20-4	22-0	25-8
7-8	14	6.57	11	17-11	19-3	21-3	22-0	26-7
8-0	14	6.86	11	17-11	19-3	21-3	22-11	26-7
8-4	15	6.67	11	18-10	20-2	22-2	23-10	27-6
8-8	15	6.93	11	18-10	20-2	22-2	23-10	27-6
9-0	16	6.75	11	19-9	21-1	23-1	24-9	28-5
9-4	16	7.00	11	19-9	21-1	23-1	24-9	28-5
9-8	17	6.82	11	20-8	22-0	24-0	25-8	29-4
10-0	18	6.67	11	21-7	22-11	24-11	26-7	30-3
10-4	18	6.89	11	21-7	22-11	24-11	26-7	30-3
10-8	19	6.74	11	22-6	23-10	25-10	27-6	31-2
11-0	19	6.95	11	22-6	23-10	25-10	27-6	31-2
11-4	20	6.80	11	23-5	24-9	26-9	28-5	32-1
11-8	20	7.00	11	23-5	24-9	26-9	28-5	32-1
12-0	21	6.86	11	24-4	25-8	27-8	29-4	33-0

Stairway widths may be determined rapidly by using the tables and graphs on pages 239–265.

ONE-FLIGHT STAIR

ONE-FLIGHT STAIR: METRIC UNITS

Floor-to-Floor Height (m)	Number of Risers	Riser Height (mm)	Tread Depth (mm)	Overall Inside Length of Stair Enclosure (m)				
				900-mm Width	1100-mm Width	1400-mm Width	1650-mm Width	2200-mm Width
0.500	3	167	280	2.360	2.760	3.360	3.860	4.960
0.600	4	150	280	2.640	3.040	3.640	4.140	5.240
0.700	4	180	280	2.640	3.040	3.640	4.140	5.240
0.800	5	160	280	2.920	3.320	3.920	4.420	5.520
0.900	5	180	280	2.920	3.320	3.920	4.420	5.520
1.000	6	167	280	3.200	3.600	4.200	4.700	5.800
1.100	6	183	280	3.200	3.600	4.200	4.700	5.800
1.200	7	171	280	3.480	3.880	4.480	4.980	6.080
1.300	7	186	280	3.480	3.880	4.480	4.980	6.080
1.400	8	175	280	3.760	4.160	4.760	5.260	6.360
1.500	8	188	280	3.760	4.160	4.760	5.260	6.360
1.600	9	178	280	4.040	4.440	5.040	5.540	6.640
1.700	10	170	280	4.320	4.720	5.320	5.820	6.920
1.800	10	180	280	4.320	4.720	5.320	5.820	6.920
1.900	11	173	280	4.600	5.000	5.600	6.100	7.200
2.000	11	182	280	4.600	5.000	5.600	6.100	7.200
2.100	12	175	280	4.880	5.280	5.880	6.380	7.480
2.200	12	183	280	4.880	5.280	5.880	6.380	7.480
2.300	13	177	280	5.160	5.560	6.160	6.660	7.760
2.400	13	185	280	5.160	5.560	6.160	6.660	7.760
2.500	14	179	280	5.440	5.840	6.440	6.940	8.040
2.600	14	186	280	5.440	5.840	6.440	6.940	8.040
2.700	15	180	280	5.720	6.120	6.720	7.220	8.320
2.800	15	187	280	5.720	6.120	6.720	7.220	8.320
2.900	16	181	280	6.000	6.400	7.000	7.500	8.600
3.000	16	188	280	6.000	6.400	7.000	7.500	8.600
3.100	17	182	280	6.280	6.680	7.280	7.780	8.880
3.200	18	178	280	6.560	6.960	7.560	8.060	9.160
3.300	18	183	280	6.560	6.960	7.560	8.060	9.160
3.400	19	179	280	6.840	7.240	7.840	8.340	9.440
3.500	19	184	280	6.840	7.240	7.840	8.340	9.440
3.600	20	180	280	7.120	7.520	8.120	8.620	9.720
3.700	20	185	280	7.120	7.520	8.120	8.620	9.720

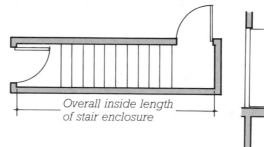

Overall inside length of stair enclosure

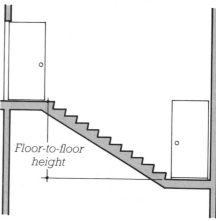

Floor-to-floor height

TWO-FLIGHT STAIR

TWO-FLIGHT STAIR: ENGLISH UNITS

Floor-to-Floor Height (ft-in.)	Number of Risers	Riser Height (in.)	Tread Depth (in.)	Overall Inside Length of Stair Enclosure (ft-in.)				
				36" Width	44" Width	56" Width	66" Width	88" Width
7-8*	14	6.57	11	11-6	12-10	14-10	16-6	20-2
8-0*	14	6.86	11	11-6	12-10	14-10	16-6	20-2
8-4	15	6.67	11	12-5	13-9	15-9	17-5	21-1
8-8	15	6.93	11	12-5	13-9	15-9	17-5	21-1
9-0	16	6.75	11	12-5	13-9	15-9	17-5	21-1
9-4	16	7.00	11	12-5	13-9	15-9	17-5	21-1
9-8	17	6.82	11	13-4	14-8	16-8	18-4	22-0
10-0	18	6.67	11	13-4	14-8	16-8	18-4	22-0
10-4	18	6.89	11	13-4	14-8	16-8	18-4	22-0
10-8	19	6.74	11	14-3	15-7	17-7	19-3	22-11
11-0	19	6.95	11	14-3	15-7	17-7	19-3	22-11
11-4	20	6.80	11	14-3	15-7	17-7	19-3	22-11
11-8	20	7.00	11	14-3	15-7	17-7	19-3	22-11
12-0	21	6.86	11	15-2	16-6	18-6	20-2	23-10
12-4	22	6.73	11	15-2	16-6	18-6	20-2	23-10
12-8	22	6.91	11	15-2	16-6	18-6	20-2	23-10
13-0	23	6.78	11	16-1	17-5	19-5	21-1	24-9
13-4	23	6.96	11	16-1	17-5	19-5	21-1	24-9
13-8	24	6.83	11	16-1	17-5	19-5	21-1	24-9
14-0	24	7.00	11	16-1	17-5	19-5	21-1	24-9
14-4	25	6.88	11	17-0	18-4	20-4	22-0	25-8
14-8	26	6.77	11	17-0	18-4	20-4	22-0	25-8
15-0	26	6.92	11	17-0	18-4	20-4	22-0	25-8
16-0	28	6.86	11	17-11	19-3	21-3	22-11	26-7
17-0	30	6.80	11	18-10	20-2	22-2	23-10	27-6
18-0	31	6.97	11	19-9	21-1	23-1	24-9	28-5
19-0	33	6.91	11	20-8	22-0	24-0	25-8	29-4
20-0	35	6.86	11	21-7	22-11	24-11	26-7	30-3
21-0	36	7.00	11	21-7	22-11	24-11	26-7	30-3
22-0	38	6.95	11	22-6	23-10	25-10	27-6	31-2
23-0	40	6.90	11	23-5	24-9	26-9	28-5	32-1
24-0	42	6.86	11	24-4	25-8	27-8	29-4	33-0

*The headroom in these stairs may be deficient, depending on the detailing of the stair structure.

Stairway widths may be determined rapidly by using the tables and graphs on pages 239–265.

TWO-FLIGHT STAIR

TWO-FLIGHT STAIR: METRIC UNITS

Floor-to-Floor Height (m)	Number of Risers	Riser Height (mm)	Tread Depth (mm)	Overall Inside Length of Stair Enclosure (m)				
				900-mm Width	1100-mm Width	1400-mm Width	1650-mm Width	2200-mm Width
2.300	13	177	280	3.480	3.880	4.480	4.980	6.080
2.400	13	185	280	3.480	3.880	4.480	4.980	6.080
2.500	14	179	280	3.480	3.880	4.480	4.980	6.080
2.600	14	186	280	3.480	3.880	4.480	4.980	6.080
2.700	15	180	280	3.760	4.160	4.760	5.260	6.360
2.800	15	187	280	3.760	4.160	4.760	5.260	6.360
2.900	16	181	280	3.760	4.160	4.760	5.260	6.360
3.000	16	188	280	3.760	4.160	4.760	5.260	6.360
3.100	17	182	280	4.040	4.440	5.040	5.540	6.640
3.200	18	178	280	4.040	4.440	5.040	5.540	6.640
3.300	18	183	280	4.040	4.440	5.040	5.540	6.640
3.400	19	179	280	4.320	4.720	5.320	5.820	6.920
3.500	19	184	280	4.320	4.720	5.320	5.820	6.920
3.600	20	180	280	4.320	4.720	5.320	5.820	6.920
3.700	20	185	280	4.320	4.720	5.320	5.820	6.920
3.800	21	181	280	4.600	5.000	5.600	6.100	7.200
3.900	21	186	280	4.600	5.000	5.600	6.100	7.200
4.000	22	182	280	4.600	5.000	5.600	6.100	7.200
4.100	23	178	280	4.880	5.280	5.880	6.380	7.480
4.200	23	183	280	4.880	5.280	5.880	6.380	7.480
4.300	24	179	280	4.880	5.280	5.880	6.380	7.480
4.400	24	183	280	4.880	5.280	5.880	6.380	7.480
4.500	25	180	280	5.160	5.560	6.160	6.660	7.760
4.800	26	185	280	5.160	5.560	6.160	6.660	7.760
5.100	28	182	280	5.440	5.840	6.440	6.940	8.040
5.400	29	186	280	5.720	6.120	6.720	7.220	8.320
5.700	31	184	280	6.000	6.400	7.000	7.500	8.600
6.000	33	182	280	6.280	6.680	7.280	7.780	8.880
6.300	35	180	280	6.560	6.960	7.560	8.060	9.160
6.600	37	178	280	6.840	7.240	7.840	8.340	9.440
6.900	38	182	280	6.840	7.240	7.840	8.340	9.440
7.200	40	180	280	7.120	7.520	8.120	8.620	9.720

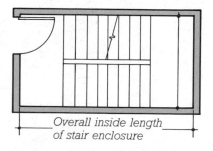

Overall inside length of stair enclosure

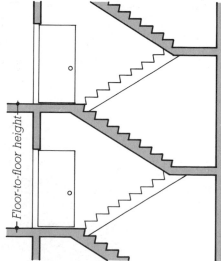

Floor-to-floor height

THREE-FLIGHT STAIR

THREE-FLIGHT STAIR: ENGLISH UNITS

Floor-to-Floor Height (ft-in.)	Number of Risers	Riser Height (in.)	Tread Depth (in.)	Overall Inside Length of Stair Enclosure (ft-in.)				
				36" Width	44" Width	56" Width	66" Width	88" Width
12-0	21	6.86	11	11-6	12-10	14-10	16-6	20-2
12-4	22	6.73	11	12-5	13-9	15-9	17-5	21-1
12-8	22	6.91	11	12-5	13-9	15-9	17-5	21-1
13-0	23	6.78	11	12-5	13-9	15-9	17-5	21-1
13-4	23	6.96	11	12-5	13-9	15-9	17-5	21-1
13-8	24	6.83	11	12-5	13-9	15-9	17-5	21-1
14-0	24	7.00	11	12-5	13-9	15-9	17-5	21-1
14-4	25	6.88	11	13-4	14-8	16-8	18-4	22-0
14-8	26	6.77	11	13-4	14-8	16-8	18-4	22-0
15-0	26	6.92	11	13-4	14-8	16-8	18-4	22-0
16-0	28	6.86	11	14-3	15-7	17-7	19-3	22-11
17-0	30	6.80	11	14-3	15-7	17-7	19-3	22-11
18-0	31	6.97	11	15-2	16-6	18-6	20-2	23-10
19-0	33	6.91	11	15-2	16-6	18-6	20-2	23-10
20-0	35	6.86	11	16-1	17-5	19-5	21-1	24-9
21-0	36	7.00	11	16-1	17-5	19-5	21-1	24-9
22-0	38	6.95	11	17-0	18-4	20-4	22-0	25-8
23-0	40	6.90	11	17-11	19-3	21-3	22-11	26-7
24-0	42	6.86	11	17-11	19-3	21-3	22-11	26-7

Stairway widths may be determined rapidly by using the tables and graphs on pages 239–265.

THREE-FLIGHT STAIR

THREE-FLIGHT STAIR: METRIC UNITS

Floor-to-Floor Height (m)	Number of Risers	Riser Height (mm)	Tread Depth (mm)	Overall Inside Length of Stair Enclosure (m)				
				900-mm Width	1100-mm Width	1400-mm Width	1650-mm Width	2200-mm Width
3.600	20	180	280	3.480	3.880	4.480	4.980	6.080
3.700	20	185	280	3.480	3.880	4.480	4.980	6.080
3.800	21	181	280	3.480	3.880	4.480	4.980	6.080
3.900	21	186	280	3.480	3.880	4.480	4.980	6.080
4.000	22	182	280	3.760	4.160	4.760	5.260	6.360
4.100	23	178	280	3.760	4.160	4.760	5.260	6.360
4.200	23	183	280	3.760	4.160	4.760	5.260	6.360
4.300	24	179	280	3.760	4.160	4.760	5.260	6.360
4.400	24	183	280	3.760	4.160	4.760	5.260	6.360
4.500	25	180	280	4.040	4.440	5.040	5.540	6.640
4.800	26	185	280	4.040	4.440	5.040	5.540	6.640
5.100	28	182	280	4.320	4.720	5.320	5.820	6.920
5.400	29	186	280	4.320	4.720	5.320	5.820	6.920
5.700	31	184	280	4.600	5.000	5.600	6.100	7.200
6.000	33	182	280	4.600	5.000	5.600	6.100	7.200
6.300	35	180	280	4.880	5.280	5.880	6.380	7.480
6.600	37	178	280	5.160	5.560	6.160	6.660	7.760
6.900	38	182	280	5.160	5.560	6.160	6.660	7.760
7.200	40	180	280	5.440	5.840	6.440	6.940	8.040

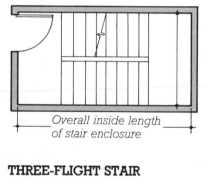

Overall inside length of stair enclosure

THREE-FLIGHT STAIR

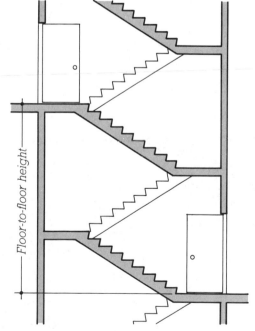

Floor-to-floor height

FOUR-FLIGHT STAIR

FOUR-FLIGHT STAIR: ENGLISH UNITS

Floor-to-Floor Height (ft-in.)	Number of Risers	Riser Height (in.)	Tread Depth (in.)	Overall Inside Length of Stair Enclosure (ft-in.)				
				36" Width	44" Width	56" Width	66" Width	88" Width
16-0	28	6.86	11	11-6	12-10	14-10	16-6	20-2
17-0	30	6.80	11	12-5	13-9	15-9	17-5	21-1
18-0	31	6.97	11	12-5	13-9	15-9	17-5	21-1
19-0	33	6.91	11	13-4	14-8	16-8	18-4	22-0
20-0	35	6.86	11	13-4	14-8	16-8	18-4	22-0
21-0	36	7.00	11	13-4	14-8	16-8	18-4	22-0
22-0	38	6.95	11	14-3	15-7	17-7	19-3	22-11
23-0	40	6.90	11	14-3	15-7	17-7	19-3	22-11
24-0	42	6.86	11	15-2	16-6	18-6	20-2	23-10

Stairway widths may be determined rapidly by using the tables and graphs on pages 239–265.

FOUR-FLIGHT STAIR

FOUR-FLIGHT STAIR: METRIC UNITS

Floor-to-Floor Height (m)	Number of Risers	Riser Height (mm)	Tread Depth (mm)	Overall Inside Length of Stair Enclosure (m)				
				900-mm Width	1100-mm Width	1400-mm Width	1650-mm Width	2200-mm Width
4.800	26	185	280	3.480	3.880	4.480	4.980	6.080
5.100	28	182	280	3.480	3.880	4.480	4.980	6.080
5.400	29	186	280	3.760	4.160	4.760	5.260	6.360
5.700	31	184	280	3.760	4.160	4.760	5.260	6.360
6.000	33	182	280	4.040	4.440	5.040	5.540	6.640
6.300	35	180	280	4.040	4.440	5.040	5.540	6.640
6.600	37	178	280	4.320	4.720	5.320	5.820	6.920
6.900	38	182	280	4.320	4.720	5.320	5.820	6.920
7.200	40	180	280	4.320	4.720	5.320	5.820	6.920

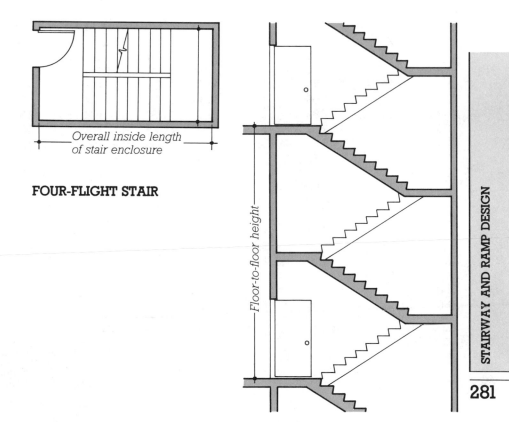

Overall inside length of stair enclosure

Floor-to-floor height

FOUR-FLIGHT STAIR

STAIRWAY AND RAMP DESIGN

281

DOUGHNUT STAIR

DOUGHNUT STAIR: ENGLISH UNITS

Floor-to-Floor Height (ft-in.)	Number of Risers	Riser Height (in.)	Tread Depth (in.)	Overall Inside Dimensions of Stair Enclosure—Length × Width (ft-in.)				
				36" Width	44" Width	56" Width	66" Width	88" Width
7-8	14	6.57	11	7-10 × 8-9	9-2 × 10-1	11-2 × 12-1	12-10 × 13-9	16-6 × 17-5
8-0	14	6.86	11	7-10 × 8-9	9-2 × 10-1	11-2 × 12-1	12-10 × 13-9	16-6 × 17-5
8-4	15	6.67	11	8-9 × 8-9	10-1 × 10-1	12-1 × 12-1	13-9 × 13-9	17-5 × 17-5
8-8	15	6.93	11	8-9 × 8-9	10-1 × 10-1	12-1 × 12-1	13-9 × 13-9	17-5 × 17-5
9-0	16	6.75	11	8-9 × 8-9	10-1 × 10-1	12-1 × 12-1	13-9 × 13-9	17-5 × 17-5
9-4	16	7.00	11	8-9 × 8-9	10-1 × 10-1	12-1 × 12-1	13-9 × 13-9	17-5 × 17-5
9-8	17	6.82	11	8-9 × 9-8	10-1 × 11-0	12-1 × 13-0	13-9 × 14-8	17-5 × 18-4
10-0	18	6.67	11	8-9 × 9-8	10-1 × 11-0	12-1 × 13-0	13-9 × 14-8	17-5 × 18-4
10-4	18	6.89	11	8-9 × 9-8	10-1 × 11-0	12-1 × 13-0	13-9 × 14-8	17-5 × 18-4
10-8	19	6.74	11	9-8 × 9-8	11-0 × 11-0	13-0 × 13-0	14-8 × 14-8	18-4 × 18-4
11-0	19	6.95	11	9-8 × 9-8	11-0 × 11-0	13-0 × 13-0	14-8 × 14-8	18-4 × 18-4
11-4	20	6.80	11	9-8 × 9-8	11-0 × 11-0	13-0 × 13-0	14-8 × 14-8	18-4 × 18-4
11-8	20	7.00	11	9-8 × 9-8	11-0 × 11-0	13-0 × 13-0	14-8 × 14-8	18-4 × 18-4
12-0	21	6.86	11	9-8 × 10-7	11-0 × 11-11	13-0 × 13-11	14-8 × 15-7	18-4 × 19-3
12-4	22	6.73	11	9-8 × 10-7	11-0 × 11-11	13-0 × 13-11	14-8 × 15-7	18-4 × 19-3
12-8	22	6.91	11	9-8 × 10-7	11-0 × 11-11	13-0 × 13-11	14-8 × 15-7	18-4 × 19-3
13-0	23	6.78	11	10-7 × 10-7	11-11 × 11-11	13-11 × 13-11	15-7 × 15-7	19-3 × 19-3
13-4	23	6.96	11	10-7 × 10-7	11-11 × 11-11	13-11 × 13-11	15-7 × 15-7	19-3 × 19-3
13-8	24	6.83	11	10-7 × 10-7	11-11 × 11-11	13-11 × 13-11	15-7 × 15-7	19-3 × 19-3
14-0	24	7.00	11	10-7 × 10-7	11-11 × 11-11	13-11 × 13-11	15-7 × 15-7	19-3 × 19-3
14-4	25	6.88	11	10-7 × 11-6	11-11 × 12-10	13-11 × 14-10	15-7 × 16-6	19-3 × 20-2
14-8	26	6.77	11	10-7 × 11-6	11-11 × 12-10	13-11 × 14-10	15-7 × 16-6	19-3 × 20-2
15-0	26	6.92	11	10-7 × 11-6	11-11 × 12-10	13-11 × 14-10	15-7 × 16-6	19-3 × 20-2
16-0	28	6.86	11	11-6 × 11-6	12-10 × 12-10	14-10 × 14-10	16-6 × 16-6	20-2 × 20-2
17-0	30	6.80	11	11-6 × 12-5	12-10 × 13-9	14-10 × 15-9	16-6 × 17-5	20-2 × 21-1
18-0	31	6.97	11	12-5 × 12-5	13-9 × 13-9	15-9 × 15-9	17-5 × 17-5	21-1 × 21-1
19-0	33	6.91	11	12-5 × 13-4	13-9 × 14-8	15-9 × 16-8	17-5 × 18-4	21-1 × 22-0
20-0	35	6.86	11	13-4 × 13-4	14-8 × 14-8	16-8 × 16-8	18-4 × 18-4	22-0 × 22-0
21-0	36	7.00	11	13-4 × 13-4	14-8 × 14-8	16-8 × 16-8	18-4 × 18-4	22-0 × 22-0
22-0	38	6.95	11	13-4 × 14-3	14-8 × 15-7	16-8 × 17-7	18-4 × 19-3	22-0 × 22-11
23-0	40	6.90	11	14-3 × 14-3	15-7 × 15-7	17-7 × 17-7	19-3 × 19-3	22-11 × 22-11
24-0	42	6.86	11	14-3 × 15-2	15-7 × 16-6	17-7 × 18-6	19-3 × 20-2	22-11 × 23-10

Stairway widths may be determined rapidly by using the tables and graphs on pages 239–265.

DOUGHNUT STAIR

DOUGHNUT STAIR: METRIC UNITS

Floor-to-Floor Height (m)	Number of Risers	Riser Height (mm)	Tread Depth (mm)	Overall Inside Dimensions of Stair Enclosure—Length × Width (m)				
				900-mm Width	1100-mm Width	1400-mm Width	1650-mm Width	2200-mm Width
2.300	13	177	280	2.360 × 2.640	2.760 × 3.040	3.360 × 3.640	3.860 × 4.140	4.960 × 5.240
2.400	13	185	280	2.360 × 2.640	2.760 × 3.040	3.360 × 3.640	3.860 × 4.140	4.960 × 5.240
2.500	14	179	280	2.360 × 2.640	2.760 × 3.040	3.360 × 3.640	3.860 × 4.140	4.960 × 5.240
2.600	14	186	280	2.360 × 2.640	2.760 × 3.040	3.360 × 3.640	3.860 × 4.140	4.960 × 5.240
2.700	15	180	280	2.640 × 2.640	3.040 × 3.040	3.640 × 3.640	4.140 × 4.140	5.240 × 5.240
2.800	15	187	280	2.640 × 2.640	3.040 × 3.040	3.640 × 3.640	4.140 × 4.140	5.240 × 5.240
2.900	16	181	280	2.640 × 2.640	3.040 × 3.040	3.640 × 3.640	4.140 × 4.140	5.240 × 5.240
3.000	16	188	280	2.640 × 2.640	3.040 × 3.040	3.640 × 3.640	4.140 × 4.140	5.240 × 5.240
3.100	17	182	280	2.640 × 2.920	3.040 × 3.320	3.640 × 3.920	4.140 × 4.420	5.240 × 5.520
3.200	18	178	280	2.640 × 2.920	3.040 × 3.320	3.640 × 3.920	4.140 × 4.420	5.240 × 5.520
3.300	18	183	280	2.640 × 2.920	3.040 × 3.320	3.640 × 3.920	4.140 × 4.420	5.240 × 5.520
3.400	19	179	280	2.920 × 2.920	3.320 × 3.320	3.920 × 3.920	4.420 × 4.420	5.520 × 5.520
3.500	19	184	280	2.920 × 2.920	3.320 × 3.320	3.920 × 3.920	4.420 × 4.420	5.520 × 5.520
3.600	20	180	280	2.920 × 2.920	3.320 × 3.320	3.920 × 3.920	4.420 × 4.420	5.520 × 5.520
3.700	20	185	280	2.920 × 2.920	3.320 × 3.320	3.920 × 3.920	4.420 × 4.420	5.520 × 5.520
3.800	21	181	280	2.920 × 3.200	3.320 × 3.600	3.920 × 4.200	4.420 × 4.700	5.520 × 5.800
3.900	21	186	280	2.920 × 3.200	3.320 × 3.600	3.920 × 4.200	4.420 × 4.700	5.520 × 5.800
4.000	22	182	280	2.920 × 3.200	3.320 × 3.600	3.920 × 4.200	4.420 × 4.700	5.520 × 5.800
4.100	23	178	280	3.200 × 3.200	3.600 × 3.600	4.200 × 4.200	4.700 × 4.700	5.800 × 5.800
4.200	23	183	280	3.200 × 3.200	3.600 × 3.600	4.200 × 4.200	4.700 × 4.700	5.800 × 5.800
4.300	24	179	280	3.200 × 3.200	3.600 × 3.600	4.200 × 4.200	4.700 × 4.700	5.800 × 5.800
4.400	24	183	280	3.200 × 3.200	3.600 × 3.600	4.200 × 4.200	4.700 × 4.700	5.800 × 5.800
4.500	25	180	280	3.200 × 3.480	3.600 × 3.880	4.200 × 4.480	4.700 × 4.980	5.800 × 6.080
4.800	26	185	280	3.200 × 3.480	3.600 × 3.880	4.200 × 4.480	4.700 × 4.980	5.800 × 6.080
5.100	28	182	280	3.480 × 3.480	3.880 × 3.880	4.480 × 4.480	4.980 × 4.980	6.080 × 6.080
5.400	29	186	280	3.480 × 3.760	3.880 × 4.160	4.480 × 4.760	4.980 × 5.260	6.080 × 6.360
5.700	31	184	280	3.760 × 3.760	4.160 × 4.160	4.760 × 4.760	5.260 × 5.260	6.360 × 6.360
6.000	33	182	280	3.760 × 4.040	4.160 × 4.440	4.760 × 5.040	5.260 × 5.540	6.360 × 6.640
6.300	35	180	280	4.040 × 4.040	4.440 × 4.440	5.040 × 5.040	5.540 × 5.540	6.640 × 6.640
6.600	37	178	280	4.040 × 4.320	4.440 × 4.720	5.040 × 5.320	5.540 × 5.820	6.640 × 6.920
6.900	38	182	280	4.040 × 4.320	4.440 × 4.720	5.040 × 5.320	5.540 × 5.820	6.640 × 6.920
7.200	40	180	280	4.320 × 4.320	4.720 × 4.720	5.320 × 5.320	5.820 × 5.820	6.920 × 6.920

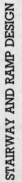
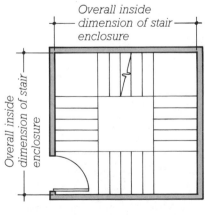

Overall inside dimension of stair enclosure

Overall inside dimension of stair enclosure

DOUGHNUT STAIR

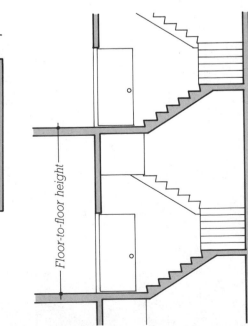

Floor-to-floor height

APPENDIXES

APPENDIX A: HEIGHT AND AREA LIMITATIONS

This section will help you determine which Construction Types are legally permitted for a building of a given height and area under any of the model building codes.

287

All building codes place limitations on building heights and areas in relation to the type of construction employed and the use or uses to which the building will be put. This is done in order to assure a minimum standard of fire safety for the occupants of the building and surrounding buildings. Height and area limitations, because they dictate the types of construction from which the designer may choose for a given building massing, have the largest impact on building design of any building code provisions. They often cause the designer to mass the building rather differently than might have been done otherwise, simply to enable it to be built using the most economical construction system possible.

Though somewhat similar in their approaches to limiting building heights and areas, the four model building codes used in North America are quite different in detail and in their degrees of permissiveness. To the maximum extent possible, these differences in detail have been minimized here by presenting the data from the four codes in a unified format so that the designer may work as readily with one code as another. The authors have adopted the names "3-Hour," "2-Hour," and so on, for the noncombustible Construction Types. These names are based on the required fire resistances of the floor structures in each Construction Type and are used instead of the various and inconsistent names used in the four model codes. The numerical factors in each code for basic allowable floor area and reductions in floor area for increasing height have been precalculated for instant reference.

One difference among the codes that it was impossible to resolve is that three of the model codes present their area limitations in terms of area per floor, while the Uniform Building Code tabulates the total area for all

Use the following indexes to find the height and area limitations table for the building code and use group you are working with.

BOCA NATIONAL BUILDING CODE

HEIGHT AND AREA LIMITATIONS

floors of the building; note carefully the basis on which each table has been constructed, as indicated at the lower left-hand corner. Building heights and areas are also measured somewhat differently from one code to another, as explained in the notes accompanying each table.

Each code has seemingly endless exceptions to its own basic height and area limitations. The most important exceptions deal with height and area increases permitted in exchange for approved automatic sprinkler systems and excess street frontage. The increases for sprinklered buildings have been incorporated fully into the tables, while the frontage increases are tabulated prominently in the accompanying notes. Other important exceptions have been noted in the text accompanying each table. A few exceptions are so complex that they could not reasonably be digested into these pages; for these you are directed to the code itself by notes accompanying the appropriate tables. Some exceptions were deemed by the authors to be so minor as not to warrant their inclusion here. For this reason, you must carry out a thorough investigation of the building code itself as a building design progresses into its developmental stage.

Under all the model codes, allowable floor areas may be multiplied by dividing the building with fire walls so as to make it, in effect, two or more separate buildings. This feature is summarized on page 424.

Listings of typical construction systems that satisfy the requirements for each Construction Type are presented on pages 425–433. These will be helpful in relating the information in the tables of height and area limitations to specific construction materials and framing systems.

NATIONAL BUILDING CODE OF CANADA

Use Group	Page
A-1	330–331
A-2	332–333
A-3	334–335
A-4	336–337
B-1	338–339
B-2	340–341
C	342–343
D	344–345
E	346–347
F-1	348–349
F-2	350–351
F-3	352–353
Open-air garages	354–355

STANDARD BUILDING CODE

Use Group	Page
A-1	358–361
A-2	362–365
B	366–367
E	368–369
F	370–371
H	372–373
I	374–377
M	378–379
R	380–381
S	382–383
Open parking garages	384–385

UNIFORM BUILDING CODE

Use Group	Page
A-1	388–389
A-2	390–391
A-2.1	390–391
A-3	392–393
A-4	392–393
B-1	394–395
B-2	394–395
B-3	394–395
B-4	396–397
E	398–399
H-1	400–401
H-2	402–403
H-3	404–405
H-4	404–405
H-5	404–405
H-6	406–407
I-1	408–409
I-2	410–411
I-3	412–413
R-1	414–415
R-3	416–417
Open parking garages	418–419

HOW TO USE THE TABLES OF HEIGHT AND AREA LIMITATIONS FOR THE BOCA NATIONAL BUILDING CODE

1. Be sure you are consulting the tables for the proper building code. If you are not sure which code you are working under, see page 7.

2. The Use Group is given at the upper left-hand corner of the table. If you are not sure about the Use Group into which your building falls, consult the index of Use Groups on page 8.

3. Noncombustible Construction Types are tabulated on the left-hand page, combustible Construction Types on the right-hand page.

4. Each pair of columns represents one Construction Type. For specific information on the different materials and modes of construction that conform to that Construction Type, follow the page reference given here.

5. The paired columns tabulate height and area information for both sprinklered and unsprinklered buildings of each Construction Type.

6. The significance of the floor area numbers in the chart, which varies from one model code to another, is explained at the lower left-hand corner.

290

300

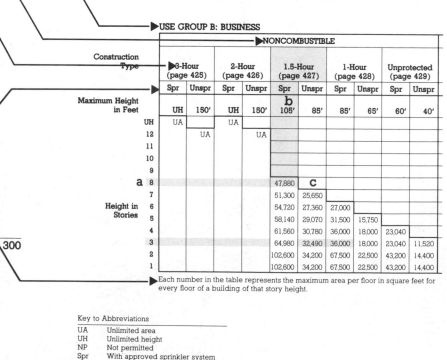

HEIGHT AND AREA LIMITATIONS

USE GROUP B: BUSINESS

Sprinklers
An approved sprinkler system is required in this Use Group for buildings taller than 12 stories or 150 ft. In buildings of this Use Group without approved sprinkler systems, each story shall be divided into two or more areas of approximately the same size, with no single area exceeding 15,000 sq ft,

in order to provide horizontal exits and areas of refuge—see page 229.

Unlimited Area
In this Use Group, a single-story building not more than 85 ft tall of construction other than Wood Light Frame and provided with an approved sprinkler system is not limited in area provided it is separated from adjacent buildings by at least 30 ft, and has exterior walls of 2-Hour construction if such separation is less than 50 ft.

Fire Walls
For multiplication of the allowable area by subdividing the building with fire walls, see page 424.

Excess Frontage
If more than 25% of the building perimeter fronts on a street or unoccupied space at least 30 ft wide that is accessible to firefighting vehicles, the tabulated area limitations may be increased 2% for each 1% of such excess frontage.

USE GROUP B: BUSINESS

Construction Type		3-Hour (page 425)		2-Hour (page 426)		1.5-Hour (page 427)		1-Hour (page 428)		Unprotected (page 429)	
		Spr	Unspr	Spr	Unspr	Spr	Unspr	Spr	Unspr	Spr	Unspr
Maximum Height in Feet		UH	150'	UH	150'	105' (b)	85'	85'	65'	60'	40'
Height in Stories	UH	UA		UA							
	12		UA		UA						
	11										
	10										
	9										
a	8					47,880	c				
	7					51,300	25,650				
	6					54,720	27,360	27,000			
	5					58,140	29,070	31,500	15,750		
	4					61,560	30,780	36,000	18,000	23,040	
	3					64,980	32,490	36,000	18,000	23,040	11,520
	2					102,600	34,200	67,500	22,500	43,200	14,400
	1					102,600	34,200	67,500	22,500	43,200	14,400

Each number in the table represents the maximum area per floor in square feet for every floor of a building of that story height.

Key to Abbreviations

UA	Unlimited area
UH	Unlimited height
NP	Not permitted
Spr	With approved sprinkler system
Unspr	Without approved sprinkler system

7. As an example of the use of this chart, a sprinklered building of Use Group B, 1.5-Hour construction, under the BOCA National Building Code, may be no more than

a. 8 stories, or

b. 105 ft tall, whichever is less,

c. with no floor larger in area than 47,880 sq ft.

8. As another example, if we wish to construct a 3-story unsprinklered building with 31,500 sq ft per floor, we must use 1.5-Hour construction as a minimum. Looking to the right along the same row of the chart, we see that the addition of sprinklers would allow us to use 1-Hour, Mill, or Ordinary construction. By following the page references at the heads of these columns, we can determine exactly what each of these Construction Types is and proceed to preliminary configuration and sizing of the structural system we select.

BOCA NATIONAL BUILDING CODE

Measurements
Height is measured from the average finished ground level adjoining the building to the top of the highest roof beams of a flat roof, or the average level of the highest sloping roof. Floor area is measured within exterior walls or exterior walls and fire walls, exclusive of courtyards.

Further Information
For information on Use Group classifications, see page 8. For information on mixed-use buildings, see page 12. For information on which code to consult, see page 7.

Unit Conversions
1 ft = 304.8 mm, 1 sq ft = 0.0929 m².

				COMBUSTIBLE							
		Ordinary				Wood Light Frame					
Mill (page 430)		1-Hour (page 431)		Unprotected (page 431)		1-Hour (page 433)		Unprotected (page 433)		Construction Type	
Spr	Unspr	Spr	Unspr	Spr	Unspr	Spr	Unspr	Spr	Unspr		
85'	65'	70'	50'	60'	40'	60'	40'	50'	30'	Maximum Height in Feet	
										UH	
										12	
										11	
										10	
										9	
										8	
										7	
25,920										6	Height in Stories
30,240	15,120	27,720								5	
34,560	17,280	31,680	15,840	23,040		24,480				4	
34,560	17,280	31,680	15,840	23,040	11,520	24,480	12,240	11,520		3	
64,800	21,600	59,400	19,800	43,200	14,400	45,900	15,300	21,600	7,200	2	
64,800	21,600	59,400	19,800	43,200	14,400	45,900	15,300	21,600	7,200	1	

This table was compiled from information contained in The BOCA® National Building Code/1987. It does not represent an official interpretation by the organization that issues the BOCA National Building Code.

301

HEIGHT AND AREA LIMITATIONS

291

HEIGHT AND AREA LIMITATIONS

USE GROUP A-1: ASSEMBLY, THEATERS

Sprinklers

An approved sprinkler system is required in this Use Group in all areas except auditoriums, foyers, lobbies, and toilet rooms.

Fire Walls

For multiplication of the allowable area by subdividing the building with fire walls, see page 424.

Excess Frontage

If more than 25% of the building perimeter fronts on a street or unoccupied space at least 30 ft wide that is accessible to firefighting vehicles, the tabulated area limitations may be increased 2% for each 1% of such excess frontage.

Measurements

Height is measured from the average finished ground level adjoining the building to the top of the highest roof beams of a flat roof, or the average level of the highest sloping roof. Floor area is measured within exterior walls or exterior walls and fire walls, exclusive of courtyards.

USE GROUP A-1: ASSEMBLY, THEATERS

Construction Type	NONCOMBUSTIBLE									
	3-Hour (page 425)		2-Hour (page 426)		1.5-Hour (page 427)		1-Hour (page 428)		Unprotected (page 429)	
	Spr	Unspr	Spr	Unspr	Spr	Unspr	Spr	Unspr	Spr	Unspr
Maximum Height in Feet	UH	UH	UH	UH	85′	65′	60′	40′	50′	30′
UH	UA	UA	UA	UA						
10										
9										
8										
7										
Height in Stories 6					31,920					
5					33,916	16,958				
4					35,910	17,955	21,000			
3					37,906	18,953	21,000	10,500	13,440	
2					59,850	19,950	39,375	13,125	25,200	8,400
1					59,850	19,950	39,375	13,125	25,200	8,400

Each number in the table represents the maximum area per floor in square feet for every floor of a building of that story height.

Key to Abbreviations

UA	Unlimited area
UH	Unlimited height
NP	Not permitted
Spr	With approved sprinkler system
Unspr	Without approved sprinkler system

BOCA NATIONAL BUILDING CODE

Further Information
For information on Use Group classifications, see page 8. For information on mixed-use buildings, see page 12. For information on which code to consult, see page 7.

Unit Conversions
1 ft = 304.8 mm, 1 sq ft = 0.0929 m².

COMBUSTIBLE										
		Ordinary				Wood Light Frame				
Mill (page 430)		1-Hour (page 431)		Unprotected (page 431)		1-Hour (page 433)		Unprotected (page 433)		
Spr	Unspr	Spr	Unspr	Spr	Unspr	Spr	Unspr	Spr	Unspr	Height in Stories
60'	40'	60'	40'	50'	30'	40'	20'	40'	20'	
										UH
										10
										9
										8
										7
										6
										5
20,160		18,480								4
20,160	10,080	18,480	9,240	13,440						3
37,800	12,600	34,650	11,550	25,200	8,400	26,775		12,600		2
37,800	12,600	34,650	11,550	25,200	8,400	26,775	8,925	12,600	4,200	1

Construction Type

Maximum Height in Feet

Height in Stories

HEIGHT AND AREA LIMITATIONS

This table was compiled from information contained in The BOCA® National Building Code/1987. It does not represent an official interpretation by the organization that issues the BOCA National Building Code.

293

HEIGHT AND AREA LIMITATIONS

USE GROUP A-2: ASSEMBLY, NIGHT CLUBS, AND SIMILAR USES

Sprinklers
An approved sprinkler system is required in this Use Group for buildings larger than 5000 sq ft or taller than one story.

Fire Walls
For multiplication of the allowable area by subdividing the building with fire walls, see page 424.

Excess Frontage
If more than 25% of the building perimeter fronts on a street or unoccupied space at least 30 ft wide that is accessible to firefighting vehicles, the tabulated area limitations may be increased 2% for each 1% of such excess frontage.

Measurements
Height is measured from the average finished ground level adjoining the building to the top of the highest roof beams of a flat roof, or the average level of the highest sloping roof. Floor area is measured within exterior walls or exterior walls and fire walls, exclusive of courtyards.

USE GROUP A-2: ASSEMBLY, NIGHT CLUBS, AND SIMILAR USES

Construction Type	NONCOMBUSTIBLE									
	3-Hour (page 425)		2-Hour (page 426)		1.5-Hour (page 427)		1-Hour (page 428)		Unprotected (page 429)	
	Spr	Unspr	Spr	Unspr	Spr	Unspr	Spr	Unspr	Spr	Unspr
Maximum Height in Feet	UH	UH	70'	50'	60'	40'	50'	30'	40'	20'
UH	UA									
10										
9										
8										
7										
6										
5			12,240							
4			12,960		10,260					
3			13,680		10,830		6,000			
2			21,600		17,100		11,250		7,200	
1		5,000	21,600	5,000	17,100	5,000	11,250	3,750	7,200	2,400

Each number in the table represents the maximum area per floor in square feet for every floor of a building of that story height.

Key to Abbreviations

UA	Unlimited area
UH	Unlimited height
NP	Not permitted
Spr	With approved sprinkler system
Unspr	Without approved sprinkler system

BOCA NATIONAL BUILDING CODE

Further Information

For information on Use Group classifications, see page 8. For information on mixed-use buildings, see page 12. For information on which code to consult, see page 7.

Unit Conversions

1 ft = 304.8 mm, 1 sq ft = 0.0929 m².

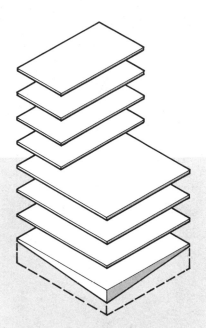

		COMBUSTIBLE									
Mill (page 430)		Ordinary				Wood Light Frame					Construction Type
		1-Hour (page 431)		Unprotected (page 431)		1-Hour (page 433)		Unprotected (page 433)			
Spr	Unspr	Spr	Unspr	Spr	Unspr	Spr	Unspr	Spr	Unspr		
50′	30′	50′	30′	40′	20′	40′	20′	40′	20′		Maximum Height in Feet
										UH	
										10	
										9	
										8	
										7	
										6	Height in Stories
										5	
										4	
5,760		5,280								3	
10,800		9,900		7,200		7,650		3,600		2	
10,800	3,600	9,900	3,300	7,200	2,400	7,650	2,550	3,600	1,200	1	

This table was compiled from information contained in The BOCA® National Building Code/1987. It does not represent an official interpretation by the organization that issues the BOCA National Building Code.

HEIGHT AND AREA LIMITATIONS

USE GROUP A-3: ASSEMBLY

Sprinklers
An approved sprinkler system is required in this Use Group for buildings larger than 12,000 sq ft.

Unlimited Area
In this Use Group, a single-story building not more than 85 ft tall of construction other than Wood Light Frame and provided with an approved sprinkler system is not limited in area provided it is separated from adjacent buildings by at least 30 ft and has exterior walls of 2-Hour construction if such separation is less than 50 ft.

Indoor participant sport areas are not limited in area and need not have a sprinkler system if exits open directly to the outdoors. See Section 504 of the BOCA National Building Code for details.

Fire Walls
For multiplication of the allowable area by subdividing the building with fire walls, see page 424.

Excess Frontage
If more than 25% of the building perimeter fronts on a street or unoccupied space at least 30 ft wide that is accessible to firefighting vehicles, the tabulated area limitations may be increased 2% for each 1% of such excess frontage.

USE GROUP A-3: ASSEMBLY

Construction Type	NONCOMBUSTIBLE									
	3-Hour (page 425)		2-Hour (page 426)		1.5-Hour (page 427)		1-Hour (page 428)		Unprotected (page 429)	
	Spr	Unspr	Spr	Unspr	Spr	Unspr	Spr	Unspr	Spr	Unspr
Maximum Height in Feet	UH	UH	UH	UH	85'	65'	60'	40'	50'	30'
UH	UA	12,000	UA	12,000						
10										
9										
8										
7										
6					31,920					
5					33,916	12,000				
4					35,910	12,000	21,000			
3					37,906	12,000	21,000	12,000	13,440	
2					59,850	12,000	39,375	12,000	25,200	8,400
1					59,850	12,000	39,375	12,000	25,200	8,400

Height in Stories (rows UH, 10, 9, 8, 7, 6, 5, 4, 3, 2, 1)

Each number in the table represents the maximum area per floor in square feet for every floor of a building of that story height.

Key to Abbreviations

UA	Unlimited area
UH	Unlimited height
NP	Not permitted
Spr	With approved sprinkler system
Unspr	Without approved sprinkler system

BOCA NATIONAL BUILDING CODE

Measurements

Height is measured from the average finished ground level adjoining the building to the top of the highest roof beams of a flat roof, or the average level of the highest sloping roof. Floor area is measured within exterior walls or exterior walls and fire walls, exclusive of courtyards.

Further Information

For information on Use Group classifications, see page 8. For information on mixed-use buildings, see page 12. For information on which code to consult, see page 7.

Unit Conversions

1 ft = 304.8 mm, 1 sq ft = 0.0929 m².

Construction Type

Maximum Height in Feet

Height in Stories

HEIGHT AND AREA LIMITATIONS

	COMBUSTIBLE									Maximum Height in Feet	Height in Stories
Mill (page 430)		Ordinary				Wood Light Frame					
		1-Hour (page 431)		Unprotected (page 431)		1-Hour (page 433)		Unprotected (page 433)			
Spr	Unspr	Spr	Unspr	Spr	Unspr	Spr	Unspr	Spr	Unspr		
60'	40'	60'	40'	50'	30'	40'	20'	40'	20'		
										UH	
										10	
										9	
										8	
										7	
										6	
										5	
20,160		18,480								4	
20,160	10,080	18,480	9,240	13,440						3	
37,800	12,000	34,650	11,550	25,200	8,400	26,775		12,600		2	
37,800	12,000	34,650	11,550	25,200	8,400	26,775	8,925	12,600	4,200	1	

This table was compiled from information contained in The BOCA® National Building Code/1987. It does not represent an official interpretation by the organization that issues the BOCA National Building Code.

HEIGHT AND AREA LIMITATIONS

USE GROUP A-4: ASSEMBLY, CHURCHES

Fire Walls

For multiplication of the allowable area by subdividing the building with fire walls, see page 424.

Excess Frontage

If more than 25% of the building perimeter fronts on a street or unoccupied space at least 30 ft wide that is accessible to firefighting vehicles, the tabulated area limitations may be increased 2% for each 1% of such excess frontage.

Measurements

Height is measured from the average finished ground level adjoining the building to the top of the highest roof beams of a flat roof, or the average level of the highest sloping roof. Floor area is measured within exterior walls or exterior walls and fire walls, exclusive of courtyards.

USE GROUP A-4: ASSEMBLY, CHURCHES

Construction Type	NONCOMBUSTIBLE									
	3-Hour (page 425)		2-Hour (page 426)		1.5-Hour (page 427)		1-Hour (page 428)		Unprotected (page 429)	
	Spr	Unspr	Spr	Unspr	Spr	Unspr	Spr	Unspr	Spr	Unspr
Maximum Height in Feet	UH	UH	UH	UH	85′	65′	85′	65′	65′	45′
UH	UA	UA	UA	UA						
10										
9										
8										
7										
6					54,720					
5					58,140	29,070				
4					61,560	30,780	36,000			
3					64,980	32,490	36,000	18,000	23,040	
2					102,600	34,200	67,500	22,500	43,200	14,400
1					102,600	34,200	67,500	22,500	43,200	14,400

(Left axis label: **Height in Stories**)

Each number in the table represents the maximum area per floor in square feet for every floor of a building of that story height.

Key to Abbreviations

UA	Unlimited area
UH	Unlimited height
NP	Not permitted
Spr	With approved sprinkler system
Unspr	Without approved sprinkler system

BOCA NATIONAL BUILDING CODE

Further Information

For information on Use Group classifications, see page 8. For information on mixed-use buildings, see page 12. For information on which code to consult, see page 7.

Unit Conversions

1 ft = 304.8 mm, 1 sq ft = 0.0929 m².

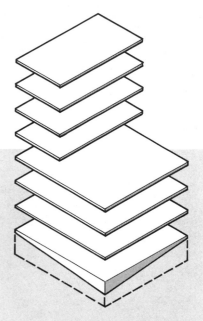

Construction Type

COMBUSTIBLE											
		Ordinary				Wood Light Frame					
Mill (page 430)		1-Hour (page 431)		Unprotected (page 431)		1-Hour (page 433)		Unprotected (page 433)			
Spr	Unspr	Spr	Unspr	Spr	Unspr	Spr	Unspr	Spr	Unspr		**Maximum Height in Feet**
85'	65'	85'	65'	65'	45'	85'	65'	65'	45'		
										UH	
										10	
										9	
										8	
										7	
										6	**Height in Stories**
										5	
34,560		31,680								4	
34,560	17,280	31,680	15,840	23,040						3	
64,800	21,600	59,400	19,800	43,200	14,400	45,900		21,600		2	
64,800	21,600	59,400	19,800	43,200	14,400	45,900	15,300	21,600	7,200	1	

This table was compiled from information contained in The BOCA® National Building Code/1987. It does not represent an official interpretation by the organization that issues the BOCA National Building Code.

HEIGHT AND AREA LIMITATIONS

USE GROUP B: BUSINESS

Sprinklers

An approved sprinkler system is required in this Use Group for buildings taller than 12 stories or 150 ft. In buildings of this Use Group without approved sprinkler systems, each story shall be divided into two or more areas of approximately the same size, with no single area exceeding 15,000 sq ft, in order to provide horizontal exits and areas of refuge—see page 229.

Unlimited Area

In this Use Group, a single-story building not more than 85 ft tall of construction other than Wood Light Frame and provided with an approved sprinkler system is not limited in area provided it is separated from adjacent buildings by at least 30 ft, and has exterior walls of 2-Hour construction if such separation is less than 50 ft.

Fire Walls

For multiplication of the allowable area by subdividing the building with fire walls, see page 424.

Excess Frontage

If more than 25% of the building perimeter fronts on a street or unoccupied space at least 30 ft wide that is accessible to firefighting vehicles, the tabulated area limitations may be increased 2% for each 1% of such excess frontage.

USE GROUP B: BUSINESS

Construction Type	NONCOMBUSTIBLE									
	3-Hour (page 425)		2-Hour (page 426)		1.5-Hour (page 427)		1-Hour (page 428)		Unprotected (page 429)	
	Spr	Unspr	Spr	Unspr	Spr	Unspr	Spr	Unspr	Spr	Unspr
Maximum Height in Feet	UH	150'	UH	150'	105'	85'	85'	65'	60'	40'
Height in Stories UH	UA		UA							
12		UA		UA						
11										
10										
9										
8					47,880					
7					51,300	25,650				
6					54,720	27,360	27,000			
5					58,140	29,070	31,500	15,750		
4					61,560	30,780	36,000	18,000	23,040	
3					64,980	32,490	36,000	18,000	23,040	11,520
2					102,600	34,200	67,500	22,500	43,200	14,400
1					102,600	34,200	67,500	22,500	43,200	14,400

Each number in the table represents the maximum area per floor in square feet for every floor of a building of that story height.

Key to Abbreviations

UA	Unlimited area
UH	Unlimited height
NP	Not permitted
Spr	With approved sprinkler system
Unspr	Without approved sprinkler system

Measurements

Height is measured from the average finished ground level adjoining the building to the top of the highest roof beams of a flat roof, or the average level of the highest sloping roof. Floor area is measured within exterior walls or exterior walls and fire walls, exclusive of courtyards.

Further Information

For information on Use Group classifications, see page 8. For information on mixed-use buildings, see page 12. For information on which code to consult, see page 7.

Unit Conversions

1 ft = 304.8 mm, 1 sq ft = 0.0929 m².

COMBUSTIBLE										Construction Type	Height in Stories
Mill (page 430)		Ordinary				Wood Light Frame					
		1-Hour (page 431)		Unprotected (page 431)		1-Hour (page 433)		Unprotected (page 433)		Maximum Height in Feet	
Spr	Unspr	Spr	Unspr	Spr	Unspr	Spr	Unspr	Spr	Unspr		
85'	65'	70'	50'	60'	40'	60'	40'	50'	30'		
										UH	
										12	
										11	
										10	
										9	
										8	
										7	
25,920										6	
30,240	15,120	27,720								5	
34,560	17,280	31,680	15,840	23,040		24,480				4	
34,560	17,280	31,680	15,840	23,040	11,520	24,480	12,240	11,520		3	
64,800	21,600	59,400	19,800	43,200	14,400	45,900	15,300	21,600	7,200	2	
64,800	21,600	59,400	19,800	43,200	14,400	45,900	15,300	21,600	7,200	1	

This table was compiled from information contained in The BOCA® National Building Code/1987. It does not represent an official interpretation by the organization that issues the BOCA National Building Code.

HEIGHT AND AREA LIMITATIONS

USE GROUP E: EDUCATIONAL

Direct Exits
When every classroom of a single-story school building has at least one door opening directly to the exterior of the building, these area limitations may be increased by 200%. At least half of the exits from any assembly room must also open directly to the exterior for this increase to be allowed.

Fire Walls
For multiplication of the allowable area by subdividing the building with fire walls, see page 424.

Excess Frontage
If more than 25% of the building perimeter fronts on a street or unoccupied space at least 30 ft wide that is accessible to firefighting vehicles, the tabulated area limitations may be increased 2% for each 1% of such excess frontage.

Measurements
Height is measured from the average finished ground level adjoining the building to the top of the highest roof beams of a flat roof, or the average level of the highest sloping roof. Floor area is measured within exterior walls or exterior walls and fire walls, exclusive of courtyards.

USE GROUP E: EDUCATIONAL

Construction Type	NONCOMBUSTIBLE									
	3-Hour (page 425)		2-Hour (page 426)		1.5-Hour (page 427)		1-Hour (page 428)		Unprotected (page 429)	
	Spr	Unspr	Spr	Unspr	Spr	Unspr	Spr	Unspr	Spr	Unspr
Maximum Height in Feet	UH	UH	UH	UH	85'	65'	60'	40'	50'	30'
UH	UA	UA	UA	UA						
10										
9										
8										
7										
6					54,720					
5					58,140	29,070				
4					61,560	30,780	36,000			
3					64,980	32,490	36,000	18,000	23,040	
2					102,600	34,200	67,500	22,500	43,200	14,400
1					102,600	34,200	67,500	22,500	43,200	14,400

Height in Stories

Each number in the table represents the maximum area per floor in square feet for every floor of a building of that story height.

Key to Abbreviations

UA	Unlimited area
UH	Unlimited height
NP	Not permitted
Spr	With approved sprinkler system
Unspr	Without approved sprinkler system

BOCA NATIONAL BUILDING CODE

Further Information

For information on Use Group classifications, see page 8. For information on mixed-use buildings, see page 12. For information on which code to consult, see page 7.

Unit Conversions

1 ft = 304.8 mm, 1 sq ft = 0.0929 m².

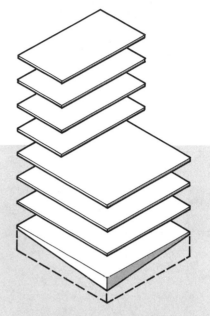

COMBUSTIBLE										Construction Type
Mill (page 430)		Ordinary				Wood Light Frame				
		1-Hour (page 431)		Unprotected (page 431)		1-Hour (page 433)		Unprotected (page 433)		
Spr	Unspr	Spr	Unspr	Spr	Unspr	Spr	Unspr	Spr	Unspr	
60'	40'	60'	40'	50'	30'	40'	20'	40'	20'	Maximum Height in Feet
										UH
										10
										9
										8
										7
										6 — Height in Stories
										5
34,560		31,680								4
34,560	17,280	31,680	15,840	23,040						3
64,800	21,600	59,400	19,800	43,200	14,400	45,900		21,600		2
64,800	21,600	59,400	19,800	43,200	14,400	45,900	15,300	21,600	7,200	1

This table was compiled from information contained in The BOCA® National Building Code/1987. It does not represent an official interpretation by the organization that issues the BOCA National Building Code.

HEIGHT AND AREA LIMITATIONS

303

USE GROUP F: FACTORY AND INDUSTRIAL

Unlimited Area

In this Use Group, a single-story building not more than 85 ft tall of construction other than Wood Light Frame and provided with an approved sprinkler system is not limited in area provided it is separated from adjacent buildings by at least 30 ft, and has exterior walls of 3-Hour construction if such separation is less than 50 ft.

Exemptions

Buildings for low-hazard industrial processes such as production of electric, gas, or steam power; rolling mills; structural metal fabrication shops and foundries; requiring large areas and unusual heights, are exempt from the limitations of this table.

Fire Walls

For multiplication of the allowable area by subdividing the building with fire walls, see page 424.

Excess Frontage

If more than 25% of the building perimeter fronts on a street or unoccupied space at least 30 ft wide that is accessible to firefighting vehicles, the tabulated area limitations may be increased 2% for each 1% of such excess frontage.

USE GROUP F: FACTORY AND INDUSTRIAL

	NONCOMBUSTIBLE									
Construction Type	**3-Hour (page 425)**		**2-Hour (page 426)**		**1.5-Hour (page 427)**		**1-Hour (page 428)**		**Unprotected (page 429)**	
	Spr	**Unspr**	**Spr**	**Unspr**	**Spr**	**Unspr**	**Spr**	**Unspr**	**Spr**	**Unspr**
Maximum Height in Feet	**UH**	**UH**	**UH**	**UH**	**95′**	**75′**	**70′**	**50′**	**50′**	**30′**
Height in Stories UH	UA	UA	UA	UA						
10										
9										
8										
7					34,200					
6					36,480	18,240				
5					38,760	19,380	21,000			
4					41,040	20,520	24,000	12,000		
3					43,320	21,660	24,000	12,000	15,360	
2					68,400	22,800	45,000	15,000	28,800	9,600
1					68,400	22,800	45,000	15,000	28,800	9,600

Each number in the table represents the maximum area per floor in square feet for every floor of a building of that story height.

Key to Abbreviations

UA	Unlimited area
UH	Unlimited height
NP	Not permitted
Spr	With approved sprinkler system
Unspr	Without approved sprinkler system

BOCA NATIONAL BUILDING CODE

Measurements

Height is measured from the average finished ground level adjoining the building to the top of the highest roof beams of a flat roof, or the average level of the highest sloping roof. Floor area is measured within exterior walls or exterior walls and fire walls, exclusive of courtyards.

Further Information

For information on Use Group classifications, see page 8. For information on mixed-use buildings, see page 12. For information on which code to consult, see page 7.

Unit Conversions

1 ft = 304.8 mm, 1 sq ft = 0.0929 m².

COMBUSTIBLE										
Mill (page 430)		Ordinary				Wood Light Frame				
		1-Hour (page 431)		Unprotected (page 431)		1-Hour (page 433)		Unprotected (page 433)		Height in Stories
Spr	Unspr	Spr	Unspr	Spr	Unspr	Spr	Unspr	Spr	Unspr	
70'	50'	60'	40'	50'	30'	50'	30'	40'	20'	
										UH
										10
										9
										8
										7
										6
20,160										5
23,040	11,520	21,120								4
23,040	11,520	21,120	10,560	15,360		16,320				3
43,200	14,400	39,600	13,200	28,800	9,600	30,600	10,200	14,400		2
43,200	14,400	39,600	13,200	28,800	9,600	30,600	10,200	14,400	4,800	1

Construction Type

Maximum Height in Feet

Height in Stories

HEIGHT AND AREA LIMITATIONS

305

This table was compiled from information contained in The BOCA® National Building Code/1987. It does not represent an official interpretation by the organization that issues the BOCA National Building Code.

HEIGHT AND AREA LIMITATIONS

USE GROUP H: HIGH HAZARD

Specific Hazards
This is a diverse Use Group with many special requirements for various specific occupancies; consult the BOCA National Building Code, Article 6, for details.

Fire Walls
For multiplication of the allowable area by subdividing the building with fire walls, see page 424.

Excess Frontage
If more than 25% of the building perimeter fronts on a street or unoccupied space at least 30 ft wide that is accessible to firefighting vehicles, the tabulated area limitations may be increased 2% for each 1% of such excess frontage.

Measurements
Height is measured from the average finished ground level adjoining the building to the top of the highest roof beams of a flat roof, or the average level of the highest sloping roof. Floor area is measured within exterior walls or exterior walls and fire walls, exclusive of courtyards.

USE GROUP H: HIGH HAZARD

Construction Type	NONCOMBUSTIBLE									
	3-Hour (page 425)		2-Hour (page 426)		1.5-Hour (page 427)		1-Hour (page 428)		Unprotected (page 429)	
	Spr	Unspr	Spr	Unspr	Spr	Unspr	Spr	Unspr	Spr	Unspr
Maximum Height in Feet	65′		40′		40′		30′		20′	
UH										
10										
9										
8										
7										
Height in Stories 6										
5	14,280									
4	15,120									
3	15,960		13,680		10,830					
2	16,800		14,400		11,400		7,500			
1	16,800	NP	14,400	NP	11,400	NP	7,500	NP	4,800	NP

Each number in the table represents the maximum area per floor in square feet for every floor of a building of that story height.

Key to Abbreviations

UA	Unlimited area
UH	Unlimited height
NP	Not permitted
Spr	With approved sprinkler system
Unspr	Without approved sprinkler system

BOCA NATIONAL BUILDING CODE

Further Information

For information on Use Group classifications, see page 8. For information on mixed-use buildings, see page 12. For information on which code to consult, see page 7.

Unit Conversions

1 ft = 304.8 mm, 1 sq ft = 0.0929 m².

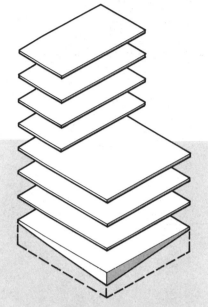

COMBUSTIBLE										
		Ordinary				Wood Light Frame				
Mill (page 430)		1-Hour (page 431)		Unprotected (page 431)		1-Hour (page 433)		Unprotected (page 433)		
Spr	Unspr	Spr	Unspr	Spr	Unspr	Spr	Unspr	Spr	Unspr	
30′		30′		20′		20′				Maximum Height in Feet
										UH
										10
										9
										8
										7
										6 — Height in Stories
										5
										4
										3
7,200		6,600								2
7,200	NP	6,600	NP	4,800	NP	5,100	NP	NP	NP	1

Construction Type

This table was compiled from information contained in The BOCA® National Building Code/1987. It does not represent an official interpretation by the organization that issues the BOCA National Building Code.

HEIGHT AND AREA LIMITATIONS

USE GROUP I-1: INSTITUTIONAL, RESIDENTIAL CARE

Sprinklers
An approved sprinkler system is required in this Use Group for any building with an occupant load of 20 persons or more.

Fire Walls
For multiplication of the allowable area by subdividing the building with fire walls, see page 424.

Excess Frontage
If more than 25% of the building perimeter fronts on a street or unoccupied space at least 30 ft wide that is accessible to firefighting vehicles, the tabulated area limitations may be increased 2% for each 1% of such excess frontage.

Measurements
Height is measured from the average finished ground level adjoining the building to the top of the highest roof beams of a flat roof, or the average level of the highest sloping roof. Floor area is measured within exterior walls or exterior walls and fire walls, exclusive of courtyards.

USE GROUP I-1: INSTITUTIONAL, RESIDENTIAL CARE

Construction Type	NONCOMBUSTIBLE									
	3-Hour (page 425)		2-Hour (page 426)		1.5-Hour (page 427)		1-Hour (page 428)		Unprotected (page 429)	
	Spr	Unspr	Spr	Unspr	Spr	Unspr	Spr	Unspr	Spr	Unspr
Maximum Height in Feet	UH	UH	UH	UH	120'	100'	70'	50'	60'	40'
UH	UA		UA							
10					23,940					
9					25,936					
8					27,930					
7					29,926					
6					31,920					
5					33,916		18,375			
4					35,910		21,000		13,440	
3					37,906		21,000		13,440	
2		UA		UA	59,850	19,950	39,375	13,125	25,200	8,400
1					59,850	19,950	39,375	13,125	25,200	8,400

Height in Stories (labels 10–1 on left)

Each number in the table represents the maximum area per floor in square feet for every floor of a building of that story height.

Key to Abbreviations

UA	Unlimited area
UH	Unlimited height
NP	Not permitted
Spr	With approved sprinkler system
Unspr	Without approved sprinkler system

BOCA NATIONAL BUILDING CODE

Further Information

For information on Use Group classifications, see page 8. For information on mixed-use buildings, see page 12. For information on which code to consult, see page 7.

Unit Conversions

1 ft = 304.8 mm, 1 sq ft = 0.0929 m².

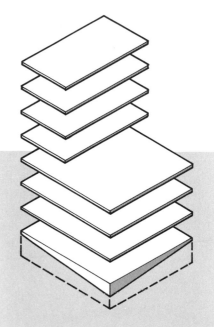

Construction Type

Maximum Height in Feet

Height in Stories

	COMBUSTIBLE										
		Ordinary				Wood Light Frame					
Mill (page 430)		1-Hour (page 431)		Unprotected (page 431)		1-Hour (page 433)		Unprotected (page 433)			
Spr	Unspr	Spr	Unspr	Spr	Unspr	Spr	Unspr	Spr	Unspr		
70'	50'	70'	50'	60'	40'	60'	40'	55'	35'		
										UH	
										10	
										9	
										8	
										7	
										6	
17,640		16,170								5	
20,160		18,480		13,440		14,280				4	
20,160		18,480		13,440		14,280		6,720		3	
37,800	12,600	34,650	11,550	25,200	8,400	26,775	8,925	12,600	4,200	2	
37,800	12,600	34,650	11,550	25,200	8,400	26,775	8,925	12,600	4,200	1	

This table was compiled from information contained in The BOCA® National Building Code/1987. It does not represent an official interpretation by the organization that issues the BOCA National Building Code.

HEIGHT AND AREA LIMITATIONS

309

HEIGHT AND AREA LIMITATIONS

USE GROUP I-2: INSTITUTIONAL, INCAPACITATED

Sprinklers
An approved sprinkler system is required in this Use Group for nursing homes more than a single story high. An approved sprinkler system is also required for child care facilities more than a single story high, or with more than 100 children, or without direct exits from each room to the outside.

Unlimited Area
In this Use Group, a single-story building not more than 85 ft tall of construction other than Wood Light Frame and provided with an approved sprinkler system is not limited in area provided it is separated from adjacent buildings by at least 30 ft, and has exterior walls of 2-Hour construction if such separation is less than 50 ft.

Fire Walls
For multiplication of the allowable area by subdividing the building with fire walls, see page 424.

Excess Frontage
If more than 25% of the building perimeter fronts on a street or unoccupied space at least 30 ft wide that is accessible to firefighting vehicles, the tabulated area limitations may be increased 2% for each 1% of such excess frontage.

USE GROUP I-2: INSTITUTIONAL, INCAPACITATED

Construction Type	NONCOMBUSTIBLE									
	3-Hour (page 425)		2-Hour (page 426)		1.5-Hour (page 427)		1-Hour (page 428)		Unprotected (page 429)	
	Spr	Unspr	Spr	Unspr	Spr	Unspr	Spr	Unspr	Spr	Unspr
Maximum Height in Feet	UH	75'	110'	45'	70'	50'	50'	30'	40'	20'
Height in Stories										
UH	UA									
10										
9			28,080							
8			30,240							
7			32,400							
6			34,560							
5		UA	36,720		29,070					
4			38,880		30,780					
3			43,200	20,520	32,490		21,375			
2			64,800	21,600	51,300		33,750	11,250		
1			64,800	21,600	51,300	17,100	33,750	11,250	21,600	7,200

Each number in the table represents the maximum area per floor in square feet for every floor of a building of that story height.

Key to Abbreviations

UA	Unlimited area
UH	Unlimited height
NP	Not permitted
Spr	With approved sprinkler system
Unspr	Without approved sprinkler system

BOCA NATIONAL BUILDING CODE

Measurements

Height is measured from the average finished ground level adjoining the building to the top of the highest roof beams of a flat roof, or the average level of the highest sloping roof. Floor area is measured within exterior walls or exterior walls and fire walls, exclusive of courtyards.

Further Information

For information on Use Group classifications, see page 8. For information on mixed-use buildings, see page 12. For information on which code to consult, see page 7.

Unit Conversions

1 ft = 304.8 mm, 1 sq ft = 0.0929 m².

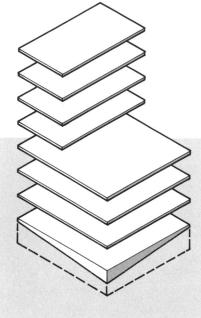

		COMBUSTIBLE								Construction Type
		Ordinary				Wood Light Frame				
Mill (page 430)		1-Hour (page 431)		Unprotected (page 431)		1-Hour (page 433)		Unprotected (page 433)		
Spr	Unspr	Spr	Unspr	Spr	Unspr	Spr	Unspr	Spr	Unspr	Maximum Height in Feet
40'	20'	40'	20'			40'	20'			UH
										10
										9
										8
										7
										6 Height in
										5 Stories
										4
										3
										2
32,400	10,800	29,700	9,900	NP	NP	22,950	7,650	NP	NP	1

This table was compiled from information contained in The BOCA® National Building Code/1987. It does not represent an official interpretation by the organization that issues the BOCA National Building Code.

HEIGHT AND AREA LIMITATIONS

311

USE GROUP I-3: INSTITUTIONAL, RESTRAINED

Sprinklers
An approved sprinkler system is required in this Use Group for any building with an occupant load greater than 5 persons.

Fire Walls
For multiplication of the allowable area by subdividing the building with fire walls, see page 424.

Excess Frontage
If more than 25% of the building perimeter fronts on a street or unoccupied space at least 30 ft wide that is accessible to firefighting vehicles, the tabulated area limitations may be increased 2% for each 1% of such excess frontage.

Measurements
Height is measured from the average finished ground level adjoining the building to the top of the highest roof beams of a flat roof, or the average level of the highest sloping roof. Floor area is measured within exterior walls or exterior walls and fire walls, exclusive of courtyards.

USE GROUP I-3: INSTITUTIONAL, RESTRAINED

Construction Type	NONCOMBUSTIBLE									
	3-Hour (page 425)		2-Hour (page 426)		1.5-Hour (page 427)		1-Hour (page 428)		Unprotected (page 429)	
	Spr	Unspr	Spr	Unspr	Spr	Unspr	Spr	Unspr	Spr	Unspr
Maximum Height in Feet	UH	UH	95'	75'	70'	50'	50'	30'	40'	20'
UH	UA	UA								
10										
9										
8										
7			27,000							
6			28,800	14,400						
5			30,600	15,300	24,225					
4			32,400	16,200	25,650	12,825				
3			34,200	17,100	27,076	13,538	15,000			
2			54,000	18,000	42,750	14,250	28,125	9,375	18,000	
1			54,000	18,000	42,750	14,250	28,125	9,375	18,000	6,000

Height in Stories (rows UH through 1)

Each number in the table represents the maximum area per floor in square feet for every floor of a building of that story height.

Key to Abbreviations

UA	Unlimited area
UH	Unlimited height
NP	Not permitted
Spr	With approved sprinkler system
Unspr	Without approved sprinkler system

BOCA NATIONAL BUILDING CODE

Further Information
For information on Use Group classifications, see page 8. For information on mixed-use buildings, see page 12. For information on which code to consult, see page 7.

Unit Conversions
1 ft = 304.8 mm, 1 sq ft = 0.0929 m².

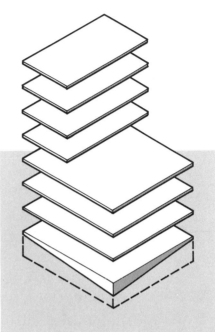

		COMBUSTIBLE									Construction Type
		Ordinary				Wood Light Frame					
Mill (page 430)		1-Hour (page 431)		Unprotected (page 431)		1-Hour (page 433)		Unprotected (page 433)			
Spr	Unspr	Spr	Unspr	Spr	Unspr	Spr	Unspr	Spr	Unspr		
50'	30'	50'	30'	40'	20'	40'	20'				Maximum Height in Feet
										UH	
										10	
										9	
										8	
										7	
										6	Height in Stories
										5	
										4	
14,400		13,200								3	
27,000	9,000	24,750	8,250	18,000		19,125				2	
27,000	9,000	24,750	8,250	18,000	6,000	19,125	6,375	NP	NP	1	

This table was compiled from information contained in The BOCA® National Building Code/1987. It does not represent an official interpretation by the organization that issues the BOCA National Building Code.

HEIGHT AND AREA LIMITATIONS

USE GROUP M: MERCANTILE

Sprinklers
An approved sprinkler system is required in this Use Group for buildings larger than 12,000 sq ft on any one floor, or a total of 24,000 sq ft on all floors.

Unlimited Area
In this Use Group, a single-story building not more than 85 ft tall of construction other than Wood Light Frame and provided with an approved sprinkler system is not limited in area provided it is separated from adjacent buildings by at least 30 ft and has exterior walls of 3-Hour construction if such separation is less than 50 ft.

Fire Walls
For multiplication of the allowable area by subdividing the building with fire walls, see page 424.

Excess Frontage
If more than 25% of the building perimeter fronts on a street or unoccupied space at least 30 ft wide that is accessible to firefighting vehicles, the tabulated area limitations may be increased 2% for each 1% of such excess frontage.

USE GROUP M: MERCANTILE

Construction Type	NONCOMBUSTIBLE									
	3-Hour (page 425)		2-Hour (page 426)		1.5-Hour (page 427)		1-Hour (page 428)		Unprotected (page 429)	
	Spr	Unspr	Spr	Unspr	Spr	Unspr	Spr	Unspr	Spr	Unspr
Maximum Height in Feet	UH	UH	UH	UH	95'	75'	70'	50'	50'	30'
UH	UA		UA							
10										
9										
8										
7					34,200					
6					36,480					
5					38,760		21,000			
4					41,040		24,000			
3		12,000		12,000	43,320	12,000	24,000	12,000	15,360	
2		12,000		12,000	68,400	12,000	45,000	12,000	28,800	9,600
1		12,000		12,000	68,400	12,000	45,000	12,000	28,800	9,600

Row label for stories 3–1 area: **Height in Stories**

Each number in the table represents the maximum area per floor in square feet for every floor of a building of that story height.

Key to Abbreviations

UA	Unlimited area
UH	Unlimited height
NP	Not permitted
Spr	With approved sprinkler system
Unspr	Without approved sprinkler system

BOCA NATIONAL BUILDING CODE

Measurements

Height is measured from the average finished ground level adjoining the building to the top of the highest roof beams of a flat roof, or the average level of the highest sloping roof. Floor area is measured within exterior walls or exterior walls and fire walls, exclusive of courtyards.

Further Information

For information on Use Group classifications, see page 8. For information on mixed-use buildings, see page 12. For information on which code to consult, see page 7.

Unit Conversions

1 ft = 304.8 mm, 1 sq ft = 0.0929 m².

COMBUSTIBLE										Construction Type
		Ordinary				Wood Light Frame				
Mill (page 430)		1-Hour (page 431)		Unprotected (page 431)		1-Hour (page 433)		Unprotected (page 433)		
Spr	Unspr	Spr	Unspr	Spr	Unspr	Spr	Unspr	Spr	Unspr	
70'	50'	60'	40'	50'	30'	50'	30'	40'	20'	Maximum Height in Feet
										UH
										10
										9
										8
										7
										6 Height in Stories
20,160										5
23,040		21,120								4
23,040	12,000	21,120	12,000	15,360		16,320				3
43,200	12,000	39,600	12,000	28,800	9,600	30,600	10,200	14,400		2
43,200	12,000	39,600	12,000	28,800	9,600	30,600	10,200	14,400	4,800	1

This table was compiled from information contained in the BOCA National Building Code, 1987 Edition. It does not represent an official interpretation by the organization that issues the BOCA National Building Code.

USE GROUP R-1: RESIDENTIAL, HOTELS

Fire Walls
For multiplication of the allowable area by subdividing the building with fire walls, see page 424.

Excess Frontage
If more than 25% of the building perimeter fronts on a street or unoccupied space at least 30 ft wide that is accessible to firefighting vehicles, the tabulated area limitations may be increased 2% for each 1% of such excess frontage.

Measurements
Height is measured from the average finished ground level adjoining the building to the top of the highest roof beams of a flat roof, or the average level of the highest sloping roof. Floor area is measured within exterior walls or exterior walls and fire walls, exclusive of courtyards.

USE GROUP R-1: RESIDENTIAL, HOTELS

Construction Type	NONCOMBUSTIBLE									
	3-Hour (page 425)		2-Hour (page 426)		1.5-Hour (page 427)		1-Hour (page 428)		Unprotected (page 429)	
	Spr	Unspr	Spr	Unspr	Spr	Unspr	Spr	Unspr	Spr	Unspr
Maximum Height in Feet	UH	150'	UH	150'	120'	100'	70'	50'	60'	40'
UH	UA		UA							
12		UA		UA						
11										
10					27,360					
9					29,640	14,820				
8					31,920	15,960				
7					34,200	17,100				
6					36,480	18,240				
5					38,760	19,380	21,000			
4					41,040	20,520	24,000	12,000	15,360	
3					43,320	21,660	24,000	12,000	15,360	7,680
2					68,400	22,800	45,000	15,000	28,800	9,600
1					68,400	22,800	45,000	15,000	28,800	9,600

Each number in the table represents the maximum area per floor in square feet for every floor of a building of that story height.

Key to Abbreviations

UA	Unlimited area
UH	Unlimited height
NP	Not permitted
Spr	With approved sprinkler system
Unspr	Without approved sprinkler system

BOCA NATIONAL BUILDING CODE

Further Information

For information on Use Group classifications, see page 8. For information on mixed-use buildings, see page 12. For information on which code to consult, see page 7.

Unit Conversions

1 ft = 304.8 mm, 1 sq ft = 0.0929 m²

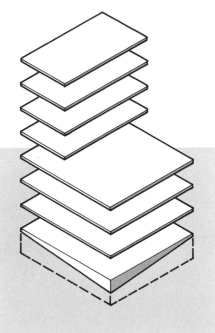

COMBUSTIBLE											
		Ordinary				Wood Light Frame					
Mill (page 430)		1-Hour (page 431)		Unprotected (page 431)		1-Hour (page 433)		Unprotected (page 433)		**Construction Type**	
Spr	Unspr	Spr	Unspr	Spr	Unspr	Spr	Unspr	Spr	Unspr		
70'	50'	70'	50'	60'	40'	60'	40'	55'	35'	**Maximum Height in Feet**	
											UH
											12
											11
											10
											9
											8
											7
										Height in Stories	6
20,160		18,480									5
23,040	11,520	21,120	10,560	15,360		16,320					4
23,040	11,520	21,120	10,560	15,360	7,680	16,320	8,160	7,680			3
43,200	14,400	39,600	13,200	28,800	9,600	30,600	10,200	14,400	4,800		2
43,200	14,400	39,600	13,200	28,800	9,600	30,600	10,200	14,400	4,800		1

This table was compiled from information contained in the BOCA National Building Code, 1987 Edition. It does not represent an official interpretation by the organization that issues the BOCA National Building Code.

USE GROUP R-2: RESIDENTIAL, MULTIFAMILY

Fire Walls

For multiplication of the allowable area by subdividing the building with fire walls, see page 424.

Excess Frontage

If more than 25% of the building perimeter fronts on a street or unoccupied space at least 30 ft wide that is accessible to firefighting vehicles, the tabulated area limitations may be increased 2% for each 1% of such excess frontage.

Measurements

Height is measured from the average finished ground level adjoining the building to the top of the highest roof beams of a flat roof, or the average level of the highest sloping roof. Floor area is measured within exterior walls or exterior walls and fire walls, exclusive of courtyards.

USE GROUP R-2: RESIDENTIAL, MULTIFAMILY

Construction Type	NONCOMBUSTIBLE									
	3-Hour (page 425)		2-Hour (page 426)		1.5-Hour (page 427)		1-Hour (page 428)		Unprotected (page 429)	
	Spr	Unspr	Spr	Unspr	Spr	Unspr	Spr	Unspr	Spr	Unspr
Maximum Height in Feet	UH	150'	UH	150'	120'	100'	70'	50'	60'	40'
UH	UA		UA							
12		UA		UA						
11										
10					27,360					
9					29,640	14,820				
8					31,920	15,960				
7					34,200	17,100				
6					36,480	18,240				
5					38,760	19,380	21,000			
4					41,040	20,520	24,000	12,000	15,360	
3					43,320	21,660	24,000	12,000	15,360	7,680
2					68,400	22,800	45,000	15,000	28,800	9,600
1					68,400	22,800	45,000	15,000	28,800	9,600

(Height in Stories — rows 1 through UH above)

Each number in the table represents the maximum area per floor in square feet for every floor of a building of that story height.

Key to Abbreviations

UA	Unlimited area
UH	Unlimited height
NP	Not permitted
Spr	With approved sprinkler system
Unspr	Without approved sprinkler system

BOCA NATIONAL BUILDING CODE

Further Information
For information on Use Group classifications, see page 8. For information on mixed-use buildings, see page 12. For information on which code to consult, see page 7.

Unit Conversions
1 ft = 304.8 mm, 1 sq ft = 0.0929 m².

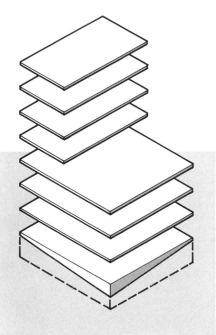

Mill (page 430)		Ordinary				Wood Light Frame				Construction Type
		1-Hour (page 431)		Unprotected (page 431)		1-Hour (page 433)		Unprotected (page 433)		

<div style="combustible header spans Ordinary and Wood Light Frame above>

COMBUSTIBLE										
Mill (page 430)		**Ordinary**				**Wood Light Frame**				
		1-Hour (page 431)		**Unprotected (page 431)**		**1-Hour (page 433)**		**Unprotected (page 433)**		**Construction Type**
Spr	Unspr	Spr	Unspr	Spr	Unspr	Spr	Unspr	Spr	Unspr	
70′	50′	70′	50′	60′	40′	60′	40′	55′	35′	**Maximum Height in Feet**
										UH
										12
										11
										10
										9
										8
										7
										6 **Height in Stories**
20,160		18,480								5
23,040	11,520	21,120	10,560	15,360		16,320				4
23,040	11,520	21,120	10,560	15,360	7,680	16,320	8,160	7,680		3
43,200	14,400	39,600	13,200	28,800	9,600	30,600	10,200	14,400	4,800	2
43,200	14,400	39,600	13,200	28,800	9,600	30,600	10,200	14,400	4,800	1

This table was compiled from information contained in the BOCA National Building Code, 1987 Edition. It does not represent an official interpretation by the organization that issues the BOCA National Building Code.

HEIGHT AND AREA LIMITATIONS

USE GROUP R-3: RESIDENTIAL, ONE- AND TWO-FAMILY

Fire Walls
For multiplication of the allowable area by subdividing the building with fire walls, see page 424.

Excess Frontage
If more than 25% of the building perimeter fronts on a street or unoccupied space at least 30 ft wide that is accessible to firefighting vehicles, the tabulated area limitations may be increased 2% for each 1% of such excess frontage.

Measurements
Height is measured from the average finished ground level adjoining the building to the top of the highest roof beams of a flat roof, or the average level of the highest sloping roof. Floor area is measured within exterior walls or exterior walls and fire walls, exclusive of courtyards.

USE GROUP R-3: RESIDENTIAL, ONE- AND TWO-FAMILY

Construction Type	NONCOMBUSTIBLE									
	3-Hour (page 425)		2-Hour (page 426)		1.5-Hour (page 427)		1-Hour (page 428)		Unprotected (page 429)	
	Spr	Unspr	Spr	Unspr	Spr	Unspr	Spr	Unspr	Spr	Unspr
Maximum Height in Feet	UH	UH	UH	UH	70'	50'	70'	50'	60'	40'
UH	UA	UA	UA	UA						
10										
9										
8										
7										
6										
5					38,760		21,000			
4					41,040	20,520	24,000	12,000	15,360	
3					43,320	21,660	24,000	12,000	15,360	7,680
2					68,400	22,800	45,000	15,000	28,800	9,600
1					68,400	22,800	45,000	15,000	28,800	9,600

Height in Stories labels rows 6 through 1.

Each number in the table represents the maximum area per floor in square feet for every floor of a building of that story height.

Key to Abbreviations

UA	Unlimited area
UH	Unlimited height
NP	Not permitted
Spr	With approved sprinkler system
Unspr	Without approved sprinkler system

Further Information

For information on Use Group classifications, see page 8. For information on mixed-use buildings, see page 12. For information on which code to consult, see page 7.

Unit Conversions

1 ft = 304.8 mm, 1 sq ft = 0.0929 m².

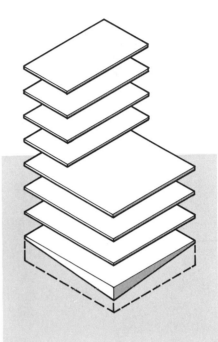

COMBUSTIBLE											
Mill (page 430)		Ordinary				Wood Light Frame				Construction Type	
		1-Hour (page 431)		Unprotected (page 431)		1-Hour (page 433)		Unprotected (page 433)			
Spr	Unspr	Spr	Unspr	Spr	Unspr	Spr	Unspr	Spr	Unspr	Maximum Height in Feet	
70'	50'	70'	50'	60'	40'	60'	40'	55'	35'		Height in Stories
										UH	
										10	
										9	
										8	
										7	
										6	Height in Stories
20,160		18,480								5	
23,040	11,520	21,120	10,560	15,360		16,320				4	
23,040	11,520	21,120	10,560	15,360	7,680	16,320	8,160	7,680		3	
43,200	14,400	39,600	13,200	28,800	9,600	30,600	10,200	14,400	4,800	2	
43,200	14,400	39,600	13,200	28,800	9,600	30,600	10,200	14,400	4,800	1	

This table was compiled from information contained in The BOCA® National Building Code/1987. It does not represent an official interpretation by the organization that issues the BOCA National Building Code.

HEIGHT AND AREA LIMITATIONS

321

USE GROUP S-1: STORAGE, MODERATE

Sprinklers

An approved sprinkler system is required in this Use Group for buildings larger than 12,000 sq ft per floor, or 24,000 sq ft total for all floors, or three stories in height.

Unlimited Area

In this Use Group, a single-story building not more than 85 ft tall of construction other than Wood Light Frame and provided with an approved sprinkler system is not limited in area provided it is separated from adjacent buildings by at least 30 ft, and has exterior walls of 3-Hour construction if such separation is less than 50 ft.

Fire Walls

For multiplication of the allowable area by subdividing the building with fire walls, see page 424.

Excess Frontage

If more than 25% of the building perimeter fronts on a street or unoccupied space at least 30 ft wide that is accessible to firefighting vehicles, the tabulated area limitations may be increased 2% for each 1% of such excess frontage.

USE GROUP S-1: STORAGE, MODERATE

	NONCOMBUSTIBLE									
Construction Type	3-Hour (page 425)		2-Hour (page 426)		1.5-Hour (page 427)		1-Hour (page 428)		Unprotected (page 429)	
	Spr	Unspr	Spr	Unspr	Spr	Unspr	Spr	Unspr	Spr	Unspr
Maximum Height in Feet	UH	UH	UH	UH	85′	65′	70′	50′	50′	30′
Height in Stories UH	UA		UA							
10										
9										
8										
7										
6					31,920					
5					33,916		18,375			
4					35,910		21,000			
3		12,000		12,000	37,906	12,000	21,000	12,000	13,440	
2		12,000		12,000	59,850	12,000	39,375	12,000	25,200	8,400
1		12,000		12,000	59,850	12,000	39,375	12,000	25,200	8,400

Each number in the table represents the maximum area per floor in square feet for every floor of a building of that story height.

Key to Abbreviations

UA	Unlimited area
UH	Unlimited height
NP	Not permitted
Spr	With approved sprinkler system
Unspr	Without approved sprinkler system

BOCA NATIONAL BUILDING CODE

Measurements
Height is measured from the average finished ground level adjoining the building to the top of the highest roof beams of a flat roof, or the average level of the highest sloping roof. Floor area is measured within exterior walls or exterior walls and fire walls, exclusive of courtyards.

Further Information
For information on Use Group classifications, see page 8. For information on mixed-use buildings, see page 12. For information on which code to consult, see page 7.

Unit Conversions
1 ft = 304.8 mm, 1 sq ft = 0.0929 m².

COMBUSTIBLE										Construction Type
Mill (page 430)		Ordinary				Wood Light Frame				
		1-Hour (page 431)		Unprotected (page 431)		1-Hour (page 433)		Unprotected (page 433)		
Spr	Unspr	Spr	Unspr	Spr	Unspr	Spr	Unspr	Spr	Unspr	
70'	50'	60'	40'	50'	30'	50'	30'	40'	20'	Maximum Height in Feet
										UH
										10
										9
										8
										7
										6 Height in Stories
17,640										5
20,160		18,480								4
20,160	12,000	18,480	9,240	13,440		14,280				3
37,800	12,000	34,650	11,550	25,200	8,400	26,775	8,925	12,600		2
37,800	12,000	34,650	11,550	25,200	8,400	26,775	8,925	12,600	4,200	1

This table was compiled from information contained in The BOCA® National Building Code/1987. It does not represent an official interpretation by the organization that issues the BOCA National Building Code.

HEIGHT AND AREA LIMITATIONS

323

USE GROUP S-2: STORAGE, LOW

Unlimited Area
In this Use Group, a single-story building not more than 85 ft tall of construction other than Wood Light Frame and provided with an approved sprinkler system is not limited in area provided it is separated from adjacent buildings by at least 30 ft, and has exterior walls of 2-Hour construction if such separation is less than 50 ft.

Fire Walls
For multiplication of the allowable area by subdividing the building with fire walls, see page 424.

Excess Frontage
If more than 25% of the building perimeter fronts on a street or unoccupied space at least 30 ft wide that is accessible to firefighting vehicles, the tabulated area limitations may be increased 2% for each 1% of such excess frontage.

Measurements
Height is measured from the average finished ground level adjoining the building to the top of the highest roof beams of a flat roof, or the average level of the highest sloping roof. Floor area is measured within exterior walls or exterior walls and fire walls, exclusive of courtyards.

USE GROUP S-2: STORAGE, LOW

Construction Type	NONCOMBUSTIBLE									
	3-Hour (page 425)		2-Hour (page 426)		1.5-Hour (page 427)		1-Hour (page 428)		Unprotected (page 429)	
	Spr	Unspr	Spr	Unspr	Spr	Unspr	Spr	Unspr	Spr	Unspr
Maximum Height in Feet	UH	UH	UH	UH	105'	85'	85'	65'	60'	40'
UH	UA	UA	UA	UA						
10										
9										
8					47,880					
7					51,300	25,650				
6					54,720	27,360	27,000			
5					58,140	29,070	31,500	15,750		
4					61,560	30,780	36,000	18,000	23,040	
3					64,980	32,490	36,000	18,000	23,040	11,520
2					102,600	34,200	67,500	22,500	43,200	14,400
1					102,600	34,200	67,500	22,500	43,200	14,400

Height in Stories

Each number in the table represents the maximum area per floor in square feet for every floor of a building of that story height.

324

Key to Abbreviations

UA	Unlimited area
UH	Unlimited height
NP	Not permitted
Spr	With approved sprinkler system
Unspr	Without approved sprinkler system

BOCA NATIONAL BUILDING CODE

Further Information

For information on Use Group classifications, see page 8. For information on mixed-use buildings, see page 12. For information on which code to consult, see page 7.

Unit Conversions

1 ft = 304.8 mm, 1 sq ft = 0.0929 m².

COMBUSTIBLE											
		Ordinary				Wood Light Frame					Construction Type
Mill (page 430)		1-Hour (page 431)		Unprotected (page 431)		1-Hour (page 433)		Unprotected (page 433)			
Spr	Unspr	Spr	Unspr	Spr	Unspr	Spr	Unspr	Spr	Unspr		
85'	65'	70'	50'	60'	40'	60'	40'	50'	30'		Maximum Height in Feet
										UH	
										10	
										9	
										8	
										7	
25,920										6	Height in Stories
30,240	15,120	27,720								5	
34,560	17,280	31,680	15,840	23,040		24,480				4	
34,560	17,280	31,680	15,840	23,040	11,520	24,480	12,240	11,520		3	
64,800	21,600	59,400	19,800	43,200	14,400	45,900	15,300	21,600	7,200	2	
64,800	21,600	59,400	19,800	43,200	14,400	45,900	15,300	21,600	7,200	1	

This table was compiled from information contained in The BOCA® National Building Code/1987. It does not represent an official interpretation by the organization that issues the BOCA National Building Code.

HEIGHT AND AREA LIMITATIONS

325

USE GROUP: OPEN PARKING GARAGES

Unlimited Area*

If open on all sides and the distance from any point on a floor to an open wall does not exceed 200 ft, the maximum height is 75 ft and the area is not limited. Alternatively, floors may be of unlimited area if the building height does not exceed 2 stories and 25 ft.

Definition

To qualify as an open parking garage, two or more sides of the structure must be substantially open to the passage of air. Parking is permitted on the roof.

Fire Walls

For multiplication of the allowable area by subdividing the building with fire walls, see page 424.

Excess Frontage

If more than 25% of the building perimeter fronts on a street or unoccupied space at least 30 ft wide that is accessible to firefighting vehicles, the tabulated area limitations may be increased 2% for each 1% of such excess frontage.

USE GROUP: OPEN PARKING GARAGES

Construction Type	NONCOMBUSTIBLE									
	3-Hour (page 425)		2-Hour (page 426)		1.5-Hour (page 427)		1-Hour (page 428)		Unprotected (page 429)	
	Spr	Unspr	Spr	Unspr	Spr	Unspr	Spr	Unspr	Spr	Unspr
Maximum Height in Feet	UH	UH	UH	UH	120'	120'	100'	100'	85'	85'
UH	UA	UA	UA	UA						
10					UA	UA				
9										
8							UA	*50,000		
7								*50,000		
6								*50,000	UA	*50,000
5								*50,000		*50,000
4								*50,000		*50,000
3								*50,000		*50,000
2								*50,000		*50,000
1								*50,000		*50,000

Height in Stories

Each number in the table represents the maximum area per floor in square feet for every floor of a building of that story height.

Key to Abbreviations

UA	Unlimited area
UH	Unlimited height
NP	Not permitted
Spr	With approved sprinkler system
Unspr	Without approved sprinkler system

BOCA NATIONAL BUILDING CODE

Measurements

Height is measured from the average finished ground level adjoining the building to the top of the highest roof beams of a flat roof, or the average level of the highest sloping roof. Floor area is measured within exterior walls or exterior walls and fire walls, exclusive of courtyards.

Further Information

For information on Use Group classifications, see page 8. For information on mixed-use buildings, see page 12. For information on which code to consult, see page 7.

Unit Conversions

1 ft = 304.8 mm, 1 sq ft = 0.0929 m^2

COMBUSTIBLE										Construction Type	Maximum Height in Feet / Height in Stories
Mill (page 430)		Ordinary				Wood Light Frame					
		1-Hour (page 431)		Unprotected (page 431)		1-Hour (page 433)		Unprotected (page 433)			
Spr	Unspr	Spr	Unspr	Spr	Unspr	Spr	Unspr	Spr	Unspr		
											UH
											10
											9
											8
											7
											6
											5
											4
											3
											2
NP	NP	NP	NP	NP	NP	NP	NP	NP	NP		1

This table was compiled from information contained in The BOCA® National Building Code/1987. It does not represent an official interpretation by the organization that issues the BOCA National Building Code.

HEIGHT AND AREA LIMITATIONS

HOW TO USE THE TABLES OF HEIGHT AND AREA LIMITATIONS FOR THE NATIONAL BUILDING CODE OF CANADA

1. Be sure you are consulting the tables for the proper building code. If you are not sure which code you are working under, see page 7.

2. The Use Group is given at the upper left-hand corner of the table. If you are not sure about the Use Group into which your building falls, consult the index of Use Groups on page 9.

3. Noncombustible Construction Types are tabulated on the left-hand page, and both noncombustible and combustible Construction Types are tabulated on the right-hand page.

4. Each pair of columns represents one Construction Type. For specific information on the different materials and modes of construction that conform to that Construction Type, follow the page reference given here.

5. The paired columns tabulate height and area information for both sprinklered and unsprinklered buildings of each Construction Type.

328

6. The significance of the floor area numbers in the chart, which varies from one model code to another, is explained at the lower left-hand corner.

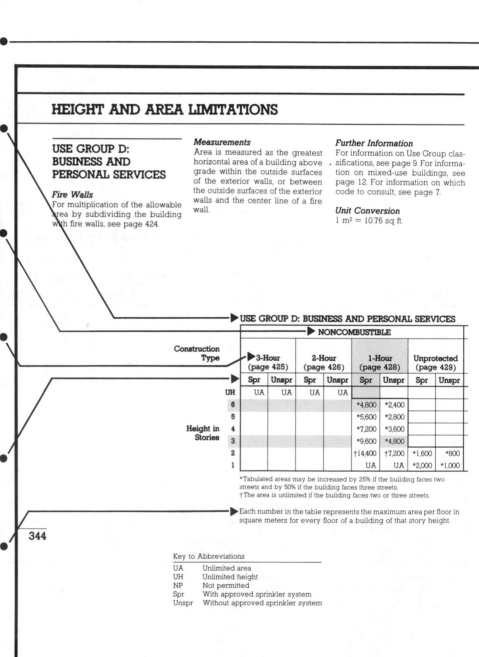

HEIGHT AND AREA LIMITATIONS

**USE GROUP D:
BUSINESS AND
PERSONAL SERVICES**

Fire Walls
For multiplication of the allowable area by subdividing the building with fire walls, see page 424.

Measurements
Area is measured as the greatest horizontal area of a building above grade within the outside surfaces of the exterior walls, or between the outside surfaces of the exterior walls and the center line of a fire wall.

Further Information
For information on Use Group classifications, see page 9. For information on mixed-use buildings, see page 12. For information on which code to consult, see page 7.

Unit Conversion
1 m² = 10.76 sq ft.

USE GROUP D: BUSINESS AND PERSONAL SERVICES

NONCOMBUSTIBLE

Construction Type		3-Hour (page 425)		2-Hour (page 426)		1-Hour (page 428)		Unprotected (page 429)	
		Spr	Unspr	Spr	Unspr	Spr	Unspr	Spr	Unspr
	UH	UA	UA	UA	UA				
	6					*4,800	*2,400		
	5					*5,600	*2,800		
Height in Stories	4					*7,200	*3,600		
	3					*9,600	*4,800		
	2					†14,400	†7,200	*1,600	*800
	1					UA	UA	*2,000	*1,000

*Tabulated areas may be increased by 25% if the building faces two streets and by 50% if the building faces three streets.
†The area is unlimited if the building faces two or three streets.

Each number in the table represents the maximum area per floor in square meters for every floor of a building of that story height.

344

Key to Abbreviations

UA	Unlimited area
UH	Unlimited height
NP	Not permitted
Spr	With approved sprinkler system
Unspr	Without approved sprinkler system

NATIONAL BUILDING CODE OF CANADA

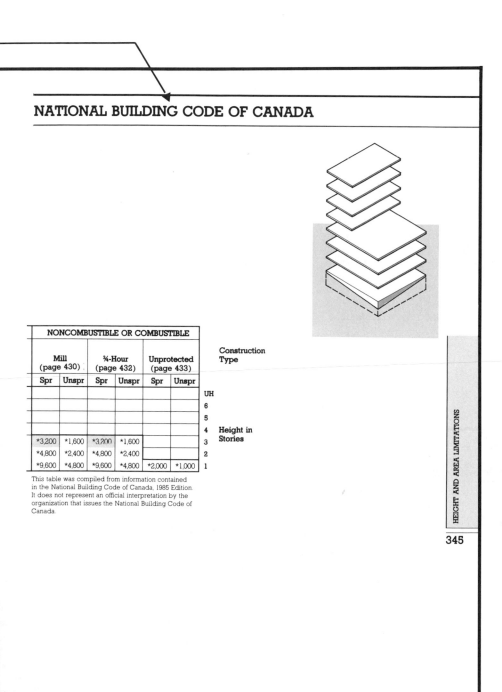

NATIONAL BUILDING CODE OF CANADA

NONCOMBUSTIBLE OR COMBUSTIBLE						Construction Type	
Mill (page 430)		¾-Hour (page 432)		Unprotected (page 433)			
Spr	Unspr	Spr	Unspr	Spr	Unspr		
						UH	
						6	
						5	
						4	Height in Stories
*3,200	*1,600	*3,200	*1,600			3	
*4,800	*2,400	*4,800	*2,400			2	
*9,600	*4,800	*9,600	*4,800	*2,000	*1,000	1	

This table was compiled from information contained in the National Building Code of Canada, 1985 Edition. It does not represent an official interpretation by the organization that issues the National Building Code of Canada.

345

7. As an example of the use of this chart, a sprinklered building of Use Group D, 1-Hour construction, under the National Building Code of Canada, may be no more than 6 stories tall, with no floor larger in area than 4800 m².

8. As another example, if we wish to construct a 3-story unsprinklered building with 3150 m² per floor, we must use 1-Hour construction as a minimum. Looking to the right along the same row of the chart, we see that the addition of sprinklers would allow us to use Mill or ¾-Hour construction. By following the page references at the heads of these columns, we can determine exactly what each of these Construction Types is, and proceed to preliminary configuration and sizing of the structural system we select.

HEIGHT AND AREA LIMITATIONS

329

The reference tables appearing on pages 328–355 are for preliminary design purposes only. They represent the authors' interpretation of certain major provisions of the National Building Code of Canada, 1985. No official interpretation has been sought from or granted by the Associate Committee on the National Building Code. For design development work and final preparation of building plans, you must consult the National Building Code of Canada, 1985, issued by the Associate Committee on the National Building Code, National Research Council of Canada, NRCC No. 23174, copyright © National Research Council of Canada, 1985.

HEIGHT AND AREA LIMITATIONS

USE GROUP A-1: ASSEMBLY BUILDINGS

Fire Walls

For multiplication of the allowable area by subdividing the building with fire walls, see page 424.

Measurements

Area is measured as the greatest horizontal area of a building above grade within the outside surfaces of the exterior walls, or between the outside surfaces of the exterior walls and the center line of a fire wall.

Further Information

For information on Use Group classifications, see page 9. For information on mixed-use buildings, see page 12. For information on which code to consult, see page 7.

Unit Conversion

$1 \text{ m}^2 = 10.76 \text{ sq ft.}$

USE GROUP A-1: ASSEMBLY BUILDINGS

Construction Type	NONCOMBUSTIBLE							
	3-Hour (page 425)		2-Hour (page 426)		1-Hour (page 428)		Unprotected (page 429)	
Height in Stories	Spr	Unspr	Spr	Unspr	Spr	Unspr	Spr	Unspr
UH	UA	UA	UA	UA				
6								
5								
4								
3								
2								
1					†UA	†UA	NP	NP

*40% of the area may be two stories high, and the occupant load of the building may not exceed 600 persons.
†The occupant load of the auditorium may not exceed 300 persons.

Each number in the table represents the maximum area per floor in square meters for every floor of a building of that story height.

Key to Abbreviations

UA	Unlimited area
UH	Unlimited height
NP	Not permitted
Spr	With approved sprinkler system
Unspr	Without approved sprinkler system

NONCOMBUSTIBLE OR COMBUSTIBLE						Construction Type
Mill (page 430)		¾-Hour (page 432)		Unprotected (page 433)		
Spr	Unspr	Spr	Unspr	Spr	Unspr	
						UH
						6
						5
						4 Height in
						3 Stories
						2
*600	*600	†UA	†UA	NP	NP	1

This table was compiled from information contained in the National Building Code of Canada, 1985 Edition. It does not represent an official interpretation by the organization that issues the National Building Code of Canada.

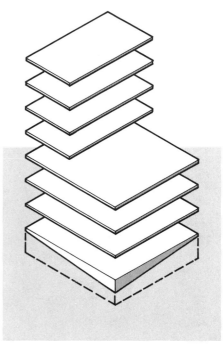

USE GROUP A-2: ASSEMBLY BUILDINGS

Fire Walls
For multiplication of the allowable area by subdividing the building with fire walls, see page 424.

Measurements
Area is measured as the greatest horizontal area of a building above grade within the outside surfaces of the exterior walls, or between the outside surfaces of the exterior walls and the center line of a fire wall.

Further Information
For information on Use Group classifications, see page 9. For information on mixed-use buildings, see page 12. For information on which code to consult, see page 7.

Unit Conversion
1 m² = 10.76 sq ft.

USE GROUP A-2: ASSEMBLY BUILDINGS

Construction Type	NONCOMBUSTIBLE							
	3-Hour (page 425)		2-Hour (page 426)		1-Hour (page 428)		Unprotected (page 429)	
Height in Stories	Spr	Unspr	Spr	Unspr	Spr	Unspr	Spr	Unspr
UH	UA	UA	UA	UA				
6								
5					UA	UA		
4								
3								
2							*400	
1							*800	*400

*Tabulated areas may be increased by 25% if the building faces two streets and by 50% if the building faces three streets.

Each number in the table represents the maximum area per floor in square meters for every floor of a building of that story height.

Key to Abbreviations

UA	Unlimited area
UH	Unlimited height
NP	Not permitted
Spr	With approved sprinkler system
Unspr	Without approved sprinkler system

NATIONAL BUILDING CODE OF CANADA

NONCOMBUSTIBLE OR COMBUSTIBLE							Construction Type
Mill (page 430)		¾-Hour (page 432)		Unprotected (page 433)			
Spr	Unspr	Spr	Unspr	Spr	Unspr		
						UH	
						6	
						5	
						4	Height in Stories
						3	
		*1,600	*800	*400		2	
6,400	3,200	*3,200	*1,600	*800	*400	1	

This table was compiled from information contained in the National Building Code of Canada, 1985 Edition. It does not represent an official interpretation by the organization that issues the National Building Code of Canada.

USE GROUP A-3: ASSEMBLY, ARENA TYPE

Fire Walls

For multiplication of the allowable area by subdividing the building with fire walls, see page 424.

Measurements

Area is measured as the greatest horizontal area of a building above grade within the outside surfaces of the exterior walls, or between the outside surfaces of the exterior walls and the center line of a fire wall.

Further Information

For information on Use Group classifications, see page 9. For information on mixed-use buildings, see page 12. For information on which code to consult, see page 7.

Unit Conversion

$1 \text{ m}^2 = 10.76 \text{ sq ft.}$

USE GROUP A-3: ASSEMBLY, ARENA TYPE

Construction Type	NONCOMBUSTIBLE							
	3-Hour (page 425)		2-Hour (page 426)		1-Hour (page 428)		Unprotected (page 429)	
Height in Stories	Spr	Unspr	Spr	Unspr	Spr	Unspr	Spr	Unspr
UH	UA	UA	UA	UA				
6								
5								
4								
3								
2					*4,000	*2,000		
1					*8,000	*4,000	*2,000	*1,000

*Tabulated areas may be increased by 25% if the building faces two streets and by 50% if the building faces three streets.

Each number in the table represents the maximum area per floor in square meters for every floor of a building of that story height.

Key to Abbreviations

UA	Unlimited area
UH	Unlimited height
NP	Not permitted
Spr	With approved sprinkler system
Unspr	Without approved sprinkler system

NATIONAL BUILDING CODE OF CANADA

NONCOMBUSTIBLE OR COMBUSTIBLE							
Mill (page 430)		¾-Hour (page 432)		Unprotected (page 433)		**Construction Type**	
Spr	Unspr	Spr	Unspr	Spr	Unspr		
						UH	
						6	
						5	
						4	**Height in Stories**
						3	
						2	
*4,800	*2,400	*4,800	*2,400	*2,000	*1,000	1	

This table was compiled from information contained in the National Building Code of Canada, 1985 Edition. It does not represent an official interpretation by the organization that issues the National Building Code of Canada.

HEIGHT AND AREA LIMITATIONS

USE GROUP A-4: ASSEMBLY, OPEN AIR

Fire Walls
For multiplication of the allowable area by subdividing the building with fire walls, see page 424.

Measurements
Area is measured as the greatest horizontal area of a building above grade within the outside surfaces of the exterior walls, or between the outside surfaces of the exterior walls and the center line of a fire wall.

Further Information
For information on Use Group classifications, see page 9. For information on mixed-use buildings, see page 12. For information on which code to consult, see page 7.

Unit Conversion
$1 \text{ m}^2 = 10.76 \text{ sq ft}$.

USE GROUP A-4: ASSEMBLY, OPEN AIR

Construction Type		NONCOMBUSTIBLE							
		3-Hour (page 425)		2-Hour (page 426)		1-Hour (page 428)		Unprotected (page 429)	
		Spr	Unspr	Spr	Unspr	Spr	Unspr	Spr	Unspr
Height in Stories	UH								
	6								
	5								
	4								
	3								
	2								
	1	*UA	*UA	*UA	*UA	*UA	*UA	*UA	*UA

*Roof assemblies may be of Heavy Timber construction.
†The occupant load may not exceed 1500 persons, and the building must be at least 6 m from a property line or another building.

Each number in the table represents the maximum area per floor in square meters for every floor of a building of that story height.

Key to Abbreviations

UA	Unlimited area
UH	Unlimited height
NP	Not permitted
Spr	With approved sprinkler system
Unspr	Without approved sprinkler system

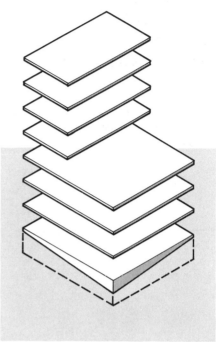

NONCOMBUSTIBLE OR COMBUSTIBLE							
Mill (page 430)		¾-Hour (page 432)		Unprotected (page 433)		Construction Type	
Spr	Unspr	Spr	Unspr	Spr	Unspr		
						UH	
						6	
						5	
						4	Height in
						3	Stories
						2	
†UA	†UA	†UA	†UA	†UA	†UA	1	

This table was compiled from information contained in the National Building Code of Canada, 1985 Edition. It does not represent an official interpretation by the organization that issues the National Building Code of Canada.

HEIGHT AND AREA LIMITATIONS

337

HEIGHT AND AREA LIMITATIONS

USE GROUP B-1: INSTITUTIONAL, DETENTION

Fire Walls
For multiplication of the allowable area by subdividing the building with fire walls, see page 424.

Measurements
Area is measured as the greatest horizontal area of a building above grade within the outside surfaces of the exterior walls, or between the outside surfaces of the exterior walls and the center line of a fire wall.

Further Information
For information on Use Group classifications, see page 9. For information on mixed-use buildings, see page 12. For information on which code to consult, see page 7.

Unit Conversion
1 m² = 10.76 sq ft.

USE GROUP B-1: INSTITUTIONAL, DETENTION

Construction Type	NONCOMBUSTIBLE							
	3-Hour (page 425)		2-Hour (page 426)		1-Hour (page 428)		Unprotected (page 429)	
Height in Stories	Spr	Unspr	Spr	Unspr	Spr	Unspr	Spr	Unspr
UH	UA	UA	UA	UA				
6								
5								
4								
3								
2								
1					NP	NP	NP	NP

Each number in the table represents the maximum area per floor in square meters for every floor of a building of that story height.

Key to Abbreviations

UA	Unlimited area
UH	Unlimited height
NP	Not permitted
Spr	With approved sprinkler system
Unspr	Without approved sprinkler system

NONCOMBUSTIBLE OR COMBUSTIBLE							
Mill (page 430)		¾-Hour (page 432)		Unprotected (page 433)			**Construction Type**
Spr	Unspr	Spr	Unspr	Spr	Unspr		
						UH	
						6	
						5	
						4	**Height in Stories**
						3	
						2	
NP	NP	NP	NP	NP	NP	1	

This table was compiled from information contained in the National Building Code of Canada, 1985 Edition. It does not represent an official interpretation by the organization that issues the National Building Code of Canada.

HEIGHT AND AREA LIMITATIONS

USE GROUP B-2: INSTITUTIONAL, RESTRAINED

Fire Walls
For multiplication of the allowable area by subdividing the building with fire walls, see page 424.

Measurements
Area is measured as the greatest horizontal area of a building above grade within the outside surfaces of the exterior walls, or between the outside surfaces of the exterior walls and the center line of a fire wall.

Further Information
For information on Use Group classifications, see page 9. For information on mixed-use buildings, see page 12. For information on which code to consult, see page 7.

Unit Conversion
1 m² = 10.76 sq ft.

USE GROUP B-2: INSTITUTIONAL, RESTRAINED

Construction Type	NONCOMBUSTIBLE							
	3-Hour (page 425)		2-Hour (page 426)		1-Hour (page 428)		Unprotected (page 429)	
Height in Stories	Spr	Unspr	Spr	Unspr	Spr	Unspr	Spr	Unspr
UH	UA	UA	UA	UA				
6								
5								
4								
3					8,000			
2					12,000	500		
1					UA	1,000	500	250

Each number in the table represents the maximum area per floor in square meters for every floor of a building of that story height.

Key to Abbreviations

UA	Unlimited area
UH	Unlimited height
NP	Not permitted
Spr	With approved sprinkler system
Unspr	Without approved sprinkler system

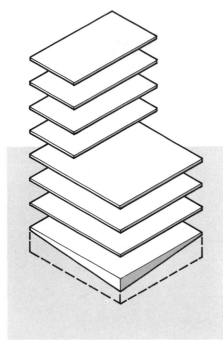

NONCOMBUSTIBLE OR COMBUSTIBLE						Construction Type
Mill (page 430)		¾-Hour (page 432)		Unprotected (page 433)		
Spr	Unspr	Spr	Unspr	Spr	Unspr	
						UH
						6
						5
						4 Height in Stories
						3
1,600	500	1,600	500			2
2,400	1,000	2,400	1,000	500	250	1

This table was compiled from information contained in the National Building Code of Canada, 1985 Edition. It does not represent an official interpretation by the organization that issues the National Building Code of Canada.

HEIGHT AND AREA LIMITATIONS

341

USE GROUP C: RESIDENTIAL

Fire Walls
For multiplication of the allowable area by subdividing the building with fire walls, see page 424.

Measurements
Area is measured as the greatest horizontal area of a building above grade within the outside surfaces of the exterior walls, or between the outside surfaces of the exterior walls and the center line of a fire wall.

Further Information
For information on Use Group classifications, see page 9. For information on mixed-use buildings, see page 12. For information on which code to consult, see page 7.

Unit Conversion
1 m^2 = 10.76 sq ft.

USE GROUP C: RESIDENTIAL

Construction Type / Height in Stories	NONCOMBUSTIBLE							
	3-Hour (page 425)		2-Hour (page 426)		1-Hour (page 428)		Unprotected (page 429)	
	Spr	Unspr	Spr	Unspr	Spr	Unspr	Spr	Unspr
UH	UA	UA	UA	UA				
6					*4,000	*2,000		
5					*4,800	*2,400		
4					*6,000	*3,000		
3					*8,000	*4,000	‡*1,200	‡*600
2					†12,000	†6,000	‡*1,800	‡*900
1					UA	UA	*2,400	*1,200

*Tabulated areas may be increased by 25% if the building faces two streets and by 50% if the building faces three streets.
†The area is unlimited if the building faces two or three streets.
‡Applies only to buildings where there is no dwelling unit over another.

Each number in the table represents the maximum area per floor in square meters for every floor of a building of that story height.

Key to Abbreviations

UA	Unlimited area
UH	Unlimited height
NP	Not permitted
Spr	With approved sprinkler system
Unspr	Without approved sprinkler system

NONCOMBUSTIBLE OR COMBUSTIBLE						Construction Type
Mill (page 430)		¾-Hour (page 432)		Unprotected (page 433)		
Spr	Unspr	Spr	Unspr	Spr	Unspr	
						UH
						6
						5
						4 Height in Stories
*1,200	*600	*1,200	*600	‡*1,200	‡*600	3
*1,800	*900	*1,800	*900	‡*1,800	‡*900	2
*2,400	*1,200	*2,400	*1,200	*2,400	‡*1,200	1

This table was compiled from information contained in the National Building Code of Canada, 1985 Edition. It does not represent an official interpretation by the organization that issues the National Building Code of Canada.

HEIGHT AND AREA LIMITATIONS

343

USE GROUP D: BUSINESS AND PERSONAL SERVICES

Fire Walls
For multiplication of the allowable area by subdividing the building with fire walls, see page 424.

Measurements
Area is measured as the greatest horizontal area of a building above grade within the outside surfaces of the exterior walls, or between the outside surfaces of the exterior walls and the center line of a fire wall.

Further Information
For information on Use Group classifications, see page 9. For information on mixed-use buildings, see page 12. For information on which code to consult, see page 7.

Unit Conversion
$1 \text{ m}^2 = 10.76 \text{ sq ft.}$

USE GROUP D: BUSINESS AND PERSONAL SERVICES

Construction Type	NONCOMBUSTIBLE							
	3-Hour (page 425)		2-Hour (page 426)		1-Hour (page 428)		Unprotected (page 429)	
	Spr	Unspr	Spr	Unspr	Spr	Unspr	Spr	Unspr
UH	UA	UA	UA	UA				
6					*4,800	*2,400		
5					*5,600	*2,800		
4					*7,200	*3,600		
3					*9,600	*4,800		
2					†14,400	†7,200	*1,600	*800
1					UA	UA	*2,000	*1,000

(Row labels "Height in Stories" apply to rows UH through 1.)

*Tabulated areas may be increased by 25% if the building faces two streets and by 50% if the building faces three streets.
†The area is unlimited if the building faces two or three streets.

Each number in the table represents the maximum area per floor in square meters for every floor of a building of that story height.

344

Key to Abbreviations

UA	Unlimited area
UH	Unlimited height
NP	Not permitted
Spr	With approved sprinkler system
Unspr	Without approved sprinkler system

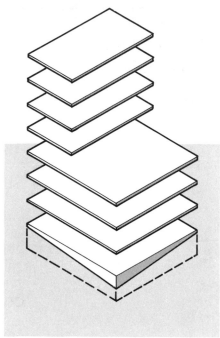

NONCOMBUSTIBLE OR COMBUSTIBLE						Construction Type
Mill (page 430)		¾-Hour (page 432)		Unprotected (page 433)		
Spr	Unspr	Spr	Unspr	Spr	Unspr	
						UH
						6
						5
						4 · Height in Stories
*3,200	*1,600	*3,200	*1,600			3
*4,800	*2,400	*4,800	*2,400			2
*9,600	*4,800	*9,600	*4,800	*2,000	*1,000	1

This table was compiled from information contained in the National Building Code of Canada, 1985 Edition. It does not represent an official interpretation by the organization that issues the National Building Code of Canada.

HEIGHT AND AREA LIMITATIONS

345

USE GROUP E: MERCANTILE BUILDINGS

Sprinklers
High buildings of this Use Group must be sprinklered; consult section 3.2.6.6.(1) of the National Building Code of Canada for details.

Fire Walls
For multiplication of the allowable area by subdividing the building with fire walls, see page 424.

Measurements
Area is measured as the greatest horizontal area of a building above grade within the outside surfaces of the exterior walls, or between the outside surfaces of the exterior walls and the center line of a fire wall.

Further Information
For information on Use Group classifications, see page 9. For information on mixed-use buildings, see page 12. For information on which code to consult, see page 7.

Unit Conversion
1 m² = 10.76 sq ft.

USE GROUP E: MERCANTILE BUILDINGS

Construction Type / Height in Stories	NONCOMBUSTIBLE							
	3-Hour (page 425)		2-Hour (page 426)		1-Hour (page 428)		Unprotected (page 429)	
	Spr	Unspr	Spr	Unspr	Spr	Unspr	Spr	Unspr
UH	UA	UA						
6			*2,500					
5			*3,000					
4			*3,750					
3			*5,000	1,500	*1,600	*800		
2			†7,500	1,500	*2,400	*1,200		
1			UA	1,500	*4,800	*1,500	*2,000	*1,000

*Tabulated areas may be increased by 25% if the building faces two streets and by 50% if the building faces three streets.
†The area is unlimited if the building faces two or three streets.

Each number in the table represents the maximum area per floor in square meters for every floor of a building of that story height.

Key to Abbreviations

UA	Unlimited area
UH	Unlimited height
NP	Not permitted
Spr	With approved sprinkler system
Unspr	Without approved sprinkler system

NONCOMBUSTIBLE OR COMBUSTIBLE						Construction Type
Mill (page 430)		¾-Hour (page 432)		Unprotected (page 433)		
Spr	Unspr	Spr	Unspr	Spr	Unspr	
						UH
						6
						5
						4 — Height in Stories
*1,600	*800	*1,600	*800			3
*2,400	*1,200	*2,400	*1,200			2
*4,800	*1,500	*4,800	*1,500	*2,000	*1,000	1

This table was compiled from information contained in the National Building Code of Canada, 1985 Edition. It does not represent an official interpretation by the organization that issues the National Building Code of Canada.

HEIGHT AND AREA LIMITATIONS

HEIGHT AND AREA LIMITATIONS

USE GROUP F-1: INDUSTRIAL, HIGH HAZARD

Sprinklers
High buildings of this Use Group must be sprinklered; consult section 3.2.6.6.(1) of the National Building Code of Canada for details.

Fire Walls
For multiplication of the allowable area by subdividing the building with fire walls, see page 424.

Measurements
Area is measured as the greatest horizontal area of a building above grade within the outside surfaces of the exterior walls, or between the outside surfaces of the exterior walls and the center line of a fire wall.

Further Information
For information on Use Group classifications, see page 9. For information on mixed-use buildings, see page 12. For information on which code to consult, see page 7.

Unit Conversion
1 m² = 10.76 sq ft.

USE GROUP F-1: INDUSTRIAL, HIGH HAZARD

Construction Type		NONCOMBUSTIBLE							
		3-Hour (page 425)		2-Hour (page 426)		1-Hour (page 428)		Unprotected (page 429)	
		Spr	Unspr	Spr	Unspr	Spr	Unspr	Spr	Unspr
Height in Stories	UH								
	6								
	5								
	4	*1,500		*1,200					
	3	*2,000		*1,600					
	2	*3,000		*2,400		*800			
	1	*6,000	NP	*4,800	NP	*1,600	NP	*4,800	NP

*Tabulated areas may be increased by 25% if the building faces two streets and by 50% if the building faces three streets.

Each number in the table represents the maximum area per floor in square meters for every floor of a building of that story height.

Key to Abbreviations

UA	Unlimited area
UH	Unlimited height
NP	Not permitted
Spr	With approved sprinkler system
Unspr	Without approved sprinkler system

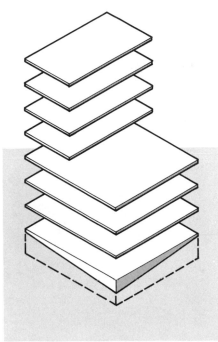

NONCOMBUSTIBLE OR COMBUSTIBLE							
Mill (page 430)		¾-Hour (page 432)		Unprotected (page 433)		**Construction Type**	
Spr	Unspr	Spr	Unspr	Spr	Unspr		
						UH	
						6	
						5	
						4	**Height in Stories**
*800						3	
*1,200		*800				2	
*2,400	NP	*1,600	NP	*1,600	NP	1	

This table was compiled from information contained in the National Building Code of Canada, 1985 Edition. It does not represent an official interpretation by the organization that issues the National Building Code of Canada.

HEIGHT AND AREA LIMITATIONS

HEIGHT AND AREA LIMITATIONS

USE GROUP F-2: INDUSTRIAL, MEDIUM HAZARD

Sprinklers
High buildings of this Use Group must be sprinklered; consult section 3.2.6.6.(1) of the National Building Code of Canada for details.

Fire Walls
For multiplication of the allowable area by subdividing the building with fire walls, see page 424.

Measurements
Area is measured as the greatest horizontal area of a building above grade within the outside surfaces of the exterior walls, or between the outside surfaces of the exterior walls and the center line of a fire wall.

Further Information
For information on Use Group classifications, see page 9. For information on mixed-use buildings, see page 12. For information on which code to consult, see page 7.

Unit Conversion
$1 \text{ m}^2 = 10.76 \text{ sq ft.}$

USE GROUP F-2: INDUSTRIAL, MEDIUM HAZARD

Construction Type	NONCOMBUSTIBLE							
	3-Hour (page 425)		2-Hour (page 426)		1-Hour (page 428)		Unprotected (page 429)	
	Spr	Unspr	Spr	Unspr	Spr	Unspr	Spr	Unspr
UH	UA							
6		*1,500	*3,000	*1,500				
5		*1,800	*3,600	*1,800				
4		*2,250	*4,500	*2,250	*3,000	*1,500		
3		*3,000	*6,000	*3,000	*4,000	*2,000		
2		*4,500	*9,000	*4,500	*6,000	*3,000	*1,200	*600
1		*9,000	*18,000	*9,000	*12,000	*6,000	*3,000	*1,000

(Left label: **Height in Stories**)

*Tabulated areas may be increased by 25% if the building faces two streets and by 50% if the building faces three streets.

Each number in the table represents the maximum area per floor in square meters for every floor of a building of that story height.

Key to Abbreviations

UA	Unlimited area
UH	Unlimited height
NP	Not permitted
Spr	With approved sprinkler system
Unspr	Without approved sprinkler system

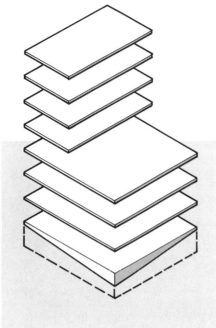

NONCOMBUSTIBLE OR COMBUSTIBLE						Construction Type
Mill (page 430)		¾-Hour (page 432)		Unprotected (page 433)		
Spr	Unspr	Spr	Unspr	Spr	Unspr	
						UH
						6
						5
*1,600	*800	*1,600	*800			4 Height in Stories
*2,140	*1,070	*2,140	*1,070			3
*3,200	*1,600	*3,200	*1600			2
*6,400	*3,200	*6,400	*3,200	*3,000	*1,000	1

This table was compiled from information contained in the National Building Code of Canada, 1985 Edition. It does not represent an official interpretation by the organization that issues the National Building Code of Canada.

HEIGHT AND AREA LIMITATIONS

USE GROUP F-3: INDUSTRIAL, LOW HAZARD

Unlimited Area
Single-story power-generating plants or plants for the manufacture or storage of incombustible materials are not limited in area if they are of noncombustible construction.

Fire Walls
For multiplication of the allowable area by subdividing the building with fire walls, see page 424.

Measurements
Area is measured as the greatest horizontal area of a building above grade within the outside surfaces of the exterior walls, or between the outside surfaces of the exterior walls and the center line of a fire wall.

Further Information
For information on Use Group classifications, see page 9. For information on mixed-use buildings, see page 12. For information on which code to consult, see page 7.

Unit Conversion
1 m^2 = 10.76 sq ft.

USE GROUP F-3: INDUSTRIAL, LOW HAZARD

Construction Type	NONCOMBUSTIBLE							
	3-Hour (page 425)		2-Hour (page 426)		1-Hour (page 428)		Unprotected (page 429)	
Height in Stories	Spr	Unspr	Spr	Unspr	Spr	Unspr	Spr	Unspr
UH	UA	UA	UA	UA				
6					*4,800	*2,440		
5					*5,760	*2,880		
4					*7,200	*3,600		
3					*9,600	*4,800		
2					*14,400	*7,200		
1					UA	UA	*11,200	*5,600

*Tabulated areas may be increased by 25% if the building faces two streets and by 50% if the building faces three streets.

Each number in the table represents the maximum area per floor in square meters for every floor of a building of that story height.

Key to Abbreviations

UA	Unlimited area
UH	Unlimited height
NP	Not permitted
Spr	With approved sprinkler system
Unspr	Without approved sprinkler system

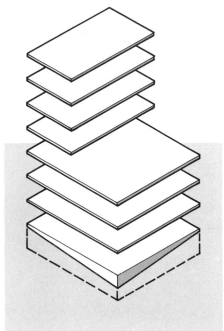

NONCOMBUSTIBLE OR COMBUSTIBLE						Construction Type
Mill (page 430)		¾-Hour (page 432)		Unprotected (page 433)		
Spr	Unspr	Spr	Unspr	Spr	Unspr	
						UH
						6
						5
*2,400	*1,200	*2,400	*1,200			4 Height in Stories
*3,200	*1,600	*3,200	*1,600			3
*4,800	*2,400	*4,800	*2,400			2
*11,200	*5,600	*9,600	*4,800	*4,800	*1,600	1

This table was compiled from information contained in the National Building Code of Canada, 1985 Edition. It does not represent an official interpretation by the organization that issues the National Building Code of Canada.

HEIGHT AND AREA LIMITATIONS

HEIGHT AND AREA LIMITATIONS

USE GROUP: OPEN-AIR GARAGES

Maximum Height
The maximum height permitted is 22 m.

Definition
These limits apply to open-air garages with no other occupancy above, in which no portion of a floor lies more than 60 m from an exterior wall opening. Other storage garages are governed by the requirements for Use Group F-3.

Fire Walls
For multiplication of the allowable area by subdividing the building with fire walls, see page 424.

Measurements
Area is measured as the greatest horizontal area of a building above grade within the outside surfaces of the exterior walls, or between the outside surfaces of the exterior walls and the center line of a fire wall.

USE GROUP: OPEN-AIR GARAGES

Construction Type		NONCOMBUSTIBLE							
		3-Hour (page 425)		2-Hour (page 426)		1-Hour (page 428)		Unprotected (page 429)	
		Spr	Unspr	Spr	Unspr	Spr	Unspr	Spr	Unspr
Height in Stories	UH	10,000	10,000	10,000	10,000	10,000	10,000	10,000	10,000
	6	10,000	10,000	10,000	10,000	10,000	10,000	10,000	10,000
	5	10,000	10,000	10,000	10,000	10,000	10,000	10,000	10,000
	4	10,000	10,000	10,000	10,000	10,000	10,000	10,000	10,000
	3	10,000	10,000	10,000	10,000	10,000	10,000	10,000	10,000
	2	10,000	10,000	10,000	10,000	10,000	10,000	10,000	10,000
	1	10,000	10,000	10,000	10,000	10,000	10,000	10,000	10,000

Each number in the table represents the maximum area per floor in square meters for every floor of a building of that story height.

Key to Abbreviations

UA	Unlimited area
UH	Unlimited height
NP	Not permitted
Spr	With approved sprinkler system
Unspr	Without approved sprinkler system

NATIONAL BUILDING CODE OF CANADA

Further Information

For information on Use Group classifications, see page 9. For information on mixed-use buildings, see page 12. For information on which code to consult, see page 7.

Unit Conversions

1 m = 3.28 ft, 1 m² = 10.76 sq ft.

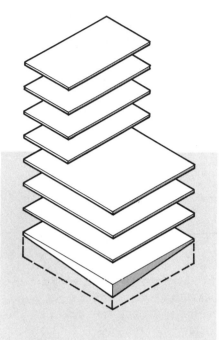

NONCOMBUSTIBLE OR COMBUSTIBLE						Construction Type
Mill (page 430)		¾-Hour (page 432)		Unprotected (page 433)		
Spr	Unspr	Spr	Unspr	Spr	Unspr	
						UH
						6
						5
						4 Height in
						3 Stories
						2
NP	NP	NP	NP	NP	NP	1

This table was compiled from information contained in the National Building Code of Canada, 1985 Edition. It does not represent an official interpretation by the organization that issues the National Building Code of Canada.

HEIGHT AND AREA LIMITATIONS

HOW TO USE THE TABLES OF HEIGHT AND AREA LIMITATIONS FOR THE STANDARD BUILDING CODE

1. Be sure you are consulting the tables for the proper building code. If you are not sure which code you are working under, see page 7.

2. The Use Group is given at the upper left-hand corner of the table. If you are not sure about the Use Group into which your building falls, consult the index of Use Groups on page 10.

3. Noncombustible Construction Types are tabulated on the left-hand page, combustible Construction Types on the right-hand page.

4. Each pair of columns represents one Construction Type. For specific information on the different materials and modes of construction that conform to that Construction Type, follow the page reference given here.

5. The paired columns tabulate height and area information for both sprinklered and unsprinklered buildings of each Construction Type.

6. The significance of the floor area numbers in the chart, which varies from one model code to another, is explained at the lower left-hand corner.

HEIGHT AND AREA LIMITATIONS

USE GROUP B: BUSINESS

Fire Walls
For multiplication of the allowable area by subdividing the building with fire walls, see page 424.

Excess Frontage
If more than 25% of the building perimeter fronts on streets, public spaces, or separations at least 30 ft

wide, the tabulated area limitations may be increased 1.33% for each 1% of such excess frontage.

Unlimited Area
If a single-story sprinklered building of this Use Group is surrounded on all sides with permanent open space at least 60 ft wide, its area is not limited.

Tall Buildings
Buildings of this Use Group having floors used for human occupancy located more than 75 ft

above the lowest level of fire department vehicle access shall either be sprinklered or have any story exceeding 15,000 sq ft in area divided by fire separations into two or more areas having a maximum floor area of 15,000 sq ft each. Buildings higher than 12 stories or 150 ft shall be sprinklered throughout. For provisions relating to smoke control in tall buildings, see Article 506.5 of the Standard Building Code.

USE GROUP B: BUSINESS

Construction Type	NONCOMBUSTIBLE							
	3-Hour (page 425)		2-Hour (page 426)		1-Hour (page 428)		Unprotected (page 429)	
	Spr	Unspr	Spr	Unspr	Spr	Unspr	Spr	Unspr
Maximum Height in Feet	UH	UH	80′	80′	**b** 65′	65′	55′	55′
Height in Stories UH	UA	UA	UA	UA				
6								
a 5					**c** 51,000	25,500	34,000	
4					51,000	25,500	34,000	
3					51,000	25,500	34,000	
2					51,000	25,500	34,000	17,000
1					76,500	25,500	51,000	17,000

Each number in the table represents the maximum area per floor in square feet for every floor of a building of that story height.

Key to Abbreviations

UA	Unlimited area
UH	Unlimited height
NP	Not permitted
Spr	With approved sprinkler system
Unspr	Without approved sprinkler system

STANDARD BUILDING CODE

Measurements

Height is measured from the average finished ground level adjoining the building to the surface of the highest flat roof, or to the average height of the highest sloping roof. Area is measured to the inside perimeter of exterior walls, not including areas within the building that are open to the sky.

Further Information

For information on Use Group classifications, see page 10. For information on mixed-use buildings, see page 12. For information on which code to consult, see page 7.

Unit Conversions

1 ft = 304.8 mm, 1 sq ft = 0.0929 m².

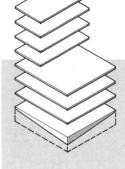

COMBUSTIBLE											
		Ordinary				Wood Light Frame					
Mill (page 430)		1-Hour (page 431)		Unprotected (page 431)		1-Hour (page 433)		Unprotected (page 433)		Construction Type	
Spr	Unspr	Spr	Unspr	Spr	Unspr	Spr	Unspr	Spr	Unspr		
65′	65′	65′	65′	55′	55′	50′	50′	40′	40′	Maximum Height in Feet	
										UH	
										6	
51,000	25,500	42,000	21,000	28,000						5	Height in Stories
51,000	25,500	42,000	21,000	28,000						4	
51,000	25,500	42,000	21,000	28,000						3	
51,000	25,500	42,000	21,000	28,000	14,000	27,000	13,500	18,000	9,000	2	
76,500	25,500	63,000	21,000	42,000	14,000	40,500	13,500	27,000	9,000	1	

This table was compiled from information contained in the Standard Building Code, 1985 Edition. It does not represent an official interpretation by the organization that issues the Standard Building Code.

7. As an example of the use of this chart, a sprinklered building of Use Group B, 1-Hour construction, under the Standard Building Code, may be no more than

a. 5 stories, or

b. 65 ft tall, whichever is less,

c. with no floor larger in area than 51,000 sq ft.

8. As another example, if we wish to construct a 3-story unsprinklered building with 31,500 sq ft per floor, we must use 2-Hour construction as a minimum. Looking to the right along the same row of the chart, we see that the addition of sprinklers would allow us to use 1-Hour, Unprotected, Mill, or 1-Hour Ordinary construction. By following the page references at the heads of these columns, we can determine exactly what each of these Construction Types is and proceed to preliminary configuration and sizing of the structural system we select.

HEIGHT AND AREA LIMITATIONS

USE GROUP A-1: ASSEMBLY, LARGE, WITH WORKING STAGE

Sprinklers

An approved sprinkler system is required in this Use Group in all areas except auditoriums, foyers, lobbies, and over electrical equipment.

Fire Walls

For multiplication of the allowable area by subdividing the building with fire walls, see page 424.

Excess Frontage

If more than 25% of the building perimeter fronts on streets, public spaces, or separations at least 30 ft wide, the tabulated area limitations may be increased 1.33% for each 1% of such excess frontage.

Measurements

Height is measured from the average finished ground level adjoining the building to the surface of the highest flat roof, or to the average height of the highest sloping roof. Area is measured to the inside perimeter of exterior walls, not including areas within the building that are open to the sky.

USE GROUP A-1: ASSEMBLY, LARGE, WITH WORKING STAGE

Construction Type	NONCOMBUSTIBLE							
	3-Hour (page 425)		2-Hour (page 426)		1-Hour (page 428)		Unprotected (page 429)	
	Spr	Unspr	Spr	Unspr	Spr	Unspr	Spr	Unspr
Maximum Height in Feet	UH	UH	80'	80'				
UH	UA	UA	UA	UA				
6								
5								
Height in Stories 4								
3								
2								
1					NP	NP	NP	NP

Each number in the table represents the maximum area per floor in square feet for every floor of a building of that story height.

358

Key to Abbreviations

UA	Unlimited area
UH	Unlimited height
NP	Not permitted
Spr	With approved sprinkler system
Unspr	Without approved sprinkler system

STANDARD BUILDING CODE

Further Information
For information on Use Group classifications, see page 10. For information on mixed-use buildings, see page 12. For information on which code to consult, see page 7.

Unit Conversions
1 ft = 304.8 mm, 1 sq ft = 0.0929 m².

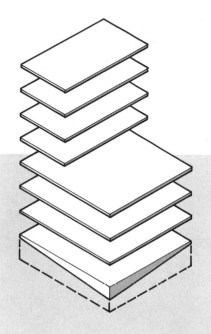

	COMBUSTIBLE										
		Ordinary				Wood Light Frame					
Mill (page 430)		1-Hour (page 431)		Unprotected (page 431)		1-Hour (page 433)		Unprotected (page 433)		Construction Type	
Spr	Unspr	Spr	Unspr	Spr	Unspr	Spr	Unspr	Spr	Unspr		
											Maximum Height in Feet
											UH
											6
											5
											4 — Height in Stories
											3
											2
NP	NP	NP	NP	NP	NP	NP	NP	NP	NP		1

This table was compiled from information contained in the Standard Building Code, 1985 Edition. It does not represent an official interpretation by the organization that issues the Standard Building Code.

HEIGHT AND AREA LIMITATIONS

USE GROUP A-1: ASSEMBLY, LARGE, WITHOUT WORKING STAGE

Sprinklers
Areas greater than 15,000 sq ft that could be used for the display, sale, or storage of combustible goods must be sprinklered.

Fire Walls
For multiplication of the allowable area by subdividing the building with fire walls, see page 424.

Excess Frontage
If more than 25% of the building perimeter fronts on streets, public spaces, or separations at least 30 ft wide, the tabulated area limitations may be increased 1.33% for each 1% of such excess frontage.

Unlimited Area
If a single-story sprinklered building of this Use Group is surrounded on all sides by at least 60 ft of permanent open space, has its assembly floor within 21 in. of grade level, has all of its exits via ramps of a slope not exceeding 1:10, and is constructed of 1-Hour, Mill, or 1-Hour Ordinary construction, it is not limited in area.

USE GROUP A-1: ASSEMBLY, LARGE, WITHOUT WORKING STAGE

Construction Type	NONCOMBUSTIBLE							
	3-Hour (page 425)		2-Hour (page 426)		1-Hour (page 428)		Unprotected (page 429)	
	Spr	Unspr	Spr	Unspr	Spr	Unspr	Spr	Unspr
Maximum Height in Feet	UH	UH	80'	80'	65'	65'	55'	55'
UH	UA	UA	UA	UA				
6								
5								
4								
3								
2								
1					36,000	12,000	24,000	8,000

(Height in Stories: UH, 6, 5, 4, 3, 2, 1)

Each number in the table represents the maximum area per floor in square feet for every floor of a building of that story height.

Key to Abbreviations

UA	Unlimited area
UH	Unlimited height
NP	Not permitted
Spr	With approved sprinkler system
Unspr	Without approved sprinkler system

STANDARD BUILDING CODE

Area Increase

If a building of this Use Group has no balconies or galleries, has its assembly floor within 21 in. of grade level, and has all its exits via ramps of a slope not exceeding 1:10, the tabulated areas may be increased by 50%.

Measurements

Height is measured from the average finished ground level adjoining the building to the surface of the highest flat roof, or to the average height of the highest sloping roof. Area is measured to the inside perimeter of exterior walls, not including areas within the building that are open to the sky.

Further Information

For information on Use Group classifications, see page 10. For information on mixed-use buildings, see page 12. For information on which code to consult, see page 7.

Unit Conversions

1 ft = 304.8 mm, 1 sq ft = 0.0929 m².

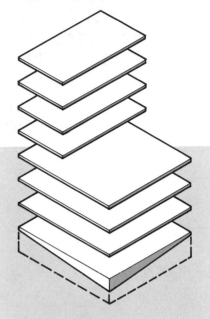

		COMBUSTIBLE									
Mill (page 430)		Ordinary				Wood Light Frame					Construction Type
		1-Hour (page 431)		Unprotected (page 431)		1-Hour (page 433)		Unprotected (page 433)			
Spr	Unspr	Spr	Unspr	Spr	Unspr	Spr	Unspr	Spr	Unspr		
65'	65'	65'	65'	55'	55'						Maximum Height in Feet
										UH	
										6	
										5	
										4	Height in Stories
										3	
										2	
36,000	12,000	36,000	12,000	24,000	8,000	NP	NP	NP	NP	1	

This table was compiled from information contained in the Standard Building Code, 1985 Edition. It does not represent an official interpretation by the organization that issues the Standard Building Code.

HEIGHT AND AREA LIMITATIONS

361

HEIGHT AND AREA LIMITATIONS

USE GROUP A-2: ASSEMBLY, SMALL, WITH WORKING STAGE

Fire Walls

For multiplication of the allowable area by subdividing the building with fire walls, see page 424.

Excess Frontage

If more than 25% of the building perimeter fronts on streets, public spaces, or separations at least 30 ft wide, the tabulated area limitations may be increased 1.33% for each 1% of such excess frontage.

Area Increase

If a building of this Use Group has no balconies or galleries, has its assembly floor within 21 in. of grade level, and has all its exits via ramps of a slope not exceeding 1:10, the tabulated areas may be increased by 50%.

Measurements

Height is measured from the average finished ground level adjoin-

USE GROUP A-2: ASSEMBLY, SMALL, WITH WORKING STAGE

Construction Type		NONCOMBUSTIBLE							
		3-Hour (page 425)		2-Hour (page 426)		1-Hour (page 428)		Unprotected (page 429)	
		Spr	Unspr	Spr	Unspr	Spr	Unspr	Spr	Unspr
Maximum Height in Feet		UH	UH	80'	80'	65'	65'	55'	55'
	UH	UA	UA	UA	UA				
	6								
	5								
Height in Stories	4								
	3								
	2								
	1					30,000	10,000	18,000	6,000

Each number in the table represents the maximum area per floor in square feet for every floor of a building of that story height.

Key to Abbreviations

UA	Unlimited area
UH	Unlimited height
NP	Not permitted
Spr	With approved sprinkler system
Unspr	Without approved sprinkler system

ing the building to the surface of the highest flat roof, or to the average height of the highest sloping roof. For this Use Group, a basement containing classrooms or assembly rooms shall be counted as a story. Area is measured to the inside perimeter of exterior walls, not including areas within the building that are open to the sky.

Further Information

For information on Use Group classifications, see page 10. For information on mixed-use buildings, see page 12. For information on which code to consult, see page 7.

Unit Conversions

1 ft = 304.8 mm, 1 sq ft = 0.0929 m^2.

Construction Type

Maximum Height in Feet

Height in Stories

	COMBUSTIBLE										
		Ordinary				Wood Light Frame					
Mill (page 430)		1-Hour (page 431)		Unprotected (page 431)		1-Hour (page 433)		Unprotected (page 433)			
Spr	Unspr	Spr	Unspr	Spr	Unspr	Spr	Unspr	Spr	Unspr		
65′	65′	65′	65′	55′	55′	50′	50′	40′	40′		UH
											6
											5
											4
											3
											2
30,000	10,000	30,000	10,000	18,000	6,000	13,500	4,500	9,000	3,000		1

This table was compiled from information contained in the Standard Building Code, 1985 Edition. It does not represent an official interpretation by the organization that issues the Standard Building Code.

HEIGHT AND AREA LIMITATIONS

USE GROUP A-2: ASSEMBLY, SMALL, WITHOUT WORKING STAGE

Fire Walls

For multiplication of the allowable area by subdividing the building with fire walls, see page 424.

Excess Frontage

If more than 25% of the building perimeter fronts on streets, public spaces, or separations at least 30 ft wide, the tabulated area limitations may be increased 1.33% for each 1% of such excess frontage.

Unlimited Area

If a single-story sprinklered building of this Use Group is surrounded on all sides with permanent open space at least 60 ft wide, has its assembly floor within 21 in. of grade level, has all its exits via ramps of a slope not exceeding 1:10, and is constructed of 1-Hour, Mill, or 1-Hour Ordinary construction, its area is not limited.

Area Increase

If a building of this Use Group has no balconies or galleries, has its as-

USE GROUP A-2: ASSEMBLY, SMALL, WITHOUT WORKING STAGE

Construction Type		NONCOMBUSTIBLE							
		3-Hour (page 425)		2-Hour (page 426)		1-Hour (page 428)		Unprotected (page 429)	
		Spr	Unspr	Spr	Unspr	Spr	Unspr	Spr	Unspr
Maximum Height in Feet		UH	UH	80′	80′	65′	65′	55′	55′
	UH	UA	UA	UA	UA				
	6								
	5								
Height in Stories	4								
	3								
	2					24,000	12,000	16,000	8,000
	1					36,000	12,000	24,000	8,000

Each number in the table represents the maximum area per floor in square feet for every floor of a building of that story height.

Key to Abbreviations

UA	Unlimited area
UH	Unlimited height
NP	Not permitted
Spr	With approved sprinkler system
Unspr	Without approved sprinkler system

STANDARD BUILDING CODE

sembly floor within 21 in. of grade level, and has all its exits via ramps of a slope not exceeding 1:10, the tabulated areas may be increased by 50%.

Place of Worship

For a place of worship, the tabulated areas may be increased by one-third.

Measurements

Height is measured from the average finished ground level adjoining the building to the surface of the highest flat roof, or to the average height of the highest sloping roof. Area is measured to the inside perimeter of exterior walls, not including areas within the building that are open to the sky.

Further Information

For information on Use Group classifications, see page 10. For information on mixed-use buildings, see page 12. For information on which code to consult, see page 7.

Unit Conversions

1 ft = 304.8 mm, 1 sq ft = 0.0929 m².

Construction Type

Maximum Height in Feet

	COMBUSTIBLE											
			Ordinary				Wood Light Frame					
	Mill (page 430)		1-Hour (page 431)		Unprotected (page 431)		1-Hour (page 433)		Unprotected (page 433)			
	Spr	Unspr	Spr	Unspr	Spr	Unspr	Spr	Unspr	Spr	Unspr		
	65'	65'	65'	65'	55'	55'	50'	50'	40'	40'		UH
												6
												5
												4
												3
	24,000	12,000	24,000	12,000	16,000	8,000						2
	36,000	12,000	36,000	12,000	24,000	8,000	22,500	7,500	15,000	5,000		1

Height in Stories

This table was compiled from information contained in the Standard Building Code, 1985 Edition. It does not represent an official interpretation by the organization that issues the Standard Building Code.

USE GROUP B: BUSINESS

Fire Walls

For multiplication of the allowable area by subdividing the building with fire walls, see page 424.

Excess Frontage

If more than 25% of the building perimeter fronts on streets, public spaces, or separations at least 30 ft wide, the tabulated area limitations may be increased 1.33% for each 1% of such excess frontage.

Unlimited Area

If a single-story sprinklered building of this Use Group is surrounded on all sides with permanent open space at least 60 ft wide, its area is not limited.

Tall Buildings

Buildings of this Use Group having floors used for human occupancy located more than 75 ft above the lowest level of fire department vehicle access shall either be sprinklered or have any story exceeding 15,000 sq ft in area divided by fire separations into two or more areas having a maximum floor area of 15,000 sq ft each. Buildings higher than 12 stories or 150 ft shall be sprinklered throughout. For provisions relating to smoke control in tall buildings, see Article 506.5 of the Standard Building Code.

USE GROUP B: BUSINESS

Construction Type	NONCOMBUSTIBLE							
	3-Hour (page 425)		2-Hour (page 426)		1-Hour (page 428)		Unprotected (page 429)	
	Spr	Unspr	Spr	Unspr	Spr	Unspr	Spr	Unspr
Maximum Height in Feet	UH	UH	80'	80'	65'	65'	55'	55'
Height in Stories								
UH	UA	UA	UA	UA				
6								
5					51,000	25,500	34,000	
4					51,000	25,500	34,000	
3					51,000	25,500	34,000	
2					51,000	25,500	34,000	17,000
1					76,500	25,500	51,000	17,000

Each number in the table represents the maximum area per floor in square feet for every floor of a building of that story height.

Key to Abbreviations

UA	Unlimited area
UH	Unlimited height
NP	Not permitted
Spr	With approved sprinkler system
Unspr	Without approved sprinkler system

STANDARD BUILDING CODE

Measurements

Height is measured from the average finished ground level adjoining the building to the surface of the highest flat roof, or to the average height of the highest sloping roof. Area is measured to the inside perimeter of exterior walls, not including areas within the building that are open to the sky.

Further Information

For information on Use Group classifications, see page 10. For information on mixed-use buildings, see page 12. For information on which code to consult, see page 7.

Unit Conversions

1 ft = 304.8 mm, 1 sq ft = 0.0929 m².

COMBUSTIBLE										
		Ordinary				Wood Light Frame				
Mill (page 430)		1-Hour (page 431)		Unprotected (page 431)		1-Hour (page 433)		Unprotected (page 433)		
Spr	Unspr	Spr	Unspr	Spr	Unspr	Spr	Unspr	Spr	Unspr	
65'	65'	65'	65'	55'	55'	50'	50'	40'	40'	
										UH
										6
51,000	25,500	42,000	21,000	28,000						5
51,000	25,500	42,000	21,000	28,000						4
51,000	25,500	42,000	21,000	28,000						3
51,000	25,500	42,000	21,000	28,000	14,000	27,000	13,500	18,000	9,000	2
76,500	25,500	63,000	21,000	42,000	14,000	40,500	13,500	27,000	9,000	1

Construction Type

Maximum Height in Feet

Height in Stories

This table was compiled from information contained in the Standard Building Code, 1985 Edition. It does not represent an official interpretation by the organization that issues the Standard Building Code.

HEIGHT AND AREA LIMITATIONS

USE GROUP E: EDUCATIONAL

Fire Walls
For multiplication of the allowable area by subdividing the building with fire walls, see page 424.

Excess Frontage
If more than 25% of the building perimeter fronts on streets, public spaces, or separations at least 30 ft wide, the tabulated area limitations may be increased 1.33% for each 1% of such excess frontage.

Area Increase
If a single-story building of this Use Group is built of other than Wood Light Frame construction, is surrounded on all sides by permanent open space at least 60 ft wide, and has at least two exits per classroom, one of which opens directly to the outdoors, the tabulated areas may be increased by 100%. This increase may be added to any increase for excess frontage.

USE GROUP E: EDUCATIONAL

Construction Type	NONCOMBUSTIBLE							
	3-Hour (page 425)		2-Hour (page 426)		1-Hour (page 428)		Unprotected (page 429)	
	Spr	Unspr	Spr	Unspr	Spr	Unspr	Spr	Unspr
Maximum Height in Feet	UH	UH	80'	80'	65'	65'	55'	55'
Height in Stories UH	UA	UA	UA	UA				
6								
5								
4								
3								
2					36,000	18,000		
1					54,000	18,000	36,000	12,000

Each number in the table represents the maximum area per floor in square feet for every floor of a building of that story height.

Key to Abbreviations

UA	Unlimited area
UH	Unlimited height
NP	Not permitted
Spr	With approved sprinkler system
Unspr	Without approved sprinkler system

STANDARD BUILDING CODE

Measurements

Height is measured from the average finished ground level adjoining the building to the surface of the highest flat roof, or to the average height of the highest sloping roof. A basement containing classrooms shall be counted as a story. Area is measured to the inside perimeter of exterior walls, not including areas within the building that are open to the sky.

Further Information

For information on Use Group classifications, see page 10. For information on mixed-use buildings, see page 12. For information on which code to consult, see page 7.

Unit Conversions

1 ft = 304.8 mm, 1 sq ft = 0.0929 m²

		COMBUSTIBLE									
		Ordinary				Wood Light Frame					**Construction Type**
Mill (page 430)		1-Hour (page 431)		Unprotected (page 431)		1-Hour (page 433)		Unprotected (page 433)			
Spr	Unspr	Spr	Unspr	Spr	Unspr	Spr	Unspr	Spr	Unspr		
65'	65'	65'	65'	55'	55'	50'	50'	40'	40'		**Maximum Height in Feet**
										UH	
										6	
										5	
										4	**Height in Stories**
										3	
36,000	18,000	36,000	18,000			24,000	12,000			2	
54,000	18,000	54,000	18,000	36,000	12,000	36,000	12,000	24,000	8,000	1	

This table was compiled from information contained in the Standard Building Code, 1985 Edition. It does not represent an official interpretation by the organization that issues the Standard Building Code.

HEIGHT AND AREA LIMITATIONS

369

USE GROUP F: FACTORY-INDUSTRIAL

Fire Walls
For multiplication of the allowable area by subdividing the building with fire walls, see page 424.

Excess Frontage
If more than 25% of the building perimeter fronts on streets, public spaces, or separations at least 30 ft wide, the tabulated area limitations may be increased 1.33% for each 1% of such excess frontage.

Unlimited Area
If a single-story sprinklered building of this Use Group is surrounded on all sides with permanent open space at least 60 ft wide, its area is not limited.

USE GROUP F: FACTORY-INDUSTRIAL

Construction Type	NONCOMBUSTIBLE							
	3-Hour (page 425)		2-Hour (page 426)		1-Hour (page 428)		Unprotected (page 429)	
	Spr	Unspr	Spr	Unspr	Spr	Unspr	Spr	Unspr
Maximum Height in Feet	UH	UH	UH	UH	UH	UH	UH	UH
UH	UA	UA	UA	UA				
6								
5								
Height in Stories 4					63,000		42,000	
3					63,000		42,000	
2					63,000	31,500	42,000	21,000
1					94,500	31,500	63,000	21,000

Each number in the table represents the maximum area per floor in square feet for every floor of a building of that story height.

370

Key to Abbreviations

UA	Unlimited area
UH	Unlimited height
NP	Not permitted
Spr	With approved sprinkler system
Unspr	Without approved sprinkler system

STANDARD BUILDING CODE

Measurements
Height is measured from the average finished ground level adjoining the building to the surface of the highest flat roof, or to the average height of the highest sloping roof. Area is measured to the inside perimeter of exterior walls, not including areas within the building that are open to the sky.

Further Information
For information on Use Group classifications, see page 10. For information on mixed-use buildings, see page 12. For information on which code to consult, see page 7.

Unit Conversions
1 ft = 304.8 mm, 1 sq ft = 0.0929 m².

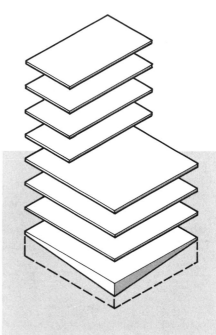

Construction Type

Maximum Height in Feet

Height in Stories

COMBUSTIBLE										Height in Stories
Mill (page 430)		Ordinary				Wood Light Frame				
		1-Hour (page 431)		Unprotected (page 431)		1-Hour (page 433)		Unprotected (page 433)		
Spr	Unspr	Spr	Unspr	Spr	Unspr	Spr	Unspr	Spr	Unspr	
UH	UH	UH	UH	UH	UH	UH	UH	UH	UH	
										UH
63,000										6
63,000										5
63,000		45,000		30,000						4
63,000	31,500	45,000		30,000						3
63,000	31,500	45,000	22,500	30,000	15,000					2
94,500	31,500	67,500	22,500	45,000	15,000	45,000	15,000	30,000	10,000	1

This table was compiled from information contained in the Standard Building Code, 1985 Edition. It does not represent an official interpretation by the organization that issues the Standard Building Code.

USE GROUP H: HAZARDOUS

Specific Hazards

This is a diverse Use Group with many special requirements for various specific occupancies; consult the Standard Building Code, Article 408, for details.

Fire Walls

For multiplication of the allowable area by subdividing the building with fire walls, see page 424.

Measurements

Height is measured from the average finished ground level adjoining the building to the surface of the highest flat roof, or to the average height of the highest sloping roof. Area is measured to the inside perimeter of exterior walls, not including areas within the building that are open to the sky.

USE GROUP H: HAZARDOUS

Construction Type	NONCOMBUSTIBLE							
	3-Hour (page 425)		2-Hour (page 426)		1-Hour (page 428)		Unprotected (page 429)	
	Spr	Unspr	Spr	Unspr	Spr	Unspr	Spr	Unspr
Maximum Height in Feet	UH		80'		65'		55'	
UH								
6								
5								
Height in Stories 4	11,500							
3	11,500		8,300					
2	11,500		8,300					
1	11,500	NP	8,300	NP	5,000	NP	5,000	NP

Each number in the table represents the maximum area per floor in square feet for every floor of a building of that story height.

Key to Abbreviations

UA	Unlimited area
UH	Unlimited height
NP	Not permitted
Spr	With approved sprinkler system
Unspr	Without approved sprinkler system

Further Information

For information on Use Group classifications, see page 10. For information on mixed-use buildings, see page 12. For information on which code to consult, see page 7.

Unit Conversions

1 ft = 304.8 mm, 1 sq ft = 0.0929 m².

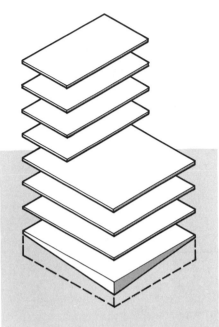

		COMBUSTIBLE								
		Ordinary				Wood Light Frame				
Mill (page 430)		1-Hour (page 431)		Unprotected (page 431)		1-Hour (page 433)		Unprotected (page 433)		
Spr	Unspr	Spr	Unspr	Spr	Unspr	Spr	Unspr	Spr	Unspr	
65'		65'		65'						
										UH
										6
										5
										4
										3
7,500										2
7,500	NP	5,000	NP	5,000	NP	NP	NP	NP	NP	1

Construction Type

Maximum Height in Feet

Height in Stories

This table was compiled from information contained in the Standard Building Code, 1985 Edition. It does not represent an official interpretation by the organization that issues the Standard Building Code.

HEIGHT AND AREA LIMITATIONS

USE GROUP I: INSTITUTIONAL, RESTRAINED

Fire Walls

For multiplication of the allowable area by subdividing the building with fire walls, see page 424.

Excess Frontage

If more than 25% of the building perimeter fronts on streets, public spaces, or separations at least 30 ft wide, the tabulated area limitations may be increased 1.33% for each 1% of such excess frontage.

Measurements

Height is measured from the average finished ground level adjoining the building to the surface of the highest flat roof, or to the average height of the highest sloping roof. Area is measured to the inside perimeter of exterior walls, not including areas within the building that are open to the sky.

USE GROUP I: INSTITUTIONAL, RESTRAINED

Construction Type	NONCOMBUSTIBLE							
	3-Hour (page 425)		2-Hour (page 426)		1-Hour (page 428)		Unprotected (page 429)	
	Spr	Unspr	Spr	Unspr	Spr	Unspr	Spr	Unspr
Maximum Height in Feet	UH		80'		65'		55'	
UH	UA		UA					
6								
5								
4								
3					30,000			
2					30,000		20,000	
1		NP		NP	45,000	NP	30,000	NP

Each number in the table represents the maximum area per floor in square feet for every floor of a building of that story height.

374

Key to Abbreviations

UA	Unlimited area
UH	Unlimited height
NP	Not permitted
Spr	With approved sprinkler system
Unspr	Without approved sprinkler system

STANDARD BUILDING CODE

Further Information

For information on Use Group classifications, see page 10. For information on mixed-use buildings, see page 12. For information on which code to consult, see page 7.

Unit Conversions

1 ft = 304.8 mm, 1 sq ft = 0.0929 m².

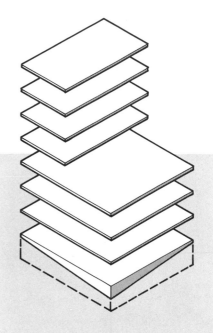

COMBUSTIBLE											
		Ordinary				Wood Light Frame					
Mill (page 430)		1-Hour (page 431)		Unprotected (page 431)		1-Hour (page 433)		Unprotected (page 433)			**Construction Type**
Spr	Unspr	Spr	Unspr	Spr	Unspr	Spr	Unspr	Spr	Unspr		
65′		65′		55′		50′		40′			**Maximum Height in Feet**
										UH	
										6	
										5	
										4	**Height in Stories**
		21,000				15,000				3	
24,000		21,000		14,000		15,000		10,000		2	
36,000	NP	31,500	NP	21,000	NP	22,500	NP	15,000	NP	1	

This table was compiled from information contained in the Standard Building Code, 1985 Edition. It does not represent an official interpretation by the organization that issues the Standard Building Code.

HEIGHT AND AREA LIMITATIONS

USE GROUP I: INSTITUTIONAL, UNRESTRAINED

Fire Walls
For multiplication of the allowable area by subdividing the building with fire walls, see page 424.

Excess Frontage
If more than 25% of the building perimeter fronts on streets, public spaces, or separations at least 30 ft wide, the tabulated area limitations may be increased 1.33% for each 1% of such excess frontage.

Measurements
Height is measured from the average finished ground level adjoining the building to the surface of the highest flat roof, or to the average height of the highest sloping roof. Area is measured to the inside perimeter of exterior walls, not including areas within the building that are open to the sky.

USE GROUP I: INSTITUTIONAL, UNRESTRAINED

Construction Type	NONCOMBUSTIBLE							
	3-Hour (page 425)		2-Hour (page 426)		1-Hour (page 428)		Unprotected (page 429)	
	Spr	Unspr	Spr	Unspr	Spr	Unspr	Spr	Unspr
Maximum Height in Feet	80'	80'	80'	80'	65'	65'	55'	
UH	NL	NL	NL	NL				
6								
5								
4								
3					30,000			
2					30,000			
1					45,000	15,000	30,000	NP

Height in Stories

Each number in the table represents the maximum area per floor in square feet for every floor of a building of that story height.

Key to Abbreviations

UA	Unlimited area
UH	Unlimited height
NP	Not permitted
Spr	With approved sprinkler system
Unspr	Without approved sprinkler system

STANDARD BUILDING CODE

Further Information

For information on Use Group classifications, see page 10. For information on mixed-use buildings, see page 12. For information on which code to consult, see page 7.

Unit Conversions

1 ft = 304.8 mm, 1 sq ft = 0.0929 m².

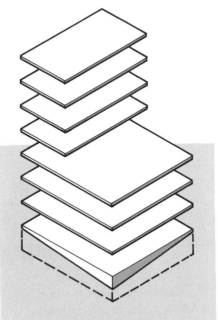

		COMBUSTIBLE								
		Ordinary				Wood Light Frame				
Mill (page 430)		1-Hour (page 431)		Unprotected (page 431)		1-Hour (page 433)		Unprotected (page 433)		
Spr	Unspr	Spr	Unspr	Spr	Unspr	Spr	Unspr	Spr	Unspr	
65'		65'				50'				
										UH
										6
										5
										4
										3
24,000		21,000								2
36,000	NP	31,500	NP	NP	NP	22,500	NP	NP	NP	1

Construction Type

Maximum Height in Feet

Height in Stories

This table was compiled from information contained in the Standard Building Code, 1985 Edition. It does not represent an official interpretation by the organization that issues the Standard Building Code.

HEIGHT AND AREA LIMITATIONS

HEIGHT AND AREA LIMITATIONS

USE GROUP M: MERCANTILE

Sprinklers
Stores that display combustible goods and have an area greater than 15,000 sq ft per floor must be sprinklered.

Fire Walls
For multiplication of the allowable area by subdividing the building with fire walls, see page 424.

Excess Frontage
If more than 25% of the building perimeter fronts on streets, public spaces, or separations at least 30 ft wide, the tabulated area limitations may be increased 1.33% for each 1% of such excess frontage. An unsprinklered building of this Use Group shall not exceed 15,000 sq ft per floor after this increase.

Unlimited Area
If a single-story sprinklered building of this Use Group is surrounded on all sides with permanent open space at least 60 ft wide, its area is not limited.

USE GROUP M: MERCANTILE

Construction Type	NONCOMBUSTIBLE							
	3-Hour (page 425)		2-Hour (page 426)		1-Hour (page 428)		Unprotected (page 429)	
	Spr	Unspr	Spr	Unspr	Spr	Unspr	Spr	Unspr
Maximum Height in Feet	UH	UH	80'	80'	65'	65'	55'	55'
UH	UA	15,000	UA	15,000				
6		15,000		15,000				
5		15,000		15,000	27,000	13,500	18,000	
4		15,000		15,000	27,000	13,500	18,000	
3		15,000		15,000	27,000	13,500	18,000	
2		15,000		15,000	27,000	13,500	18,000	9,000
1		15,000		15,000	40,500	13,500	27,000	9,000

(Height in Stories: rows UH, 6, 5, 4, 3, 2, 1)

Each number in the table represents the maximum area per floor in square feet for every floor of a building of that story height.

378

Key to Abbreviations

UA	Unlimited area
UH	Unlimited height
NP	Not permitted
Spr	With approved sprinkler system
Unspr	Without approved sprinkler system

STANDARD BUILDING CODE

Measurements
Height is measured from the average finished ground level adjoining the building to the surface of the highest flat roof, or to the average height of the highest sloping roof. Area is measured to the inside perimeter of exterior walls, not including areas within the building that are open to the sky.

Further Information
For information on Use Group classifications, see page 10. For information on mixed-use buildings, see page 12. For information on which code to consult, see page 7.

Unit Conversions
1 ft = 304.8 mm, 1 sq ft = 0.0929 m².

Construction Type

Maximum Height in Feet

Height in Stories

COMBUSTIBLE										Stories
Mill (page 430)		Ordinary				Wood Light Frame				
		1-Hour (page 431)		Unprotected (page 431)		1-Hour (page 433)		Unprotected (page 433)		
Spr	Unspr	Spr	Unspr	Spr	Unspr	Spr	Unspr	Spr	Unspr	
65'	65'	65'	65'	55'	55'	50'	50'	40'	40'	
										UH
										6
27,000	13,500	27,000	13,500	18,000						5
27,000	13,500	27,000	13,500	18,000						4
27,000	13,500	27,000	13,500	18,000						3
27,000	13,500	27,000	13,500	18,000	9,000	18,000	9,000	12,000	6,000	2
40,500	13,500	40,500	13,500	27,000	9,000	27,000	9,000	18,000	6,000	1

This table was compiled from information contained in the Standard Building Code, 1985 Edition. It does not represent an official interpretation by the organization that issues the Standard Building Code.

HEIGHT AND AREA LIMITATIONS

379

USE GROUP R: RESIDENTIAL

Fire Walls

For multiplication of the allowable area by subdividing the building with fire walls, see page 424.

Excess Frontage

If more than 25% of the building perimeter fronts on streets, public spaces, or separations at least 30 ft wide, the tabulated area limitations may be increased 1.33% for each 1% of such excess frontage.

Tall Buildings

Buildings of this Use Group having floors used for human occupancy located more than 75 ft above the lowest level of fire department vehicle access shall either be sprinklered or have any story exceeding 15,000 sq ft in area divided by fire separations into two or more areas having a maximum floor area of 15,000 sq ft each. Buildings higher than 12 stories or 150 ft shall be sprinklered throughout. For provisions relating to smoke control in tall buildings, see Article 506.5 of the Standard Building Code.

USE GROUP R: RESIDENTIAL

Construction Type	NONCOMBUSTIBLE							
	3-Hour (page 425)		2-Hour (page 426)		1-Hour (page 428)		Unprotected (page 429)	
	Spr	Unspr	Spr	Unspr	Spr	Unspr	Spr	Unspr
Maximum Height in Feet	UH	UH	80'	80'	65'	65'	55'	55'
UH	UA	UA	UA	UA				
6								
5					36,000	18,000	24,000	
4					36,000	18,000	24,000	
3					36,000	18,000	24,000	
2					36,000	18,000	24,000	12,000
1					54,000	18,000	36,000	12,000

(Height in Stories: UH, 6, 5, 4, 3, 2, 1)

Each number in the table represents the maximum area per floor in square feet for every floor of a building of that story height.

Key to Abbreviations

UA	Unlimited area
UH	Unlimited height
NP	Not permitted
Spr	With approved sprinkler system
Unspr	Without approved sprinkler system

STANDARD BUILDING CODE

Measurements

Height is measured from the average finished ground level adjoining the building to the surface of the highest flat roof, or to the average height of the highest sloping roof. If a building of this Use Group is built above a single-story parking structure of 3-Hour or 2-Hour construction, or a single-story open parking structure of Mill construction, the story height is counted from the top of the parking structure. Area is measured to the inside perimeter of exterior walls, not including areas within the building that are open to the sky.

Further Information

For information on Use Group classifications, see page 10. For information on mixed-use buildings, see page 12. For information on which code to consult, see page 7.

Unit Conversions

1 ft = 304.8 mm, 1 sq ft = 0.0929 m².

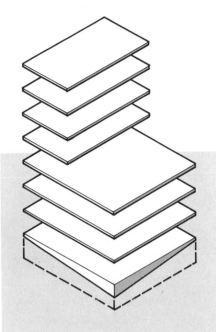

Construction Type

Maximum Height in Feet

Height in Stories

COMBUSTIBLE									
		Ordinary				Wood Light Frame			
Mill (page 430)		1-Hour (page 431)		Unprotected (page 431)		1-Hour (page 433)		Unprotected (page 433)	
Spr	Unspr	Spr	Unspr	Spr	Unspr	Spr	Unspr	Spr	Unspr
65'	65'	65'	65'	55'	55'	50'	50'	40'	40'
		36,000	18,000	24,000					
		36,000	18,000	24,000					
36,000	18,000	36,000	18,000	24,000		21,000	10,500		
36,000	18,000	36,000	18,000	24,000	12,000	21,000	10,500	14,000	7,000
54,000	18,000	54,000	18,000	36,000	12,000	31,500	10,500	21,000	7,000

(Height in Stories, right side: UH, 6, 5, 4, 3, 2, 1)

This table was compiled from information contained in the Standard Building Code, 1985 Edition. It does not represent an official interpretation by the organization that issues the Standard Building Code.

HEIGHT AND AREA LIMITATIONS

HEIGHT AND AREA LIMITATIONS

USE GROUP S: STORAGE

Fire Walls

For multiplication of the allowable area by subdividing the building with fire walls, see page 424.

Excess Frontage

If more than 25% of the building perimeter fronts on streets, public spaces, or separations at least 30 ft wide, the tabulated area limitations may be increased 1.33% for each 1% of such excess frontage.

Unlimited Area

If a single-story sprinklered building of this Use Group is surrounded on all sides with permanent open space at least 60 ft wide, its area is not limited.

USE GROUP S: STORAGE

Construction Type	NONCOMBUSTIBLE							
	3-Hour (page 425)		2-Hour (page 426)		1-Hour (page 428)		Unprotected (page 429)	
	Spr	Unspr	Spr	Unspr	Spr	Unspr	Spr	Unspr
Maximum Height in Feet	UH	UH	UH	UH	UH	UH	UH	UH
UH	UA	UA						
6			60,000	30,000				
5			60,000	30,000				
Height in Stories 4			60,000	30,000	48,000		32,000	
3			60,000	30,000	48,000		32,000	
2			60,000	30,000	48,000	24,000	32,000	16,000
1			90,000	30,000	72,000	24,000	48,000	16,000

Each number in the table represents the maximum area per floor in square feet for every floor of a building of that story height.

Key to Abbreviations

UA	Unlimited area
UH	Unlimited height
NP	Not permitted
Spr	With approved sprinkler system
Unspr	Without approved sprinkler system

STANDARD BUILDING CODE

Measurements

Height is measured from the average finished ground level adjoining the building to the surface of the highest flat roof, or to the average height of the highest sloping roof. Area is measured to the inside perimeter of exterior walls, not including areas within the building that are open to the sky.

Further Information

For information on Use Group classifications, see page 10. For information on mixed-use buildings, see page 12. For information on which code to consult, see page 7.

Unit Conversions

1 ft = 304.8 mm, 1 sq ft = 0.0929 m^2.

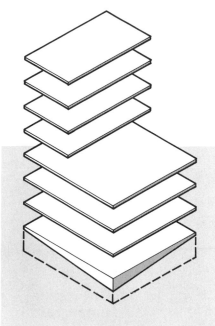

COMBUSTIBLE											Construction Type
Mill (page 430)		Ordinary				Wood Light Frame					
		1-Hour (page 431)		Unprotected (page 431)		1-Hour (page 433)		Unprotected (page 433)			
Spr	Unspr	Spr	Unspr	Spr	Unspr	Spr	Unspr	Spr	Unspr		
UH	UH	UH	UH	UH	UH	UH	UH	UH	UH		Maximum Height in Feet
										UH	
48,000										6	
48,000										5	
48,000		48,000		32,000						4	Height in Stories
48,000		48,000		32,000						3	
48,000	24,000	48,000	24,000	32,000	16,000					2	
72,000	24,000	72,000	24,000	48,000	16,000	27,000	9,000	18,000	6,000	1	

This table was compiled from information contained in the Standard Building Code, 1985 Edition. It does not represent an official interpretation by the organization that issues the Standard Building Code.

HEIGHT AND AREA LIMITATIONS

USE GROUP: OPEN PARKING GARAGES

General Notes

Roof parking is permitted. Enclosed parking structures may be constructed to the limits defined for Group S buildings.

Fire Walls

For multiplication of the allowable area by subdividing the building with fire walls, see page 424.

Excess Frontage

If more than 25% of the building perimeter fronts on streets, public spaces, or separations at least 30 ft wide, the tabulated area limitations may be increased 1.33% for each 1% of such excess frontage.

Measurements

Height is measured from the average finished ground level adjoining the building to the surface of the highest flat roof, or to the average height of the highest sloping roof. Area is measured to the inside perimeter of exterior walls, not including areas within the building that are open to the sky.

USE GROUP: OPEN PARKING GARAGES

Construction Type	NONCOMBUSTIBLE							
	3-Hour (page 425)		2-Hour (page 426)		1-Hour (page 428)		Unprotected (page 429)	
	Spr	Unspr	Spr	Unspr	Spr	Unspr	Spr	Unspr
Maximum Height in Feet	UH	UH	80'	80'	75'	75'	75'	75'
UH	UA	UA	UA	UA				
6					400,000	400,000	400,000	400,000
5					400,000	400,000	400,000	400,000
4					400,000	400,000	400,000	400,000
3					400,000	400,000	400,000	400,000
2					400,000	400,000	400,000	400,000
1					400,000	400,000	400,000	400,000

(Rows 6–1 labeled "Height in Stories")

Each number in the table represents the maximum area per floor in square feet for every floor of a building of that story height.

384

Key to Abbreviations

UA	Unlimited area
UH	Unlimited height
NP	Not permitted
Spr	With approved sprinkler system
Unspr	Without approved sprinkler system

Further Information

For information on Use Group classifications, see page 10. For information on mixed-use buildings, see page 12. For information on which code to consult, see page 7.

Unit Conversions

1 ft = 304.8 mm, 1 sq ft = 0.0929 m².

		COMBUSTIBLE									
		Ordinary				Wood Light Frame					
Mill (page 430)		1-Hour (page 431)		Unprotected (page 431)		1-Hour (page 433)		Unprotected (page 433)			
Spr	Unspr	Spr	Unspr	Spr	Unspr	Spr	Unspr	Spr	Unspr		
40'	40'										UH
											6
											5
											4
											3
30,000	30,000										2
30,000	30,000	NP	NP	NP	NP	NP	NP	NP	NP		1

Construction Type

Maximum Height in Feet

Height in Stories

This table is compiled from information contained in the Standard Building Code, 1985 Edition. It does not represent an official interpretation by the organization that issues the Standard Building Code.

HEIGHT AND AREA LIMITATIONS

385

HEIGHT AND AREA LIMITATIONS

HOW TO USE THE TABLES OF HEIGHT AND AREA LIMITATIONS FOR THE UNIFORM BUILDING CODE

1. Be sure you are consulting the tables for the proper building code. If you are not sure which code you are working under, see page 7.

2. The Use Group is given at the upper left-hand corner of the table. If you are not sure about the Use Group into which your building falls, consult the index of Use Groups on page 11.

3. Noncombustible Construction Types are tabulated on the left-hand page, combustible Construction Types on the right-hand page.

4. Each pair of columns represents one Construction Type. For specific information on the different materials and modes of construction that conform to that Construction Type, follow the page reference given here.

5. The paired columns tabulate height and area information for both sprinklered and unsprinklered buildings of each Construction Type.

6. The significance of the floor area numbers in the chart, which varies from one model code to another, is explained at the lower left-hand corner.

386

HEIGHT AND AREA LIMITATIONS

USE GROUPS B-1, B-2, AND B-3: BUSINESS

Sprinklers
An approved sprinkler system is required in this Use Group in covered mall buildings and in Use Group B-2 buildings larger than 12,000 sq ft per floor or 24,000 sq ft total or greater than three stories in height.

Fire Walls
For multiplication of the allowable area by subdividing the building with fire walls, see page 424.

Excess Frontage
If a building adjoins public ways or yards on more than one side, the tabulated floor areas may be increased by the following percentages for each foot by which the minimum width of the public ways or yards exceeds 20 ft:

a. For frontage on two sides, 1.25% for each foot, up to a maximum of 50%.

b. For frontage on three sides, 2.5% for each foot, up to a maximum of 100%.

c. For frontage on all sides, 5% for each foot, up to a maximum of 100%.

There is no limit on these increases for Use Group B-3 aircraft hangars with open space on all sides.

Tall Buildings
Use Group B-2 office buildings with floors used for human occupancy that are more than 75 ft above the lowest level of fire department vehicle access shall either be sprinklered or provide safe ar-

394

USE GROUP B-1, B-2, B-3: BUSINESS

Construction Type	3-Hour (page 425)		2-Hour (page 426)		1-Hour (page 428)		Unprotected (page 429)	
	Spr	Unspr	Spr	Unspr	Spr	Unspr	Spr	Unspr
Maximum Height in Feet	UH	UH	160'	160'	65' b	65'	55'	55'
UH	UA	UA						
13			79,800					
12			159,600	79,800				
11			159,600	79,800				
10			159,600	79,800				
9			159,600	79,800				
8			159,600	79,800				
7			159,600	79,800				
6			159,600	79,800				
5 a			159,600	79,800	36,000			
4			159,600	79,800	72,000	36,000		
3			159,600	79,800	72,000	36,000	24,000	
2			159,600	79,800	72,000	36,000	48,000	24,000
1			119,700	39,900	54,000	18,000	36,000	12,000

Height in Stories

Each number in the table represents the maximum total floor area in square feet for an entire building of that story height.

The floor area of any story may not exceed the area permitted for a single-story building of the same Construction Type.

Key to Abbreviations

UA	Unlimited area	Spr	With approved sprinkler system
UH	Unlimited height	Unspr	Without approved sprinkler system
NP	Not permitted		

UNIFORM BUILDING CODE

7. As an example of the use of this chart, a sprinklered building of Use Group B-2, 1-Hour construction, under the Uniform Building Code, may be no more than

a. 5 stories, or

b. 65 ft tall, whichever is less,

c. with a total floor area for an entire building of this height of no more than 36,000 sq ft.

Notice that under the Uniform Building Code, we can build a building larger than this if the height is reduced—the same building, if 2 to 4 stories tall, can have a total floor area of up to 72,000 sq ft.

8. As another example, if we wish to construct a 3-story unsprinklered building with 21,500 sq ft per floor, a total of 64,500 sq ft, we must use 3-Hour or 2-Hour construction. Looking to the right along the same row of the chart, we see that the addition of sprinklers would allow us to use 1-Hour, Mill, or 1-Hour Ordinary construction. By following the page references at the heads of these columns, we can determine exactly what each of these Construction Types is and proceed to preliminary configuration and sizing of the structural system we select.

UNIFORM BUILDING CODE

eas of refuge by dividing every story into at least two more or less equal areas, each having a maximum floor area of 15,000 sq ft and each provided with at least one elevator and one enclosed exit stairway.

Measurements

Height is measured from an elevation 10 ft higher than the lowest grade, or from the elevation of the highest adjacent sidewalk or ground surface within 5 ft horizontally of the building, whichever is lower. Height is measured to the highest point of the coping of a flat roof, to the deck line of a mansard roof, or to the average height of the highest sloping roof. Area is measured within the surrounding walls, exclusive of vent shafts and courts.

Further Information

For information on Use Group classifications, see page 11. For information on mixed-use buildings, see page 12. For information on which code to consult, see page 7.

Unit Conversions

1 ft = 304.8 mm, 1 sq ft = 0.0929 m².

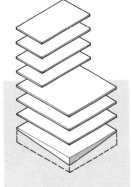

| Construction Type |
| Maximum Height in Feet |
| Height in Stories |

		COMBUSTIBLE										
		Ordinary				Wood Light Frame						
Mill (page 430)		1-Hour (page 431)		Unprotected (page 431)		1-Hour (page 433)		Unprotected (page 433)				
Spr	Unspr	Spr	Unspr	Spr	Unspr	Spr	Unspr	Spr	Unspr			
65′	65′	65′	65′	55′	55′	50′	50′	40′	40′			
											UH	
											13	
											12	
											11	
											10	
											9	
											8	Height in
											7	Stories
											6	
36,000		36,000									5	
72,000	36,000	72,000	36,000			28,000					4	
72,000	36,000	72,000	36,000	24,000		56,000	28,000	16,000			3	
72,000	36,000	72,000	36,000	48,000	24,000	56,000	28,000	32,000	16,000		2	
54,000	18,000	54,000	18,000	36,000	12,000	42,000	14,000	24,000	8,000		1	

This table was compiled from information contained in the Uniform Building Code, 1985 Edition. It does not represent an official interpretation by the organization that issues the Uniform Building Code.

HEIGHT AND AREA LIMITATIONS

USE GROUP A-1: ASSEMBLY BUILDING WITH STAGE AND WITH OCCUPANT LOAD OF 1000 OR MORE

Sprinklers

An approved sprinkler system is required in this Use Group in stages and backstage areas, in basements larger than 1500 sq ft, and in nightclubs and discos larger than 5000 sq ft.

Fire Walls

For multiplication of the allowable area by subdividing the building with fire walls, see page 424.

Excess Frontage

If a building adjoins public ways or yards on more than one side, the tabulated floor areas may be increased by the following percentages for each foot by which the minimum width of the public ways or yards exceeds 20 ft:

a. For frontage on two sides, 1.25% for each foot, up to a maximum of 50%.

b. For frontage on three sides, 2.5% for each foot, up to a maximum of 100%.

c. For frontage on all sides, 5% for each foot, up to a maximum of 100%.

Measurements

Height is measured from an elevation 10 ft higher than the low-

USE GROUP A-1: ASSEMBLY BUILDING WITH STAGE AND WITH OCCUPANT LOAD OF 1000 OR MORE

Construction Type	NONCOMBUSTIBLE							
	3-Hour (page 425)		2-Hour (page 426)		1-Hour (page 428)		Unprotected (page 429)	
	Spr	Unspr	Spr	Unspr	Spr	Unspr	Spr	Unspr
Maximum Height in Feet	UH	UH	160'	160'				
UH	UA	UA						
13								
12								
11								
10								
9								
8								
7								
6								
5			59,800					
4			119,600	59,800				
3			119,600	59,800				
2			119,600	59,800				
1			89,700	29,900	NP	NP	NP	NP

Each number in the table represents the maximum total floor area in square feet for an entire building of that story height.

The floor area of any story may not exceed the area permitted for a single-story building of the same Construction Type.

Key to Abbreviations

UA	Unlimited area	Spr	With approved sprinkler system
UH	Unlimited height	Unspr	Without approved sprinkler system
NP	Not permitted		

UNIFORM BUILDING CODE

est grade, or from the elevation of the highest adjacent sidewalk or ground surface within 5 ft horizontally of the building, whichever is lower. Height is measured to the highest point of the coping of a flat roof, to the deck line of a mansard roof, or to the average height of the highest sloping roof. Area is measured within the surrounding walls, exclusive of vent shafts and courts.

Further Information

For information on Use Group classifications, see page 11. For information on mixed-use buildings, see page 12. For information on which code to consult, see page 7.

Unit Conversions

1 ft = 304.8 mm, 1 sq ft = 0.0929 m².

COMBUSTIBLE										Construction Type
		Ordinary				Wood Light Frame				
Mill (page 430)		1-Hour (page 431)		Unprotected (page 431)		1-Hour (page 433)		Unprotected (page 433)		
Spr	Unspr	Spr	Unspr	Spr	Unspr	Spr	Unspr	Spr	Unspr	
										Maximum Height in Feet
										UH
										13
										12
										11
										10
										9
										8 Height in
										7 Stories
										6
										5
										4
										3
										2
NP	NP	NP	NP	NP	NP	NP	NP	NP	NP	1

This table was compiled from information contained in the Uniform Building Code, 1985 Edition. It does not represent an official interpretation by the organization that issues the Uniform Building Code.

USE GROUP A-2: ASSEMBLY BUILDING WITH STAGE AND WITH OCCUPANT LOAD OF LESS THAN 1000, AND USE GROUP A-2.1: ASSEMBLY BUILDING WITHOUT STAGE AND WITH OCCUPANT LOAD OF 300 OR MORE

Sprinklers

An approved sprinkler system is required in this Use Group in stages and backstage areas, in basements larger than 1500 sq ft, in exhibition or display spaces larger than 12,000 sq ft, and in nightclubs and discos larger than 5000 sq ft.

Fire Walls

For multiplication of the allowable area by subdividing the building with fire walls, see page 424.

Excess Frontage

If a building adjoins public ways or yards on more than one side, the tabulated floor areas may be increased by the following percentages for each foot by which the minimum width of the public ways or yards exceeds 20 ft:

a. For frontage on two sides, 1.25% for each foot, up to a maximum of 50%.

b. For frontage on three sides, 2.5% for each foot, up to a maximum of 100%.

USE GROUP A-2: ASSEMBLY BUILDING WITH STAGE AND WITH OCCUPANT LOAD OF LESS THAN 1000, AND
USE GROUP A-2.1: ASSEMBLY BUILDING WITHOUT STAGE AND WITH OCCUPANT LOAD OF 300 OR MORE

Construction Type	NONCOMBUSTIBLE							
	3-Hour (page 425)		2-Hour (page 426)		1-Hour (page 428)		Unprotected (page 429)	
	Spr	Unspr	Spr	Unspr	Spr	Unspr	Spr	Unspr
Maximum Height in Feet	UH	UH	160′	160′	65′	65′		
Height in Stories: UH	UA	UA						
13								
12								
11								
10								
9								
8								
7								
6								
5			59,800					
4			119,600	59,800				
3			119,600	59,800	27,000			
2			119,600	59,800	54,000	27,000		
1			89,700	29,900	40,500	13,500	NP	NP

Each number in the table represents the maximum total floor area in square feet for an entire building of that story height.

The floor area of any story may not exceed the area permitted for a single-story building of the same Construction Type.

Key to Abbreviations

UA	Unlimited area	Spr	With approved sprinkler system
UH	Unlimited height	Unspr	Without approved sprinkler system
NP	Not permitted		

UNIFORM BUILDING CODE

c. For frontage on all sides, 5% for each foot, up to a maximum of 100%.

Measurements

Height is measured from an elevation 10 ft higher than the lowest grade, or from the elevation of the highest adjacent sidewalk or ground surface within 5 ft horizontally of the building, whichever is lower. Height is measured to the highest point of the coping of a flat roof, to the deck line of a mansard roof, or to the average height of the highest sloping roof. Area is measured within the surrounding walls, exclusive of vent shafts and courts.

Further Information

For information on Use Group classifications, see page 11. For information on mixed-use buildings, see page 12. For information on which code to consult, see page 7.

Unit Conversions

1 ft = 304.8 mm, 1 sq ft = 0.0929 m²

COMBUSTIBLE										Construction Type	
Mill (page 430)		Ordinary				Wood Light Frame					
		1-Hour (page 431)		Unprotected (page 431)		1-Hour (page 433)		Unprotected (page 433)			
Spr	Unspr	Spr	Unspr	Spr	Unspr	Spr	Unspr	Spr	Unspr	Maximum Height in Feet	
65'	65'	65'	65'			50'	50'				
										UH	
										13	
										12	
										11	
										10	
										9	
										8	Height in
										7	Stories
										6	
										5	
										4	
27,000		27,000				21,000				3	
54,000	27,000	54,000	27,000			42,000	21,000			2	
40,500	13,500	40,500	13,500	NP	NP	31,500	10,500	NP	NP	1	

This table was compiled from information contained in the Uniform Building Code, 1985 Edition. It does not represent an official interpretation by the organization that issues the Uniform Building Code.

HEIGHT AND AREA LIMITATIONS

USE GROUP A-3: ASSEMBLY BUILDING WITHOUT STAGE AND WITH OCCUPANT LOAD OF 300 OR LESS, AND USE GROUP A-4: STADIUMS, REVIEWING STANDS, AND AMUSEMENT PARK STRUCTURES

Sprinklers

An approved sprinkler system is required in this Use Group in base-ments larger than 1500 sq ft, in exhibition or display spaces larger than 12,000 sq ft, and in nightclubs and discos larger than 5000 sq ft.

Fire Walls

For multiplication of the allowable area by subdividing the building with fire walls, see page 424.

Excess Frontage

If a building adjoins public ways or yards on more than one side, the tabulated floor areas may be increased by the following percentages for each foot by which the minimum width of the public ways or yards exceeds 20 ft:

a. For frontage on two sides, 1.25% for each foot, up to a maximum of 50%.

b. For frontage on three sides, 2.5% for each foot, up to a maximum of 100%.

USE GROUP A-3: ASSEMBLY BUILDING WITHOUT STAGE AND WITH OCCUPANT LOAD OF 300 OR LESS, AND
USE GROUP A-4: STADIUMS, REVIEWING STANDS, AND AMUSEMENT PARK STRUCTURES

Construction Type	NONCOMBUSTIBLE							
	3-Hour (page 425)		2-Hour (page 426)		1-Hour (page 428)		Unprotected (page 429)	
	Spr	Unspr	Spr	Unspr	Spr	Unspr	Spr	Unspr
Maximum Height in Feet	UH	UH	160'	160'	65'	65'	55'	55'
UH	UA	UA						
13			59,800					
12			119,600	59,800				
11			119,600	59,800				
10			119,600	59,800				
9			119,600	59,800				
8			119,600	59,800				
7			119,600	59,800				
6			119,600	59,800				
5			119,600	59,800				
4			119,600	59,800				
3			119,600	59,800	27,000			
2			119,600	59,800	54,000	27,000	18,200	
1			89,700	29,900	40,500	13,500	27,300	9,100

(Row label "Height in Stories" applies to the story-height rows 1–UH.)

Each number in the table represents the maximum total floor area in square feet for an entire building of that story height.

The floor area of any story may not exceed the area permitted for a single-story building of the same Construction Type.

Key to Abbreviations

UA	Unlimited area	Spr	With approved sprinkler system
UH	Unlimited height	Unspr	Without approved sprinkler system
NP	Not permitted		

392

UNIFORM BUILDING CODE

c. For frontage on all sides, 5% for each foot, up to a maximum of 100%.

Measurements
Height is measured from an elevation 10 ft higher than the lowest grade, or from the elevation of the highest adjacent sidewalk or ground surface within 5 ft horizontally of the building, whichever is lower. Height is measured to the highest point of the coping of a flat roof, to the deck line of a mansard roof, or to the average height of the highest sloping roof. Area is measured within the surrounding walls, exclusive of vent shafts and courts.

Further Information
For information on Use Group classifications, see page 11. For information on mixed-use buildings, see page 12. For information on which code to consult, see page 7.

Unit Conversions
1 ft = 304.8 mm, 1 sq ft = 0.0929 m².

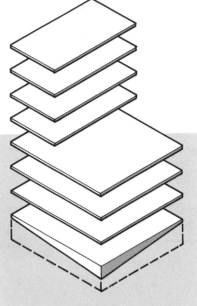

COMBUSTIBLE										Construction Type		Height in Stories
Mill (page 430)		Ordinary				Wood Light Frame						
		1-Hour (page 431)		Unprotected (page 431)		1-Hour (page 433)		Unprotected (page 433)				
Spr	Unspr	Spr	Unspr	Spr	Unspr	Spr	Unspr	Spr	Unspr			
65'	65'	65'	65'	55'	55'	50'	50'	40'	40'		UH	
											13	
											12	
											11	
											10	
											9	
											8	
											7	
											6	
											5	
											4	
27,000		27,000				21,000					3	
54,000	27,000	54,000	27,000	18,200		42,000	21,000	12,000			2	
40,500	13,500	40,500	13,500	27,300	9,100	31,500	10,500	18,000	6,000		1	

Maximum Height in Feet

This table was compiled from information contained in the Uniform Building Code, 1985 Edition. It does not represent an official interpretation by the organization that issues the Uniform Building Code.

HEIGHT AND AREA LIMITATIONS

USE GROUPS B-1, B-2, AND B-3: BUSINESS

Sprinklers

An approved sprinkler system is required in this Use Group in covered mall buildings and in Use Group B-2 buildings larger than 12,000 sq ft per floor or 24,000 sq ft total or greater than three stories in height.

Fire Walls

For multiplication of the allowable area by subdividing the building with fire walls, see page 424.

Excess Frontage

If a building adjoins public ways or yards on more than one side, the tabulated floor areas may be increased by the following percentages for each foot by which the minimum width of the public ways or yards exceeds 20 ft:

a. For frontage on two sides, 1.25% for each foot, up to a maximum of 50%.

b. For frontage on three sides, 2.5% for each foot, up to a maximum of 100%.

c. For frontage on all sides, 5% for each foot, up to a maximum of 100%.

There is no limit on these increases for Use Group B-3 aircraft hangars with open space on all sides.

Tall Buildings

Use Group B-2 office buildings with floors used for human occupancy that are more than 75 ft above the lowest level of fire department vehicle access shall either be sprinklered or provide safe ar-

USE GROUP B-1, B-2, B-3: BUSINESS

Construction Type	NONCOMBUSTIBLE							
	3-Hour (page 425)		2-Hour (page 426)		1-Hour (page 428)		Unprotected (page 429)	
	Spr	Unspr	Spr	Unspr	Spr	Unspr	Spr	Unspr
Maximum Height in Feet	UH	UH	160'	160'	65'	65'	55'	55'
Height in Stories								
UH	UA	UA						
13			79,800					
12			159,600	79,800				
11			159,600	79,800				
10			159,600	79,800				
9			159,600	79,800				
8			159,600	79,800				
7			159,600	79,800				
6			159,600	79,800				
5			159,600	79,800	36,000			
4			159,600	79,800	72,000	36,000		
3			159,600	79,800	72,000	36,000	24,000	
2			159,600	79,800	72,000	36,000	48,000	24,000
1			119,700	39,900	54,000	18,000	36,000	12,000

Each number in the table represents the maximum total floor area in square feet for an entire building of that story height.

The floor area of any story may not exceed the area permitted for a single-story building of the same Construction Type.

Key to Abbreviations

UA	Unlimited area	Spr	With approved sprinkler system
UH	Unlimited height	Unspr	Without approved sprinkler system
NP	Not permitted		

eas of refuge by dividing every story into at least two more or less equal areas, each having a maximum floor area of 15,000 sq ft and each provided with at least one elevator and one enclosed exit stairway.

Measurements

Height is measured from an elevation 10 ft higher than the lowest grade, or from the elevation of the highest adjacent sidewalk or ground surface within 5 ft horizontally of the building, whichever is lower. Height is measured to the highest point of the coping of a flat roof, to the deck line of a mansard roof, or to the average height of the highest sloping roof. Area is measured within the surrounding walls, exclusive of vent shafts and courts.

Further Information

For information on Use Group classifications, see page 11. For information on mixed-use buildings, see page 12. For information on which code to consult, see page 7.

Unit Conversions

1 ft = 304.8 mm, 1 sq ft = 0.0929 m².

COMBUSTIBLE											Construction Type	Height in Stories
Mill (page 430)		Ordinary				Wood Light Frame						
		1-Hour (page 431)		Unprotected (page 431)		1-Hour (page 433)		Unprotected (page 433)				
Spr	Unspr	Spr	Unspr	Spr	Unspr	Spr	Unspr	Spr	Unspr		Maximum Height in Feet	
65'	65'	65'	65'	55'	55'	50'	50'	40'	40'			
										UH		
										13		
										12		
										11		
										10		
										9		
										8	Height in Stories	
										7		
										6		
36,000		36,000								5		
72,000	36,000	72,000	36,000			28,000				4		
72,000	36,000	72,000	36,000	24,000		56,000	28,000	16,000		3		
72,000	36,000	72,000	36,000	48,000	24,000	56,000	28,000	32,000	16,000	2		
54,000	18,000	54,000	18,000	36,000	12,000	42,000	14,000	24,000	8,000	1		

This table was compiled from information contained in the Uniform Building Code, 1985 Edition. It does not represent an official interpretation by the organization that issues the Uniform Building Code.

HEIGHT AND AREA LIMITATIONS

USE GROUP B-4: BUSINESS

Fire Walls

For multiplication of the allowable area by subdividing the building with fire walls, see page 424.

Excess Frontage

If a building adjoins public ways or yards on more than one side, the tabulated floor areas may be increased by the following percentages for each foot by which the minimum width of the public ways or yards exceeds 20 ft:

a. For frontage on two sides, 1.25% for each foot, up to a maximum of 50%.

b. For frontage on three sides, 2.5% for each foot, up to a maximum of 100%.

c. For frontage on all sides, 5% for each foot, up to a maximum of 100%.

There is no limit on these increases for Use Group B-4 occupancies of one or two stories in height.

Measurements

Height is measured from an elevation 10 ft higher than the lowest grade, or from the elevation of the highest adjacent sidewalk or ground surface within 5 ft horizontally of the building, whichever is lower. Height is measured to the highest point of the coping of a flat roof, to the deck line of a mansard roof, or to the average height of the highest sloping roof. Area is measured within the surrounding walls, exclusive of vent shafts and courts.

USE GROUP B-4: BUSINESS

Construction Type	NONCOMBUSTIBLE							
	3-Hour (page 425)		2-Hour (page 426)		1-Hour (page 428)		Unprotected (page 429)	
	Spr	Unspr	Spr	Unspr	Spr	Unspr	Spr	Unspr
Maximum Height in Feet	UH	UH	160'	160'	65'	65'	55'	55'
UH	UA	UA						
13			119,800					
12			239,600	119,800				
11			239,600	119,800				
10			239,600	119,800				
9			239,600	119,800				
8			239,600	119,800				
7			239,600	119,800				
6			239,600	119,800				
5			239,600	119,800	54,000			
4			239,600	119,800	108,000	54,000		
3			239,600	119,800	108,000	54,000	36,000	
2			239,600	119,800	108,000	54,000	72,000	36,000
1			179,700	59,900	81,000	27,000	54,000	18,000

Height in Stories (label for rows 13 through 1)

Each number in the table represents the maximum total floor area in square feet for an entire building of that story height.

The floor area of any story may not exceed the area permitted for a single-story building of the same Construction Type.

Key to Abbreviations

UA	Unlimited area	Spr	With approved sprinkler system
UH	Unlimited height	Unspr	Without approved sprinkler system
NP	Not permitted		

396

UNIFORM BUILDING CODE

Unlimited Area

If a single-story sprinklered building of this Use Group is surrounded on all sides with permanent open space at least 60 ft wide, its area is not limited. If an unsprinklered single-story building of this Use Group is of Noncombustible, Mill, or 1-Hour Ordinary construction, its area is not limited.

Further Information

For information on Use Group classifications, see page 11. For information on mixed-use buildings, see page 12. For information on which code to consult, see page 7.

Unit Conversions

1 ft = 304.8 mm, 1 sq ft = 0.0929 m².

Construction Type

COMBUSTIBLE											
	Mill (page 430)		Ordinary				Wood Light Frame				
			1-Hour (page 431)		Unprotected (page 431)		1-Hour (page 433)		Unprotected (page 433)		
	Spr	Unspr	Spr	Unspr	Spr	Unspr	Spr	Unspr	Spr	Unspr	Maximum Height in Feet
	65'	65'	65'	65'	55'	55'	50'	50'	40'	40'	Height in Stories
UH											
13											
12											
11											
10											
9											
8											
7											
6											
5	54,000		54,000								
4	108,000	54,000	108,000	54,000			42,000				
3	108,000	54,000	108,000	54,000	36,000		84,000	42,000	24,000		
2	108,000	54,000	108,000	54,000	72,000	36,000	84,000	42,000	48,000	24,000	
1	81,000	27,000	81,000	27,000	54,000	18,000	63,000	21,000	36,000	12,000	

This table was compiled from information contained in the Uniform Building Code, 1985 Edition. It does not represent an official interpretation by the organization that issues the Uniform Building Code.

USE GROUP E: EDUCATIONAL

Sprinklers
An approved sprinkler system is required in Use Group E-1 basements larger than 1500 sq ft.

Fire Walls
For multiplication of the allowable area by subdividing the building with fire walls, see page 424.

Excess Frontage
If a building adjoins public ways or yards on more than one side, the tabulated floor areas may be increased by the following percentages for each foot by which the minimum width of the public ways or yards exceeds 20 ft:

a. For frontage on two sides, 1.25% for each foot, up to a maximum of 50%.

b. For frontage on three sides, 2.5% for each foot, up to a maximum of 100%.

c. For frontage on all sides, 5% for each foot, up to a maximum of 100%.

Area Increase
An increase of 50% in the allowable areas is permitted if egress travel distance is reduced by 50%; see section 802(a) of the Uniform Building Code.

USE GROUP E: EDUCATIONAL

Construction Type	NONCOMBUSTIBLE							
	3-Hour (page 425)		2-Hour (page 426)		1-Hour (page 428)		Unprotected (page 429)	
	Spr	Unspr	Spr	Unspr	Spr	Unspr	Spr	Unspr
Maximum Height in Feet	UH	UH	160′	160′	65′	65′	55′	55′
UH	UA	UA						
13								
12								
11								
10								
9								
8								
7								
6								
5			90,400					
4			180,800	90,400				
3			180,800	90,400	40,400			
2			180,800	90,400	80,800	40,400	27,000	
1			135,600	45,200	60,600	20,200	40,500	13,500

(Rows 13–1 under "Height in Stories")

Each number in the table represents the maximum total floor area in square feet for an entire building of that story height.

The floor area of any story may not exceed the area permitted for a single-story building of the same Construction Type.

Key to Abbreviations

UA	Unlimited area	Spr	With approved sprinkler system
UH	Unlimited height	Unspr	Without approved sprinkler system
NP	Not permitted		

UNIFORM BUILDING CODE

Measurements
Height is measured from an elevation 10 ft higher than the lowest grade, or from the elevation of the highest adjacent sidewalk or ground surface within 5 ft horizontally of the building, whichever is lower. Height is measured to the highest point of the coping of a flat roof, to the deck line of a mansard roof, or to the average height of the highest sloping roof. Area is measured within the surrounding walls, exclusive of vent shafts and courts.

Further Information
For information on Use Group classifications, see page 11. For information on mixed-use buildings, see page 12. For information on which code to consult, see page 7.

Unit Conversions
1 ft = 304.8 mm, 1 sq ft = 0.0929 m².

COMBUSTIBLE										Construction Type	Maximum Height in Feet	Height in Stories
	Ordinary				Wood Light Frame							
Mill (page 430)		1-Hour (page 431)		Unprotected (page 431)		1-Hour (page 433)		Unprotected (page 433)				
Spr	Unspr	Spr	Unspr	Spr	Unspr	Spr	Unspr	Spr	Unspr			
65'	65'	65'	65'	55'	55'	50'	50'	40'	40'			
											UH	
											13	
											12	
											11	
											10	
											9	
											8	
											7	
											6	
											5	
											4	
40,400		40,400				31,400					3	
80,800	40,400	80,800	40,400	27,000		62,800	31,400	18,200			2	
60,600	20,200	60,600	20,200	40,500	13,500	47,100	15,700	27,300	9,100		1	

This table was compiled from information contained in the Uniform Building Code, 1985 Edition. It does not represent an official interpretation by the organization that issues the Uniform Building Code.

HEIGHT AND AREA LIMITATIONS

USE GROUP H-1: HAZARDOUS

Specific Hazards
This is a diverse Use Group with many special requirements for various specific occupancies; consult the Uniform Building Code, Chapter 9, for details.

Location on Site
A building of this Use Group must be located at least 60 ft from all property lines.

Fire Walls
For multiplication of the allowable area by subdividing the building with fire walls, see page 424.

Excess Frontage
If a building adjoins public ways or yards on more than one side, the tabulated floor areas may be increased by the following percentages for each foot by which the minimum width of the public ways or yards exceeds 20 ft:

a. For frontage on two sides, 1.25% for each foot, up to a maximum of 50%.

b. For frontage on three sides, 2.5% for each foot, up to a maximum of 100%.

c. For frontage on all sides, 5% for each foot, up to a maximum of 100%.

Measurements
Height is measured from an elevation 10 ft higher than the lowest grade, or from the elevation of

USE GROUP H-1: HAZARDOUS

		NONCOMBUSTIBLE							
Construction Type		**3-Hour (page 425)**		**2-Hour (page 426)**		**1-Hour (page 428)**		**Unprotected (page 429)**	
		Spr	Unspr	Spr	Unspr	Spr	Unspr	Spr	Unspr
Maximum Height in Feet		UH	UH	160'	160'	65'	65'	55'	55'
	UH	30,000	1,500						
	13	30,000	1,500						
	12	30,000	1,500						
	11	30,000	1,500						
	10	30,000	1,500						
	9	30,000	1,500						
Height in Stories	8	30,000	1,500						
	7	30,000	1,500						
	6	30,000	1,500						
	5	30,000	1,500						
	4	30,000	1,500						
	3	30,000	1,500						
	2	30,000	1,500	24,800	1,500				
	1	15,000	1,500	12,400	1,500	5,600	1,500	3,700	1,500

Each number in the table represents the maximum total floor area in square feet for an entire building of that story height.

The floor area of any story may not exceed the area permitted for a single-story building of the same Construction Type.

Key to Abbreviations

UA	Unlimited area	Spr	With approved sprinkler system
UH	Unlimited height	Unspr	Without approved sprinkler system
NP	Not permitted		

400

the highest adjacent sidewalk or ground surface within 5 ft horizontally of the building, whichever is lower. Height is measured to the highest point of the coping of a flat roof, to the deck line of a mansard roof, or to the average height of the highest sloping roof. Area is measured within the surrounding walls, exclusive of vent shafts and courts.

Further Information

For information on Use Group classifications, see page 11. For information on mixed-use buildings, see page 12. For information on which code to consult, see page 7.

Unit Conversions

1 ft = 304.8 mm, 1 sq ft = 0.0929 m².

				COMBUSTIBLE						
		Ordinary				Wood Light Frame				
Mill (page 430)		1-Hour (page 431)		Unprotected (page 431)		1-Hour (page 433)		Unprotected (page 433)		
Spr	Unspr	Spr	Unspr	Spr	Unspr	Spr	Unspr	Spr	Unspr	
65'	65'	65'	65'	55'	55'	50'	50'	40'	40'	
										UH
										13
										12
										11
										10
										9
										8
										7
										6
										5
										4
										3
										2
5,600	1,500	5,600	1,500	3,700	1,500	4,400	1,500	2,500	1,500	1

Construction Type

Maximum Height in Feet

Height in Stories

HEIGHT AND AREA LIMITATIONS

This table was compiled from information contained in the Uniform Building Code, 1985 Edition. It does not represent an official interpretation by the organization that issues the Uniform Building Code.

USE GROUP H-2: HAZARDOUS

Specific Hazards

This is a diverse Use Group with many special requirements for various specific occupancies; consult the Uniform Building Code, Chapter 9, for details.

Fire Walls

For multiplication of the allowable area by subdividing the building with fire walls, see page 424.

Excess Frontage

If a building adjoins public ways or yards on more than one side, the tabulated floor areas may be increased by the following percentages for each foot by which the minimum width of the public ways or yards exceeds 20 ft:

a. For frontage on two sides, 1.25% for each foot, up to a maximum of 50%.

b. For frontage on three sides, 2.5% for each foot, up to a maximum of 100%.

c. For frontage on all sides, 5% for each foot, up to a maximum of 100%.

Measurements

Height is measured from an elevation 10 ft higher than the lowest grade, or from the elevation of the highest adjacent sidewalk or ground surface within 5 ft horizontally of the building, whichever is lower. Height is measured to the highest point of the coping of a flat roof, to the deck line of a mansard

USE GROUP H-2: HAZARDOUS

Construction Type		NONCOMBUSTIBLE							
		3-Hour (page 425)		2-Hour (page 426)		1-Hour (page 428)		Unprotected (page 429)	
		Spr	Unspr	Spr	Unspr	Spr	Unspr	Spr	Unspr
Maximum Height in Feet		UH	UH	160'	160'	65'	65'	55'	55'
	UH	30,000	1,500						
	13	30,000	1,500						
	12	30,000	1,500						
	11	30,000	1,500						
	10	30,000	1,500						
	9	30,000	1,500						
Height in Stories	8	30,000	1,500						
	7	30,000	1,500						
	6	30,000	1,500						
	5	30,000	1,500	24,800	1,500				
	4	30,000	1,500	24,800	1,500				
	3	30,000	1,500	24,800	1,500				
	2	30,000	1,500	24,800	1,500	11,200	1,500		
	1	15,000	1,500	12,400	1,500	5,600	1,500	3,700	1,500

Each number in the table represents the maximum total floor area in square feet for an entire building of that story height.

The floor area of any story may not exceed the area permitted for a single-story building of the same Construction Type.

Key to Abbreviations

UA	Unlimited area	Spr	With approved sprinkler system
UH	Unlimited height	Unspr	Without approved sprinkler system
NP	Not permitted		

roof, or to the average height of the highest sloping roof. Area is measured within the surrounding walls, exclusive of vent shafts and courts.

Further Information

For information on Use Group classifications, see page 11. For information on mixed-use buildings, see page 12. For information on which code to consult, see page 7.

Unit Conversions

1 ft = 304.8 mm, 1 sq ft = 0.0929 m².

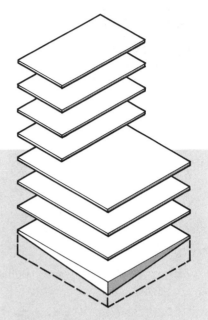

		COMBUSTIBLE										
			Ordinary				Wood Light Frame					
Mill (page 430)		1-Hour (page 431)		Unprotected (page 431)		1-Hour (page 433)		Unprotected (page 433)		**Construction Type**		
Spr	Unspr	Spr	Unspr	Spr	Unspr	Spr	Unspr	Spr	Unspr			
65'	65'	65'	65'	55'	55'	50'	50'	40'	40'	**Maximum Height in Feet**		
										UH		
										13		
										12		
										11		
										10		
										9		
										8	**Height in Stories**	
										7		
										6		
										5		
										4		
										3		
11,200	1,500	11,200	1,500			8,800	1,500			2		
5,600	1,500	5,600	1,500	3,700	1,500	4,400	1,500	2,500	1,500	1		

This table was compiled from information contained in the Uniform Building Code, 1985 Edition. It does not represent an official interpretation by the organization that issues the Uniform Building Code.

USE GROUPS H-3, H-4, H-5: HAZARDOUS

Specific Hazards

These are diverse Use Groups with many special requirements for various specific occupancies; consult the Uniform Building Code, Chapter 9, for details.

Sprinklers

An approved automatic sprinkler system is required in Use Group H-3 buildings larger than 3000 sq ft and in Use Group H-4 buildings more than one story in height.

Fire Walls

For multiplication of the allowable area by subdividing the building with fire walls, see page 424.

Excess Frontage

If a building adjoins public ways or yards on more than one side, the tabulated floor areas may be increased by the following percentages for each foot by which the minimum width of the public ways or yards exceeds 20 ft:

a. For frontage on two sides, 1.25% for each foot, up to a maximum of 50%.

b. For frontage on three sides, 2.5% for each foot, up to a maximum of 100%.

c. For frontage on all sides, 5% for each foot, up to a maximum of 100%. Use Group H-5 aircraft repair hangars one story in height with open space on all sides may be increased in area up to a maximum of 500%. Use Group H-5 aircraft repair hangars surrounded on all sides with at least 60 ft of open space, if sprinklered, are not limited in area.

USE GROUPS H-3, H-4, H-5: HAZARDOUS

Construction Type	NONCOMBUSTIBLE							
	3-Hour (page 425)		2-Hour (page 426)		1-Hour (page 428)		Unprotected (page 429)	
	Spr	Unspr	Spr	Unspr	Spr	Unspr	Spr	Unspr
Maximum Height in Feet	UH	UH	160'	160'	65'	65'	55'	55'
UH	UA	UA						
13								
12								
11								
10								
9								
8								
7								
6			49,600					
5			99,200	49,600				
4			99,200	49,600				
3			99,200	49,600	22,400			
2			99,200	49,600	44,800	22,400	15,000	
1			74,400	24,800	33,600	11,200	22,500	7,500

Height in Stories (rows UH through 1)

Each number in the table represents the maximum total floor area in square feet for an entire building of that story height.

The floor area of any story may not exceed the area permitted for a single-story building of the same Construction Type.

Key to Abbreviations

UA	Unlimited area	Spr	With approved sprinkler system
UH	Unlimited height	Unspr	Without approved sprinkler system
NP	Not permitted		

UNIFORM BUILDING CODE

Measurements
Height is measured from an elevation 10 ft higher than the lowest grade, or from the elevation of the highest adjacent sidewalk or ground surface within 5 ft horizontally of the building, whichever is lower. Height is measured to the highest point of the coping of a flat roof, to the deck line of a mansard roof, or to the average height of the highest sloping roof. Area is measured within the surrounding walls, exclusive of vent shafts and courts.

Further Information
For information on Use Group classifications, see page 11. For information on mixed-use buildings, see page 12. For information on which code to consult, see page 7.

Unit Conversions
1 ft = 304.8 mm, 1 sq ft = 0.0929 m².

	COMBUSTIBLE										Construction Type
Mill (page 430)		Ordinary				Wood Light Frame				
		1-Hour (page 431)		Unprotected (page 431)		1-Hour (page 433)		Unprotected (page 433)		
Spr	Unspr	Spr	Unspr	Spr	Unspr	Spr	Unspr	Spr	Unspr	Maximum Height in Feet
65'	65'	65'	65'	55'	55'	50'	50'	40'	40'	
										UH
										13
										12
										11
										10
										9
										8 Height in Stories
										7
										6
										5
										4
22,400		22,400				17,600				3
44,800	22,400	44,800	22,400	15,000		35,200	17,600	20,400		2
33,600	11,200	33,600	11,200	22,500	7,500	26,400	8,800	15,300	5,100	1

This table was compiled from information contained in the Uniform Building Code, 1985 Edition. It does not represent an official interpretation by the organization that issues the Uniform Building Code.

HEIGHT AND AREA LIMITATIONS

USE GROUP H-6: HAZARDOUS

Specific Hazards
This is a diverse Use Group with many special requirements for various specific occupancies; consult the Uniform Building Code, Chapter 9, for details.

Fire Walls
For multiplication of the allowable area by subdividing the building with fire walls, see page 424.

Excess Frontage
If a building adjoins public ways or yards on more than one side, the tabulated floor areas may be increased by the following percentages for each foot by which the minimum width of the public ways or yards exceeds 20 ft:

a. For frontage on two sides, 1.25% for each foot, up to a maximum of 50%.

b. For frontage on three sides, 2.5% for each foot, up to a maximum of 100%.

c. For frontage on all sides, 5% for each foot, up to a maximum of 100%.

Measurements
Height is measured from an elevation 10 ft higher than the lowest grade, or from the elevation of the highest adjacent sidewalk or ground surface within 5 ft horizontally of the building, whichever is lower. Height is measured to the highest point of the coping of a flat roof, to the deck line of a mansard

USE GROUP H-6: HAZARDOUS

Construction Type	NONCOMBUSTIBLE							
	3-Hour (page 425)		2-Hour (page 426)		1-Hour (page 428)		Unprotected (page 429)	
	Spr	Unspr	Spr	Unspr	Spr	Unspr	Spr	Unspr
Maximum Height in Feet	UH		160'		65"		55"	
UH								
13								
12								
11								
10								
9								
8								
7								
6								
5								
4								
3	UA		79,800		36,000			
2			79,800		36,000		24,000	
1		NP	39,900	NP	18,000	NP	12,000	NP

Height in Stories (row labels UH, 13–1)

Each number in the table represents the maximum total floor area in square feet for an entire building of that story height.

The floor area of any story may not exceed the area permitted for a single-story building of the same Construction Type.

Key to Abbreviations

UA	Unlimited area	Spr	With approved sprinkler system
UH	Unlimited height	Unspr	Without approved sprinkler system
NP	Not permitted		

UNIFORM BUILDING CODE

roof, or to the average height of the highest sloping roof. Area is measured within the surrounding walls, exclusive of vent shafts and courts.

Further Information

For information on Use Group classifications, see page 11. For information on mixed-use buildings, see page 12. For information on which code to consult, see page 7.

Unit Conversions

1 ft = 304.8 mm, 1 sq ft = 0.0929 m².

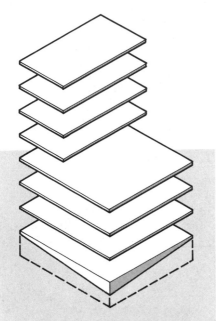

Construction Type

Maximum Height in Feet

Height in Stories

	COMBUSTIBLE									
Mill (page 430)		**Ordinary**				**Wood Light Frame**				
		1-Hour (page 431)		**Unprotected** (page 431)		**1-Hour** (page 433)		**Unprotected** (page 433)		
Spr	Unspr	Spr	Unspr	Spr	Unspr	Spr	Unspr	Spr	Unspr	
65′		65′		55′		50′		40′		
										UH
										13
										12
										11
										10
										9
										8
										7
										6
										5
										4
36,000		36,000				28,000				3
36,000		36,000		24,000		28,000				2
18,000	NP	18,000	NP	12,000	NP	14,000	NP	8,000	NP	1

This table was compiled from information contained in the Uniform Building Code, 1985 Edition. It does not represent an official interpretation by the organization that issues the Uniform Building Code.

HEIGHT AND AREA LIMITATIONS

USE GROUP I-1: INSTITUTIONAL

Fire Walls
For multiplication of the allowable area by subdividing the building with fire walls, see page 424.

Excess Frontage
If a building adjoins public ways or yards on more than one side, the tabulated floor areas may be increased by the following percentages for each foot by which the minimum width of the public ways or yards exceeds 20 ft:

a. For frontage on two sides, 1.25% for each foot, up to a maximum of 50%.

b. For frontage on three sides, 2.5% for each foot, up to a maximum of 100%.

c. For frontage on all sides, 5% for each foot, up to a maximum of 100%.

Measurements
Height is measured from an elevation 10 ft higher than the lowest grade, or from the elevation of the highest adjacent sidewalk or ground surface within 5 ft horizontally of the building, whichever is lower. Height is measured to the highest point of the coping of a flat roof, to the deck line of a mansard roof, or to the average height of the highest sloping roof. Area is measured within the surrounding walls, exclusive of vent shafts and courts.

USE GROUP I-1: INSTITUTIONAL

Construction Type	NONCOMBUSTIBLE							
	3-Hour (page 425)		2-Hour (page 426)		1-Hour (page 428)		Unprotected (page 429)	
	Spr	Unspr	Spr	Unspr	Spr	Unspr	Spr	Unspr
Maximum Height in Feet	UH		160′		65′			
UH	UA							
13								
12								
11								
10								
9								
8								
7								
6								
5								
4			30,200					
3			60,400					
2			60,400		13,600			
1		NP	45,300	NP	20,400	NP	NP	NP

Each number in the table represents the maximum total floor area in square feet for an entire building of that story height.

The floor area of any story may not exceed the area permitted for a single-story building of the same Construction Type.

Key to Abbreviations

UA	Unlimited area	Spr	With approved sprinkler system
UH	Unlimited height	Unspr	Without approved sprinkler system
NP	Not permitted		

408

UNIFORM BUILDING CODE

Further Information

For information on Use Group classifications, see page 11. For information on mixed-use buildings, see page 12. For information on which code to consult, see page 7.

Unit Conversions

1 ft = 304.8 mm, 1 sq ft = 0.0929 m².

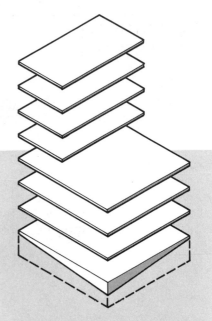

COMBUSTIBLE										
Mill (page 430)		Ordinary				Wood Light Frame				
		1-Hour (page 431)		Unprotected (page 431)		1-Hour (page 433)		Unprotected (page 433)		
Spr	Unspr	Spr	Unspr	Spr	Unspr	Spr	Unspr	Spr	Unspr	
65'		65'				50'				
										UH
										13
										12
										11
										10
										9
										8
										7
										6
										5
										4
										3
13,600		13,600				10,400				2
20,400	NP	20,400	NP	NP	NP	15,600	NP	NP	NP	1

Construction Type

Maximum Height in Feet

Height in Stories

HEIGHT AND AREA LIMITATIONS

409

This table was compiled from information contained in the Uniform Building Code, 1985 Edition. It does not represent an official interpretation by the organization that issues the Uniform Building Code.

USE GROUP I-2: INSTITUTIONAL

Fire Walls

For multiplication of the allowable area by subdividing the building with fire walls, see page 424.

Excess Frontage

If a building adjoins public ways or yards on more than one side, the tabulated floor areas may be increased by the following percentages for each foot by which the minimum width of the public ways or yards exceeds 20 ft:

a. For frontage on two sides, 1.25% for each foot, up to a maximum of 50%.

b. For frontage on three sides, 2.5% for each foot, up to a maximum of 100%.

c. For frontage on all sides, 5% for each foot, up to a maximum of 100%.

Measurements

Height is measured from an elevation 10 ft higher than the lowest grade, or from the elevation of the highest adjacent sidewalk or ground surface within 5 ft horizontally of the building, whichever is lower. Height is measured to the highest point of the coping of a flat roof, to the deck line of a mansard roof, or to the average height of the highest sloping roof. Area is measured within the surrounding walls, exclusive of vent shafts and courts.

USE GROUP I-2: INSTITUTIONAL

Construction Type	NONCOMBUSTIBLE							
	3-Hour (page 425)		2-Hour (page 426)		1-Hour (page 428)		Unprotected (page 429)	
	Spr	Unspr	Spr	Unspr	Spr	Unspr	Spr	Unspr
Maximum Height in Feet	UH		160′		65′			
Height in Stories UH	UA							
13								
12								
11								
10								
9								
8								
7								
6								
5								
4			30,200					
3			60,400		13,600			
2			60,400		27,200			
1		NP	45,300	NP	20,400	NP	NP	NP

Each number in the table represents the maximum total floor area in square feet for an entire building of that story height.

The floor area of any story may not exceed the area permitted for a single-story building of the same Construction Type.

Key to Abbreviations

UA	Unlimited area	Spr	With approved sprinkler system
UH	Unlimited height	Unspr	Without approved sprinkler system
NP	Not permitted		

UNIFORM BUILDING CODE

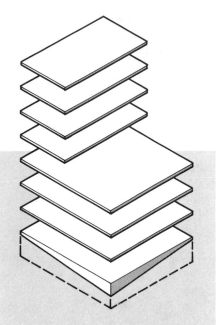

Further Information

For information on Use Group classifications, see page 11. For information on mixed-use buildings, see page 12. For information on which code to consult, see page 7.

Unit Conversions

1 ft = 304.8 mm, 1 sq ft = 0.0929 m².

Construction Type

Maximum Height in Feet

Height in Stories

	COMBUSTIBLE								
Mill (page 430)		**Ordinary**				**Wood Light Frame**			
		1-Hour (page 431)		**Unprotected** (page 431)		**1-Hour** (page 433)		**Unprotected** (page 433)	
Spr	Unspr	Spr	Unspr	Spr	Unspr	Spr	Unspr	Spr	Unspr
65′		65′				50′				UH
										13
										12
										11
										10
										9
										8
										7
										6
										5
										4
13,600		13,600				10,400				3
27,200		27,200				20,800				2
20,400	NP	20,400	NP	NP	NP	15,600	NP	NP	NP	1

This table was compiled from information contained in the Uniform Building Code, 1985 Edition. It does not represent an official interpretation by the organization that issues the Uniform Building Code.

HEIGHT AND AREA LIMITATIONS

411

USE GROUP I-3: INSTITUTIONAL

Fire Walls

For multiplication of the allowable area by subdividing the building with fire walls, see page 424.

Excess Frontage

If a building adjoins public ways or yards on more than one side, the tabulated floor areas may be increased by the following percentages for each foot by which the minimum width of the public ways or yards exceeds 20 ft:

a. For frontage on two sides, 1.25% for each foot, up to a maximum of 50%.

b. For frontage on three sides, 2.5% for each foot, up to a maximum of 100%.

c. For frontage on all sides, 5% for each foot, up to a maximum of 100%.

Measurements

Height is measured from an elevation 10 ft higher than the lowest grade, or from the elevation of the highest adjacent sidewalk or ground surface within 5 ft horizontally of the building, whichever is lower. Height is measured to the highest point of the coping of a flat roof, to the deck line of a mansard roof, or to the average height of the highest sloping roof. Area is measured within the surrounding walls, exclusive of vent shafts and courts.

USE GROUP I-3: INSTITUTIONAL

	NONCOMBUSTIBLE							
Construction Type	**3-Hour (page 425)**		**2-Hour (page 426)**		**1-Hour (page 428)**		**Unprotected (page 429)**	
	Spr	**Unspr**	**Spr**	**Unspr**	**Spr**	**Unspr**	**Spr**	**Unspr**
Maximum Height in Feet	**UH**		**160′**		**65′**			
Height in Stories UH	UA							
13								
12								
11								
10								
9								
8								
7								
6								
5								
4								
3			30,200					
2			60,400					
1		NP	45,300	NP	3,900	NP	NP	NP

Each number in the table represents the maximum total floor area in square feet for an entire building of that story height.

The floor area of any story may not exceed the area permitted for a single-story building of the same Construction Type.

Key to Abbreviations

UA	Unlimited area	Spr	With approved sprinkler system
UH	Unlimited height	Unspr	Without approved sprinkler system
NP	Not permitted		

UNIFORM BUILDING CODE

Further Information

For information on Use Group classifications, see page 11. For information on mixed-use buildings, see page 12. For information on which code to consult, see page 7.

Unit Conversions

1 ft = 304.8 mm, 1 sq ft = 0.0929 m².

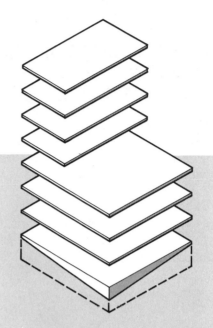

COMBUSTIBLE											
Mill (page 430)		Ordinary				Wood Light Frame				Construction Type
		1-Hour (page 431)		Unprotected (page 431)		1-Hour (page 433)		Unprotected (page 433)		
Spr	Unspr	Spr	Unspr	Spr	Unspr	Spr	Unspr	Spr	Unspr	
		65'				50'				Maximum Height in Feet
										UH
										13
										12
										11
										10
										9
										8 Height in Stories
										7
										6
										5
										4
										3
										2
NP	NP	3,900	NP	NP	NP	3,900	NP	NP	NP	1

This table was compiled from information contained in the Uniform Building Code, 1985 Edition. It does not represent an official interpretation by the organization that issues the Uniform Building Code.

USE GROUP R-1: HOTELS, APARTMENTS, CONVENTS, AND MONASTERIES

Fire Walls

For multiplication of the allowable area by subdividing the building with fire walls, see page 424.

Excess Frontage

If a building adjoins public ways or yards on more than one side, the tabulated floor areas may be increased by the following percentages for each foot by which the minimum width of the public ways or yards exceeds 20 ft:

a. For frontage on two sides, 1.25% for each foot, up to a maximum of 50%.

b. For frontage on three sides, 2.5% for each foot, up to a maximum of 100%.

c. For frontage on all sides, 5% for each foot, up to a maximum of 100%.

Tall Buildings

Buildings of this Use Group with floors used for human occupancy that are more than 75 ft above the lowest level of fire department vehicle access shall either be sprinklered or provide safe areas of refuge by dividing every story into at least two more or less equal areas, each having a maximum floor area of 15,000 sq ft, and each provided with at least one elevator and one enclosed exit stairway.

USE GROUPS R-1: HOTELS, APARTMENTS, CONVENTS, AND MONASTERIES

	NONCOMBUSTIBLE							
Construction Type	**3-Hour** (page 425)		**2-Hour** (page 426)		**1-Hour** (page 428)		**Unprotected** (page 429)	
	Spr	Unspr	Spr	Unspr	Spr	Unspr	Spr	Unspr
Maximum Height in Feet	UH	UH	160'	160'	65'	65'	55'	55'
UH	UA	UA						
13			59,800					
12			119,600	59,800				
11			119,600	59,800				
10			119,600	59,800				
9			119,600	59,800				
8			119,600	59,800				
7			119,600	59,800				
6			119,600	59,800				
5			119,600	59,800	27,000			
4			119,600	59,800	54,000	27,000		
3			119,600	59,800	54,000	27,000		
2			119,600	59,800	54,000	27,000	30,300	12,100
1			89,700	29,900	40,500	13,500	27,300	9,100

(Left-side label: **Height in Stories**)

Each number in the table represents the maximum total floor area in square feet for an entire building of that story height.

The floor area of any story may not exceed the area permitted for a single-story building of the same Construction Type.

Key to Abbreviations

UA	Unlimited area	Spr	With approved sprinkler system
UH	Unlimited height	Unspr	Without approved sprinkler system
NP	Not permitted		

UNIFORM BUILDING CODE

Measurements

Height is measured from an elevation 10 ft higher than the lowest grade, or from the elevation of the highest adjacent sidewalk or ground surface within 5 ft horizontally of the building, whichever is lower. Height is measured to the highest point of the coping of a flat roof, to the deck line of a mansard roof, or to the average height of the highest sloping roof. Area is measured within the surrounding walls, exclusive of vent shafts and courts.

Further Information

For information on Use Group classifications, see page 11. For information on mixed-use buildings, see page 12. For information on which code to consult, see page 7.

Unit Conversions

1 ft = 304.8 mm, 1 sq ft = 0.0929 m².

	COMBUSTIBLE										
	Mill (page 430)		Ordinary				Wood Light Frame				
			1-Hour (page 431)		Unprotected (page 431)		1-Hour (page 433)		Unprotected (page 433)		Construction Type / Maximum Height in Feet / Height in Stories
	Spr	Unspr	Spr	Unspr	Spr	Unspr	Spr	Unspr	Spr	Unspr	
Max Height	65'	65'	65'	65'	55'	55'	50'	50'	40'	40'	
UH											UH
13											13
12											12
11											11
10											10
9											9
8											8
7											7
6											6
5	27,000		27,000								5
4	54,000	27,000	54,000	27,000			21,000				4
3	54,000	27,000	54,000	27,000			42,000	21,000			3
2	54,000	27,000	54,000	27,000	30,300	12,100	42,000	21,000	21,000	9,000	2
1	40,500	13,500	40,500	13,500	27,300	9,100	31,500	10,500	18,000	6,000	

This table was compiled from information contained in the Uniform Building Code, 1985 Edition. It does not represent an official interpretation by the organization that issues the Uniform Building Code.

USE GROUP R-3: DWELLINGS AND LODGING HOUSES

Fire Walls

For multiplication of the allowable area by subdividing the building with fire walls, see page 424.

Excess Frontage

If a building adjoins public ways or yards on more than one side, the tabulated floor areas may be increased by the following percentages for each foot by which the minimum width of the public ways or yards exceeds 20 ft:

a. For frontage on two sides, 1.25% for each foot, up to a maximum of 50%.

b. For frontage on three sides, 2.5% for each foot, up to a maximum of 100%.

c. For frontage on all sides, 5% for each foot, up to a maximum of 100%.

Measurements

Height is measured from an elevation 10 ft higher than the lowest grade, or from the elevation of the highest adjacent sidewalk or ground surface within 5 ft horizontally of the building, whichever is lower. Height is measured to the highest point of the coping of a flat roof, to the deck line of a mansard roof, or to the average height of the highest sloping roof. Area is measured within the surrounding walls, exclusive of vent shafts and courts.

USE GROUP R-3: DWELLINGS AND LODGING HOUSES

Construction Type	NONCOMBUSTIBLE							
	3-Hour (page 425)		2-Hour (page 426)		1-Hour (page 428)		Unprotected (page 429)	
	Spr	Unspr	Spr	Unspr	Spr	Unspr	Spr	Unspr
Maximum Height in Feet	UH	UH	160'	160'	65'	65'	55'	55'
UH	UA	UA						
13								
12								
11								
10								
9								
8								
7								
6								
5								
4								
3			UA	UA	UA	UA	UA	UA
2								
1								

(Left column label: "Height in Stories")

Each number in the table represents the maximum total floor area in square feet for an entire building of that story height.

The floor area of any story may not exceed the area permitted for a single-story building of the same Construction Type.

Key to Abbreviations

UA	Unlimited area	Spr	With approved sprinkler system
UH	Unlimited height	Unspr	Without approved sprinkler system
NP	Not permitted		

UNIFORM BUILDING CODE

Further Information

For information on Use Group classifications, see page 11. For information on mixed-use buildings, see page 12. For information on which code to consult, see page 7.

Unit Conversions

1 ft = 304.8 mm, 1 sq ft = 0.0929 m².

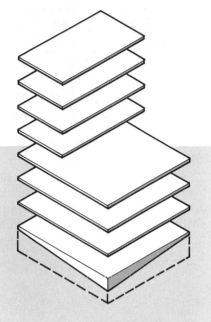

		COMBUSTIBLE									
Mill (page 430)		Ordinary				Wood Light Frame					Construction Type
		1-Hour (page 431)		Unprotected (page 431)		1-Hour (page 433)		Unprotected (page 433)			
Spr	Unspr	Spr	Unspr	Spr	Unspr	Spr	Unspr	Spr	Unspr		
65'	65'	65'	65'	55'	55'	50'	50'	40'	40'		Maximum Height in Feet
										UH	
										13	
										12	
										11	
										10	
										9	
										8	Height in Stories
										7	
										6	
										5	
										4	
UA	UA	UA	UA	UA	UA	UA	UA	UA	UA	3	
										2	
										1	

This table was compiled from information contained in the Uniform Building Code, 1985 Edition. It does not represent an official interpretation by the organization that issues the Uniform Building Code.

HEIGHT AND AREA LIMITATIONS

417

USE GROUP: OPEN PARKING GARAGES

General Notes

The tabulated areas are for a garage that is open on two sides. If three sides are open, the tabulated areas may be increased by 25% and the heights by one story. If the entire perimeter is open, the areas may be increased by 50% and the heights by one story. A garage of a height less than the maximum permitted for a given Construction Type may be built to the gross total floor area permitted if at least three sides are open and no part of the floor lies more than 200 ft from an opening.

Unlimited Area

A garage of Noncombustible construction is not limited in area if all its sides are open and its height does not exceed 75 ft.

Fire Walls

For multiplication of the allowable area by subdividing the building with fire walls, see page 424.

Excess Frontage

If a building adjoins public ways or yards on more than one side, the tabulated floor areas may be increased by the following percentages for each foot by which the minimum width of the public ways or yards exceeds 20 ft:

a. For frontage on two sides, 1.25% for each foot, up to a maximum of 50%.

b. For frontage on three sides, 2.5% for each foot, up to a maximum of 100%.

USE GROUP: OPEN PARKING GARAGES

Construction Type	NONCOMBUSTIBLE							
	3-Hour (page 425)		2-Hour (page 426)		1-Hour (page 428)		Unprotected (page 429)	
	Spr	Unspr	Spr	Unspr	Spr	Unspr	Spr	Unspr
Maximum Height in Feet	UH	UH						
UH	UA	UA						
13								
12			125,000	125,000				
11			125,000	125,000				
10			125,000	125,000	50,000	50,000		
9			125,000	125,000	50,000	50,000		
8			125,000	125,000	50,000	50,000	30,000	30,000
7			125,000	125,000	50,000	50,000	30,000	30,000
6			125,000	125,000	50,000	50,000	30,000	30,000
5			125,000	125,000	50,000	50,000	30,000	30,000
4			125,000	125,000	50,000	50,000	30,000	30,000
3			125,000	125,000	50,000	50,000	30,000	30,000
2			125,000	125,000	50,000	50,000	30,000	30,000
1			125,000	125,000	50,000	50,000	30,000	30,000

(Left label for story rows: **Height in Stories**)

Each number in the table represents the maximum total floor area in square feet for an entire building of that story height.

The floor area of any story may not exceed the area permitted for a single-story building of the same Construction Type.

Key to Abbreviations

UA	Unlimited area	Spr	With approved sprinkler system
UH	Unlimited height	Unspr	Without approved sprinkler system
NP	Not permitted		

418

UNIFORM BUILDING CODE

c. For frontage on all sides, 5% for each foot, up to a maximum of 100%.

Measurements

Height is measured from an elevation 10 ft higher than the lowest grade, or from the elevation of the highest adjacent sidewalk or ground surface within 5 ft horizontally of the building, whichever is lower. Height is measured to the highest point of the coping of a flat roof, to the deck line of a mansard roof, or to the average height of the highest sloping roof. Area is measured within the surrounding walls, exclusive of vent shafts and courts.

Further Information

For information on Use Group classifications, see page 11. For information on mixed-use buildings, see page 12. For information on which code to consult, see page 7.

Unit Conversions

1 ft = 304.8 mm, 1 sq ft = 0.0929 m².

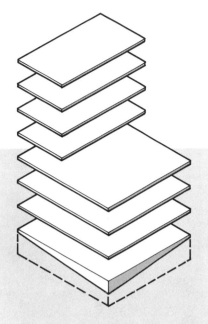

COMBUSTIBLE										Construction Type	Maximum Height in Feet
Mill (page 430)		Ordinary				Wood Light Frame					
		1-Hour (page 431)		Unprotected (page 431)		1-Hour (page 433)		Unprotected (page 433)			
Spr	Unspr	Spr	Unspr	Spr	Unspr	Spr	Unspr	Spr	Unspr		
											UH
											13
											12
											11
											10
											9
											8 — Height in Stories
											7
											6
											5
											4
											3
											2
NP	NP	NP	NP	NP	NP	NP	NP	NP	NP		1

This table was compiled from information contained in the Uniform Building Code, 1985 Edition. It does not represent an official interpretation by the organization that issues the Uniform Building Code.

APPENDIX B: CONSTRUCTION TYPES

This section will help you relate the building code height and area limitations to specific structural materials and systems. The fire-resistance requirements for the four model building codes have been simplified and consolidated into the single chart on pages 422–423. The pages following this chart define each Construction Type in terms of specific structural materials and minimum material thicknesses.

REQUIRED FIRE-RESISTANCE RATINGS OF ELEMENTS OF BUILDINGS (IN HOURS)

This table is a consolidation and simplification of the definitions of Construction Types as given in the four model building codes.

Construction Type	NONCOMBUSTIBLE				
	3-Hour	2-Hour	1.5-Hour	1-Hour	Unprotected
Floor Construction	3	2	1.5	1	0
Columns and Loadbearing Walls	4	3	2	1	0
Roof Construction	0–2	0–1½	0–1	0	0
Exterior Walls	Variable, depending on the distances from property				
Party Walls and Fire Walls—see page 424	4	3–4	2–4	2–4	2–4
Tenant Space Separations	1	1	1	1	0
Dwelling Unit Separations	1	1	1	1	1
Other Nonbearing Partitions	Noncombustible				
Exit Access Corridors	1	1	1	1	1
Enclosures of Exits, Exit Hallways, Stairways	2	2	2	2	2
Shaft Enclosures	2	2	2	2	2

REQUIRED FIRE-RESISTANCE RATINGS OF ELEMENTS OF BUILDINGS (IN HOURS)

	COMBUSTIBLE					Construction Type
		Ordinary		Wood Light Frame		
Mill	1-Hour	Unprotected	1-Hour	¾-Hour	Unprotected	
Heavy Timber	1	0	1	¾	0	Floor Construction
2 or Heavy Timber	1	0	1	¾	0	Columns and Loadbearing Walls
Heavy Timber	0	0	0	0	0	Roof Construction
lines and adjacent buildings—consult the appropriate code for details.						Exterior Walls
2–4	2–4	2–4	2–4	2–4	2–4	Party Walls and Fire Walls—see page 424
1	1	0	1	1	0	Tenant Space Separations
1	1	1	1	1	1	Dwelling Unit Separations
0	0	0	0	0	0	Other Nonbearing Partitions
1	1	1	1	1	1	Exit Access Corridors
2	2	2	2	2	2	Enclosures of Exits, Exit Hallways, Stairways
2	2	2	0	0	0	Shaft Enclosures

FIRE WALLS

Under all four model building codes, each portion of a building separated from the remainder of the building by fire walls may be considered as a separate building for purposes of calculating allowable heights and areas. This allows a building of any Construction Type to be unlimited in horizontal extent so long as it is subdivided by fire walls into compartments that are each of a size that does not exceed the height and area limitations prescribed by the building code.

A fire wall must be constructed so that it will remain stable even if the construction on one side or the other of it collapses during a fire. It must extend from the foundation through the roof to a parapet wall, except that in some instances a fire wall may terminate at the underside of a noncombustible roof. Fire walls may be built of masonry or concrete, or of gypsum plaster or gypsum wallboard supported by noncombustible framing. The required fire-resistance rating for a fire wall may be from one to four hours, depending on the occupancy of the building, the construction type, and the applicable building code. Openings through a fire wall are restricted to a minor percentage of the length of the wall and must be protected with self-closing fire doors. For more detailed specifications for fire walls and their openings, consult the appropriate building code. For purposes of showing a fire wall on preliminary design drawings, a wall thickness of 6 to 8 in. (150 to 200 mm) and a parapet height of 32 in. (800 mm) are generally sufficient.

3-HOUR NONCOMBUSTIBLE CONSTRUCTION

3-Hour Noncombustible construction requires a fire-resistance rating of 3 hours for floor construction and 4 hours for columns and bearing walls.

☐ **Structural Steel** columns, beams, joists, and decking must be protected to these values with applied fireproofing materials or an appropriately fire-resistive ceiling of plaster, gypsum board, or fibrous panels (see pages 90–103).

☐ **Reinforced Concrete** columns must be at least 14 in. (356 mm) in dimension, and loadbearing walls must be at least 6.5 in. (165 mm) thick. Floor slabs must be at least 6.2 in. (157 mm) thick. Concrete one-way and two-way joist systems (ribbed slabs and waffle slabs) with slabs thinner than 6.2 in. (157 mm) between joists re-quire protection with applied fireproofing materials or an appropriately fire-resistive ceiling of plaster, gypsum board, or fibrous panels (see pages 105–121).

☐ **Posttensioned Concrete** floor slabs must be at least 6.2 in. (157 mm) thick (see pages 112–121).

☐ **Precast Concrete** columns must be at least 12 in. (305 mm) in dimension, and beams at least 9.5 in. (241 mm) wide. Loadbearing wall panels must be at least 6.5 in. (165 mm) thick. Solid slabs may not be less than 6.2 in. (157 mm) thick. Hollow core slabs must be at least 8 in. (203 mm) deep and must have a minimum topping of 2 in. (51 mm) of concrete. Double and single tees require applied fireproofing materials or an appropriately fire-resistive ceiling of plaster, gypsum board, or fibrous panels (see pages 123–133).

☐ **Brick Masonry** loadbearing walls must be at least 8 in. (203 mm) thick. Vaults and domes must be at least 8 in. (203 mm) deep with a rise not less than one-twelfth the span (see pages 72–73).

☐ **Concrete Masonry** loadbearing walls must be at least 8 in. (203 mm) thick. Depending on the composition and design of the masonry unit, applied plaster or stucco facings may also be required (see pages 80–81).

Fire-resistive requirements for nonloadbearing walls and partitions are summarized on pages 422–423.

CONSTRUCTION TYPES

425

2-HOUR NONCOMBUSTIBLE CONSTRUCTION

2-Hour Noncombustible construction requires a fire-resistance rating of 2 hours for floor construction and 3 hours for columns and bearing walls.

☐ **Structural Steel** columns, beams, joists, and decking must be protected to these values with applied fireproofing materials or an appropriately fire-resistive ceiling of plaster, gypsum board, or fibrous panels (see pages 90–103).

☐ **Reinforced Concrete** columns must be at least 12 in. (305 mm) in dimension, and loadbearing walls must be at least 6 in. (152 mm) thick. Floor slabs must be at least 5 in. (127 mm) thick. Concrete one-way and two-way joist systems (ribbed slabs and waffle slabs) with slabs thinner than 5 in. (127 mm) between joists require protection with applied fireproofing materials or an appropriately fire-resistive ceiling of plaster, gypsum board, or fibrous panels (see pages 105–121).

☐ **Posttensioned Concrete** floor slabs must be at least 5 in. (127 mm) thick (see pages 112–121).

☐ **Precast Concrete** columns must be at least 10 in. (254 mm) in dimension, and beams at least 7 in. (178 mm) wide. Loadbearing wall panels must be at least 6 in. (152 mm) thick. Solid slabs may not be less than 5 in. (127 mm) thick. Hollow core slabs must be at least 8 in. (203 mm) deep and may be used without a topping. Double and single tees require applied fireproofing materials or an appropriately fire-resistive ceiling of plaster, gypsum board, or fibrous panels, unless a concrete topping 3.25 in. (83 mm) thick is poured (see pages 123–133).

☐ **Brick Masonry** loadbearing walls must be at least 6 in. (152 mm) thick. Vaults and domes must be at least 8 in. (203 mm) deep with a rise not less than one-twelfth the span (see pages 72–73).

☐ **Concrete Masonry** loadbearing walls must be at least 8 in. (203 mm) thick. Depending on the composition and design of the masonry unit, appied plaster or stucco facings may also be required (see pages 80–81).

Fire-resistive requirements for nonloadbearing walls and partitions are summarized on pages 422–423.

1½-HOUR NONCOMBUSTIBLE CONSTRUCTION

1½-Hour Noncombustible construction requires a fire-resistance rating of 1½ hours for floor construction and 2 hours for columns and bearing walls.

☐ **Structural Steel** columns, beams, joists, and decking must be protected to these values with applied fireproofing materials or an appropriately fire-resistive ceiling of plaster, gypsum board, or fibrous panels (see pages 90–103).

☐ **Reinforced Concrete** columns must be at least 10 in. (254 mm) in dimension, and loadbearing walls must be at least 5 in. (127 mm) thick. Floor slabs must be at least 4.3 in. (109 mm) thick. Concrete one-way and two-way joist systems (ribbed slabs and waffle slabs) with slabs thinner than 4.3 in. (109 mm) between joists re-

quire protection with applied fireproofing materials or an appropriately fire-resistive ceiling of plaster, gypsum board, or fibrous panels (see pages 105–121).

☐ **Posttensioned Concrete** floor slabs must be at least 4.25 in. (108 mm) thick (see pages 112–121).

☐ **Precast Concrete** columns must be at least 8 in. (203 mm) in dimension, and beams at least 7 in. (178 mm) wide. Loadbearing wall panels must be at least 5 in. (127 mm) thick. Solid slabs may not be less than 4.3 in. (109 mm) thick. Hollow core slabs must be at least 8 in. (203 mm) deep and may be used without a topping. Double and single tees require applied fireproofing materials or an ap-

propriately fire-resistive ceiling of plaster, gypsum board, or fibrous panels unless a concrete topping 2.75 in. (70 mm) thick is poured (see pages 123–133).

☐ **Brick Masonry** loadbearing walls must be at least 6 in. (152 mm) thick. Vaults and domes must be at least 6 in. (152 mm) deep with a rise not less than one-twelfth the span (see pages 72–73).

☐ **Concrete Masonry** loadbearing walls must be at least 6 in. (152 mm) thick. Depending on the composition and design of the masonry unit, applied plaster, gypsum board, or stucco facings may also be required (see pages 80–81).

Fire-resistive requirements for nonloadbearing walls and partitions are summarized on pages 422–423.

CONSTRUCTION TYPES

1-HOUR NONCOMBUSTIBLE CONSTRUCTION

1-Hour Noncombustible construction requires a fire-resistance rating of 1 hour for floor construction and 1 hour for columns and bearing walls.

☐ **Structural Steel** columns, beams, joists, and decking must be protected to these values with applied fireproofing materials or an appropriately fire-resistive ceiling of plaster, gypsum board, or fibrous panels (see pages 90–103).

☐ **Light Gauge Steel** floor joists must be protected with a ceiling of two layers of ½-in. Type X gypsum board or its equivalent. Loadbearing walls framed with light gauge steel studs must be faced on both sides with single layers of ⅝-in. Type X gypsum board or its equivalent (see pages 86–89).

☐ **Reinforced Concrete** columns must be at least 8 in. (203 mm) in dimension, and loadbearing walls must be at least 3.5 in. (89 mm) thick. Floor slabs must be at least 3.5 in. (89 mm) thick. Concrete one-way and two-way joist systems (ribbed slabs, skip-joist slabs, and waffle slabs) require protection with applied fireproofing materials or an appropriately fire-resistive ceiling of plaster, gypsum board, or acoustical panels unless the slab thickness is at least 3.5 in. between joists (see pages 105–121).

☐ **Posttensioned Concrete** floor slabs must be at least 3.5 in. (89 mm) thick (see pages 112–121).

☐ **Precast Concrete** columns must be at least 6 in. (152 mm) in dimension, and beams at least 4 in. (102 mm) wide. Loadbearing wall panels must be at least 3.5 in. (89 mm) thick. Solid slabs may not be less than 3.5 in. (89 mm) thick. Hollow core slabs must be at least 8 in. (203 mm) deep and may be used without a topping. Double and single tees require applied fireproofing materials or an appropriately fire-resistive ceiling of plaster, gypsum board, or acoustical panels unless a concrete topping 1.75 in. (44 mm) thick is poured (see pages 123–133).

☐ **Brick Masonry** loadbearing walls must be at least 4 in. (102 mm) thick. Vaults and domes must be at least 4 in. (102 mm) deep with a rise not less than one-twelfth the span (see pages 72–73).

☐ **Concrete Masonry** loadbearing walls must be at least 4 in. (102 mm) thick. Depending on the composition and design of the masonry unit, applied plaster, gypsum board, or stucco facings may also be required (see pages 80–81).

Fire-resistive requirements for nonloadbearing walls and partitions are summarized on pages 422–423.

428

UNPROTECTED NONCOMBUSTIBLE CONSTRUCTION

Unprotected Noncombustible construction has no fire-resistive requirements for floor construction, columns, or bearing walls, except that they must be constructed of noncombustible materials.

☐ **Structural Steel** columns, beams, joists, and decking may be used without applied fireproofing materials or fire-resistive ceilings (see pages 90–103).

☐ **Light Gauge Steel Framing** may be used with minimum facings of gypsum board or its equivalent to brace the studs and joists against buckling (see pages 86–89).

☐ **Reinforced Concrete** structures of all types may be designed to the minimum dimensions dictated by structural considerations, without need for applied fireproofing materials (see pages 105–121).

☐ **Posttensioned Concrete** structures of all types may be designed to the minimum dimensions dictated by structural considerations, without need for applied fireproofing materials (see pages 105–121).

☐ **Precast Concrete** structures of all types may be designed to the minimum dimensions dictated by structural considerations, without need for applied fireproofing materials (see pages 123–133).

☐ **Masonry Structures** of all types may be designed to the minimum dimensions dictated by structural considerations, without need for applied fireproofing materials (see pages 69–83).

Fire-resistive requirements for nonloadbearing walls and partitions are summarized on pages 422–423.

CONSTRUCTION TYPES

MILL CONSTRUCTION (HEAVY TIMBER)

Mill construction depends for its fire-resistive properties on timbers and decking whose thickness is such that they are slow to catch fire and burn. Either solid or glue-laminated timbers and decking may be used. Thickness requirements vary slightly from code to code, but the following dimensions are appropriate for preliminary design purposes:

☐ **Columns** supporting floor loads must be at least 8×8 nominal dimensions (7.5 × 7.5 in., or 184 × 184 mm). Columns supporting a roof and ceiling only may be no smaller than 6×8 (5.5 × 7.5 in., or 140 × 184 mm).

☐ **Beams and Girders** supporting a floor must be at least 6×10 nom-inal dimensions (5.5 × 9.5 in., or 140 × 235 mm). If supporting a roof and ceiling only, they may be no smaller than 4×6 (3.5 × 5.5 in., or 89 × 140 mm).

☐ **Trusses** must be made of members no smaller than 8×8 nominal dimensions (7.5 × 7.5 in., or 184 mm × 184 mm), except that roof trusses may be made up of members as small as 4×6 nominal dimensions (3.5 × 5.5 in., or 89 × 140 mm).

☐ **Decking** for floors must consist nominally of 3-in. structural deck-ing with a 1-in. finish floor laid at right angles on top (2.5 in. plus ¾ in., or 64 mm plus 19 mm). Roof decking may be nominally 2 in. thick (actually 1.5 in., or 38 mm), or 1⅛-in. (29-mm) plywood.

☐ **Exterior Walls** must be noncom-bustible; traditionally they have been made of loadbearing ma-sonry. The degree of fire resis-tance required for exterior walls varies from zero to 4 hours de-pending on the occupancy of the building, the distance of the wall from the property line and adja-cent buildings, and the applicable building code.

See pages 48–65 for structural information on the timber mem-bers of Mill construction and pages 69–83 for information on loadbear-ing walls. Fire-resistive require-ments for nonloadbearing walls and partitions are summarized on pages 422–423.

ORDINARY CONSTRUCTION

So-called "Ordinary" construction consists of noncombustible exterior walls and an interior structure that is usually wood light framing but may be of metal or concrete.

☐ **Interior Framing** members of wood may not be less than 2 in. nominal dimension (actual dimension 1.5 in., or 38 mm). Walls and partitions are framed with studs, floors with joists, and roofs with rafters or light trusses, usually at spacings of 16 or 24 in. (406 or 610 mm). In 1-Hour Ordinary construction, all roofs, loadbearing walls, and floors must have 1 hour of fire protection. In Unprotected Ordinary construction, no fire protection is required on these elements of the structure. One hour of protection may be provided on walls by applying ⅝-in. (15.9-mm) Type X gypsum board or its equivalent to each face of the studs. On ceilings, a layer of ⅝-in. Type X gypsum board or its equivalent is required for a 1-hour rating, assuming that the floor above consists of 1-in. nominal subflooring and 1-in. nominal finish flooring (actual dimensions ¾ in., or 19 mm, each).

☐ **Exterior Walls** must be noncombustible; traditionally they have been made of loadbearing masonry. The degree of fire resistance required for exterior walls varies from zero to 4 hours depending on the occupancy of the building, the distance of the wall from the property line and adjacent buildings, and the applicable building code.

See pages 50–57 for structural information on the wood members of Ordinary construction and pages 69–83 for information on masonry loadbearing walls. Fire-resistive requirements for nonloadbearing walls and partitions are summarized on pages 422–423.

¾-HOUR NONCOMBUSTIBLE OR COMBUSTIBLE CONSTRUCTION

¾-Hour Noncombustible or Combustible construction is a classification established by the National Building Code of Canada. While the classification is very broad, including any construction materials that will satisfy the requirements tabulated on pages 422–423, in practice this classification is most generally applied to light framing of wood or light gauge steel framing. Heavy Timber construction is also considered to be the equivalent of ¾-Hour construction under the National Building Code of Canada.

☐ **Loadbearing Walls** framed with wood or light gauge steel studs may be given a ¾-hour fire-resistance rating by applying ⅝-in. (15.9-mm) Type X gypsum board or its equivalent to both faces of the framing, or by using ordinary ½-in. (12.7-mm) gypsum board or its equivalent on each face, and inserting a mineral fiber batt of certain minimum specifications in the cavity. Exterior walls framed with wood or steel studs and finished on the outside with wood sheathing and siding require an interior finish of ½-in. (12.7-mm) gypsum board or its equivalent and the insertion of mineral fiber batts in the cavities.

☐ **Ceilings below Floors and Roofs** framed with wood or metal require ⅝-in. (15.9-mm) Type X gypsum board or its equivalent to achieve a ¾-hour fire-resistance rating.

See pages 50–57 for structural information on wood light framing and pages 86–89 for information on light gauge steel framing. Fire-resistive requirements for nonloadbearing walls and partitions are summarized on pages 422–423.

WOOD LIGHT FRAME CONSTRUCTION

Floors, walls, and roofs of Wood Light Frame construction are framed with wood members not less than 2 in. in nominal thickness (actually 1.5 in., or 38 mm). These members are usually spaced at center-to-center distances of either 16 or 24 in. (406 or 610 mm) and covered with any of a very wide range of sheathing and finish materials.

☐ **Unprotected Wood Light Frame Construction** allows the structure of the building to remain exposed or to be finished with materials that do not have a sufficient fire-resistance rating to satisfy a higher classification of construction, such as wood paneling or thin gypsum board.

☐ **1-Hour Wood Light Frame Construction** requires that loadbearing walls and floors have 1-hour fire-resistance ratings. A 1-hour wall may be constructed of wood studs by applying ⅝-in. (15.9-mm) Type X gypsum board or its equivalent to each face of the studs. A floor with 1-in. nominal subflooring and finish flooring (actual dimensions ¾ in., or 19 mm each) has a 1-hour fire-resistance rating if it is finished below with a ceiling of ⅝-in. (15.9-mm) Type X gypsum board or its equivalent.

For structural information on Wood Light Frame construction, see pages 50–57. Fire-resistive requirements for nonloadbearing walls and partitions are summarized on pages 422–423.

APPENDIX C: MEZZANINES AND ATRIUMS

This section will assist you in designing multistory open spaces in accordance with building code requirements.

MEZZANINES

A mezzanine is an intermediate floor level placed between the floor and ceiling of a room. Under all four model codes, a mezzanine is not counted as a story for purposes of determining the maximum of height of a building in stories. While detailed requirements vary somewhat from one building code to another, a preliminary design for a mezzanine may be prepared in accordance with the following simplified guidelines:

• There may be more than one mezzanine area in a room or on a story, but the aggregate total area of the mezzanines may not exceed one-third the area of the story on which they are located; otherwise they must be counted as a separate story. (The National Building Code of Canada allows the total area of mezzanines to be 40% of the area of the story).

• There may be more than one level of mezzanines in a room. (The Uniform Building Code limits the number of mezzanine levels per story to two).

• The construction of a mezzanine must be consistent with the construction type of the floor on which it is located (The Uniform Building Code allows 1-Hour Non-combustible construction to be used for mezzanines in a building of a higher construction type if the mezzanine is unenclosed).

• A mezzanine is usually required to be open to the room in which it is placed. An enclosed portion that does not exceed 10% of the mezzanine area and has an occupancy load not exceeding 10 persons is generally permitted.

• One or two exits to the room below are required, depending on the size of the mezzanine, the occupant load, and the travel distance to exits. These exits may be by way of open stairways.

ATRIUMS

An atrium, as defined in the building codes, is a roofed, inhabited, multistory open space contained within a building. Atriums are commonly used for lobbies and shopping arcades.

While detailed requirements vary slightly from one building code to another, the major requirements of the four model codes that bear on the form of an atrium are these:

• A building containing an atrium must be protected throughout by an approved system of automatic sprinklers.

• The ceiling of an atrium must be provided with a mechanical smoke exhaust system that would be activated in case of fire by any of four means: automatically by smoke detectors, the fire alarm system, or water flow in the sprinkler system; and manually by firefighters. All four means of activation must be provided. A standby power supply is required so that the smoke exhaust system will operate even if there has been a power interruption. In an atrium up to 55 ft (17 m) high, the exhaust system may draw fresh air through gravity supply inlets at the floor of the atrium. If the atrium is taller than this, fresh air must be supplied mechanically, also at floor level.

• Except for the open balconies that may surround an atrium, adjacent spaces must be separated from the atrium by a 1-hour enclosing wall. The wall area may include windows, but window area is restricted under some codes, and these windows must be glazed with fixed lights of tempered, wired, or laminated glass. Windows in this enclosing wall must also be protected by automatic sprinkler heads that completely wet the entire surface of the glass when actuated. *Under all four model codes, atrium enclosing walls may be omitted entirely from any three floors of the building. For example, the ground floor, the floor above, and the top floor of a building may be left completely open to the atrium.*

• A minimum atrium width of 20 ft (6 m) is required by some codes. The Uniform Building Code further requires a minimum width of 30 ft (9 m) for atriums in buildings of 5 to 7 stories and 48 ft (14.6 m) in buildings taller than 7 stories.

APPENDIX D: CODE REQUIREMENTS FOR TOILET ROOMS

This section presents a summary of the fixture requirements for toilet rooms as prescribed by the model codes.

THE BOCA NATIONAL PLUMBING CODE/1987

To determine the number of occupants for the purpose of finding the minimum number of fixtures, see pages 244–245.

SECTION P-1202.0 MINIMUM PLUMBING FACILITIES

P-1202.1 Minimum number of fixtures: Plumbing fixtures shall be provided for the type of building occupancy and in the minimum number(s) shown in Table P-1202.1. Types of building occupancy not shown in Table P-1202.1 shall be considered individually by the code official. The number of occupants shall be determined by the building code listed in Appendix A.

P-1202.2 Separate facilities: In other than residential installations, where plumbing fixtures are required, separate facilities shall be provided for each sex.

> **Exception:** Separate employees facilities shall not be required when 15 or less people are employed.

P-1202.3 Number of occupants of each sex: The number of fixtures shall be based on an occupant load composed of 50 percent of each sex.

P-1202.4 Location of employee toilet facilities: Toilet facilities shall be accessible within the employees' regular working area. The path of travel to the facilities shall not exceed a travel distance of 500 feet (152 m) or traverse more than one flight of stairs. Employee facilities shall be either separate facilities or public customer facilities.

> **Exception:** Facilities required for employees in storage buildings or kiosks located in adjacent buildings under the same ownership, lease, or control, shall be a maximum distance of travel of 500 feet (152 m) from the employees' regular working area to the facilities.

P-1202.5 Customer facilities: Customers, patrons and visitors shall be provided with public toilet facilities in restaurants, nightclubs, places of public assembly and mercantile buildings. In shopping centers and shopping malls, required facilities shall be based on total square footage and facilities shall be installed in individual stores or in a central toilet area if the distance of travel from the main entrance of any store does not exceed 500 feet (152 m) or more than one flight of stairs.

> **Exceptions**
> 1. Customer facilities are not required in buildings with a customer occupant load of less than 150 which do not serve food or beverage.
> 2. Customer facilities are not required in facilities which serve food or beverage with a customer occupant load of 15 or less.

SECTION P-1203.0 HANDICAP PLUMBING FACILITIES

P-1203.1 Toilet rooms: In all buildings other than hotels, motels and multi-family dwellings, toilet rooms containing required fixtures shall have at least one water closet and lavatory accessible to and usable by physically handicapped persons. In hotels, motels and multi-family dwellings, handicap facilities shall be provided in accordance with the building code listed in Appendix A.

> **Exceptions**
> 1. If required plumbing fixtures are installed in two or more toilet rooms for use by the same sex on the same floor, fixtures in only one room are required to comply with these provisions, provided that the room is accessible and marked to indicate that handicap facilities are available therein.
> 2. Use Groups R-3, S, H and U.
> 3. Single-occupant handicap restrooms for use by both sexes.

P-1203.2 Water closet compartment: The clear width between the face of a water closet compartment and a wall shall not be less than 48 inches (1219 mm). The compartment shall be not less than 60 inches (1524 mm) wide by 59

CODE REQUIREMENTS FOR TOILET ROOMS

441

(continued)

inches (1499 mm) deep when the water closet is accessible from the side and not less than 36 inches (914 mm) wide by 69 inches (1753 mm) deep when the water closet is accessible from the front. Where wall-mounted water closets are used, the required depth of the compartment shall be reduced by 3 inches (76 mm). The compartment shall have an out-swinging door at least 32 inches (813 mm) wide or an opening at least 32 inches (813 mm). Handrails shall be provided at the rear and on the side closest to the water closet and mounted 33 inches (838 mm) above and parallel to the floor. The side handrail shall be not less than 42 inches (1067 mm) long, with the back end positioned 12 inches (305 mm) from the rear wall. The rear handrail shall be not less than 36 inches (914 mm) long with the front end positioned 24 inches (610 mm) beyond the centerline of the water closet. Handrails for children shall be mounted 28 inches (711 mm) above the floor. Handrails shall be mounted with a minimum and maximum clearance of 1½ inches (38 mm) between the rail and wall.

P-1203.3 Water closets: A water closet shall have a seat 16 to 19 inches (406 to 483 mm) from the floor. The trap shall not extend in front of, or be flush with, the lip of the bowl.

P-1203.4 Lavatory: A lavatory shall be located a maximum of 32 inches (813 mm) from the floor to the top of the lavatory. An unobstructed knee clearance a minimum of 27 inches (686 mm) high by 8 inches (203 mm) deep from the face of the lavatory shall be provided. An unobstructed toe clearance a minimum of 9 inches (229 mm) high by 9 inches (229 mm) deep from the lavatory wall shall also be provided.

P-1203.5 Drinking fountain: Where a drinking fountain is required, 5 percent or not less than one drinking fountain or other water dispensing means shall be accessible to, and usable by physically handicapped persons. A floor-type, wall-mounted, or semirecessed (fully recessed not acceptable) drinking fountain or cooler shall have a spout and hand control near the front of the unit with the basin located not more than 30 inches (762 mm) above the floor.

P-1203.6 Use Group A: Where showers are provided in gymnasium facilities in conjunction with sports activities, a minimum of one shower shall be provided for the handicapped in accordance with ANSI A117.1 listed in Appendix A.

Table P-1202.1
MINIMUM NUMBER OF PLUMBING FACILITIES[a]
Fixtures (Number of fixtures per number of occupants)
(see Sections P-1202.2 and P-1202.3)

	Building use group	Water closets (Urinals see Section P-1206.2)	Lavatories	Bathtubs/showers	Drinking fountains	Others
A-1	Assembly, theaters	1 per 125	1 per 200		1 per 1,000	1 service sink
A-2	Assembly, nightclubs	1 per 40	1 per 75		1 per 500 (see Section P-1221.1)	
A-3	Assembly, restaurants	1 per 75	1 per 200		1 per 500 (see Section P-1221.1)	1 service sink
	Halls, museums, etc.	1 per 125	1 per 200		1 per 1,000	1 service sink
A-4	Assembly, churches[b]	1 per 150	1 per 200		1 per 1,000	1 service sink
A-5	Assembly, stadiums, pools, etc.	1 per 100	1 per 150		1 per 1,000 (see Section P-1221.1)	1 service sink
B	Business (see Sections P-1202.2 and P-1202.4)	1 per 25	1 per 40		1 per 100 (see Section P-1221.1)	1 service sink
E	Educational	1 per 50	1 per 50		1 per 100	1 service sink
F	Factory and industrial	1 per 15	1 per 20	(see Section P-1223.0)	1 per 100 (see Section P-1221.1)	1 service sink
H	High hazard (see Sections P-1202.2 and P-1202.4)	1 per 100	1 per 100	(see Section P-1223.0)	1 per 1,000 (see Section P-1221.1)	1 service sink
I-1	Institutional, residential care	1 per 10	1 per 10	1 per 8	1 per 100	1 service sink
I-2	Institutional, hospitals[c]	1 per room	1 per room	1 per 15	1 per 100	1 service sink per floor
	Day nurseries, sanitariums, etc.	1 per 15	1 per 15	1 per 15	1 per 100	1 service sink
	Employees[c]	1 per 25	1 per 35		1 per 100	
	Visitors	1 per 75	1 per 100		1 per 500	
I-3	Institutional, prisons[c]	1 per cell	1 per cell	1 per 15	1 per 100	1 service sink
	Asylums, reformatories, etc.[c]	1 per 15	1 per 15	1 per 15	1 per 100	1 service sink
	Employees[c]	1 per 25	1 per 35		1 per 100	
	Visitors	1 per 75	1 per 100		1 per 500	
M	Mercantile (see Sections P-1202.2, P-1202.4, and P-1202.5)	1 per 500	1 per 750		1 per 1,000	1 service sink
R-1	Residential, hotels, motels	1 per guest room	1 per guest room	1 per guest room		1 service sink
	Lodges	1 per 10	1 per 10	1 per 8	1 per 100 (see Section P-1221.1)	1 service sink
R-2	Residential, multifamily	1 per dwelling unit	1 per dwelling unit	1 per dwelling unit		1 kitchen sink per dwelling unit; 1 automatic clothes washer connection per 20 dwelling units
	Dormitories	1 per 10	1 per 10	1 per 8	1 per 100 (see Section P-1221.1)	1 service sink
R-3	Residential, one & two family dwelling	1 per dwelling unit	1 per dwelling unit	1 per dwelling unit		1 kitchen sink per dwelling unit; 1 automatic clothes washer connection per dwelling unit[d]
S	Storage (see Sections P-1202.2 and P-1202.4)	1 per 100	1 per 100	(see Section P-1223.0)	1 per 1,000 (see Section P-1221.1)	1 service sink

Note a. The fixtures shown are based on one fixture being the minimum required for the number of persons indicated or any fraction of persons. The number of occupants shall be determined by the building code listed in Appendix A.
Note b. Fixtures located in adjacent buildings under the ownership or control of the church shall be accessible during periods the church is occupied.
Note c. Toilet facilities for employees shall be separate from facilities for inmates or patients.
Note d. For attached one- and two-family dwellings, one automatic clothes washer connection shall be required per 20 dwelling units.

Section 1206.2 states that in each bathroom or toilet room, urinals shall not be substituted for more than 50 percent of the required water closets.

CODE REQUIREMENTS FOR TOILET ROOMS

To determine the number of persons for the purpose of finding the minimum number of fixtures, see page 250.

To determine the number of persons for the purpose of finding the minimum number of fixtures, see page 250.

SUBSECTION 3.6.4. PLUMBING FACILITIES

Systems required

3.6.4.1.(1) Each *building* situated on property that abuts on a *street* in which a public or municipal water main is located shall be provided with or have accessible to its occupants a *plumbing system* including a potable water supply, a *sanitary drainage system* and toilet fixtures.

(2) When the installation of a *sanitary drainage system* is not possible because of the absence of a water supply, sanitary privies, chemical closets or other means for the disposal of human waste shall be provided.

Minimum number of fixtures

3.6.4.2.(1) Water closets shall be provided for each sex in accordance with the anticipated proportion of each sex in the *occupancy* when this can be determined with reasonable accuracy, except that when such a determination cannot be made with reasonable accuracy, it shall be assumed that the *occupancy* is equally divided between the sexes.

(2) Where water closets are required in this Subsection, urinals may be substituted for ⅔ of the required number of water closets and may be counted as water closets, except that where only 2 water closets are required, 1 urinal may be substituted for 1 of the water closets.

(3) Except as provided in Sentence (4), at least 1 lavatory shall be provided in a room containing 1 or 2 water closets or urinals, and at least 1 additional lavatory shall be provided for each additional 2 such fixtures.

(4) Wash fountains in circular form may be provided in lieu of lavatories required in Sentence (3) provided each 500 mm of circumference is considered to be the equivalent of 1 lavatory.

(5) The number of water closets required for Group A, Division 1, 3, and 4 *occupancies* and for auditoria, gymnasia, lecture halls, secondary schools, non-residential colleges and similar occupancies shall conform to Table 3.6.4.A.

Table 3.6.4.A.
Forming Part of Sentence 3.6.4.2.(5)

Number of Persons of Each Sex	Minimum Number of Water Closets	
	Male	Female
1– 25	1	1
26– 50	1	2
51– 75	2	3
76–100	2	4
101–150	3	5
151–200	4	6
201–300	5	7
301–400	6	8
Over 400	7 plus 1 for each additional increment of 200 males	9 plus 1 for each additional increment of 150 females
Column 1	2	3

(6) Except as provided in Sentence (13), the number of water closets required for Group D *occupancies* and for restaurants, nonresidential clubs, bowling alleys, community halls, lodge rooms, passenger stations and depots, art galleries, exhibition halls, libraries, museums, court rooms and similar *occupancies* shall conform to Table 3.6.4.B.

Table 3.6.4.B.
Forming Part of Sentence 3.6.4.2.(6)

Number of Persons of Each Sex	Minimum Number of Water Closets for Each Sex
1–25	1
26–50	2
Over 50	3 plus 1 for each additional increment of 50 persons of each sex
Column 1	2

(7) The number of water closets required for primary schools and day-care centres shall be at least 1 fixture for each 30 males and 1 fixture for each 25 females.

(8) The number of water closets required for places of worship and undertaking premises shall be at least 1 fixture for each 150 persons of each sex.

(9) The number of water closets required for *institutional occupancies* shall be determined on the basis of the special needs of such *occupancies*.

(10) Except as provided in Sentence (13), the number of water closets required for *residential occupancies* shall be at least 1 fixture for each 10 persons of each sex, except that *dwelling units* shall conform to the requirements in Part 9.

(11) Except as provided in Sentence (13), the number of water closets required for *mercantile occupancies* shall be at least 1 fixture for each 300 males and 1 fixture for each 150 females.

(12) Except as provided in Sentence (13), the number of water closets required for *industrial occupancies* shall conform to Table 3.6.4.C.

Table 3.6.4.C.
Forming Part of Sentence 3.6.4.2.(12)

Number of Persons of Each Sex	Minimum Number of Water Closets for Each Sex
1– 10	1
11– 25	2
26– 50	3
51– 75	4
76–100	5
Over 100	6 plus 1 for each additional increment of 30 persons of each sex
Column 1	2

Exception for small occupant load

(13) Where the *occupant load* in an *occupancy* described in Sentences (6), (10) and (12) does not exceed 10 persons, or where the total area in a Group E *occupancy* does not exceed 100 m^2, both sexes may be served by 1 water closet.

Service building for mobile homes

(14) Where mobile homes do not have individual sanitary facilities connected to a central water supply and drainage system, a service *building* shall be provided for public use and shall contain a least 1 water closet for each sex where the facilities serve not more than 10 mobile homes, and where the facilities serve more than 10 mobile homes, an additional water closet for each sex shall be provided for each additional 10 mobile homes.

(15) Where a service *building* is required by Sentence (14), it shall contain lavatories as required in Sentence (3) and at least
  (a) 1 laundry tray or similar facility, and
  (b) 1 bathtub or shower for each sex.

Glass around showers or bathtubs

3.6.4.3. Glass, other than safety glass, shall not be used for a shower or bathtub enclosure.

SUBSECTION 3.6.5. MEDICAL GAS PIPING SYSTEMS

3.6.5.1. Non-flammable medical gas piping systems shall be installed in conformance with CSA Z305.1, "Non-Flammable Medical Gas Piping Systems."

SECTION 3.7 BARRIER-FREE DESIGN

SUBSECTION 3.7.1. GENERAL

3.7.1.1. The requirements of this Section apply to all *buildings* except
  (a) houses, including semi-detached, duplexes, triplexes, town houses, row houses and boarding houses,
  (b) *buildings* of Group F, Division 1 *major occupancy*, and
  (c) *buildings* which are not intended to be occupied on a daily or full time basis, including automatic telephone exchanges, pumphouses and substations.

(continued)

3.7.1.2. Every *building* in Article 3.7.1.1. shall have at least 1 entrance intended for general use by the public or the occupants designed in conformance with Article 3.7.3.3., opening to the outdoors at sidewalk level or to a ramp conforming to Article 3.7.3.4. leading to a sidewalk. (See Appendix A.)

Accessible entrance

3.7.1.3.(1) Except as permitted in Subsection 3.7.3., every *barrier-free access* shall provide an unobstructed width of at least 920 mm for the passage of wheelchairs.

Barrier-free access

(2) Floor *surfaces* along a *barrier-free access* shall have no opening that will permit the passage of a sphere larger than 13 mm diam.

(3) Except as provided in Article 3.7.3.5., controls for the operation of *building* services or safety devices, located in a *barrier-free access* and intended to be operated by the occupant, including electrical switches, thermostats and intercom switches, shall be accessible to a person in a wheelchair and shall be mounted at not more than 1.4 m above the floor.

SUBSECTION 3.7.2. OCCUPANCY REQUIREMENTS

3.7.2.1.(1) A *barrier-free access* shall be provided on the entrance *storey* and on each *storey* served by a passenger type elevator or other platform equipped passenger elevating device from the entrance described in Article 3.7.1.2.

Areas requiring barrier-free access

    (a) into each *suite*,
    (b) into rooms or areas that serve the public or are designated for use by visitors, including areas in *assembly occupancies* with fixed seats, display areas and merchandising departments,
    (c) into rooms or areas for student use in *assembly occupancies*,
    (d) into general work areas, including office areas,
    (e) into general use or general service areas, including shared laundry areas in *residential occupancies*, recreational areas, cafeteria, lounge rooms, lunch rooms and infirmaries,
    (f) into patients' rooms,
    (g) into at least 1 passenger type elevator or elevating device conforming to Article 3.7.3.5.,
    (h) into washrooms described in Article 3.7.2.3.,
    (i) to any facility required by this Section to be designed to accommodate disabled persons,
    (j) onto every balcony provided in conformance with Sentence 3.3.1.5.(1), and
    (k) to ticket counters, refreshment stands, drinking fountains and checkout counters (see Appendix A).

(See Appendix A.)
(See Article 3.3.1.5. for additional requirements for *floor areas* above the first *storey* with *barrier-free access*.)

(2) The number of spaces designated for wheelchair use in Clause 3.7.2.1.(1)(b) shall conform to Table 3.7.2.A. (See Appendix A.)

Wheelchair space in seating areas

Table 3.7.2.A.
Forming Part of Sentence 3.7.2.1.(2)

Number of Fixed Seats in Seating Area	Number of Spaces Required for Wheelchairs
up to 200	2
201 to 300	3
301 to 400	4
401 to 600	5
601 to 800	6
801 to 1 000	7
Over 1 000	8 plus 1 for each additional increment of 1 000 seats to a maximum of 20
Column 1	2

Access to parking areas

3.7.2.2.(1) A *barrier-free access* shall be provided from the entrance described in Article 3.7.1.2. to

    (a) an exterior parking area where exterior parking is provided (see Appendix A), and

    (b) at least 1 parking level where a passenger elevator serves an indoor parking level.

Washrooms for disabled persons

3.7.2.3.(1) Except as provided in Sentence (2), washrooms shall be designed to accommodate disabled persons in conformance with the appropriate requirements in Articles 3.7.3.6. to 3.7.3.9.

(2) Washrooms need not conform to the requirements in Sentence (1) provided

    (a) they are located on a *floor area* to which *barrier-free access* is not provided,

    (b) they are located within *suites* of *residential occupancy*, or

    (c) other washrooms designed to accommodate disabled persons are available in locations providing equivalent convenience.

SUBSECTION 3.7.3.   DESIGN STANDARDS

Accessibility signs

3.7.3.1.(1) Where a *building* is required to have an entrance to accommodate disabled persons, signs incorporating the international symbol of accessibility for disabled persons shall be installed where necessary to indicate the location of that entrance.

(2) Where a washroom, elevator or parking area is required to accommodate disabled persons, it shall be identified by a sign consisting of the international symbol of accessibility for disabled persons and such other graphic or written directions as are needed to indicate clearly the type of facility available. (See Appendix A.)

Exterior walks

3.7.3.2.(1) Exterior walks that form part of a *barrier-free access* shall

    (a) have a slip-resistant, continuous and even surface,

    (b) be at least 1 100 mm in width, and

    (c) have a level area adjacent to the entrance doorway conforming to Clause 3.7.3.4.(1)(c).

Doors in a barrier-free access

3.7.3.3.(1) Every doorway that is located in a *barrier-free access* shall have a clear width of at least 760 mm when the door is in the open position.

(2) The doorway to at least 1 bathroom within a *suite* of *residential occupancy* shall have a clear width of at least 760 mm when the door is in the open position. (See Appendix A.)

(3) Thresholds for doorways in Sentences (1) and (2) shall not exceed 13 mm in height above the finished floor surface and shall be bevelled to facilitate the passage of wheelchairs.

Door closers

(4) Except for doors to *dwelling units*, door closers for doors in a *barrier-free access* shall be designed to permit

    (a) doors to open when a force of not more than 38 N is applied to the handles, push plates or latch-releasing devices for exterior doors and not more than 22 N for interior doors, and

    (b) interior doors to have a closing period of at least 3 s measured from the door in an open position of 70° to the doorway to a point 75 mm from the closed position measured from the leading edge of the latch side of the door.

Vestibules in a barrier-free access

(5) Vestibules located in a *barrier-free access* shall be arranged to allow the movement of wheelchairs between doors and shall

    (a) provide a distance between 2 doors in series of at least 1.2 m plus the width of any door that swings into the space in the path of travel from one door to another, and

    (b) have a clear space, beyond the latch side of each door, of at least 600 mm when the door swings into the vestibule and at least 300 mm when the door swings away from the vestibule (see A-3.7.3.4.(1)(c) in Appendix A).

CODE REQUIREMENTS FOR TOILET ROOMS

447

(continued)

CODE REQUIREMENTS FOR TOILET ROOMS

Ramps in a barrier-free access

3.7.3.4.(1) Ramps located in a *barrier-free access* shall
  (a) have a minimum width of 870 mm between handrails,
  (b) have a maximum gradient of 1 in 12, except that a gradient not exceeding 1 in 10 is permitted where the length of ramp does not exceed 3 m,
  (c) have a level area of least 1.5 m by 1.5 m at the top and bottom and at intermediate levels of a ramp leading to a door, so that the level area extends at least 600 mm beyond the latch side of the door opening, except that where the door opens away from the ramp, the area extending beyond the latch side of the door opening may be reduced to 300 mm (see Appendix A),
  (d) have a level area at least 1.2 m long and at least the same width as the ramp
     (i) at intervals of not more than 9 m along its length, and
     (ii) where there is an abrupt change in the direction of the ramp, and
  (e) be equipped with handrails and *guards* conforming to Articles 3.4.7.5. and 3.4.7.6.

(2) Floors or walks in a *barrier-free access* having a slope steeper than 1 in 20 shall be designed as ramps.

Elevators

3.7.3.5.(1) The passenger-type elevator in Article 3.7.2.1. shall conform to Appendix E of CSA B44, "Safety Code for Elevators, Dumbwaiters, Escalators and Moving Walks."

Other elevating devices

(2) The passenger-type elevating device in Article 3.7.2.1. shall conform to CAN3-B355, "Safety Code for Elevating Devices for the Handicapped."

Water closet stalls for disabled persons

3.7.3.6.(1) Where a washroom is required by Article 3.7.2.3. to accommodate disabled persons, at least 1 water closet stall or enclosure shall
  (a) be at least 1.5 m in width by 1.5 m in depth,
  (b) be equipped with a door which shall
     (i) be capable of being locked from the inside,
     (ii) provide a clear opening of at least 760 mm with the door in the open position,
     (iii) swing outward, unless sufficient room is provided within the stall or enclosure to permit the door to be closed without interfering with the wheelchair,
     (iv) be provided with a door pull on the inside located so that the centreline is between 200 mm and 300 mm from the hinged side of the door, and
     (v) be provided with a door pull on the outside, near the latch side of the door,
  (c) have a water closet located so that its centreline is not less than 460 mm and not more than 480 mm from an adjacent side wall on 1 side,
  (d) be equipped with grab bars which shall
     (i) be mounted on the side wall closest to the water closet extending from a point not more than 300 mm from the rear wall to at least 450 mm in front of the water closet seat,
     (ii) be mounted on the wall behind the water closet so that it extends the full width of the toilet bowl where the water closet does not have a water tank,
     (iii) be mounted from 840 mm to 920 mm above the floor level,
     (iv) be installed to resist a load of at least 1.3 kN applied vertically or horizontally,
     (v) be not less than 30 mm and not more than 40 mm in diameter, and
     (vi) have a clearance of 35 mm to 45 mm from the wall,
  (e) be equipped with a coat hook mounted not more than 1.4 m above the floor on a side wall and projecting not more than 25 mm from the wall,
  (f) have a clearance of at least 1.7 m between the outside of the stall face and the face of an in-swinging washroom door and 1.4 m between the outside of the stall face and any wall-mounted fixture.

(See Appendix A.)

Water closets for disabled persons

3.7.3.7.(1) Water closets for disabled persons shall
- (a) be equipped with seats located at not less than 400 mm and not more than 460 mm above the floor level,
- (b) be equipped with hand-operated flushing controls that are easily accessible to a cheelchair user,
- (c) be equipped with a back support such as a seat lid, and
- (d) not have a spring-activated seat.

(See Appendix A.)

Lavatories for disabled persons

3.7.3.8.(1) Where a washroom is required to accommodate disabled persons, it shall
- (a) be equipped with a lavatory which shall
  - (i) be mounted so that the distance between the centreline of the fixture and the side wall is at least 460 mm,
  - (ii) have a clearance of at least 660 mm beneath the bottom of the lavatory to a point at least 260 mm in from the front,
  - (iii) have insulated waste outlet pipes where the waste pipes constitute a burn hazard,
  - (iv) have faucet handles of the lever type that are not spring-loaded, and
  - (v) have no shelves or other projections located above it so as to create a hazard,

Soap and towel dispensers

- (b) have soap and towel dispensers located not more than 1.4 m above the floor and accessible to persons in wheelchairs.

Special washrooms

3.7.3.9.(1) Where a special washroom is provided primarily for the use of disabled persons of both sexes in lieu of facilities for disabled persons in washrooms used by the general public, such washrooms shall
- (a) be equipped with doors capable of being locked from the inside and released from the outside,
- (b) be provided with a lavatory conforming to Article 3.7.3.8.,
- (c) be equipped with a water closet conforming to Article 3.7.3.7.,
- (d) be equipped with grab bars conforming to Clause 3.7.3.6.(1)(d),
- (e) have no dimension less than 1.7 m,
- (f) have fixture clearances conforming to the fixture clearances described in Articles 3.7.3.6. to 3.7.3.8., and
- (g) have a doorway conforming to Article 3.7.3.3.

Shower stalls for disabled persons

(See Appendix A.)

3.7.3.10.(1) Where individual shower stalls are provided in *buildings* of *assembly occupancy*, at least 1 shower stall shall be provided for disabled persons which shall
- (a) have no dimension less than 920 mm,
- (b) be equipped with a hinged seat that is not spring loaded,
- (c) be equipped with grab bars mounted approximately 900 mm above the floor on the wall opposite the seat, extending around at least 300 mm along the adjacent wall,
- (d) be equipped with pressure-balanced single lever controls,
- (e) be equipped with a hand-held shower head with at least 1.5 m of flexible hose capable of being used as a fixed shower head mounted approximately 450 mm in from the front of the shower and approximately 1.2 m above the floor,
- (f) have a bevelled threshold not exceeding 13 mm in height above the finished floor, and
- (g) have a slip-resistant floor.

CODE REQUIREMENTS FOR TOILET ROOMS

449

922 — REQUIRED MINIMUM FACILITIES

922.1 — GENERAL

922.1.1 In new construction or building additions and in changes of occupancy as defined in the Standard Building Code, at least the minimum facilities provided for in this section shall be installed, and the minimum number of each type of fixture shall be in accordance with Table 922.2.

922.1.2 Wherever plumbing fixtures are installed, the minimum number of each type of fixture installed shall be in accordance with Table 922.2, unless otherwise specifically provided.

922.1.3 The number of occupants of a building shall be determined by the square feet of habitable floor space in accordance with Table 922.2. In determining the habitable space, the square foot area of permanent structural building components, public kitchens, toilet rooms, corridors, stairways, vertical shafts and equipment rooms, when necessary for the operation of building utilities only, may be deducted from the total aggregate floor area.

922.1.4 Tenancies, rental units or other habitable areas within a building when separated from the required toilet facilities by walls or partitions without common access openings shall be considered independently from the remainder of the building, and shall be provided with separate facilities in accordance with this chapter regardless of the type of occupancy.

922.2 — TABLE 922.2 — GENERAL

922.2.1 In applying the schedule of facilities recorded in the following Table 922.2, consideration must be given to the accessibility of the fixtures. Conformity purely on a numerical basis may not result in an installation suitable to the need of the individual establishment. For example, schools should be provided with toilet facilities on each floor having classrooms.

922.2.2 Temporary facilities for use by workmen during building construction, not included in Table 922.2, shall consist of at least one water closet or chemical toilet and one urinal for each 30 workmen.

922.2.3 . Every building and each subdivision thereof intended for public use shall be provided with facilities in accordance with this chapter. Required facilities shall be directly accessible to the public through direct openings or corridors from the area or areas they are intended to serve. Required facilities shall be free and designated by legible signs for each sex. Pay facilities may be installed when in excess of the required minimum facilities.

Publisher and copyright holder: Southern Building Code Congress International, 900 Montclair Road, Birmingham, Alabama 35213. Copyright © 1985.

TABLE 922.2 — MINIMUM FACILITIES[1] AND OCCUPANT CONTENT[2]

Type of Building or Occupancy[2]	Occupant Content Sq. Ft. = One Person	Water Closets		Urinals	Lavatories		Bathtubs or Showers	Miscellaneous Fixtures[3][5]
Dwelling or Apt. House[4]	Not applicable	1 for each dwelling or apartment unit			1 for each dwelling or apartment unit.		1 for each dwelling or apartment unit.	Washing Machine Connection per Unit[10]
Schools Pre-School, Day Care or Nursery	Classrooms 20 square feet	No. of Fixtures Each 15 children 1 Add one fixture for each 15 additional children or fraction thereof.			No. of Persons 15 Add one fixture for each 15 additional children or fraction thereof.	No. of Fixtures 1		
Elementary		No. of Fixtures Each 35 Females or less 1 Each 60 males or less 1		1 per 30 males or less	No. of Persons 60	No. of Fixtures[11] 1		Drinking fountains for each 3 classrooms but not less than one each floor.
Secondary		Each 45 Females or less 1 Each 100 Males or less 1		1 per 30 males or less	60 Over 60 same ratio.	1 persons		

TABLE 922.2 — MINIMUM FACILITIES[1] AND OCCUPANT CONTENT[2]—(Cont'd)

Type of Building or Occupancy[2]	Occupant Content Sq. Ft. = One Person	Water Closets		Urinals	Lavatories		Bathtubs or Showers	Miscellaneous Fixtures[1][8]	
Office and Public Buildings	100 square feet	No. of Persons 1- 15 16- 35 36- 55 56- 80 81-100 101-150 Add one fixture for each 40 additional persons	No. of Fixtures[13] 1 2 3 4 5 6	One urinal required for each 3 required water closets in all men's toilet rooms when accessible to the public. Wherever urinals are provided for men or women, one water closet less than the number specified may be provided for each urinal installed except that the number of required water closets in such cases shall not be reduced to less than 2/3 of the minimum specified for men and 3/4 of the minimum specified for women.	No. of Persons 1- 15 16- 35 36- 60 61-90 91-125 Add one fixture for each 45 additional persons.	No. of Fixtures[13] 1 2 3 4 5		Drinking Fountains No. of Persons No. of Fixtures 1-100 1 101-250 2 251-500 3 Not less than one fixture each floor subject to access.	
Common toilet facilities for areas of commercial buildings of multiple tenants[14][15]	Use the sq. ft. per person ratio applicable to the single type occupancy(s) occupying the greatest aggregate floor areas. (Consider separately each floor area of a divided floor)	No. of Persons 1- 15 16- 35 36- 55 56- 80 81-100 101-150 Add one fixture for each 40 additional persons	No. of Fixtures[13] 1 2 3 4 5 6	One urinal required for each 3 required water closets in all men's toilet rooms when accessible to the public. Wherever urinals are provided for men or women, one water closet less than the number specified may be provided for each urinal installed except that the number of required water closets in such cases shall not be reduced to less than 2/3 of the minimum specified for men and 3/4 of the minimum specified for women. (In no case less than one urinal for men)	No. of Persons 1- 15 16- 35 36- 60 61- 90 91-125 Add one fixture for each 45 additional persons.	No. of Fixtures[13] 1 2 3 4 5		Drinking Fountains No. of Persons No. of Fixtures 1- 100 1 101- 250 2 251- 500 3 501-1000 4 Not less than one fixture each floor subject to access.	
Retail Stores	200 square feet	No. of Persons 1- 15 16- 35 36- 55 56- 80 81-100 101-150 Add one fixture for each 40 additional persons up to 390 persons. For all over 390 persons, add one fixture for each 75 persons.	No. of Fixtures[13] 1 2 3 4 5 6	One urinal required for each 3 required water closets in all men's toilet rooms when accessible to the public. Wherever urinals are provided for men or women, one water closet less than the number specified may be provided for each urinal installed except that the number of required water closets in such cases shall not be reduced to less than 2/3 of the minimum specified for men and 3/4 of the minimum specified for women.	No. of Persons 1- 15 16- 35 36- 60 61-90 91-125 Add one fixture for each 45 additional persons up to 350 persons. For all over 350 persons, add one fixture for each 90 persons.	No. of Fixtures[13] 1 2 3 4 5		Drinking Fountains No. of No. of Persons Fixtures 1-100 1 101- 250 2 251- 500 3 501-1000 4 Not less than one fixture each floor subject to access.	
Restaurants, Clubs and Lounges[11]	40 square feet	No. of Persons 1-50 51-100 101-300	No. of Fixtures[11] 1 2 3	No. of Persons No. of Fixtures 1-50 Men 1 51-200 2 Over 200 add one fixture for each additional 200 males. Required urinals may be used in lieu of 1/3 the required water closets in either men's or women's toilet rooms.	No. of Persons 1-150 151-200 201-400 Over 400 persons add one fixture for each additional 100 persons.	No. of Fixtures[13] 1 2 3		To Comply with Board of Health requirements.	

(continued)

TABLE 922.2 — MINIMUM FACILITIES[1] AND OCCUPANT CONTENT[2]—(Cont'd)

Type of Building or Occupancy[2]	Occupant Content Sq. Ft. = One Person	Water Closets		Urinals		Lavatories		Bathtubs or Showers	Miscellaneous Fixtures[3][8]
Do It Yourself Laundries	50 square feet	No. of Persons 1-50 51-100	No. of Fixtures[13] 1 2			No. of Persons 1-100	No. of Fixtures 1		One drinking fountain and one service sink.
Beauty Shops and Barber Shops	50 square feet	No. of Persons 1-35 36-75	No. of Fixtures[13] 1 2			One fixture for each sex when located in the toilet rooms or one fixture if accessible outside of both toilet rooms.			One drinking fountain and one service or other utility sink.
Waiting Rooms Airports Railroad stations Bus stations For other areas, see office or public building as applicable	70 square feet	No. of Persons 1-100 101-200 201-400 Over 400 persons add one fixture for each additional 400 persons. In women's add additional water closets or urinals at the ratio required for urinals in men's toilets.	No. of Fixtures[13] 2 3 4	No. of Persons 1-100 101-200 201-400 401-600 Over 600, 1 additional 300 males.	No. of Fixtures 1 M. 2 3 4 for ad-	No. of Persons 1-100 101-200 201-400 401-750 Note: At least 1 for each toilet room.	No. of Fixtures 1 2 3 4		Drinking Fountains No. of Persons / No. of Fixtures[13] 1-100 / 1 101-350 / 2 Over 350 add one fixture for each 400
Manufacturing, Warehouses,[12] Workshops, Loft Buildings, Foundries and similar establishments[5][6][12]	Occupant content to be determined for the proposed use or occupancy by the owner or tenants furnishing satisfactory data to substantiate the maximum occupant content during any one shift. Also see Section 923.4(B)	No. of Persons 1 10-24 25-49 50-75 76-100 Add one additional fixture for each additional 30 employees.	No. of Fixtures[11] 1 2 3 4 5	Wherever urinals are provided for men or women, one water closet less than the number specified may be provided for each urinal installed except that the number of water closets in such cases shall not be reduced to less than 2/3 of the minimum specified for men and 3/4 of the minimum specified for women.		No. of Persons[7] 1-15 16-35 36-60 61-90 91-125 Add one fixture for each 45 additional persons.	No. of Fixtures[13] 1 2 3 4 5	1 shower for each 15 persons exposed to excessive heat or to skin contamination with poisonous, infectious, or irritating material.[13]	Drinking Fountains, One for each 75 persons.
Dormitories[9] [11]	50 square feet. (Calculated on sleeping area only)	Male: 1 for each 10 persons Female: 1 for each 8 persons Over 10 persons, add 1 fixture for each 25 additional males and 1 for each 20 additional females.		1 for each 25 men. Over 150 persons add 1 fixture for each 50 men.		1 for each 12 persons. (Separate dental lavatories should be provided in community toilet rooms. Ratio of dental lavatories for each 50 persons is recommended.) Add 1 lavatory for each 20 males, 1 foe each 15 females.[13]		1 for each 8 persons. In women's dorms add tubs in the ratio 1 for each 30 females. Over 150 persons, add 1 fixture for each 20 persons.[13]	Washing Machines may be used in lieu of laundry tubs.

TABLE 922.2 — MINIMUM FACILITIES[1] AND OCCUPANT CONTENT[2]—(Cont'd)

Type of Building or Occupancy[2]	Occupant Content Sq. Ft. = One Person	Water Closets		Urinals		Lavatories		Bathtubs or Showers	Miscellaneous Fixtures[3][1]	
Theatres, Auditoriums, and Churches[11]	70 square feet. (Calculated from assembly area.) Other areas considered separately. See office or public buildings.	No. of Persons	No. of Fixtures	No. of Persons	No. of Fixtures	No. of Persons	No. of Fixtures[13]		Drinking Fountains No. of Persons	No. of Fixtures[13]
		1-100	2	1-200	2 M.	1-200	1		1-100	1
		101-200	3	201-400	3	201-400	2		101-350	2
		201-400	4	401-600	4	401-750	3		Over 350 add one fixture for each 400.	
		Over 400 persons add one fixture for each additional 400 persons. In women's add additional water closets or urinals at the ratio required for urinals in men's toilets.		Over 600, 1 for additional 300 males. in places of worship, one less fixture may be required		Note: At least one for each toilet room. Over 750, one for each additional 500 persons.				

1. The figures shown are based upon one fixture being the minimum required for the number of persons indicated or any fraction thereof.

2. The occupant content and the number of required facilities for occupancies other than listed shall be determined by the Plumbing Official. Plumbing facilities in the occupancies or tenancies of similar use may be determined by the Plumbing Official from this table.

3. Drinking fountains shall not be installed in toilet rooms.

4. Kitchen Sinks — 1 for each dwelling or apartment unit.

5. For other than industrial areas of the occupancy, see other applicable type occupancies (applicable to facilities provided due to inaccessibility of those in main or initial occupancy).

6. As required by the American Standard Safety Code for Industrial Sanitation in Manufacturing Establishments (ANSI Z4.1-1955).

7. Where there is exposure to skin contamination with poisonous, infectious, or irritating materials, provide 1 lavatory for each 5 persons.

8. 24-lineal-in of wash sink or 18-in of a circular basin, when provided with water outlets for such space, shall be considered equivalent to 1 lavatory.

9. Laundry trays, 1 for each 50 persons. Slop sinks, 1 for each 100 persons.

10. When central washing facilities are provided, in lieu of washing machine connections in each living unit, central facilities shall be located for the building served at the ratio of not less than one washing machine for each 8 living units, but in no case less than two machines for each building of fifteen living units or less.

11. The installation of female urinals shall be optional.

12. (a) Light Storage

Light storage is that storage which can be handled without the aid of special handling equipment such as forklifts, cranes or similar equipment.

(b) Heavy Storage

Heavy storage is that storage which requires special equipment for handling such as cranes, forklifts or similar equipment.

13. See Table 922.3.

14. Common toilet facilities (separate for males and females) for each floor are acceptable in lieu of separate facilities required by this section only when the applicable building occupant content has common access from within the building. When tenancies, rental units, etc., are to be provided with separate facilities of a partial nature, such facilities are not deductible from the total common facilities required.

15. (A) Applicable to small stand-up restaurants and similar occupancies.

(B) Not applicable to do-it-yourself laundries, beauty shops and similar occupancies where persons must remain to receive personal services.

(continued)

CODE REQUIREMENTS FOR TOILET ROOMS

922.3 — DIVISION OF FACILITIES BY PERCENTAGE

Fixtures required by 922.1 and listed in Table 922.2 shall be divided in accordance with Table 922.3.

TABLE 922.3 — DIVISION OF FACILITIES

Type of Occupancy	Males %	Females %	Exceptions in Type of Occupancy
Schools	50	50	Boys' School Girls' School
Offices[4]	40	60	
Common Toilet Facilities, Commercial Buildings	Use Average % ratio applicable to the single type occupancy(s) occupying the greatest aggregate floor area.		See Footnotes 14 and 15, Table 922.2
Retail Stores[5]	30	70	
Restaurants[6]	50	50	Also Restaurant & Lounge when same area
Clubs and Lounges	65	35	
Coin Operated[7] Laundries	20	80	
Beauty Shops[8]	10	90	
Barber Shops[8]	90	10	
Waiting Rooms	50	50	

Warehouses[9]
  Light Storage
  Heavy Storage
	
	75
	90
		
		25
		10
			
			See Sect. 922.4.1
			See Sect. 922.4.1

Foundries & Heavy Manufacturing[9][1]
  Medium Mfg.[2]
  Light Mfg.[3]
	90
	75
	50
		10
		25
		50
			See Sect. 922.4.1
			See Sect. 922.4.1
			See Sect. 922.4.1

Dorms			Plans must specify whether men or women
Theatres	50	50	
Auditoriums Churches	40	60	

454

NOTES TO TABLE 922.3

1. Heavy manufacturing is applicable to those manufacturers manufacturing products requiring overhead cranes or similar equipment for the movement of raw materials and/or the finished products.

2. Medium manufacturing is applicable to those manufacturers manufacturing products requiring forklifts or similar equipment to handle the manufactured product and may require overhead cranes or similar equipment to handle the raw material used in manufacturing.

3. Light manufacturing is applicable to those manufacturers manufacturing finished products which require no special equipment to handle single finished products but may require special equipment to handle the products when packaged in containers containing multiple products.

4. A single facility may be used by both males and females when the building area is 1200 sq ft or less.

5. A single facility may be used by both males and females when the building area is 1500 sq ft or less, excluding fuel dispensing operations (i.e. service stations).

6. A single facility may be used by both males and females when the building area is 500 sq ft or less.

7. A single facility may be used by both males and females when the building area is 1400 sq ft or less.

8. A single facility may be used by both males and females when the building area is 900 sq ft or less.

9. See footnote 5 of Table 922.2.

922.4 — ADJUSTMENTS

922.4.1 The Plumbing Official may make adjustments in the percentage ratio of facilities for males and females when furnished satisfactory data to substantiate a claim that the percentage factor in the table would not provide a satisfactory ratio of facilities for the ultimate users. In any case, where deviation is permitted, in accordance with this section, the Plumbing Official may require additional facilities if the data submitted proves to be in error or if changes are made that affect such data, whether it be by the original or later owner or occupants of the building or tenancy.

922.4.2 The Plumbing Official may make adjustments in the occupant content established by Table 922.2 when, in a particular case, satisfactory data, accompanied by plans, is furnished which substantiates a claim that the occupant content of a particular building or tenancy will, at all times, be less than provided for in the above table. Approval of such data and accompanying claims shall not prevent the Plumbing Official from requiring additional facilities based on the above table, should changes be made affecting the data or plan upon which the original approval was based whether such changes be made by the original or ultimate owner or building occupant or occupants. The remainder of the facilities requirements of 922 are not affected by this paragraph.

922.5 — FACILITIES SEPARATION

The occupant content established by this Code shall not be construed to have any force or effect upon the occupant content requirements of the Building Code and is established only to calculate the number of plumbing facilities required for a building or for a tenancy within a building when such tenancy is separated from the remainder of the building by walls or partitions or when central facilities would not provide for the satisfactory needs of a tenant's patrons who must remain in a given area to receive the service rendered.

To determine the number of persons for the purpose of finding the minimum number of fixtures, see page 264.

MINIMUM PLUMBING FACILITIES[1]

Each building shall be provided with sanitary facilities, including provisions for the physically handicapped as prescribed by the Department having jurisdiction. In the absence of such requirements, this Appendix — which provides a guideline for the minimum facilities for the various types of occupancies (See Section 910, Plumbing Fixtures Required, of the Uniform Plumbing Code) may be used. For handicapped requirements, ANSI A117.1-1961 (R1971). Specifications for Making Buildings and Facilities Accessible to, and Usable by, the Physically Handicapped, may be used.

Type of Building or Occupancy[2]	Water Closets (Fixtures per person)		Urinals[10] (Fixtures per person)	Lavatories (Fixtures per person)		Bathtubs or Showers (Fixtures per person)	Drinking Fountains[3,13] (Fixtures per person)
Assembly Places — Theatres Auditoriums, Convention Halls, etc. — for permanent employee use.	*Male* 1:1-15 2:16-35 3:36-55 Over 55, add 1 fixture for each additional 40 persons	*Female* 1:1-15 2:16-35 3:36-55	1 per 50	*Male* 1 per 40	*Female* 1 per 40	————————	————————
Assembly Places — Theatres Auditoriums, Convention Halls, etc. — for public use	*Male* 1:1-100 2:101-200 3:201-400 Over 400 add 1 fixture for each additional 500 males and 2 for each 300 females	*Female* 3:1-100 6:101-200 8:201-400	1:1-100 2:101-200 3:201-400 4:401-600 Over 600 add 1 fixture for each additional 300 males	*Male* 1:1-200 2:201-400 3:401-750 Over 750, add 1 fixture for each additional 500 persons	*Female* 1:1-200 2:201-400 3:401-750	————————	1 per 75[12]
Dormitories[9] — School or Labor	*Male* 1 per 10 Add 1 fixture for each additional 25 males (over 10) and 1 for each additional 20 females (over 8)	*Female* 1 per 8	1 per 25 Over 150, add 1 fixture for each additional 50 males	*Male* 1 per 12 Over 12, add 1 fixture for each additional 20 males and 1 for each 15 females	*Female* 1 per 12	1 per 8 For female, add 1 bathtub per 30. Over 150, add 1 per 20	1 per 75[12]
Dormitories — for staff use	*Male* 1:1-15 2:16-35 3:36-55 Over 55, add 1 fixture for each additional 40 persons	*Female* 1:1-15 2:16-35 3:36-55	1 per 50	*Male* 1 per 40	*Female* 1 per 40	————————	————————
Dwellings[4] Single Dwelling Multiple Dwelling or Apartment House	1 per dwelling 1 per dwelling or apartment unit		————————	1 per dwelling 1 per dwelling or apartment unit		1 per dwelling 1 per dwelling or apartment unit	————————
Hospitals Waiting Room For employee use	1 per room *Male* 1:1-15 2:16-35 3:36-55 Over 55, add 1 fixture for each additional 40 persons	*Female* 1:1-15 2:16-35 3:36-55	1 per 50	1 per room *Male* 1 per 40	*Female* 1 per 40	————————	1 per 75[12]
Hospitals Individual Room Ward Room	1 per room 1 per 8 patients		———————— ————————	1 per room 1 per 10 patients		1 per room 1 per 20 patients	1 per 75[12]
Industrial[6] Warehouses Workshops, Foundries and similar establishments (for employee use)	*Male* 1:1-10 2:11-25 3:26-50 4:51-75 5:76-100 Over 100, add 1 fixture for each additional 30 persons	*Female* 1:1-10 2:11-25 3:26-50 4:51-75 5:76-100		Up to 100, 1 per 10 persons Over 100, 1 per 15 persons[7,8]		1 shower for each 15 persons exposed to excessive heat or to skin contamination with poisonous, infectious, or irritating material.	1 per 75[12]
Institutional—other than Hospitals or Penal Institutions (on each occupied floor)	*Male* 1 per 25	*Female* 1 per 20	1 per 50	*Male* 1 per 10	*Female* 1 per 10	1 per 8	1 per 75[12]
Institutional—other than Hospitals or Penal Institutions (on each occupied floor)—for employee use	*Male* 1:1-15 2:16-35 3:36-55 Over 55, add 1 fixture for each additional 40 persons	*Female* 1:1-15 2:16-35 3:36-55	1 per 50	*Male* 1 per 40	*Female* 1 per 40	————————	————————

MINIMUM PLUMBING FACILITIES

Type of Building or Occupancy[2]	Water Closets (Fixtures per person)		Urinals[10] (Fixtures per person)	Lavatories (Fixtures per person)		Bathtubs or Showers (Fixtures per person)	Drinking Fountains[3,13] (Fixtures per person)
Office or Public Buildings	*Male* 1:1-15 2:16-35 3:36-55 4:56-80 5:81-110 6:111-150 Over 150, add 1 fixture for each additional 40 persons	*Female* 1:1-15 2:16-35 3:36-55 4:56-80 5:81-110 6:111-150		*Male* 1:1-15 2:16-35 3:36-60 4:61-90 5:91-125 Over 125, add 1 fixture for each additional 45 persons	*Female* 1:1-15 2:16-35 3:36-60 4:61-90 5:91-125	----------------	1 per 75[12]
Office or Public Buildings For employee use	*Male* 1:1-15 2:16-35 3:36-55 Over 55, add 1 fixture for each additional 40 persons	*Female* 1:1-15 2:16-35 3:36-55	1 per 50	*Male* 1 per 40	*Female* 1 per 40	----------------	----------
Penal Institutions— For employee use	*Male* 1:1-15 2:16-35 3:36-55 Over 55, add 1 fixture for each additional 40 persons	*Female* 1:1-15 2:16-35 3:36-55	1 per 50	*Male* 1 per 40	*Female* 1 per 40	---------------- ----------------	1 per 75[12]
Penal Institutions— For prisoner use Cell Exercise Room	1 per cell 1 per exercise room		------------- 1 per exercise room	1 per cell 1 per exercise room		---------------- ----------------	1 per cell block floor 1 per exercise room
Restaurants, Pubs and Lounges[11]	*Male* 1:1-50 2:51-150 3:151-300 Over 300, add 1 fixture for each additional 200 persons	*Female* 1:1-50 2:51-150 4:151-300	1:1-150 Over 150, add 1 fixture for each additional 150 males	*Male* 1:1-150 2:151-200 3:201-400 Over 400, add 1 fixture for each additional 400 persons	*Female* 1:1-150 2:151-200 3:201-400	----------------	----------
Schools—For staff use All schools	*Male* 1:1-15 2:16-35 3:36-55 Over 55, add 1 fixture for each additional 40 persons	*Female* 1:1-15 2:16-35 3:36-55	1 per 50	*Male* 1 per 40	*Female* 1 per 40	----------------	----------
Schools[5]—For student use Nursery	*Male* 1:1-20 2:21-50 Over 50, add 1 fixture for each additional 50 persons	*Female* 1:1-20 2:21-50	-------------	*Male* 1:1-25 2:26-50 Over 50, add 1 fixture for each additional 50 persons	*Female* 1:1-25 2:26-50	----------------	1 per 75[12]
Elementary	*Male* 1 per 30	*Female* 1 per 25	1 per 75	*Male* 1 per 35	*Female* 1 per 35	----------------	1 per 75[12]
Secondary	*Male* 1 per 40	*Female* 1 per 30	1 per 35	*Male* 1 per 40	*Female* 1 per 40	----------------	1 per 75[12]
Others (Colleges, Universities, Adult Centers, etc.)	*Male* 1 per 40	*Female* 1 per 30	1 per 35	*Male* 1 per 40	*Female* 1 per 40	----------------	1 per 75[12]
Worship Places Educational and Activities Unit	*Male* 1 per 250	*Female* 1 per 125	1 per 250	1 per toilet room		----------------	1 per 75[12]
Worship Places Principal Assembly Place	*Male* 1 per 300	*Female* 1 per 150	1 per 300	1 per toilet room		----------------	1 per 75[12]

Whenever urinals are provided, one (1) water closet less than the number specified may be provided for each urinal installed, except the number of water closets in such cases shall not be reduced to less than two-thirds (⅔) of the minimum specified.

1. The figures shown are based upon one (1) fixture being the minimum required for the number of persons indicated or any fraction thereof.
2. Building categories not shown on this table shall be considered separately by the Administrative Authority.
3. Drinking fountains shall not be installed in toilet rooms.
4. Laundry trays. One (1) laundry tray or one (1) automatic washer standpipe for each dwelling unit or two (2) laundry trays or two (2) automatic washer standpipes, or combination thereof, for each ten (10) apartments. Kitchen sinks. One (1) for each dwelling or apartment unit.
5. This schedule has been adopted by the National Council on Schoolhouse Construction.
6. As required by ANSI Z4.1-1968, Sanitation in Places of Employment.
7. Where there is exposure to skin contamination with poisonous, infectious, or irritating materials, provide one (1) lavatory for each five (5) persons.
8. Twenty-four (24) lineal inches (609.6 mm) of wash sink or eighteen (18) inches (457.2 mm) of a circular basin, when provided with water outlets for such space, shall be considered equivalent to one (1) lavatory.
9. Laundry trays. One (1) for each fifty (50) persons. Slop sinks, one (1) for each hundred (100) persons.
10. General. In applying this schedule of facilities, consideration must be given to the accessibility of the fixtures. Conformity purely on a numerical basis may not result in an installation suited to the need of the individual establishment. For example, schools should be provided with toilet facilities on each floor having classrooms. Temporary workingmen facilities. One (1) water closet and one (1) urinal for each thirty (30) workmen.
    a. Surrounding materials. Wall and floor space to a point two (2) feet (0.6 m) in front of urinal lip and four (4) feet (1.2 m) above the floor, and at least two (2) feet (0.6 m) to each side of the urinal shall be lined with non-absorbent material.
    b. Trough urinals are prohibited.
11. A restaurant is defined as a business which sells food to be consumed on the premises.
    a. The number of occupants for a drive-in restaurant shall be considered as equal to the number of parking stalls.
    b. Employee toilet facilities are not to be included in the above restaurant requirements. Hand washing facilities must be available in the kitchen for employees.
12. Where food is consumed indoors, water stations may be substituted for drinking fountains. Theatres, auditoriums, dormitories, offices, or public buildings for use by more than six (6) persons shall have one (1) drinking fountain for the first seventy-five (75) persons and one (1) additional fountain for each one hundred and fifty (150) persons thereafter.
13. There shall be a minimum of one (1) drinking fountain per occupied floor in schools, theatres, auditoriums, dormitories, offices or public buildings.

APPENDIX E: UNITS OF CONVERSION

English	Metric	Metric	English
1 in.	25.4 mm	1 mm	0.0394 in.
1 ft	304.8 mm	1 m	39.37 in.
1 ft	0.3048 m	1 m	3.2808 ft
1 lb	0.454 kg	1 kg	2.205 lb
1 ft^2	0.0929 m^2	1 m^2	10.76 ft^2
1 psi	6.89 kPa	1 kPa	0.145 psi
1 lb/ft^2	4.884 kg/m^2	1 kg/m^2	0.205 lb/ft^2
1 lb/ft^3	16.019 kg/m^3	1 kg/m^3	0.0624 lb/ft^3
1 ft/min	0.0051 m/sec	1 m/sec	196.85 ft/min
1 cfm	0.0005 m^3/sec	1 m^3/sec	2119 cfm
1 BTU	1.055 kJ	1 kJ	0.9479 BTU
1 BTU	3.9683 kcal	1 kcal	0.252 BTU
1 BTUH	0.2928 W	1 W	3.412 BTUH

$$1 \text{ Pa} = 0.102 \text{ kg/m}^2$$
$$1 \text{ kg/m}^2 = 9.80 \text{ Pa}$$

APPENDIX F:
REFERENCES

APPENDIX F: REFERENCES

These references are recommended as starting points if you need additional information. For those books that are not commonly available in bookstores, the publishers' mailing addresses are given.

DESIGNING THE STRUCTURE

For a more comprehensive treatment of structural design and analysis: Schodek, Daniel L. *Structures.* Englewood Cliffs, New Jersey, Prentice-Hall, Inc., 1980.

For a comprehensive discussion of construction materials and methods: Allen, Edward. *Fundamentals of Building Construction.* New York, John Wiley & Sons, Inc., 1985.

For Heavy Timber construction: American Institute of Timber Construction. *Timber Construction Manual* (3rd ed.). New York, John Wiley & Sons, Inc., 1985.

For Wood Light Frame construction: National Forest Products Association. *Span Tables for Joists and Rafters.* Washington, National Forest Products Association, 1977. (Address: 1619 Massachusetts Avenue N.W., Washington, D.C. 20036.) Also highly recommended is the literature published by the American Plywood Association, P.O. Box 11700, Tacoma, Washington 98411.

For brick masonry construction: Brick Institute of America. *Technical Notes on Brick Construction.* Reston, Virginia, various dates. (Address: 11490 Commerce Park Drive, Reston, Virginia 22091.)

For concrete masonry construction: National Concrete Masonry Association. *A Manual of Facts on Concrete Masonry.* Herndon, Virginia, various dates. (Address: 2302 Horse Pen Road, Herndon, Virginia 22070.)

For structural steel: American Institute of Steel Construction. *Manual of Steel Construction* (8th ed.). Chicago, American Institute of Steel Construction, 1980. (Address: 400 North Michigan Avenue, Chicago, Illinois 60611.)

For sitecast concrete: Concrete Reinforcing Steel Institute. *CRSI Handbook 1984* (6th ed.). Schaumburg, Illinois, Concrete Reinforcing Steel Institute, 1984. (Address: CRSI Distribution Center, P.O. Box 100125, Dept. #b38, Roswell, Georgia 30075.)

For precast concrete: Phillips, William R., and David A. Sheppard. *Plant Cast Precast and Prestressed Concrete, A Design Guide.* Chicago, Prestressed Concrete Institute, 1980. (Address: 175 West Jackson Blvd., Chicago, Illinois 60604.)

DESIGNING SPACES FOR MECHANICAL AND ELECTRICAL SERVICES

American Society of Heating, Refrigerating, and Air-Conditioning Engineers, Inc. *ASHRAE Handbook,* in four volumes entitled *Fundamentals* (1981), *Applications* (1982), *Equipment* (1983), and *Systems* (1984). Atlanta, American Society of Heating, Refrigerating, and Air-Conditioning Engineers, Inc.

Bradshaw, Vaughn. *Building Control Systems.* New York, John Wiley & Sons, 1985.

Stein, Benjamin, John S. Reynolds, and William J. McGuinness. *Mechanical and Electrical Equipment for Buildings* (7th ed.). New York, John Wiley & Sons, 1986.

DESIGNING FOR EGRESS

Lathrop, James K. (ed.). *Life Safety Code® Handbook.* Quincy, Massachusetts, National Fire Protection Association, Inc., 1988. (Address: National Fire Protection Association, Batterymarch Park, Quincy, Massachusetts 02269.)

BUILDING CODES

Associate Committee on the National Building Code, National Research Council of Canada. *National Building Code of Canada, 1985.* Ottawa, National Research Council of Canada, 1985. (Address: Associate Committee on the National Building Code, National Research Council, Ottawa, Ontario, K1A OR6.)

Building Officials & Code Administrators International, Inc. *The BOCA National Building Code/1987.* Country Club Hills, Illinois, Building Officals & Code Administrators International, Inc., 1987. (Address: 4051 W. Flossmoor Road, Country Club Hills, Illinois 60477-5795.)

International Conference of Building Officials. *Uniform Building Code* (1985 ed.). Whittier, California, International Conference of Building Officials, 1985. (Address: 5360 South Workman Mill Road, Whittier, California 90601.)

Southern Building Code Conference International, Inc. *Standard Building Code.* Birmingham, Alabama, Southern Building Code Congress International, Inc., 1985. (Address: 900 Montclair Road, Birmingham, Alabama 35213-1206.)

INDEX

INDEX

INDEX

INDEX